TRAVELS IN INDIA,
INCLUDING
SINDE AND THE PUNJAB

BY

CAPTAIN LEOPOLD VON ORLICH.

TRANSLATED FROM THE GERMAN,
BY

H. EVANS LLOYD, ESQ

IN TWO VOLUMES.

VOL. I.

GYAN

Published by

Gyan Publishing House
5, Ansari Road
Daryaganj, New Delhi-110002
Phone: 011-47034999, 9811692060
E-mail: books@gyanbooks.com

Distribution Network
gyanbooks.com
India, USA, Canada, UK, Australia, France

ISBN : 978-81-212-4148-9 (Set)
ISBN : 978-81-212-4719-1 (HB)
First Published, London, 1845

2nd Impression 2020

Printed at: Gyan Press, Delhi.

Travels in India, including Sinde and the Punjab
Author: Captain Leopold Von Orlich

TRAVELS IN INDIA, INCLUDING SINDE AND THE PUNJAB

PRINTED IN COLOURS BY HULLMANDEL & WALTON

THE CUTLEB MINAR,

OR COLUMN ERECTED BY THE EMPEROR CUTLEB AB DEEN, IN 1193

NOTICE.

The Publishers of this work beg to state that it is private property, protected by the late Copyright Act, the 5 & 6 Victoria, c. 45. They beg also to state that any person having in his possession, within the United Kingdom, for sale or hire, one or more copies printed abroad of any English work protected by the Act referred to, is liable to a penalty, which, in cases affecting their interests, they intend to enforce.

The Public are farther informed that the Act 5 & 6 Victoria, c. 47. s. 24. prohibits the importation of all works printed in foreign countries, of which the copyright is not expired. Even single copies, though for the especial use of the Importers and marked with their names, are excluded, and the Customs officers in the different ports are strictly enjoined to carry this regulation into effect.

N.B.—The above regulations are in force in all British colonies and dependencies, as well as in the United Kingdom.

TRANSLATOR'S PREFACE.

NOTWITHSTANDING the numerous works of every description which treat of India, notwithstanding the marvellous phenomenon presented by the rise, progress, and colossal magnitude of our Indian empire, it was, on the whole, too long before the English nation took an interest in the subject in any degree commensurate with its importance. The affairs of that country were regarded as the concern of the East India Company rather than as involving any national interest:—India, in fact, was looked upon as an El Dorado, where persons, enjoying the patronage of the Company, might acquire immense fortunes; and when public attention was drawn to abuses, real or supposed, it was, as in the case of Warren Hastings, rather to forward the views of a party than to vindicate the honour or to promote the interests of the mother-country.

Meantime the labours and indefatigable researches of many men of eminent learning and ability were gradually revealing to Europe, not only its natural wonders, its surpassing fertility, its richness in every production that can contribute to the support, the comfort, and the happiness of man, but likewise the treasures of its learning, the condition of its people, and, alas! independently of its absurd general idolatry, the Tantra and Sakta worship, which necessarily brutalised and enslaved a part of its people.

A decided change for the better has undoubtedly taken place within a comparatively short period; and in proportion as the English nation has been more thoroughly informed of the state of India, it has manifested a more lively sympathy in the affairs of that empire; hence public opinion has had no little influence in producing a marked improvement in the government of that remote country, which will unquestionably be still further promoted by the rapid communication now obtained by means of steam navigation.

Under these circumstances the public are now eager for the most recent and authentic information; and the work of an intelligent and impartial foreigner like Captain Von Orlich cannot, therefore, fail to be highly acceptable. The circumstance that his letters are addressed to two such eminently distinguished characters as Alexander Von Humboldt and Carl Ritter would of itself be sufficient to guarantee their inherent importance; in fact, the very cordial reception which this distinguished officer met with from the various civil and military functionaries, and the marked attention with which he was honoured by Lord Ellenborough, together with his visit to the native princes of Sinde, Lahore, and Oude, have enabled him to collect ample materials, which he has wrought into a highly interesting narrative. His account of the Ameers of Sinde, to all of whom he had a personal introduction, derives a peculiar importance from the recent transactions in that country — the dethronement of its princes, and its annexation to the British dominions, which have given rise to so many conflicting opinions respecting the policy and justice of that unexpected measure.

In the completion of my agreeable task I have had the advantage of the kind and valuable assistance of Colonel Sykes, a director of the East India Company, a personal friend of the author, and a gentleman who is thoroughly acquainted with the army and administration of India. He has most obligingly revised the proofs of the whole work, and not only supplied the most approved orthography of many of the proper names, but has also thrown fuller light upon some portions of the author's text, more especially relating to the Anglo-Indian army. To this gallant officer I am further indebted for the valuable tables of the revenue of India, which have never before been published. I have also subjoined a few notes and remarks illustrative of several facts adduced by the author.

The following pages cannot indeed fail of a cordial reception from the British nation, who will be gratified by the opinion of so enlightened and unbiassed an observer of the stability of the British power in India, which he believes to be very far from having attained its culminating point,—an opinion in which he is borne out by another distinguished German traveller, Baron Von Hûgel, who says:—

"More than two thousand times has the earth performed its revolution round the sun—a number of years, nearly equal to a third of the period of time that has elapsed since the beginning of the history of the human race—since Alexander the Great crossed the Indus, and conceived the plan of making India tributary to Greece. * * * More than two thousand years after Alexander, his stupendous plan has been carried into execution by a nation whose original possessions scarcely exceed Greece in extent. * * * This empire has within itself the elements of duration; for the cause of justice and equity, the firm upholding of the law, and implied submission to its ordinance, are the peculiar characteristics of that energetic people to whom Providence has committed the destiny of so many millions of the human race."

"Debellare superbos, parcere subjectis"

is indeed a proud motto, more truly applicable to England than to Rome.

One doubt alone arises to cloud the brilliant prospect that England seems to have before her with regard to India. Has she not too long delayed to perform her duty, holding, as she does, so high a position in the Christian world? In the schools established and supported by her government no attempt appears to be made to lead the natives to that Divine religion which she herself professes in its greatest purity. According to Captain Von Orlich, the young men trained in her schools, for the most part turn out Deists; and this assertion is painfully corroborated by the Rev. J. Weitbrecht, in his excellent little work on Missions in Bengal, and by other highly credible authorities. While this state of things obtains the zealous labours of a few pious missionaries will be wholly inadequate to stem the fearful torrent of evil which must result from furnishing the mind of the Indian youth with the superstructure of an ample store of secular knowledge, while the only solid foundation of Gospel truth is wholly wanting; a mode of procedure which will inevitably involve them in a ruin more fearful than before, while it furnishes them with weapons against ourselves. May we not fear that, unless a radical change takes place, the lines of Homer, so affectingly spoken by

Scipio on the fall of Carthage, may be applicable to England?—

> "The day shall come, the great avenging day,
> Which Troy's proud glories in the dust shall lay;
> When Priam's power and Priam's self shall fall,
> And one prodigious ruin swallow all."

But let us hope for better things, and rather look forward to the moment (may it soon arrive!) when the British Government shall be able, as it doubtless is desirous, to communicate religious as well as secular knowledge to the people committed to her charge.

H. EVANS LLOYD.

LONDON, *January*, 1845.

AUTHOR'S PREFACE.

THREE years ago, when the disastrous events in Cabool were first made known, it was generally believed that a lengthened and serious war must be the inevitable consequence. The Author of the following work participated in this opinion, and anxiously wished to be present at the approaching campaign, for the purpose of acquiring, in the ranks of the British army, that military experience, which a long peace had prevented him from obtaining in the army of his own country. His Sovereign was graciously pleased to grant the Author's request; but the necessary negotiations with the British Government delayed his departure for India, while the rapid succession of military events in the seat of war surpassed every expectation. In consequence of this unavoidable detention, the Author only joined the British army at Ferozpoor on its return from its glorious campaign, when he saw, indeed, how well the laurels graced the brows of the victors, but with the mortifying reflection that he had come too late to witness how they had been won.

The main purpose of his journey having unhappily been thus defeated, by circumstances over which he had no control, it seemed to be an imperative duty to do all that was still in his power to make himself acquainted with that remarkable country, which has been visited by very few of his countrymen. If he has not taken the fullest advantage of the favourable opportunity which he enjoyed, the fault must be attributed to the shortness of the time rather than to any remissness on the part of the Author, who met with treasures far beyond his hopes, which, though fully able to appreciate, he could not in every case turn to account. He relates plainly and faithfully, what he saw and felt, and, to supply the deficiency of actual observation, he has added other matter which he heard and learnt from men of unimpeachable credit.

The Author has had the privilege of adding to his kind patrons and friends at home, many others both in England and in India, and a grateful remembrance of them will be for ever impressed on his heart.

THE AUTHOR.

CONTENTS

OF

THE FIRST VOLUME.

LETTER I.

ADDRESSED TO ALEXANDER VON HUMBOLDT.

LETTER II.

ADDRESSED TO ALEXANDER VON HUMBOLDT.

LETTER III.

ADDRESSED TO CARL RITTER.

LETTER IV.

ADDRESSED TO ALEXANDER VON HUMBOLDT.

LETTER V.

ADDRESSED TO ALEXANDER VON HUMBOLDT.

LETTER VI.

ADDRESSED TO CARL RITTER.

LETTER VII.

ADDRESSED TO ALEXANDER VON HUMBOLDT.

TRAVELS IN INDIA.

LETTER I.

TO ALEXANDER VON HUMBOLDT.

Departure from London to Southampton.—Embarkation on the Tagus steamer.—Falmouth, Gibraltar, Malta, and Alexandria.—Voyage on the Mahmudie canal to Atfeh; Steam navigation on the Nile.—Cairo.—Journey across the Desert to Suez.—Voyage in the Berenice war steamer, on the Red Sea to Aden, and thence, on board the Cleopatra, to Bombay.—Entrance into the Harbour on the 6th August.

Bombay, August 8. 1842.

AFTER a prosperous voyage of thirty-seven days, I arrived on the 6th inst. in this land of wonders! The fact that I have been conveyed in so short a time into a new world seems like a dream, and I should doubt its reality did not all things around convince me of the truth. However, though my imagination is most powerfully excited, and I have an interminable succession of occupation, I will at once attempt to give you a sketch of my voyage hitherward.

I passed my last day in London with our hospitable Consul-General, Mr. Hebeler, who had invited some of our countrymen to meet me, and whose amiable lady gave a charm to the social entertainment by her graceful and animated conversation. I was unfortunately obliged to decline an invitation from the Duke of Sussex, with whom I had previously had a long and very interesting conversation; little thinking that it was the last time that we should meet in this life, for I had to leave London that same day, and, attended by the good wishes of our ambassador, I started by the railway for Southampton. Spite of the sailor's prejudice I embarked on Friday, 1st July, on board the splendid steamer the Tagus, of 350 horse-power. The morning was unpleasant; light showery clouds driven by the wind covered the sun, and I was wet through before I reached the vessel. Here all was bustle and activity: while the roaring and hissing of the steam announced our speedy departure, goods of all kinds were hastily put on board, and the porters and sailors ran backwards and forwards, stowing the luggage and making other preparations. Most of the passengers were on deck surrounded by their friends; here was a father giving his last advice and blessing to his son; there brethren and friends bade each other a long adieu, while husband and wife parted, perhaps for ever; and a farewell salute was given to others by friends among the crowd assembled on shore. I alone stood like an isolated being; there was none to press my hand and take my last fond wishes to my friends at home; but in spirit I sent a thousand kind remembrances to those I love. At six o'clock the first gun gave the signal for separation, and a few minutes afterwards a second announced our departure. The Tagus, which was intended for the passage to Lisbon only, was now setting out for her first voyage to Egypt, in the place of the Oriental, which was under repair: as we passed this fine vessel the crew gave us some hearty cheers, which were warmly re-echoed by our sailors.

Our company consisted of between fifty and sixty persons, chiefly officers who were going to join their regiments in India, several naval officers, merchants, and a clergyman with his family, who were bound for Malta. The spacious deck, and the splendidly furnished saloon, which was provided with a library and newspapers, were far preferable to our small uncomfortable cabins, and we all accordingly amused ourselves either with promenading the deck, or with reading, writing, and conversation.

While steering our course between the French coast and the lovely Isle of Wight, the sky cleared up, and a light fresh breeze blew ahead; but the rolling of the vessel compelled many of the passengers to pay an involuntary tribute to Neptune; I, too, felt very uncomfortable, though I did not suffer from sea-sickness either then or afterwards. On the 2d July, at nine in the morning, we came in sight of the rocks which enclose the harbour of Falmouth. Shortly before entering it we took a pilot on board, who conducted us through the narrow channel, leaving on the left hand a reef of rocks, on which stood a small black tower, and at half-past nine o'clock we cast anchor at about 800 paces from the town. Here we had to wait for the India mail, which was not brought on board till four o'clock, and consisted of fifty-six large chests of letters, and other packages. We immediately weighed anchor, and before sunset we were on the wide Atlantic, bounded on all sides by the bright blue canopy of heaven.

A ship life, unless broken by some special circumstances, is so regular, monotonous, and, in long voyages, often so wearisome, that in giving a description of one day I make you tolerably well acquainted with the general tenour of our life. Our captain is a grave, reserved man, and has little intercourse with his officers except on matters of duty. At sunrise the crew begin cleaning and scouring the deck; the ship's bell indicates the hours, and when it strikes nine we assemble in the great saloon, at breakfast, which, according to English fashion, consists of hot and cold meats, &c. After breakfast, and again at about twelve o'clock, the captain and his officers regularly determine the position of the ship, and the passengers eagerly inquire how many miles we have made in the last twenty-four hours, and what is our latitude and longitude? On Sundays and holydays, we all assemble about eleven o'clock for divine worship, which is performed by the clergyman: when there is no clergyman on board the captain reads prayers. On other days we each pursue our own occupations, or seek exercise and recreation on deck. At twelve o'clock, we take a second breakfast, and at four o'clock the steward summons us to an exceedingly good dinner which consists of three courses, and a variety of wines. After this we generally spend the evening on the quarter-deck, where tea and conversation while away the time. If the weather be fine, the pure air and the brilliancy of the starry heavens keep many of us on deck till midnight.

The only interruptions to our life in its monotonous flow are passing vessels, shoals of dolphins, or a storm of wind. We encountered a heavy squall which drove our ponderous steamer as if it had been a plaything, towards the coast of Spain, which came in sight on the morning of the 5th of July; and, when we were off Cape Finisterre, a brisk north wind swelled our sails, so that by the aid of wind and steam we proceeded at the rate of ten miles an hour. Among my fellow-passengers I was particularly interested with Colonel M'Neile, Captain Forbes, of the Madras army, and Lieutenant Miaulis, a son of the celebrated Greek admiral, who was educated at Munich, and is now serving in the British navy. His frank, cheerful manners greatly attracted me; we mutually communicated our little adventures to each other; and the enthusiastic Greek, with sparkling eyes and animated gestures, recounted the deeds of his heroic father.

On the 7th and 8th we enjoyed serene weather and pure air under the lovely blue of this southern sky. On the preceding day, about noon, we met several Portuguese schooners, as we were passing between the wild rugged Berlinga rocks, of whose proximity the navigator is warned by a lighthouse in the little Fort St. Goa, and, at three o'clock, descried the once celebrated Mafra, whose large monastery, situated on an eminence near the city, is visible at a great distance. Soon afterwards we passed Cintra; and at seven o'clock Lisbon rose before us, like a panorama, in its entire extent and all its beauty. From this point we kept at a greater distance from the coast, which we did not see again till the following morning. Several vessels passed us, one of which had lost its foremast in a storm. At sunset we sailed by the celebrated Cape Trafalgar, and approached the Straits of Gibraltar: it was a remarkably fine evening, the air was warm yet refreshing, the sky resplendent with innumerable stars, the sea slightly agitated, and profound silence prevailed on board our vessel. This, and the expectation of soon entering another sea, induced me to remain on deck till we should reach the harbour of Gibraltar. About eleven o'clock a stormy wind suddenly arose, which several times extinguished our lantern, and we were very near coming into collision with another vessel, the crew of which set up a loud cry. Their apprehensions were, however, groundless, for notwithstanding the darkness of the night, we had fortunately perceived their ship in time to avoid any accident. The nearer we approached the lighthouse, the more violent did the storm become; but as soon as we had passed it, and were in the Straits, a complete calm suddenly succeeded. About half past three o'clock on the following morning, a gun was fired as a signal to the inhabitants of Gibraltar that we had cast anchor in the road. We were not able to observe the solar eclipse which afterwards took place, as the sun was obscured by clouds.

Gibraltar lies at the foot of a rock 1437 feet high, which declines, more or less abruptly, towards every side; on the east it rises from the sea like a wall, and runs out in a rugged promontory nearly 500 paces in length into the Mediterranean. On the Spanish side it is perfectly level, and forms a semicircle around the harbour, and, opposite Gibraltar, joins other masses of rock at the entrance. This harbour is one of the finest in the world, and is capable of receiving the largest men-of-war. The town and fortress lie on the declivity towards the harbour: the fortress consists of a wall which surrounds the town with salient angles and bulwarks; they are most extensive on the flanks, and are commanded by some works situated above them, and by several batteries hewn in the rocks, the guns of which hang in chains. Gibraltar is nearly impregnable by its natural position, and on the Spanish side may be isolated by inundating the plain. Wherever the rocky soil would permit, orange trees have been planted, and gardens laid out. Cactus and aloes grow luxuriantly to the very summit of the rock, the retreat of herds of monkeys, which, like the Capitoline geese of old, were distinguished during a siege, and consequently have ever since been looked upon as sacred animals, which are not to be molested.

Accompanied by several of my fellow-passengers, I took a small boat and went on shore. I cannot describe to you the elevating yet melancholy feeling that filled my heart as I trod the beautiful soil of Spain, the most southern point of Europe. The busy life of early morning met us on our landing; mules laden with vegetables, fruit and corn, driven by peasants in their singular costume; fine vigorous men with the most expressive countenances, wearing the broad-brimmed hat, the cloak, thrown like a toga over the shoulder and presenting a most picturesque appearance, encountered us at every step. In the markets we were struck with the peculiarities and the animated manners of the natives of the South, contrasted with the calm serious deportment of the English in their scarlet uniforms and the Scotch in their Highland dress. We spent some hours in viewing the little town and the fortifications, and while we were amusing ourselves with these scenes, the women and girls riding on heavily-laden asses scrutinised us coquettishly with their piercing black eyes.

Fatigued by the heat and unwonted exercise, we went into the best inn for refreshment: here they charged us three shillings each for a very indifferent breakfast, and I was therefore not surprised, though rather amused, to hear the English call these people rogues and scorpions.

Meantime our vessel had taken in coals and provisions for the voyage to Malta. We hastened on board, and at twelve o'clock we were already in the Mediterranean, which extended before us as smooth as a mirror; the air was warm without being oppressive, and the sky unclouded. This fine weather continued till Saturday 13th, and our vessel made ten miles an hour. On Friday evening we approached the African coast, where the lofty Atlas chain with its bare, rugged limestone rocks rose above the clouds, and long bore us company. We sailed along these classic lands, rich in traditions and historical interest, where Dido founded her States, where Æneas sought protection, and where Hannibal, Scipio, Jugurtha, Cæsar, the Vandals, the Arabs, the Spaniards, and the French have borne their warlike arms. What ample stores of history, what busy, varying fortunes of nations and individuals were recalled to our minds as we glided rapidly onwards!

On Saturday towards evening the wind had collected dense black clouds over the mountains: while we were watching their ever-changing forms, we suddenly saw a globe of fire fall from heaven; it was as large as the moon, and bursting in a few seconds, it illuminated the coast and the sea with magnificent though transitory splendour; soon afterwards vivid flashes lightened up the whole scene, so that Mount Atlas often appeared as if standing in an ocean of fire. On Monday the wind and sea became more calm, and we were able to enjoy the view of the coast once more at our ease. We saw the Bay of Tunis, the site of ancient Carthage, and passed close to the rocky island of Zembra, and the island of Pantellaria, famed for its wine. On Tuesday we had a brisk east wind, and at five o'clock on the following morning we were in sight of Malta.

The entrance into a new harbour in a foreign country is an event full of expectation to a stranger, and we accordingly all came on deck, eagerly making observations and inquiries. Malta has the appearance of a bare, sterile, rocky island, which seems to owe its origin to a recent volcanic convulsion. A few orange trees, some vines and fruit trees, trained against artificial walls, and growing in soil which had been fetched from Sicily, was all that presented itself to our view. Close to the shore, at intervals of 600 or 800 paces, there are towers, some round, others square, each provided with a twenty-four pounder for the defence of the coast. We saw the flags hoisted on the lighthouse at La Valetta, to announce our arrival to the pilots and to the governor. At half past eight we took on board a pilot, who soon conducted us through a narrow channel into one of the most spacious harbours in the world. It consists of the entrance harbour and three smaller ones branching off to the east, and is bounded by calcareous rocks, from 200 to 300 feet in height, on the most westerly of which the city rises in the form of terraces. A fine sight here presented itself to our view; a large fleet of men-of-war and war steamers, under the command of Admiral Owen lying at anchor. The harbour and town are defended by innumerable works and batteries, which are admirably placed and constructed; the only fault is that there are too many of them. On the side of the principal harbour, separated from the town, is the quarantine-harbour: I refrain from any further description of this island, interesting in so many points of view, because you are well acquainted with it, and shall content myself with relating the occurrences of the two days which I passed here.

We had scarcely cast anchor, when we were surrounded by boats, from which our ears were assailed with loud, shrill cries, resembling those of Naples when passengers are about to land. I hired a boat and made for the Queen, in order to look for Lieutenant Johnston, whose father, Sir Alexander, had kindly favoured me with a letter to him. He is a fine young man, full of life and spirit, and bid me a hearty welcome, introduced me to his messmates, and conducted me over every part of this floating palace. The Queen carrying 110 guns, 204 feet long, 60 broad, and 46 deep, with a crew of 1000 men, had been launched only a few months before, and is probably at this time the largest and handsomest man-of-war in the British navy. Here, where the strictest discipline and order prevail, where simplicity with adaptation to the object are combined in the highest perfection, we are irresistibly impressed with the power of England; these are the fibres which she throws out on every side, with which she encompasses the earth, as with a spider's web, and appropriates to herself the empire of the seas. The spacious saloon and dining-room are well supplied with books and maps; in the officers' cabins a thirty-two-pounder is placed close to each bed, otherwise each is furnished according to the taste of the respective occupant, and here, too, food for the mind is never wanting. As we passed through the magazines, the arsenal, the store-rooms, and the lazaretto, I had an opportunity of remarking the regularity and order of the crew; but the finest sight was on the upper deck, where the vessel is seen at once in its entire extent, with its intricate network of cordage and ladders.

After we had spent two hours in inspecting the vessel, Lieutenant Johnston took me to the Howe of 120 guns, which, however, is nine feet narrower than the Queen; we next visited the Indus of 84 guns, which bears on the upper deck, as an admonitory warning, Nelson's celebrated words before the battle of Trafalgar—"England expects every man to do his duty." At three o'clock, we were again on board the Queen, where I dined in the company of the highly accomplished officers. Johnston afterwards accompanied me into the town, and showed me the palace, formerly belonging to the grand master, now the residence of the governor, the armoury, and the fine church of St. John's. Here we parted: my young friend was obliged by his duty to return to his ship, while I was tempted, by the coolness of the evening, to linger for some time in the town, so that it was dark when I reached the Tagus. The next morning at sun-rise I again went ashore to view the fortifications, and about twelve o'clock returned on board, quite exhausted with my fatiguing excursion. Preparations were already made to put to sea, for the steamer had arrived from Marseilles with the English mail. Meanwhile, we amused ourselves with watching the diving of some lively boys, who willingly went to the bottom of the sea, to fetch up some copper coins.

The weather was perfectly fine when we weighed anchor at three o'clock in the afternoon, but towards evening a westerly wind with rain arose. On Friday the 15th, a south-east wind cooled the air, rain alternated with sunshine, and in the evening continued flashes of lightning, in the west, illumined the sky and the sea; on Saturday, the wind abated, a total calm succeeded, and we were surrounded by a glassy sea under an unclouded sky. On Monday, however, at three o'clock in the afternoon, while we were passing the Arab towers, the sea suddenly became greatly agitated, our vessel pitched, heaved, and the waves dashed over her forepart, with such violence that we could not proceed more than seven knots an hour. We were scarcely eight miles from the coast; a scorching wind passed over the arid plains of Africa, and we saw the hot vapour floating over the dazzling white sand of the desert.

Shortly afterwards we descried the light-house of Alexandria. About two miles before the entrance into the harbour, which has a sufficient depth of water, but at one point is scarcely 200 paces broad, we had considerable difficulty in taking a pilot on board, near the vicinity of the coast, where some hundreds of small stone windmills are erected. In boarding our vessel this handsome, long-bearded Turk dropped his slippers, and seemed more disposed to leave us to our fate than to lose them. The sun was sinking towards the horizon as we entered the harbour, which presented a very animated scene — the Pacha's fleet, consisting of more than twenty men-of-war of various sizes, lying at anchor within it. While wending our way through this forest of masts a boat with Europeans, who welcomed us with waving their hats and handkerchiefs, came out to meet us; and before we had cast anchor, we were surrounded by innumerable Egyptian boats, from which arose such a medley of cries and shouts, that in truth we could not even hear ourselves speak. We were obliged, stick in hand, to force our way through this importunate crowd; and it was only by similar means that the agents of the Company succeeded in transporting our effects and securing us quiet possession of the boats we had need of. On landing, camel and ass drivers received us in the same riotous manner; however, I was resolved not to employ any of them, but, accompanied by a guide, preferred proceeding in the cool of the evening to the inn.

I was treading the classic soil of Egypt, so rich in historical reminiscences; but the images which passed before me in the twilight of evening were not like the creations of fancy. As I wandered, full of thought, through the narrow dirty streets of Alexandria, I every where encountered the Eastern world, with its peculiarities, its singular manners and customs, and its strange natural physiognomy. Here were groups of Mussulmans sitting in their picturesque costume, and smoking their pipes in gravity and silence; there women and girls closely veiled, with the exception of their eyes, fled at the approach of the infidels; in the gay bazar illuminated with lamps was seen all the bustle of a little commercial world — men and boys talking and bargaining, while asses were furiously driven amidst the throng, or heavily laden camels paced with a slow and cautious step through the crowd. No indication of joy or mirth was to be seen or heard.

After I had followed my guide for about half an hour, we suddenly entered a large square surrounded by lofty and handsome buildings belonging to the consuls: winding stairs rise to a considerable height above the flat roofs, and afford an extensive prospect over the city and the sea. Here too our inn was situated. We had barely sufficient time allowed us comfortably to partake of refreshments; and having regaled ourselves with bananas, melons, and delicious grapes, we were informed that our guides and asses were waiting. A disorderly crowd of boys and youths rushed upon us with their beasts, uttering their loud, incoherent yells in broken English. Before I well knew what was done, I was lifted upon an ass and driven away. My companions were treated in the same summary manner, and our cavalcade galloped, helter-skelter, to embark on the Mahmudic canal.

The evening, which the bright light of the moon and the total stillness rendered peculiarly agreeable, was as delightful as the most lively imagination can paint. Our route lay along groves of palm, over which passed a light sea breeze, and wafted pure reviving odours, which invigorated the breast with their balsamic fragrance. On passing through the gate of a small fort, a Turkish officer counted our little company, and we then proceeded full trot between bare stony hills, past Pompey's Pillar, and in less than an hour — it was just eleven — we were under shady sycamores, at the place of embarkation. A covered iron gondola, resembling a cage for monkeys rather than a boat, could with difficulty accommodate all the passengers. I therefore preferred, though the cool damp nights are said to be very injurious to the health, to remain on deck till the morning, wrapped up in my cloak.

The Mahmudic canal, the work of Mehemet Ali, is eighty-four miles long, fifty paces broad, and was at this time from four to six feet deep. It runs from the Nile at the village of Atfeh, to Alexandria, and serves not only for navigation, but likewise for irrigating the adjacent country. Innumerable Persian wheels turned by oxen convey the water to the canals, whence it is carried in every direction over the country, and the soil consequently yields abundance of rice, cotton, tobacco, and corn. On either side is a narrow pathway for horses and camels.

After tedious altercations we at length commenced our voyage. An Arab steersman, and two rowers of the same nation, aided by four horses, set the gondola in motion, and a man stationed in the fore-part spoke through a most discordant trumpet, at the approach of any boat. This always created a commotion; before they could resolve to which side they should respectively keep, both parties cried, shouted, and heartily abused each other; sometimes they got so entangled that our rowers were compelled to swim to the bank and take the towing line from the horses. Amidst all this din, which was increased by the monotonous creaking of the waterwheels, and the cries of birds flying over our heads, sleep was not to be thought of. Happily the moon shed so bright a light, that all objects might be pretty clearly distinguished. The navigation on the canal was extremely brisk; sometimes we met boats conveying travellers, or cargoes of cotton, corn, and mats; and then again, others laden with water jugs, poultry, and fruit. The villages lying on the banks, like most of those in Egypt, are built of clay, and consist of an irregularly constructed mass: some of the buildings are round resembling our ovens, others look like little towers, while others again are square. They are seldom more than twenty feet high, and are often without either roof or window, and in that case have only narrow loopholes. A small court-yard, enclosed by clay walls, in which the cattle are kept, or the threshing-floor is laid, is attached to most of them. The vicinity of such a village is generally indicated by date palms and bananas which surround it, and agreeably diversify the monotonous appearance of the country. Tents are set up in several spots for the troops engaged on the works, and superintendents employed by Mehemet Ali.

On the 19th of July at nine in the morning, we saw a gondola adorned with flags and streamers, which, as our boatmen informed us, was conveying a daughter of the Pacha. Behind the elegantly carved lattices of the cabin, we saw several veiled females, whose eyes were inquisitively directed towards us. A Turk of distinction, probably the husband, was seated on fine carpets in the open air, smoking a long pipe, and having coffee and various kinds of fruits and sweetmeats spread out before him. Their eunuchs, military attendants, and servants, followed in an equally pretty gondola. But this scene of splendour and luxury was succeeded by one of sorrow and misery. A large boat crowded with chained slaves, Arabs and Abyssinians, who were to be employed in the navy, followed in the track. Many of these poor wretches, we were told, often pull out their teeth or cut off a finger, in order to avoid the hard fate that awaited them.

Our voyage was very diversified and animated; — boats and gondolas filled with people in a variety of costume, forming the most picturesque groups — caravans, riders on horses or asses — post-messengers — the working of the telegraphs along the banks, and between whiles the boatmen enjoying the pleasure of swimming. I was particularly struck with the appearance, and splendid dress, of Said Pacha, who, mounted on a bay Arab, with his negro at his side, and attended by several horsemen, galloped past us at full speed. The nearer we approached the Nile, the fuller of life and activity was the scene, in the numerous craft on the canal and in the large encampments of troops on shore. The latter amused themselves with now and then wantonly discharging their muskets at us. Our progress now became more slow, as we occasionally struck on the stony bottom, and our boat was filled with water.

We were heartily glad on being informed at two o'clock that we had reached Atfeh. Here we left our gondola, and went through the village to the Nile, where the Lotus, a pretty steamer with two engines, each of sixteen horse-power, was ready to receive us, and where our luggage, which had just arrived, was being put on board. Atfeh ranks among the largest and best constructed of the Egyptian villages; it has a covered bazar, and even an inn, if a dirty house with a sign may be so designated. The Nile is here about 500 paces broad, and gradually increases in width as it approaches Cairo; in some places it flows in a bed 3000 paces in width, and is studded with sandy and clayey islands. Its banks seldom rise above fifteen feet in height, and the water, which is rendered turbid by the slimy bottom, is of an ash-grey colour. Its bed being subject to continual changes, the navigation is difficult, so that, in spite of every precaution, we twice ran aground on a sandbank, but were soon set afloat again by the power of the engines. The prospect of the richly cultivated tracts on the bank of the river, diversified by small palm groves, whose fan-like crowns rose proudly and majestically above the poor huts, or waved by the side of taper minarets, was refreshing alike to the eye and mind The little town lying on the left bank, behind Atfeh, with its numerous minarets and its neat white buildings, some of which were really handsome, presented an extremely pretty appearance. We set off in about an hour; our crew, with the exception of the engineers, consisted of Arabs, and while we sat round our dinner table on deck, watching the setting sun, our Mussulmans, one after the other, ascended the paddle-box, where they spread out their turbans, and, undisturbed by the lively conversation of the Christians at their repast, performed their stated devotions.

A fine starlight night, with a thermometer in the evening of 82° Fahrenheit, was too inviting to allow me to go early to rest, lost as I was in contemplation on the vicissitudes of human life. These reflections were awakened not only by the ample records of history, but also by the varied circumstances of inhabitants of three quarters of the globe collected together in the narrow compass of a steam-boat. Most of them could look back on a life rich in experience; but what trials and struggles may its attainment have cost them up to this very moment, and how equally chequered a future might each have to encounter ere he reached the goal! How few contented, how many dissatisfied! The epitaph in Westminster Abbey involuntarily rose to my mind:

> "Life is a jest*, and all things show it:
> I thought so once, but now I know it."

The rising sun on the 30th of July was the harbinger of

* Would not *dream* be a more appropriate word than *jest?*— H. E. L.

a fine and serene day, with an atmosphere as pure and invigorating as we had enjoyed on the preceding day. A mosque, surrounded by a grove of shady sycamore mingled with lofty date-palms, first greeted my sight; there was something mysterious and fairy-like in the magic gloom, and reminded me of the poetical scenes of the Arabian Nights. Near this mosque several of our Arab passengers went on shore, but as there was no boat to transport them to land, each one tied his scanty garments around his head, leapt naked into the river, and bidding us adieu with a *salam alekum* (peace be with thee!), swam ashore. Towards eight o'clock we came in sight of the Pyramids! from a steam-boat! What a contrast!

A mile below Cairo the country on the right bank of the Nile suddenly assumes a very busy appearance. The first object that strikes the eye is Mehemet Ali's splendid country seat, surrounded by a garden laid out with much skill and taste; more than thirty large Persian wheels are employed in its irrigation. In its immediate vicinity are some other villas, and adjoining them a row of extensive manufactories, in which, however, we did not observe any great activity. A newly-constructed road, bordered by tall, luxuriant and shady sycamores, leads from this spot, along the banks of the Nile to Cairo. Near this place we met the Atfeh steamer conveying passengers coming from India. Both parties stopped; some hurried questions were put to the few happy individuals who were hastening homewards, letters were exchanged; and we proceeded to Bulak.

Just before reaching this little town we completed our voyage of 120 miles. We had scarcely cast anchor, when boys came to meet us with asses, on which we proceeded in the usual fashion, and under a thermometer of 95° Fahrenheit, through the narrow, dirty streets of Bulak to Cairo, a distance of only three miles, which we accomplished in half an hour. On our way thither the increasing bustle and activity indicated our approach to a populous Oriental city. We met heavily-laden camels and asses, riders and pedestrians, fruitsellers, and the troops of his Highness in dirty cotton jackets: before us lay innumerable minarets; on one side the boundless valley of the Nile, and in the background the proudly towering Pyramids. With much difficulty we forced our way amidst the confused crowd, by means of the clamours and vociferations of our ruthless attendants, and passing through several narrow little streets, we rode into the courtyard of Hill's hotel. Six hours was all the time allowed us for stopping in this interesting place, and as I did not know whether circumstances would ever bring me to Cairo again, I resolved to make the best use of the scanty moments that were meted out to me.

In company with Lieutenant Bowen, an experienced traveller, and conducted by a guide, I at once set out. We rode on small asses, as is customary here, through the animated bazars, first of all to the negro slave market, for Europeans are not allowed to see that, where the whites are bought and sold. We passed through a door which was opened to admit us, into a large yard, surrounded with shady chambers, where these unhappy creatures were offered for sale, and where man may buy his fellow creature for 8*l.* up to 40*l.* Here we saw between thirty and forty male and female slaves, Abyssinians and Negroes. The women and girls, who were any thing but handsome, and clad in dirty garments which barely covered them, burst into a loud laugh on our approach: they made their observations whispering and tittering, asked us to purchase them, and jeered at us when we turned from them to the men and boys. These, who for the most part were in the prime of life, vigorous and healthy-looking, lay on rush beds in the shade, partly fettered, partly free. Their countenances bore the traces of grief and dejection; two handsome negro youths, about sixteen years of age, approached me as we were going away, and addressed a few words to me. "They want you to buy them," said our guide; "they will serve you faithfully and assiduously." "What is the price of the lads?" continued he, addressing the slave merchant, who was standing by. "Twenty pounds each," replied he. How gladly would I have given these poor youths their liberty: but this would have been of no use to them, they would have been even more destitute than before! "To give them a trifle is not advisable," said our guide, "for their tormentors would immediately take it from them."

Yet still more melancholy, nay horrible, was the sight of the mad-house. In a narrow yard, surrounded by lofty buildings, the lower rooms of which contained small cells resembling the cages of wild beasts, with iron bars, in which the inmates had barely room to lie down, there were between twenty and thirty of these unhappy beings, most of them in chains, almost naked, perishing in filth; labouring under madness which had its origin either in aberrations of hopeless love, in drunkenness, or in bodily disease. The keeper described the method adopted for their cure as very simple: — scanty food, a shower-bath three times a day, and corporal chastisement. Those who are convalescent are freed from their chains and employed in some light work, and those who can designate the days of the week and the hours of the day are discharged as cured!

Our ride to the citadel, built on a calcareous rock, about 200 feet high, in the south-eastern quarter of the city, was calculated to chase the gloomy reflections excited by the sad scenes we had quitted. From this building we enjoyed one of the finest and grandest prospects in the world: Cairo with its fifty-six minarets lay at our feet; immediately before us the barracks of the troops, and the busy scene of a market; in the background the mighty Nile, with its verdant plains, ships, country seats, and palm groves; towards the South the ancient aqueduct, the gigantic Pyramids, with a glimpse into the bare and boundless desert, and in the far distance the ruins of Memphis. A few paces off, a spot surrounded by wretched huts marks the place where Mehemet Ali destroyed the Mamelukes. From the windows of his small, one-storied marble palace this cold-blooded, artful tyrant overlooks his fine country and his mighty creations. In the vestibule of this palace we found some young men seated on carpets employed in writing at the dictation of an old grey-bearded Armenian, who was recounting the deeds of his master. The palace itself consists of a few apartments with silk divans along the walls, decorated partly in the Oriental and partly in the European style. A billiard-table serves for the recreation of Mehemet Ali, who usually plays with his Mameluke. Another building has been commenced in the vicinity of this palace, consisting of a quadrangular courtyard, surrounded by lofty marble halls supported by round and angular pillars in the Moorish style; in the centre is a covered basin, the vaulted roof of which rests upon columns; here fountains will be erected to diffuse coolness and freshness around. The whole has a grand appearance, and is executed in a skilful and pleasing style. Near these modern buildings are the ruins called by the natives Joseph's Palace. They are three thousand years old, and but little remains of them except the well, which is so deep that if a stone is thrown into it its fall can scarcely be heard.

We were quite exhausted when we reached our inn, in time, however, to fortify ourselves, by a good dinner, for our journey across the desert. Our luggage had already preceded us on forty camels. It was six o'clock when we set out in six two-wheeled carts, covered with a linen awning, and drawn by four horses, each capable of containing four persons. I had for my companions Colonel M'Neile, Captain Forbes, and my worthy subaltern officer Werner. Unfortunately, our driver was an Italian, who was to-day to make his first essay in coachmanship with untrained horses; we learnt afterwards that he had hitherto gained his livelihood as a tailor and hair-dresser, and now wished to better his condition by breaking-in horses. His setting out did not inspire us with confidence in his skill, for after spending nearly a quarter of an hour in trying to make the horses move, they broke loose and galloped full speed towards a canal twenty feet deep, into which we must inevitably have fallen, had not the man who was running at their side dexterously saved us. After we had passed through the gate, a luxuriant banana garden with a fence of tall aloes was the last indication of vegetable life that cheered us, for before us lay the stony, boundless desert. A strange feeling was awakened by the sight of half-a-dozen carriages crossing the desert in the stillness of a beautiful moonlight night, sometimes running beside, and sometimes behind, each other, in the track marked by the feet of the camels. It is not a glaring, sandy desert, as you well know, but a waste of stony earth, covered with gravel, broken by small undulating calcareous eminences, and does not assume its wild, rocky character till in the vicinity of the Red Sea. Indications that this track was once covered by the waves are every where apparent.

Before we reached the first station, our horses had refused, more than ten times, to move onwards: this obliged the other carriages to halt; the running grooms hurried to our assistance, shouted, halloed, and beat the horses; in the sequel Werner was always compelled to jump out and to set our cart in motion by pushing the wheels. After proceeding nine miles, we stopped at an isolated house, where ten horses only stood ready to relieve the wearied animals; we now went on as before, the same men running by the side eleven miles farther, to the second station, where we took coffee and rested in two large apartments till three o'clock. It was ten miles further to the third station, where some of the horses were changed, and from this place to the central station, eleven miles distant, the animals were made to exert all their strength, in order that we might reach shelter before the heat of the sun became too intense. A solitary shady thorn, called Mahomet's tree, because the great prophet is said to have rested here on his journey, and a massive anchor, give peculiar interest to this point. The house is two stories high, very roomy, and furnished with divans. Here we dined, and at five o'clock in the afternoon proceeded on our journey, the thermometer being 93° Fahr. If the road through the desert had hitherto been marked by dead camels, asses, and horses, or the graves of unfortunate travellers, it was increasingly so on this part of the journey. A large pile of stones indicated the place where only a few days before five Arabs had been struck dead by a *coup de soleil.* In two hours we reached the next halting-place, ten miles off, but hastened without stopping to the last station, which is eleven miles further on, and where we waited for the camels coming from Suez with water; we then travelled at a brisk pace to that town, which is thirteen miles distant, and alighted at the caravansary at Suez at seven o'clock in the morning.

Suez is a small dirty town, built of stone and brick, surrounded by a decayed wall, with scarcely 2000 inhabitants, who subsist by fishing and trade. It is the staple place for the coffee from Mocha, which is sent on camels to Cairo. After our luggage had been shifted and we had refreshed ourselves with sleep and food, a large boat conveyed us, at two o'clock, with the thermometer at 96°, to the war steamer Berenice, which lay about two miles off. This vessel belongs to the East India Company: it is of 646 tons burden, has an engine of 230 horse-power, and seven guns, and is commanded by Captain B——, a well-informed, able seaman, who inspired confidence by the decision of his manner, and maintained the strictest order among his crew, which consisted of thirty-six Europeans and twenty-two Lascars. A stout Arab, who has acquired great reputation by his knowledge of this sea, served as our pilot; he was the only one among the Mahometans who regularly performed his devotions on the paddle-box, at sunrise and sunset. All the arrangements were in the Indian style, and the servants were all Mussulmans and Parsees, one of whom was employed during meal-time in keeping up a fresh circulation of air by means of a large punca.

On the 22d of July at five in the afternoon we put to sea, in a dead calm; during the first thirty-six hours we saw at the same time the rocky coast and mountain chains of Egypt and Arabia. We then approached the sharp and singularly peaked eminences of Abyssinia; passed on Wednesday the 27th, at nine in the evening, the volcanic island of Zebaya, which is scarcely 800 feet high, and on the following day, the partly rocky, partly sandy islands of Jibbel, Zuger, and Harnish. Off Mocha a gun was fired to announce our arrival, and soon afterwards a boat put off which received the letters for the agent at that place. Mocha with its closely-built houses and clay huts, above which rise two minarets, surrounded by a few date-palms, appears to lie in a desert.

Our voyage on the unruffled sea would have been very agreeable, had we not been oppressed by a constant heat of 100° Fahr., which even at night fell only to 89°, and was not tempered by any breeze. Neither baths nor any other artificial means were of the slightest avail; eau de Cologne alone afforded momentary refreshment; and we passed our days in a state of languor without being able to procure sleep. But on the evening of the 28th, when we passed through the Straits of Bab-el-Mandeb into the agitated southern ocean, a cooling monsoon blew in our faces, by which the temperature of the air and sea was mitigated 10°, as you will perceive from the accompanying observations. The next morning, at 8 o'clock, we entered the Bay of Aden, which is surrounded by bare rugged rocks 1780 feet in height.

We were not even allowed sufficient time to go ashore, because the Cleopatra steamer, of 700 tons burden and 220 horse-power, was waiting for us, and we were to proceed on the voyage as soon as ever the baggage was moved from one vessel to the other. Fifty Sepoys, invalids of the regiment stationed here, together with their wives and children, were embarked with us. These brown, naked, sickly-looking people, most of them Hindoos, were uncomfortably lodged in the fore part of the vessel; and as their religion forbids them to cook on board, their only food was rice moistened with water and seasoned with spices, of which they partook so sparingly that it seemed barely sufficient to sustain life.

At 3 o'clock in the afternoon we weighed anchor. A violent storm arose at the mouth of the bay, as we put to sea; and scarcely had we passed the last rocks when the cry of fire was raised by the terrified Lascars. The engine was instantly stopped, and I saw some of the crew pouring pailfuls of water on the engine, which, not having been properly oiled, had become ignited. Matters were, however, soon set to rights, and in a quarter of an hour we were able to proceed on our voyage. The sea continued very rough; the wind, however, was not so violent as before, but the sky was covered with a grey veil, through which the sun shed only a faint melancholy gleam. Though the Cleopatra was in other respects so admirable in its arrangements, yet the cleanliness peculiar to the English was lamentably wanting. The provisions were scarcely eatable, and during the eight days we passed on board I lived almost wholly on rice and wine.

In the afternoon of the 31st we reached the region of the Monsoon: the engine was now stopped, the sails hoisted, and a strong wind carried us rapidly forward, at the rate of eight knots an hour. We had not proceeded long, and the sun was already setting, when a loud cry arose of some one overboard. It was the wife of one of the Hindoo soldiers, who, in preparing her bed for the night, lost her balance, and feeling herself going, exclaimed, "My husband! my husband!" The ship passed over her, and she instantly disappeared. The captain immediately had the sails furled; but before the vessel could be stopped and the life-boat put out, full a quarter of an hour had elapsed. An officer with six seamen, carrying a lantern as a signal, hastily steered towards the spot where the poor woman had sunk. In the darkness of the night the little boat soon vanished from our eyes, and we waited long and anxiously for its return: it was nearly half an hour ere we saw it approach us, but, as might be expected, without the body of the unfortunate Hindoo. Two days after this we buried one of our sailors. As the sun was sinking into the ocean the ship's bell was tolled; the sailors, dressed in their best suit, carried the corpse on a simple bier, charged with cannon balls and covered with a flag, to the side of the vessel: here the captain having read the incomparable burial service and pronounced the blessing, the sailors lowered the body of their comrade into its ocean-grave. It was a solemn moment! But I was shocked and astonished to see some of our passengers stand with their coffee-cups in their hands to witness this mournful ceremony!

From this time slight showers of rain occasionally passed over us, but, contrary to expectation, the nearer we approached Bombay the more pure was the air, and the more serene and lovely was the sky. The wind had abated so much that, on the 4th of August, it was found expedient to set the engine at work again. At length, on the 6th, we descried in the hazy distance the coast of Bombay; from this time we met many fishing-boats, which often go out as far as twenty miles to sea. In joyful expectation, we all stood on deck with our eyes riveted on the rocks and lighthouse of Bombay; but before we could clearly discern them, total darkness set in. The captain sent up blue lights from time to time, which were answered from the pilot-boats, by which such a magic brightness was spread around, that the ocean was illumined to a great distance, and our vessel seemed to swim in a sea of light. Towards 8 o'clock, we approached the harbour, which was full of vessels, saluting them as we entered with the thunder of our guns, and ere long the loud clank of the ponderous anchor chain, announced the happy termination of our voyage.

You may imagine that I was all impatience to set my foot on shore. Lieutenant Bowen and myself accordingly engaged the first boat; our luggage was speedily stowed in it, and in less than an hour, I trod the soil of India. But how shall I describe the impression which almost overpowered me at this moment! To find myself in the land which was the cradle of the human race, the land of poetry, and of the Arabian Nights! I could scarcely conceive that the dreams of my youth were realised. Though it was dark, the naked forms that flitted before me, the style of the architecture of the houses, and the foreign character of the scenery, told me that I was indeed in a new world. An officer, who was riding the rounds, was the first European whom we met; we of course overwhelmed him with questions respecting the army, and I was glad that he gave me hopes of being an eye-witness of some military operations. We were soon afterwards lodged in the Victoria Hotel, the only inn in this place, which much resembles our German post-houses, while the charges are on the scale of the first-rate hotel in London. We were, however, heartily glad to partake of a good supper, after which I took possession of a bed covered with a mosquito net, and soon fell into a profound sleep, from which I was awakened by the rising sun and the screams of innumerable crows.

LETTER II.

TO ALEXANDER VON HUMBOLDT.

Bombay: the town and harbour.—Native town.—Bazars.—Merchants and artizans.—Colabah.—Domestic establishments of Englishmen of distinction.—Excursions in the environs and to Malabar Point and Pareil.—Burning the dead.—The Parsees.—Gymnastic exercises of the Indians and their Jugglers.—Journey to Poonah.—The chain of Ghauts.—Poonah.—Festivities of the natives in honour of the governor.—Bayaderes.—Mode of life of the English.—Parbutty and the palace of the Peishwa.—Return to Bombay.—The rainy season.—Preparations for our journey to Kurrachee.—Establishment of the governor.

Bombay, August 3d, 1842.

HAVING accompanied me till my arrival in Bombay, permit me to give you some account of this delightful island, before I proceed to relate any particulars of my diversified mode of life within the last few weeks.

At the foot of the Western Ghauts lies a small group of islands, of which Bombay is the most important. It is situated in 18° 58′ N. L.,.and 72° 55′ E. L. from Greenwich, and is connected on its northern side by an arched stone bridge with Salsette, the larger island. It is surrounded by several others of a lofty rocky character, the most remarkable of which is Elephanta, famed for its ancient colossal Hindoo or Buddah temple, hewn in the solid rock. Back bay, as it is called, is formed by two peninsulas which stretch far into the sea: the northern of these is the rocky promontory of Malabar Point, and the southern, the narrow Colabah, is of coral formation, and scarcely rises above the surface of the water. The harbour is spacious, and is situated between Colabah, Bombay, and Salsette; four miles from its eastern extremity is Butcher's Island, which is apparently connected with Elephanta, and a little to the south lies Caranja, five miles to the south-west of which, between Toll Point and Colabah, is the entrance into the harbour of Bombay. The lighthouse stands upon a rock 150 feet above the level of the sea, at the extreme point of Colabah. The harbour is defended by numerous batteries, which would render a hostile landing next to impossible. The coast is every where adorned with palm-trees, and I was especially struck with the beauties of the slender, lofty cocoa palm, which lifts its graceful crown towards the skies.

Bombay is divided into two towns, one lying next to the sea, and surrounded by the fortifications, and the other called the Black or Native town, situated to the west, and built upon an alluvial soil. The streets of the former are narrow, the houses three stories high, and built of wood or brick; their external appearance is not unlike that of the houses in the towns of Southern Italy. They all have verandahs which rise one above the other, and are supported by wooden pillars, and small bow windows, which are adorned with neat trellis-work. In the lower part of the town are the bazars, which are narrow and dirty, and are chiefly kept by the Parsees. The only remarkable building in Bombay is the Government-house; it has a fine colonnade, and in front of it is a square planted with trees, with a fountain rising in the centre. It comprehends the several government offices, a library, and a spacious saloon, adorned with marble statues of the excellent Mountstuart Elphinstone, and Sir John Malcolm. Adjoining this building are the extensive arsenals and docks. The fleet of Bombay consists of 22 war-steamers, six of which are armed for service; there are also 18 sailing vessels, 11 of which carry 98 guns; three of these are sloops, four brigs, four schooners, and four cutters; there are besides 11 iron steam-boats for the navigation of the Indus and the Euphrates. I must not forget to mention that a school-house has been recently erected, and I am happy to say that much attention has lately been paid, both by the government and private individuals to the education of the natives. I hope to be able to give you some particulars respecting it on a future occasion.

A road leads from the extensive fortifications through a gate towards the west, across a broad esplanade to the Black Town, which is about a mile distant. On our way thither we saw several hundreds of men and women, standing in the most picturesque groups round brick wells, drawing water, washing linen, and refreshing themselves by throwing large pitchers of water over each other. The streets in the Native town are very narrow, and consist of small brick houses, two stories high: the lower story is raised but little above the ground, in which the open bazars are kept, where the dealers sit cross-legged behind their merchandise, which is piled up in baskets. Here a scene of the most busy and noisy activity constantly prevails, but especially in the evening, when the streets and bazars are lighted by numerous small lamps. Thousands of natives throng the stalls. examining the goods of the dealers, among whom the Bannia (corn chandler), and the Mittie-walla (confectioner), have the chief custom.

BANNIA.

The *Bannia* has every variety of grain, wheat, rice, barley, iowary (*Holcus Sorghum*), bagera (*Panicum spicatum*), Gram (*Cicer arietinum*), &c. exposed for sale in baskets, and in dry weather it is piled up in heaps in the street, in front of his booth. He generally has an iron pan at his side; this he keeps constantly hot, and pours maize into it, which is thus heated and roasted. It is a favourite food of the Indians, but their choicest delicacy is a cake made of flour and sugar, seethed in Ghee (clarified butter): these the *Mittie-Wallas* (p. 35.) arrange with much taste, and attract great numbers of women and children. It is, however, too sweet and indigestible to suit our refined palates, though the natives indulge in it, till they actually become ill.

MITTIE-WALLA.

The *Soottar* (carpenter) (p. 36.) employs only five tools, namely a hatchet, hammer, saw, gimblet, and knife, and with these, in a very awkward sitting posture, he not only makes the neatest furniture, but the prettiest boxes of Sandal-wood, inlaid with steel and ivory, in the most delicate and elegant patterns.

At his side is seated the *Moochee* (shoemaker) (p. 37.), manufacturing singularly formed pointed shoes, and it is remarkable that he generally works with his head uncovered.

A loud hammering indicates the workshop of the *Lohar* (smith and locksmith) (p. 38.), who performs his hard labour in a similar, inconvenient sitting posture.

The *Seikelgar* (stone and glass grinder) (p. 39.)

works in a less constrained position, and sets his small stone wheel in motion by means of a tight string.

SOOTTAR.

As soon as the cool season sets in and refreshing winds prevail, the harvest of the *Pattangh-walla* (the kite-maker) (p. 40.) commences, because old and young delight in flying the kite; and while the Mussulman selects those which are adorned with the crescent, the Hindu chooses those which are ornamented with stars and painted in gay colours.

The *Bazars* (calico printer) (p. 41.) displays much skill in printing from wooden blocks, which he holds in his hands; but his goods are not so much in vogue since the handsomer and less expensive English prints have come into fashion.

Next to the Bazars, the *Ruiwalla* (the cotton beater) (p. 42.) and *Sellogry* (the cotton weaver) (p. 43.) generally take their place. The former beats the cotton, just as it is taken from the husk, against a tightened cord, till it becomes loose.

MOOCHEE.

The *Sellogry* prepares the finest and most delicate tissue on a loom, taking off the flocks with a brush and arranging the threads.

Among the most wretched-looking people are the *Dahl-Bechnewallæ* (poor women, sellers of dhal, *Cytisus Cajan*) (p. 44.), who sit at the corners of the bazars, and carry on a little trade in fruit, spices, or flowers.

The *Batty-walla* (candle maker) (p.45.) looks almost equally miserable; during the cool evenings he sits by his hoops, which are suspended in the open air, and to which the wicks are fastened. The hoops he turns diligently over a vessel filled with hot wax or tallow, which he pours over the wicks with a ladle, and the current of air thus created quickly hardens them. Candles are, however, in request only in the cool season, and then chiefly by Europeans; lamps made of clay or glass are in general use.

LOHAR.

The *Parsee* is distinguished among the busy crowd by his lofty, vigorous form, aquiline nose, large, fine eyes, and noble Greek physiognomy, set off by his high turban. The Parsees are the most industrious of all classes; they are the best shipwrights, the most able merchants, and the richest of the natives. Their chief men are distinguished by their intellectual activity, and give entertainments in the European style. One of them, the philanthropic Sir Jamsitjee Jeejeebhoy, a man worth a million, has been knighted by the Queen, on account of his benevolent character, and has been honoured with a gold medal. Most of the Parsees are acquainted with the English language and are very conversant with English literature.

The *Hindoo* is distinguished by his smaller and more elegant figure, particularly the upper part of the

SEIKELGAR.

body, and his mild expressive features: like the Parsee, he has mustachios, and wears an upper garment of white cotton, and wide pantaloons of the same material, but his turban is flatter.

The *Marwarees* (corn-dealer) (p. 64.) are of a more robust frame of body, and wear high red turbans, and girdles ornamented with heavy, gay tassels and tufts, and the women wear ivory bracelets on their arms. The Mussulman costume is very similar; he is more animated in his movements and gesticulations than the Hindu, and suffers his beard to grow.

Bombay includes several villages and many handsome country seats. Immediately behind the Black Town begins a series of the finest country houses, enclosed by beautiful gardens; both stories being surrounded by a verandah supported by pillars. As soon

PATTANGH-WALLA.

as the hot winds set in, screens lined with aromatic reeds are placed between the pillars, and constantly kept moist by running water. These villas, which are detached, are built with every accommodation and regard to the climate, and extend as far as Pareil, the residence of the governor, which is four miles distant.

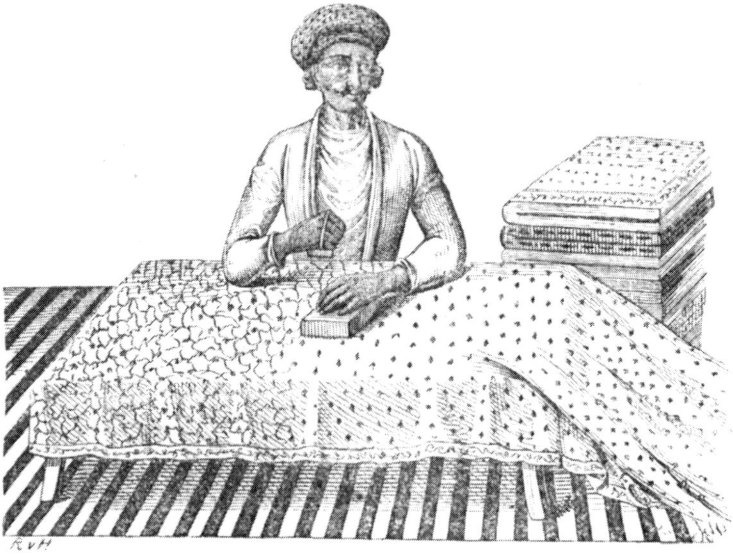

BAZARS.

Malabar Point is adorned with equally handsome country seats, the situation of which is yet more healthy and beautiful; it is the residence of the Europeans and the most distinguished of the natives. If you will bear me company in my excursion thither, you will become better acquainted with this lovely island, which is 18¼ square miles in extent, and is inhabited by about 200,000 persons, increased by a floating population of 70,000 seamen, merchants, pilgrims, and peasants. Nearly two thirds of the population are Hindus; about 20,000 Parsees, and the remainder Mussulmans, Jews, and Portuguese Christians. The latter, who have a darker complexion than the natives, were recommended to me as servants, because they are willing to perform any kind of work, and are more faithful and trustworthy than the Europeans and Mussulmans.

RUIWALLA.

The first day that I passed in India was Sunday. My companion Lieutenant Bowen, who had quitted me early to join his regiment, which had landed three days before, and was quartered in the barracks at Colabah, sent me a polite invitation to join his officers' mess. It was quite out of the question to walk thither in the burning heat of the sun; and indeed it would have been a violation of all etiquette. I therefore engaged six palanquin bearers, who carried me in an hour's time to Colabah. The motion was very pleasant, but it was quite repugnant to my feelings to be carried by my fellow beings; though these brown men (who wear no other dress than a white cotton garment round the waist) are used to it, and gladly offer their services for one rupee the whole day.*

SELLOGRY.

Colabah is joined to Bombay by a causeway, which gives it the appearance of a peninsula; as soon as we crossed this causeway, a Protestant church met our eye, and immediately behind it commenced the Bungalows. These are spacious wooden houses, of which those nearest the sea are taken down during the Monsoon. Most of them are surrounded with small gardens; and

* A rupee is equal to 16 annas, or 2 shillings sterling; a lack is 100,000 rupees, or 10,000*l.* sterling; a crore is equal to 100 lacs, or a million sterling.

the neat buildings are overshadowed by mangoes, palms, and tamarinds. I was greatly pleased with the society of my new comrades, and did not leave them till late in the evening. Two of these gentlemen, with whom I had been particularly taken, fell victims to the cholera a few days afterwards; and my travelling companion Lieutenant Bowen and some others were attacked by fever.

DAHL-BECHNEWALLEE.

As neither the governor nor the commanding general were here, I paid a visit on the following day to General Barr at Mazagon House, to whom Colonel Sykes had introduced me by letter. The general and his family were at breakfast, and I was received by all with the greatest kindness. General Barr is one of those fine, noble, manly persons who instantly produce a favourable impression; his deportment is grave and dignified; he is wholly devoted to his country and to his profession, and greatly beloved by his family, to whom, indeed, he is in every sense the kindest of husbands and fathers. His lady is the most warm-hearted and benevolent of women, and has no thought but that of ordering her family as in the sight of God. Three sons, officers in the army, and two daughters, who closely resemble their estimable parents, and one of whom has been recently

BATTY-WALLA.

married, completed this happy family circle. After some conversation, I was invited to take up my residence in the house, and you may imagine that I considered myself fortunate to be received into such a family. The same evening I was surrounded with all the comforts and conveniences of a wealthy Indian country seat.

The general has four-and-twenty servants, one of whom stands at the foot of the stairs in the hall to receive visiters; near him is generally seated the *Durzee* (man tailor), busily occupied in embroidering, or making articles of dress for the ladies.

The man with a stick in his hand, and wearing a metal plate on his breast, is the *Chuprassy*, (p.47.) who is employed as messenger or letter-carrier. He is also engaged by rich natives to precede them, and proclaim to the crowd the virtues, powers, and noble qualities of his master in flowing and poetical phrases.

DURZEE.

Another servant, who always wears a bunch of keys at his side, is the *Sirdar* (p. 48.), called the Treasurer and Superintendent, and sometimes the Butler.

The *Byhishti* (water-carrier) (p. 49.) is always seen with his leather water-bag at his side.

Early in the morning, shortly before breakfast, the *Mahli* (gardener) (p. 50.) brings a nosegay and a small basket in which fruits and vegetables are tastefully arranged; his master expresses his satisfaction by touching what he brings with his right hand.

The sole business of the *Hookaburdar* (p. 51.) is to attend to his master's hookah or pipe; he carefully rolls up the tobacco, which is composed of flowers and spices, moistened with rose-water, and throws it on the

CHUPRASSY.

charcoal fire. By means of a long tube, which is wetted from time to time with rose-water, the fumes are drawn through the water, which is in the stand, and diffuse an aromatic odour.

When the heat is very great, another servant, the *Chowree burdar*, stands behind his master's chair, cooling the air with a fan made of the silky hair of the tail of the Nepaulese cow. All the washing is done by men, and the Dobys (p. 52.), though they wash the linen in cold water, and only beat it, far surpass our laundresses in the execution of their labours.

SIRDAR.

Fresh cool beverages are a great luxury, or, I should rather say, are quite indispensable; great pains are therefore taken to cool water in porous vessels or in ice, and wine is cooled by means of saltpetre and salt, or the bottle is covered with damp linen and exposed to a current of air. The *Abdar* (p. 53.), who has the charge of this department, is the only servant who is permitted to keep on his shoes while performing his office, to prevent him from taking cold.

BYHISHTI.

The *Babatschy* (cooks) (p. 54.) are well acquainted with English cookery, and are very cleanly and teachable.

There are many other servants employed in the household, and others in the stables, each horse having its own groom, who runs by its side when the master either drives or rides out. The lowest of all in rank is the Mather (p. 55.): his name is indeed princely, but he is, as it were, the Paria, because it is his business to clear away the dirt, and to perform all the drudgery of the house.

MAHLI.

The *Ayah* (nurse or confidential servant) (p.56.) of the mistress of the house is generally represented with a casket of jewels in her hand, and those who have the charge of the younger children are usually accompanied, when they go out walking, by two men-servants, that the little ones may have protection at hand if needed. In this singular country every one attends exclusively to his own particular duty ; the Hindoo is commanded to do so by his religion, and the Mussulman follows the example as a matter of convenience. Each therefore thoroughly understands his own business; and the consequence is, that you are admirably waited upon, though the greater part of these useful people are content with eight rupees or sixteen shillings per month.

HOOKABUDRAR.

I now pass my time quite in the Indian fashion. In the morning, before sunrise, I take a ride with H——, the eldest son of my excellent host, to different parts of the island ; the refreshment of a bath succeeds, and immediately after, about half-past nine o'clock, we assemble for breakfast, after which every one follows his own occupation till two, when a slight luncheon once more unites our circle. About five o'clock we again make some little excursion, and at eight we meet

DOBY.

at dinner, where we relate to each other the little adventures of the day, and in the evening we amuse ourselves at the billiard-table. Receiving and paying visits give some diversity to our daily life. Although this is the rainy season, we continue to have the finest weather; slight showers of rain falling only in the night, so that we are frequently able to extend our rides to the most distant parts of the island.

ABDAR.

A new causeway leads from Mazagon House through the west end of the Black Town, across the marshy soil of the island, past the cemetery of the Mussulmans; not far from which it is intended to build a theatre. Immediately beyond the plain commences the Malabar peninsula; at the entrance of which stands the handsome country house of a wealthy Hindoo goldsmith, with a pagoda in front of it. The peninsula is very rocky and extends far into the sea: it is adorned with a pleasing variety of country seats, interspersed with groves of cocoa-nut trees, and traversed in all directions by good roads. We followed a winding direction round the northern extremity, and the nearer we approached the sea the more wild and rude the scenery became; shattered masses of rock lay scattered around, and the palm tree rarely enlivened this district There was something sublime in the appearance of

BABATSCHY.

this tract washed by the dashing billows of the majestic ocean. Malabar Point is formed by a rock, 60 feet high, projecting into the sea, upon which Mr. Elphinstone built a small summer residence; and not far off, close upon the beach, are the ruins of some very ancient Hindoo temples. From this point we enjoyed one of the most beautiful prospects in the world, closely resembling that of the Bay of Naples, but far exceeding it in grandeur. Before us rolled the boundless ocean, breaking with fury against the rocks, and dashing its waves aloft into the air. A fine view presented itself of the two towns which form Bombay, Colabah, and, beyond it, the port, animated with numerous ships, with the islands of Ele-

MATHER.

phanta, Caranja, and Butcher's Island, scattered like fairy flower-gardens on the bright bosom of the ocean.

One evening at sunset, as we were riding home along the road leading to the south, enjoying this varied prospect, we saw a poor Hindoo, with a small box in his hand, carefully feeding with sugar the ants that were crawling across the path. Masses of rock painted red indicated this, and some other sacred spots. At a distance on the strand, in a bay formed by Colabah and Malabar Point, we saw bright flames

AYAH.

ascending in several places; they were the funeral piles of those who had died in the course of the day. As soon as a person expires the corpse is bathed, anointed with fragrant essences, and then placed on a bed of holy grass before the door of the house. Hymns and prayers are addressed to the dead body, which is strewn with sacred leaves and flowers, and the relations, with concise exclamations of grief, instantly bear the deceased to the funeral pile. In Southern India the procession is accompanied with music, and the face of the departed is coloured with crimson paint. The mourners, who are members of a religious order, sit cross-legged in damp garments round the fire, seemingly lost in contemplation, with their eyes fixed on the dead body which is placed between blocks of wood; and, when the last remains have been burnt up, the ashes are collected, and every one returns to his home in silent meditation. The pile is not more than five feet high, and is adorned with flowers; ghee and fragrant oils are poured upon the wood to cherish the flames; and in a few short hours every trace has been effaced by the wind or the waves.

The Parsees meanwhile, turning towards the ocean, gaze upon the setting sun, and worship that luminary and the watery element; many of them holding manuscripts in their hands, the language of which they do not understand. Their burying-place is not far distant: it is planted with palm trees and surrounded by a wall; thither they bear the corpse, which, like the Hindoos, they deck with flowers, and place in the open air, and wait patiently till it is devoured by the birds. As soon as a limb has been eaten by them, and especially if they have commenced with the eyes, these poor ignorant people imagine that the life of the deceased was acceptable to God, and that his spirit is in bliss!

On one occasion I visited the temples and the fakirs, the Hindoo saints. My young friend told me of two of these men, who, for fifteen years, had subjected themselves to the greatest bodily pain. One of them held up a flower-pot in his right hand, and had performed his vow with such energy of will that his nails had grown into it; the other who, likewise naked, had suffered his hair and beard to grow, and held a lotus flower. Neither of them could put their arm into any other posture; they were held in great veneration by the members of their own religion, who daily brought them food and drink, and performed the necessary ablutions. On our arrival at the pagoda my friend inquired after them: we were sorry to learn that they had quitted the temple only the day previous, as the term of their probation had expired. We then rode to some other pagodas; in front of nearly all of them was a tank or walled pond, with flights of steps leading into the water, in which the people bathe, to wash away their sins. The Brahmins are distinguished by their foreheads being painted in a particular manner, generally red, by their white garments, and a cotton skein of thread fastened to their left shoulder and brought across the breast. The fakirs are perfectly naked, emaciated, and very dirty; their faces are deformed by all kinds of paint, and their lank, matted hair gives them a very disgusting appearance. They are regarded as saints, and every temple can boast of some of them. Others perform their devotions in luxury and indolence, satisfying themselves with frequent bathing and silent meditation, or with smoking the hookah with grave indifference. In front of the temple is the sacred bull, hewn in stone, and within the building are some of their divinities with burning lamps placed before them.

Having determined to undertake a journey to Poonah, in company with the younger son of my excellent host, the General's lady contrived to let me see some specimens of the dexterity of the natives. First of all, several men, women, and children appeared in the garden, to exhibit their skill in balancing; it is impossible for you to form any conception of the agility, distortion of limb, and pliability of body of these people: our rope-dancers would have been quite abashed in their presence; but I can tell them, for their comfort, that they would have displayed more grace in their exhibitions. They represented almost all kinds of remarkable animals, in doing which several bodies were so interlaced, that the different individuals could scarcely be distinguished. They also performed feats of strength, and one man bore on his shoulders six others, standing two and two above each other. These performances were succeeded by a band of jugglers, consisting of a long-bearded old man, accompanied by three boys and several women. They first exhibited various tricks with tamed serpents, among which was the venomous cobra de capella; these animals sometimes danced to the sound of a pipe, twined themselves together, and then suddenly disappeared. They then exhibited the most extraordinary transformations, some of which were wholly inexplicable. Thus a strapping boy fifteen years old contrived to creep into a round basket, two feet high and three feet broad, in such a manner that when the basket was opened there was nothing to be seen of him; he must have managed most cleverly to cower down into the veriest nook on that side of the basket which was nearest us. The exhibition closed with thrusting daggers down their throats, and flames issuing from their mouths.

I have likewise had an insight into social life in India, for which I am indebted to the hospitality of some of the principal families; it consists chiefly of dinners, musical entertainments, and, in the cooler season, of balls. At the former, a stranger is much struck by the appearance of the numerous attendants in their national costume, each guest being obliged to bring his own servant. Everything is in the English style, with the exception of the Punca, which is suspended over the table, and keeps up a constant circulation of air. I cannot omit speaking of the mango. This gold-coloured fruit, which is larger than our nectarine, has a most delicious fragrance, and combines in its taste the ambrosia of the pineapple, the flavour of the orange, and the juiciness of the peach. The mango of Bombay is the finest in India, and is sent by messengers to great distances; preserved in sugar, it is one of the most delicious fruits imaginable.

One fine morning, the air having been cooled during the night by a fall of rain, we rode to Pareil. On the way thither, we crossed several eminences which afforded beautiful prospects over the island and the sea towards the Ghauts. We met many country people carrying various kinds of fruits, or large vessels full of liquor (called by the English toddy), an intoxicating beverage, extracted from the palm. A mile to the left of this road is the Botanic Garden, which was formed two years ago by voluntary contributions. Pareil is a large, irregular building, and was formerly a Portugese Jesuit College; it contains some very fine and richly ornamented apartments, and is surrounded by an extensive, but ill-arranged garden. The governor generally spends the hot season at this place, and the rainy season in his country seat near Poonah. He receives the superior officers and strangers at breakfast, every Saturday.

On the evening of the same day we visited the lighthouse of Colabah. An adjacent churchyard contains the graves of the many persons who have suffered shipwreck on this coast. Two years ago, some vessels with troops from England stranded here, on board of which were several officers with their families, and above 500 men, few of whom could be saved. It was a heartrending moment to the seamen and spectators on shore, to see the despair of the people on the wreck struggling with the waves, without being able to render them the slightest assistance. I was told that in June 1837 the monsoon set in with such violence that most of the vessels in the harbours were dismasted. The prospect from the lighthouse towards Malabar Point is most beautiful: in other directions the objects lie too scattered to be comprehended in one view. Between the burying-place, to which I have before alluded, and the walls of the lighthouse, innumerable serpents have their retreat.

On the 14th of August we commenced our journey to Poonah: at 11 o'clock we went on board what is called a Banderboat, which had a small cabin, with a crew of five Mussulmans, a steersman, and four rowers. We expected to be able, by the aid of wind and tide, to reach the village of Panwelly, above thirty miles distant, in eight hours; but we had scarcely sailed a league beyond Elephanta, when we were driven between Butcher's Island and Salsette, where the wind gradually abated, and we were obliged to have recourse to our oars. A monotonous singing, and the Gurguru, or pipe producing a guttural sort of sound, passing from mouth to mouth, broken by the exhortations of the steersman, animated our indolent crew: but our misadventures had retarded us so much, that we were obliged to cast anchor at eight o'clock at the mouth of the Panwell river, where we waited for the next tide, with which we reached the Mole at four o'clock in the morning. We found our one-horse buggy waiting for us at a bungalow near the bank; and we drove along an excellent road, made by Mountstuart Elphinstone, through the neat and cheerful village of Panwell. As soon as we had passed the village, we entered a richly cultivated valley, between the most luxuriant rice fields, and at our side and in the background rose the picturesque, singularly formed chain of the Ghauts. A dingy funnel-shaped mountain, which rises like the chimney of a forge from the centre of a table mountain, in wild, jagged masses, forms a most strange contrast with the bright verdure of the foliage and meadows. This striking object is surrounded by ragged masses of rock, which tower majestically above the large-leaved teak-tree, and appear from a distance exactly like ruins of ancient castles. They rise about 3000 feet above the level of the sea. We saw scarcely a bird, excepting some green parrots and the dazzling white, long-legged Paddy bird (*Ardea*), which was seeking its food in the rice plantations. The inhabitants were ranged round the fire in their wretched clay huts, or walking in the fields covered with a mat of palm-leaves, which runs to a point above their heads, and hanging down over their shoulders, serves as a protection against the rain. Every now and then we met long trains of amply-laden Hackeries drawn by oxen carrying sacks. The creaking of the wheels of these clumsy and heavily-built Hackeries, or farmer's waggons, is heard at some distance. These wheels are made either of a solid piece of wood, or have eight spokes, two and two, placed close to each other, and traverse the axle-tree nearly at right angles. The Hackeries are used by the farmers to bring home their harvest, and to carry their productions to market. In those districts, where manure is employed in tillage, a basket is hung on the Hackery to convey it to the fields. We also occasionally met Brinjares, driving oxen, carrying sacks of corn upon their backs.

After proceeding nine miles, we reached our first stage close to a hideous Maharatta idol hewn in stone, and painted red. Here the road rises more and more, the eminences are more thickly wooded, and the valley gradually closes in at the village of Kampuly, at the side of which stands an ancient temple, dedicated to Mahadeo (the God of Death), surrounded by a large walled tank. From this place, the road leads in many windings up the Kandalla pass to the village of Kandalla or Kindalla, which is about 3000 feet above the level of the sea. Here we left our buggy, which was drawn up by men while we were carried to the summit in palanquins. The morning was delightfully cool, and the sun from time to time darted his beams through the breaking clouds: the scenery which surrounded me was luxuriant in the highest degree, and the flowery carpet of the mountain parterres lay before me in such freshness and beauty, that I found it impossible to remain any longer in my palanquin, borne on the shoulders of men. At one point of view we suddenly overlooked the whole of the valley through which we had just passed. On one side ten beautiful waterfalls, — the largest of which, the Calliani, is about 1400 feet high, — rushed down over ledges, and broken masses of rock presented a most magnificent sight which can be enjoyed only in the rainy season; while at the bottom,

MARWAREES.

deep down in the valley, lies Kampuly with its solitary temple. Turning to the other side, the chain of the Ghauts, running towards the south, and the distant wide-spread ocean, lay before us. At this moment "a solemn silence and sublime repose" reigned over the whole landscape; as if all nature was rapt in mute adoration before God.

We breakfasted with a Parsee in a bungalow at Kandalla, a little village built on the top of the Ghauts, on the most picturesque points of which stand several country houses, belonging to British officers. From hence the road gradually declines, and passes over a table land from 3000 to 4000 paces broad; the eminences at either side assume more and more an undulating character, retire to a greater distance in the vicinity of Poonah, and at length appear only in isolated masses. We found post-horses ready at every ten miles; but, as we were unfortunately obliged to reach Poonah the same day, we were forced to defer our intended excursion to the celebrated cave-temples of Carli. We did not arrive at our destination till 9 o'clock in the evening, when I was welcomed in the kindest manner in the bungalow of Captain St. Clair.

Poonah, the former residence of the Peishwa, or supreme Rajah of the Maharattas, lies on an extensive bare plateau, about 2000 feet above the sea, surrounded by strangely formed trap mountains, on the rocky summits of which are scattered ruined castles of the Maharattas. On account of the salubrity of the climate, Poonah is one of the chief stations of the British. Five thousand men were garrisoned here at this time, and Sir Thomas M'Mahon, general-in-chief, and Sir George Arthur, Governor of Bombay, were also at Poonah. The city, which in the height of its splendour contained a population of more than 140,000 inhabitants, now scarcely numbers 60,000. Most of the houses are two stories high; and are built of stone, wood, or brick. The principal streets are macadamized and very clean; the bazars broad, and planted with trees. A considerable trade is carried on, and we every where saw indications of increasing prosperity. The barracks, a Protestant church, and innumerable country houses and bungalows of the civil and military officers, surrounded with the most beautiful flower gardens and orchards, lie in a semicircle towards the east, immediately without the city, which has no gates. Besides bananas, oranges, mangoes, and pomegranates, grapes and apples grow here in perfection. Roads run in every direction, and bridges, with several arches supported by stone piers, are thrown across the Moota and Mola, which flow in a broad and stony bed.

It was a happy coincidence for me, that, on the very first day after my arrival, the principal inhabitants were preparing to give a festive reception to the Governor, who had lately arrived from Europe. Accompanied by my friend, I rode through the city to the house of a wealthy Hindoo merchant: the houses were all adorned with flowers, and crowds of persons dressed in white were standing in the streets, anxiously waiting to see the Governor pass. He was seated with Sir Charles Napier in an open carriage, preceded by a body of cavalry, and his servants, who were dressed in bright scarlet liveries; his suite followed in several other carriages, and a detachment of cavalry closed the procession. Though I had not yet been presented to Sir George Arthur, he had the goodness to invite me to be present at this interesting and unique ceremony. The houses of the gentlemen who gave the entertainment were distinguished by particularly rich garlands of flowers.

Amid the sound of unharmonious music, the host received his distinguished guest at the threshold of his gate, which opened into a quadrangle surrounded by open arcades. A narrow, dark staircase led to the very simple, low, reception room on the second floor. Here the gentlemen of the family and the servants were standing. As soon as we were seated on divans and chairs, the music (consisting of a small drum, a pipe and a kind of guitar) immediately struck up. Some of the Bayadères commenced dancing, while others at the same time crowned us with wreaths of flowers, and sprinkled us with ottar of roses. At the desire of the host, the company were presented with various kinds of gilded spices on silver salvers, and the beetle-nut, neatly folded in beetle leaves and mixed with catechu and chunam, were handed round. The Bayadères were very much ornamented with jewels, and wore massive rings in their ears and noses and around their ancles: they were dressed in gay garments, which fell in ample folds around them; and a scarf of the finest texture covered their neck and bosom, while their beautiful silky black hair hung down in braids over their shoulders. During their dance, which consisted partly in a revolving movement, partly in a springing step, they flung the shawl in various graceful forms about the body, and accompanied the music with a monotonous song. To heighten the beauty of their eyes, they had blackened the eyelids with antimony. Their hands and feet were small and delicate, and the contour of the figure and of the countenance extremely elegant and noble: if not actually beautiful, these Bayadères had a very attractive, feminine appearance.

After we had looked at the dancing for about a quarter of an hour, our host conducted us to the interior small flower garden, enclosed by the Zenana, in the centre of which was a basin with a fountain. Festoons and garlands, interspersed with innumerable lamps and painted paper lanterns, diffused a magic charm over the whole scene. While gazing around on these elegant decorations, we saw the wives and daughters of our host peeping through a wooden lattice in the second story; but no sooner did they perceive that they were remarked, than they immediately vanished from our inquisitive eyes. After taking leave of our host, we visited several other persons of distinction, and every where met with a similar reception: the more wealthy, of course, displayed greater splendour and profusion in the decorations of their houses, and likewise brought forward more numerous Bayadères.

I am living in a continual round of military and other festivities. When the gun is fired at the dawn of day, I join the troops, and much of my time is taken up with visits, and all kinds of fêtes. I cannot speak in sufficiently high terms of the hospitality of the Governor, of the general in command, and of Sir Charles Napier, and of the courtesy of the officers of all the troops, who indeed treat me like a comrade. I am particularly pleased with Dapoory, the country seat of the Governor, which is about five miles from Poonah: it is most agreeably situated, and is surrounded with a delightful flower and botanic garden. Close to it lies the village of Kirkee, where the 14th regiment of Dragoons is stationed. I have likewise attended a ball given by the officers of the 1st European regiment in their mess room. Indian luxury was here combined with European comfort. The novel sight of Indians of distinction in their picturesque costume, moving gravely and silently among the handsome ladies, and the military in their rich uniforms, furnished matter for various reflections and comparisons on the characters and manners of different nations. In the adjoining garden arbours made of artificial flowers, and tents adorned with festoons, were lighted up in every variety of style, and all the walks were laid with the richest carpets: the night was so beautiful and cool, that the company prolonged their enjoyment till the morning dawned.

Captain Keith Erskine, one of my new acquaintances, whose wit and humour is a constant source of amusement to us, undertook the wearisome task of a cicerone, and rode with me one fine morning to Parbutty, a mile south-west of the city. A short distance before reaching Parbutty we visited Heera Baugh, formerly the summer palace of the Peishwa; it is situated in a luxuriant flower garden, by the side of a large pond shaded with pipal (*Ficus religiosa*), mangoes, tamarinds, and banyan trees. We were received by Manackjy Carsetjy, a young Parsee, who had raised himself by his talents from the subordinate condition of a writer, to that of an Indian grandee. After the publication of some tolerable poems, he received, by way of encouragement, the distinguished appellation of "the Byron of the East." This, together with his subsequent travels in Europe, — where the title of prince is so lavishly bestowed upon every Indian, and where the pope and the great men of England and France, received him with special marks of distinction, and presented him with costly gifts,— tended to make him such a conceited dandy, that we can only pity the vain young man, who now really fancies himself a second Byron, for having acquired some knowledge of the civilised world.

Parbutty is an isolated peak, about 300 feet high; there are some very picturesque prospects from the summit, where several temples of Parvati, wife of Mahadeo, are built. Before us lay the pond, surrounded by a meadow, which was covered with land-crabs, and on one side of which stood the delightful Heera Baugh. Close to this palace is the Elephant park, where the Peishwa used to have combats of tigers, and behind it rose the town and numerous bungalows, amidst a forest of mango trees, above which gleamed the bright tops of the pagodas; while in the remote distance the rocky eminences were covered with Maharatta castles. Our guide was a blind Brahmin, who gave us such a vivid description, in English, of the mode of life of the Peishwa at his country-seat, of the decayed temples, and of the fine natural scenery around us, that we could scarcely persuade ourselves that he did not actually see the objects which he depicted so well. As we were going away, one of his companions asked us for an alms for him; but he himself merely expressed a wish to know our names, that he might keep us in remembrance. We returned through the ill-built and dirty south-end of the town to the old palace of the Peishwa, which is surrounded by a high wall and a moat. It is a large quadrangular building, with colonnades of elegantly carved wooden pillars, and has a kind of tower shaded by a verandah; but the whole is in such a state of decay that it is not worth the expense of repair.

The short period of eight days allotted to our stay passed rapidly away, amidst such an ample variety of objects to engage my attention. I spent the last evening at a cheerful repast with the officers of the 14th regiment of Dragoons, where, according to English custom, we had numerous toasts and speeches. With these agreeable impressions, accompanied with many good wishes, I took leave of S——, for whom I had conceived a great regard, and in two hours I was on my road to Bombay, in company with the Governor's aide-de-camp. Orders for post-horses having been sent on before, we reached Panwell early on Monday the 22d, but we were detained several hours, because the Governor's gondola did not come to fetch us till eleven o'clock. It was quite dark by the time we landed at Trombay on Salsette, whence a small carriage conveyed us along a causeway towards Colabah. The day had been very rainy, but was succeeded by a starlight night; luminous insects fluttered on every side, and every now and then some poor bird, startled by the noise of our carriage, flew across our path from the thickets, and the numerous ruined temples and Portuguese churches along the road. Our journey, which had hitherto been so prosperous, was suddenly interrupted by a slight accident: we had scarcely passed the bridge when our coachman, to avoid some carts, turned too far aside and overturned us into a ditch. My companion leaped out of the carriage window in a trice; but I waited very patiently till the door was opened, and was thankful to find myself on my legs again. Our light vehicle was soon raised by the assistance of some persons passing by at the time, and at midnight I arrived safe and sound at Mazagon House.

The following days were spent in the cheerful society of the amiable circle, in relating our adventures, and in preparations for my journey. Incessant rain, which fell like a water-spout, and obscured the sun for fourteen days, rendered it quite impossible to stir abroad. At such time the air is always so full of aqueous particles, that clothes, linen, and indeed every thing, is damp, and it is impossible to preserve arms and other articles of steel from rust: in order, in some degree, to lessen the unpleasant effects of these vapours, pans of charcoal must be constantly kept burning in the room.

With respect to my arrangements, I regret that I did not provide for them in Europe; for, with the exception of tents, every thing is incredibly bad and dear in this place. I was several days looking out for a horse, as the Arabs demand a hundred pounds for a serviceable animal, and I was obliged to rest satisfied with having procured one for 817 rupees. It is equally difficult for a stranger to obtain good servants: I have hired two Mahometans; the first, who is my butler, speaks English with tolerable fluency: he took part in the campaign in Affghanistan, and is to receive 42 rupees per month; and the latter 14 rupees. I intend to hire the other servants whom I shall want as soon as I reach the Indus.

I passed two days with the Governor at Pareil, where I had ample opportunity of making myself acquainted with the splendid establishments and luxury, of persons filling the highest offices in India. His Excellency has a band of twenty-five musicians, which performs every evening during dinner: a body guard, consisting of an officer and twenty-five men, accompanies him on his travels and on state occasions; and he has about two hundred servants, of whom more than forty are clothed in scarlet liveries. Several Parsees and Mahometans are about his person; forty are employed in the gardens, the rest in the stable and in various other departments.

Our departure for Sinde is fixed for the 10th of September at the latest; and we may hope that before that time the fury of the monsoon may have passed, and that the breakers may not prevent our landing on that coast. My next communication will probably be from the mouth of the Indus. Commending myself to your continued kindness, I beg you heartily to greet my relations and friends.

LETTER III.

TO CHARLES RITTER.

Embarkation in the war steamer Zenobia, and departure for Kurrachee.—Fearful ravages of the cholera.—Dangerous landing on the coast at Kurrachee.— Kurrachee.—Alligator Pond, Maggar Talao.— Sinde under the Hindoo Princes.— Dominion of the Moguls.— The Ameers of the family of the Talpooris. — Inhabitants of Sinde. — The Belooches. — Life and mode of government of the Ameers.— Language of the inhabitants of Sinde.— The English residents.— Voyage to Garrah.—March to Tatta.— Embarkation on board the Satellite steamer.—Hyderabad.—Audience of the Ameers.— Journey to Sehwan and Sukkur. — Inhabitants. — Preparations for the journey to Ferospoor.

Kurrachee, September 11. 1842.

When you bade me farewell, I did not anticipate that the next indication of my being alive, would be sent to you not far from the mouth of the Indus ; on whose banks your indefatigable spirit has spent so many hours in learned research. But still less could I have imagined that I should send you descriptions which, in their awful reality, reminded me of the terrific scenes delineated by Boccaccio, in such fearful colours, of the desolation of the plague at Bologna; for I, too, alas! have been an eye-witness of such melancholy scenes.

You will have learnt from my letter to Alexander von Humboldt, that I intended to go with several officers in the early part of September to the Indus, on board a war steamer belonging to Govrnment. Accounts however of disturbances in Sinde, induced the Government to hasten our departure, and the more so, as Sir Charles Napier was appointed general in command of all the troops there, and was naturally desirous to proceed as speedily as possible to his new destination. The General had the goodness to offer me, in case of hostilities, a place on his staff, which, of course, I most gratefully and joyfully accepted. With deep regret I bid farewell to the amiable family at Mazagon House, and kindly accompanied by the General and his sons, I embarked on Saturday the 3d of September at three in the afternoon, on board the Zenobia steamer of 670 tons and 284 horse-power. Besides Sir Charles Napier, we had on board 22 officers, 150 soldiers of the 28th, or Queen's regiment, 50 seapoys, 23 European soldiers' wives, 27 children, Werner, and about 60 servants. Our horses were in a boat, which was towed by the Zenobia.

We weighed anchor at sunset ; a small mizzling rain, with wind and a hollow sea, rendered our voyage very disagreeable. It was especially trying to the soldiers and women, children and servants, who were obliged to remain on deck closely crowded together without any covering. Happily the weather cleared up when we had passed the last light, and got into the open sea. But towards midnight the sky again became cloudy, a tropical rain fell in torrents, and with such violence that I was roused by it from my sleep, and, taking my cloak, I went to see how it fared with the poor people on deck. Only picture to yourself such a multitude of men, women and children, crouching together in the narrow compass of the deck, in the open air, without protection against the rain, standing in water, and at the same time completely drenched by the dashing of the waves ; the wind was bitterly cold, and not a dry spot, either to lie down, or to stand upon, was to be found. The soldiers of the 28th regiment, who had arrived three days before, with their wives and children from New South Wales, could not have suffered so much on that long voyage, as during this single night. We had besides no means of cooking warm food for so many persons; biscuits, tea, and brandy, was all that we could give them. It was a scene of misery and distress; and alas! I little thought that in four days the third part of these poor sufferers, and in less than fourteen days more than the half of them, would be launched into eternity.

On Sunday the 4th, at daybreak, the rain abated, and light clouds, through which the sun darted his scorching rays, travelled rapidly across the sky. The exhalations of the wet decks and clothes of the people crowded together, and the heat of the engine, rendered the atmosphere so suffocating, that I was obliged to give up an attempt to go to the forecastle. About nine o'clock it was reported that the cholera had broken out on board, and that three persons had been seized with it: two of them were only slightly attacked; but a woman died in the course of the same day. We had scarcely committed her to the sea on Monday morning, when nine men were seized by this frightful pestilence: in a few hours this number was so fearfully augmented, that a portion of the deck was fitted up as an hospital, and above forty of the sufferers received into it. Death often followed the attack in less than four hours; and, in order to make room for fresh cases, it was necessary to cast the dead into the sea, sown up in their beds, charged with shot, without delay, and without the usual prayers. Two medical men, the officers, and the soldiers, did their utmost to afford relief to the unhappy sufferers; but alas! neither friction nor medicines, port-wine, sago, arrow-root or brandy, were of the slightest avail.

Some of these scenes of woe can never be effaced from my memory. One fine young woman, in the prime of life, with an infant at her breast, threw herself on the ground in an agony of pain; though already struggling with death, she would not resign her beloved babe, and before sunset, the bereaved husband had committed both his treasures to the deep. Another woman, weeping and sobbing by the side of her husband, knelt down to warm his benumbed limbs with her body; "O my husband, my husband, you must die," she exclaimed, wringing her hands in the anguish of her heart, but she soon held only the cold corpse in her arms. Most affecting was the separation of a young woman from her husband and child, only three years old: in the agonies of death she embraced both; neither would let go of the other till death had cast his dark shadow over the distorted countenance. Not less moving and painful was it to see the engineer, a fine young man, in his dying moments: he was married only two days before our departure, and implored God with tears to grant that he might expire in the arms of his beloved wife. These heart-rending scenes, the cries and lamentations of the dying, the wail of the living, and the frightfully distorted countenances of the dead, must soften and move the stoutest heart. In four days we buried forty-five European soldiers, two natives, three sailors, four women, and three children, and brought about thirty cholera patients on shore.

On Tuesday the disease was at its height; on Wednesday, the 7th, the sea was more calm, and from that time we had fine weather. Under a brilliant starry heaven, but in a dark night, we came within sight of the rocky coast at midnight. The Captain, desirous to ascertain his position, ordered the vessel to steer as closely as possible to it, and soundings to be taken, when the steersman suddenly called out with all his might, in an almost unintelligible language, that we were close upon a most dangerous reef. A gun was fired twice, but no answer was returned. Like a stray wanderer pursuing a beaten tract in a forest, we steadily pursued the direction of the coast, with the rocks constantly on our left hand, sometimes just touching the rocky bed of the sea. At last, we threw out an anchor, when it appeared that, as the ebb had set in, we should not have sufficient depth of water; we, therefore, quickly weighed anchor, and again put out to sea. At length, at one o'clock A.M., we succeeded in casting anchor in a creek. When the morning dawned we perceived that we had passed Kurrachee, and had anchored ten miles beyond it, in an arm of the sea, running N. W. into the land. Accordingly, about 7 o'clock we steered our course towards that town, and in two hours came to anchor opposite the ruins of a small fort situated on a rock fifty feet high. We were soon surrounded by a host of sharks, which raised their greedy jaws out of the sea: they are ever on the watch to profit by the accidental fall of a man overboard, or the rash attempt of any person to swim to the boats coming to take the people on shore. They are, however, not so dangerous to the natives as to the Europeans. Though the sea did not appear to be much agitated, yet the breakers were so violent, that the first boat we let down was dashed against our vessel, and the poor sailor who was in it had his breast-bone broken, and he died soon after. Lord Altamont, who had had a slight attack of cholera during the preceding night, Captains West and Bennet, and myself, chose the first boat that approached, which we could only reach by means of a well-calculated leap.

From the old fort which projects into the sea a bay runs three miles inland, in an easterly direction, which, in some places, is so thickly studded with clumps of mangroves (Rhizophora), that, at a distance, they look like little islands. Wild swine have their retreat in these bushes, between which the wind drove us with such rapidity that in the space of an hour we reached the flat, sandy coast, and were carried ashore by our boatmen. The town of Kurrachee, which is only 300 paces from this bay, in the vicinity of the ancient Crocola, is a small, closely-built, dirty place. The inhabitants, 14,000 in number (9000 Hindoos and about 5000 Mahometans), subsist by trade, navigation, and fishery. The slave-trade formerly carried on by Muscat, from Zanzibar to Sinde, in Hubshys and Abyssinians, was so considerable that 600 to 700 young people, of whom three-fourths were girls, were imported here every year: Georgians were occasionally imported for the harems of the rich. The price of a handsome Abyssinian girl was sometimes as high as 250 rupees: boys were sold at from 60 to 100 rupees.*

At the eastern outlet of the town is a mosque and a pond, which, however, is often dry: but a few

* The slave trade is entirely abolished under the British rule in India.

date palms, bananas, tamarinds, and tamarisks, indicate that nature is not wholly dead. Two miles to the east of the city are the cantonments of the troops, of which there were at this time 2000 men. At present only a few houses are built of stone, most of them being constructed of clay and wood. The place marked out for the barracks of the European troops, has been very injudiciously selected in the sultry plain; a far preferable situation would have been along the elevated coast of Ghisry creek, which is constantly fanned by a pure, cool air, and where a view of the sea is refreshing alike to mind and body. Fresh water is supplied by a subterraneous spring, which runs from the town to the cantonments in a bed fifteen feet broad: every where else there is only a brackish ground. Bare, undulating, calcareous mountains extend from east to west, and form, as it were, a barrier on the north side. The sky is scarcely ever clouded except in the rainy season, and the temperature seldom rises above 95° Fahr.; as a whole year frequently elapses without a fall of rain, the small quantity of corn grown here is nourished by irrigation with Persian wheels. From May till September a dry wind prevails, and incessantly carries dark clouds of dust across the sandy plain.

We waited in a small guard-house for the servants and horses of the officers, to whom we had sent our introductions; and we expected them with the greater anxiety, because Lord Altamont's illness became more serious, and nothing short of the most careful attendance and treatment seemed likely to preserve his life. It was noon before I reached the tents of Lieutenant Manbee; and here, too, I met with the kindest welcome from the officers of the Engineers and

Artillery, and those of the 22d regiment requested that during my stay here I would consider myself their guest. I did not see Werner till the next day: he had nearly lost his life on quitting the vessel, and, in order to save himself, was compelled to sacrifice my barometer

In this camp, where nearly all live in tents, our time passes away quite in a military style, and the intercourse with such a general as Sir Charles Napier, cannot fail to be highly instructive and profitable. It unfortunately happened at a trial of rockets, two days after our arrival, that the General was wounded in the calf of his leg, by the bursting of a rocket in the tube; though I stood at the charger's side, I escaped, singularly enough, without receiving the slightest injury. I occasionally make excursions on horseback in all directions, and often ride to the town. I have been particularly struck with the athletic appearance of the men, who are very handsome, and who set off their fine countenances by a towering cap of cotton or silk, embroidered with gold and silver; the women are not nearly so handsome, but they are tall and slender, and wear very long, dirty dresses. In a moral point of view, the inhabitants have, I regret to say, a very bad reputation.

One of my most interesting excursions was a ride to the Alligator Pond at Maggar Talao, or Peer Mangar, ten miles to the north of this town, and a place of pilgrimage for the natives. Captain West, who accompanied me, chose a camel, while I mounted a horse, and we agreed to change places on our return. Our guide, a handsome Arab, dressed in white, with his sabre at his breast, sat on the saddle in front: my friend occupied the seat behind, and I followed, sometimes keeping pace with the rapid trot of the camel, sometimes galloping on before, enjoying this novel exhibition.

TWO RIDERS ON A CAMEL.

Soon after quitting our tents, we came to a few huts lying in the shade of date palms, bananas, and stunted tamarisks, and surrounded with very poor-looking corn fields, then crossing a dried arm of the Indus, fifty feet in width, we had still two miles of the plain to cross. Barren calcareous hills, to the height of 200 feet, rose before us, in undulating lines from east to west; and from their highest summits we had a fine view of the town of Kurrachee, the valley of the Indus, and the ocean. During our ride amidst these broken fragments of rock, along a narrow path, sometimes ascending, and then descending, we saw only wild pigeons, some vultures, and herds of goats, which subsist on the scanty blades of grass which grow between the boulders. The herdsmen, as well as the few travellers whom we met, were armed.

After proceeding about two hours, we reached an eminence, from which we overlooked a fine valley above 1000 paces broad, enclosed between mountain chains running parallel to each other; far below, at our right hand, lay a flourishing wood of date palms, skirted by a beautiful little grove of tamarinds. Blue and white cupolas which covered the graves of the saints, glimmered amid the luxuriant verdures, and it seems evident that a high degree of cultivation formerly existed here. After passing some huts, we stopped at a pond 200 paces long and 50 paces broad, which is overgrown with grass and reeds, and contains but little water. It is supplied by a mineral spring, which issues from the rock about a mile from this place, and which is so warm that a person cannot bear his hand in it. After issuing from its source, the water flows only a few paces above ground; it then forces its way through a rock, from which it discharges itself, at a temperature of 90° Fahrenheit, at the foot of the graves into a small bricked basin, and thence into the pond above mentioned. In this pond above fifty alligators are kept, several of which are more than twenty feet long. These animals are accounted sacred, and the pilgrims must offer a goat to obtain a sight of them, and to satisfy their rapacity. They are under the special charge of fakirs, and we had scarcely dismounted, when several of these dirty, naked men came to offer their services. One of them broke off some reeds to keep at bay the eager alligators, and cried in a mournful tone, *owh! owh!* "come, come!" Above thirty of these reptiles instantly crept out of the water, and, like so many dogs, lay in a semi-circle at the feet of their master. It was a strange scene to see these animals with wide gaping jaws, not more than four steps from you: but they were so docile that they drew back at the slightest touch with the reed. Meantime, our guide had purchased a goat for a rupee; it was slaughtered on the spot, and thrown in large pieces to the alligators, which greedily tried to snatch the morsels from their companions, and in so doing their scaly bodies struck with such violence against each other, that some of them rolled completely over. After they had finished their repast, the fakir drove them back into the pond. The largest and most sacred of these alligators, which we estimated at nearly twenty-five feet in length, was kept by itself in the basin.

Turning aside from this disgusting sight, we visited the tombs of the saints. They are built of stone, with mosaic work of coloured grey tiles, and, as I said before, are furnished with cupolas. They are scarcely 20 feet high, and have only sufficient room withinside for the stone sarcophagus, and to accommodate a few persons. Before the entrance is a small projection in the form of a canopy, supported by elegantly carved wooden pillars. The sarcophagus is decorated with painting and all sorts of fanciful ornaments, feathers, ostrich eggs, ribbons, little bells, and lamps. An old grey-bearded fakir, who lay at the entrance of the principal tomb, rose slowly at our approach, and on our asking him the date of these buildings, gravely assured us that we were looking upon monuments 2000 years old; and seemed much mortified when we intimated our incredulity. By the side of the pond stands a lofty, strikingly beautiful tamarind tree, the stem of which at the height of five feet from the ground measured 22 feet in cicumference. We sat down under its light, elegant feathery foliage, which spreading on all sides formed an impenetrable canopy, and here partook of some refreshment, and drank to the health of our friends at home. We set out on our return in a temperature of 90°, but happily under a somewhat clouded sky: I found my seat on the back of the camel very unpleasant, but by its rapid trot it brought me home so speedily, that I soon forgot the inconvenience, and in little more than an hour I was comfortably seated in my tent.

Our departure for Sukkur is fixed for the 15th; but before I ask you to accompany me through these hitherto imperfectly known countries, you must allow me to give you a short historical sketch of the princes and the people who formerly inhabited them, as well as of those who now occupy them.

Sinde derives its name from the river Sinde or Indus, which flows in a course of 320 German miles, and in the last 100 miles traverses this country. The Indus is to Sinde, what the Nile is to Egypt: its stated inundations, when the snow melts in the Himalaya mountains, and the heavy rains fall, diffuse fertility over the country, which might be one of the richest in the world, had not the destructive spirit of the Mahometan usurpers deprived it of its strength.

The traditions of the priests unfortunately give us but scanty information respecting the Hindoo dynasties who formerly reigned here. It is said that in the seventh century Shash, a Brahmin priest, won the heart of the consort of the reigning Rajah Sazee by his great personal beauty. He was a confidential friend of the prince, and the queen happening to see him one day from behind a curtain in her husband's apartment, fell so deeply in love with him, that she resolved to take him for her husband whenever the rajah should die. An understanding was soon come to between them; the rajah died shortly after, whether from poison, or from a natural cause, is not stated: the artful priest, however, became the heir of the fine and extensive kingdom of Sinde. The jealousy of many of the neighbouring princes was, indeed, aroused by this, and they endeavoured to enforce their pretensions to the throne, but were either defeated or put out of the way. Shash is said to have reigned forty years, and was succeeded by his eldest son Dahir.

During his reign several vessels, richly laden with costly goods and beautiful female slaves, which came from Ceylon and belonged to the Caliph of Bagdad, were driven into the Indus and plundered by the inhabitants. The Caliph Abdool Mulik in vain demanded satisfaction, and took up arms, but he died during the preparations for war, and left his son Valid to take vengeance upon the spoilers. This prince sent a large army furnished with all kinds of ammunition by sea and land to the Indus, under the command of the young and handsome Bin Cassim. Bin Cassim advanced victoriously in 711 to Allore, the capital of the kingdom of Sinde. Here he was met by Dahir with an immense army; 30,000 infantry were placed in front of his numerous cavalry and elephants to repel the first shock of the enemy. Dahir himself, history informs us, mounted on his largest elephant in a richly ornamented howdah, attended by two beautiful female slaves, who occasionally presented him with wine and refreshments, rode between the ranks of his warriors, encouraging them to the combat. The battle commenced with equal fury on both sides; but the elephants, driven to madness by the firing, turned round, destroyed everything in their way, and spread terror and consternation among the Hindoos. The rajah's elephant also fled, Dahir was mortally wounded in the neck by an arrow, and he expired in a few moments: in order to conceal his body from the vengeance of the enemy, it was buried on the spot; but his female slaves betrayed the melancholy end of their master. His body was instantly disinterred, and his head fixed as a trophy on the point of a spear, whilst thanksgivings for the victory were offered to Allah on the ruins of the Hindoo temple. Two daughters of the rajah fell into the hands of the conqueror, who, on account of their surpassing beauty, sent them to his master for his harem. When they appeared before Valid they accused his general of infidelity towards his master, by an outrage upon their persons; sentence of death reached Bin Cassim in his victorious career: he patiently submitted to the most dreadful tortures, and died in the space of three days. His dead body was shown to the princesses as a proof of the power, and strict justice of the caliph. Contemplating it with looks of satisfaction, they confessed that he was innocent, that their object had been to take vengeance on the murderer of their father, and that they were now ready to suffer any kind of death themselves. The caliph caused the rajah's daughters to be tied by their beautiful hair to tails of horses, and torn to pieces in the streets of Bagdad; while he erected a splendid monument to the memory of his faithful general.

Sinde remained in the hands of the Omiades till the invasion of India by Mahomet the Ghaznivide; after which the country became the prey of the Ghoorur and the Moguls. The dissensions at the court of Delhi, the weakness of its princes, and the great distance of the seat of government from Sinde, made it easy for the viceroys appointed to this country to declare themselves independent of the great Moguls. From the times of Aurengzeebe we find the sovereignty in the hands of one tribe or family, the Kaloora or Abassys, said to be descended from the Abassyde caliphs; they subsequently became tributary to Nadir Shah, at his death to Ahmed Shah Dooranee, and finally to the Mahrattas. The Kaloora, who had rendered themselves odious to the people by their cruelties, having murdered the ambassador from Judpoore, a near relative of the Beloochee family of the Talpoor dynasty in Hyderabad, in 1785, Meer Futteh Ali, the head of the family, supported by several Belooche chiefs, went against the Kaloora, succeeded in expelling them, and made himself master of the country. Only a few of them escaped, some of whom found an asylum in Judpoore, and others in Caboul with Timour Khan, and obtained the gift of jaghires, or feudal tenures. Meer Nusseer Khan, who is still alive, and was at that time a boy of only ten years of age, was witness to the dreadful ravages and desolation, with which the country was at that period afflicted, and from which it has not recovered to the present hour.

He observed to an Englishman that he should never forget the ruin of the flourishing, populous town of Sukkur, and in anticipation of his fate he often expressed a desire to dictate the history of his own times to some learned man.

Meer Futteh Ali, whom some old people affirm to to have seen tending his flocks, was at first dependent on the Affghans, but by the help of the Beloochees, many tribes of whom he invited into the country and invested with jaghires, he was enabled not only to maintain himself on the throne, but to become master of the whole country of Sinde. He however gave up two fifths of it, to two of his earliest adherents—Sohrab, to whom he gave Khyrpoor and Northern Sinde, and to Thara, Meerpoor. He retained the remaining three fifths with Hyderabad as the capital, under his own government, with the title of Ameer, and reigned in conjunction with his three brothers, Meer Gholaum Ali Khan, Meer Karam Ali Khan, and Meer Murad Ali Khan. It was agreed that the eldest of the family should always reside at Hyderabad, and exercise sovereignty over all. Meer Futteh Ali undertook not only the payment of the tribute to Caboul, but also the expenses of the government and the maintenance of the whole Talpoor family.

On his death in 1801 his next brother, Gholaum Ali Khan, became chief of the family, and on his decease in 1811 the sovereignty was assumed by Meer Karam Ali and Meer Murad Ali, after a contest with Meer Sobdur and Meer Mohammed, which ended in their submission. Karam Ali died in 1828, without male posterity, and Meer Murad Ali, the only survivor of the four brothers, contrived to maintain the sovereignty. He had four sons—Noor Mohammed,

Meer Nusseer Khan, Mohammed Khan, and Ahmed Khan, of whom the two last died without children.

When Futteh Ali and his brothers expelled the Kalooras, Khyrpoor, situated in the north, fell into the possession of Meer Sohrab Ali Khan, who had taken part in the insurrection: he died in 1830 in consequence of a fall from a verandah, and left five sons, the eldest of whom, Meer Rustam, succeeded him. Khyrpoor lies on both sides of the Indus, extends northwards to Shikarpoor and Mitan, southwards to the desert, and yields a revenue of between five and six lacs.

Meerpoor, the other territory separated from Sinde in a direct line between Cutch and Hyderabad, is the most inconsiderable of the three portions, and produces a revenue of scarcely five lacs. It was assigned by Meer Futteh Ali to two brothers, the Ameers, Meer Thara and Meer Baga: the former survived his brother and retained the sovereign power in favour of his sons, Meer Ali Morad Khan and Meer Ali, and succeeded in excluding his nephew Mallea Khan, from all participation in the government. Both Khyrpoor and Meerpoor are connected with each other, and with Hyderabad by intermarriages; and although they have at times been in a state of hostility, the Ameers of Hyderabad have hitherto maintained their influence and superior authority.

These three principalities, Hyderabad, Khyrpoor, and Meerpoor, form the country governed by the Ameers, among whom, properly speaking, only the eldest of each of these families has a right to the title of Ameer. It is remarkable that Meer Futteh Ali and two of his brothers were Sunnites; whereas Meer Morad, through the influence of his minister Isman Khan, a Persian, was educated as a strict Sheeahs.

Meer Morad Ali died in 1834: after his death a triumvirate, consisting of Meer Nur Mohammed, Nusseer Khan, and Sobdar, assumed the government; and after the death of the first in 1839 we find five Ameers in Hyderabad, the eldest of whom, Meer Nusseer Khan, was recognised as the head of the family.

A HINDOO BANKER IN SINDE.

The inhabitants of Sinde are Mahometans and Hindoos; of the former, the Belooches belong to the caste of warriors, and the Juts to that of the peasants: and it may be assumed that the fifth part of the inhabitants of the cities are Hindoos. Though so greatly oppressed in their religious and civil relations, the wealth and commerce of the country are nevertheless chiefly in their hands; and they probably form a sixth part of the million of inhabitants said to reside in this country. They suffer their beard to grow, and wear the turban of the Mussulmans, whose manners and customs they have adopted; they have the submissiveness and servility of the Jews of Europe, and are as handsome, but even more dirty than the Juts. As bankers, they enjoy such confidence that their bills pass current throughout India.

THE JUTS, PEASANTS OF SINDE.

The Hindoos and the Juts are the only people on whom the British government can depend. The Juts, who are a tall, vigorous, and handsome race of people, were originally Hindoos, and, properly speaking, are the Aborigines of the country; the women are distinguished by their beauty and modesty, which cannot be said of the Mahometan females. As they form the agricultural class, they lead a quiet and peaceful life. Besides the cultivation of the soil the

Juts are occupied in the breed of buffaloes, goats, and camels. The camel is as valuable and useful to the Jut, as the horse is to the Arab.

A BELOOCHE ON FOOT.

The Miani are employed in navigation and fishery; they live as much upon the rivers and lakes as on shore—nay, some of them have no other dwelling than their boat. The women are as vigorous, and muscular as the men, and share in their hard labours; and while the husband is mending his nets, or smoking his pipe, and the child is suspended in its network cradle to the mast, the wife guides the boat with a large oar.

The Belooches, who form scarcely a tenth part of the population, are the freebooters of the desert, and originally came from the mountains and steppes in the north-west. Their manners, and many of their customs are conformable with the mosaic laws, and their oral and written traditions, as well as their general appearance, have so much resemblance with those of the Jews, that the Belooches have been looked upon as the descendants of the lost tribes of Israel. Thus for instance, on the death of the husband, his brother is bound to marry his widow, and the children are the heirs of the deceased; and again, a man may divorce his wife, according to the forms usual among the Jews. They consider themselves as the masters of the country, and devote themselves to arms, robbery, and the chase. Some few of them engage in agriculture, and all attend to the breeding of horses and camels. Their ignorance, and the uncivilised state in which they live, renders it difficult to reduce them to obedience and discipline: each tribe obeys only its chief; but if danger threatens any one tribe, messengers on camels and horses, are despatched in every direction to summon all that can bear arms. These camels are so hardy and fleet, that it is affirmed, on credible authority, that, on the entrance of Lord Keane into the country, a camel belonging to Meer Nusseer performed the journey from Hyderabad to Sukkur, a distance of between fifty and sixty geographical miles, in two days; the rider contrived to keep up its strength by giving it plenty of rice, ghee, and intoxicating liquors.

The houses of the Belooches are as wretched, dirty, and confined, as those of the other inhabitants; and only those of the chiefs are rather more roomy, and ornamented with carpets. The women are engaged in domestic occupations, while the men enjoy themselves in smoking, drinking, sleeping, or playing with the children. The Belooches are robust, though not tall; their complexion is of a dark brown colour: they have fiery eyes, and a fine, noble expression of countenance. The men wear a coloured cap of cotton or silk, embroidered with gold and silver, an open shirt, a yellow or red silk waistcoat, wide pantaloons, and pointed shoes. They are armed with a long matchlock, sabre, shield, and bow and arrows. They do not shave either the head or the beard; and they either suffer their hair to fall in ringlets over their shoulders, or they tie it in a knot on the crown of the head. They consider the beard a great ornament, and pay much attention to it; old and holy men are fond of dyeing it red, and the Sheeahs, like the descendants of the Prophet, prefer green to every other colour. The women wear wide pantaloons, and a garment which reaches to the ground and fits close to the body, a kerchief loosely wound round the head, and their hair falls in long plaits. They very seldom change their clothes, and are so dirty that neither the colour of their dress nor even that of their face can be distinguished.

These Belooches, in their capacity of executors of the commands of the Ameers, are the blood-suckers of the poor, oppressed peasant, who is obliged to deliver to the princes more than the half of his produce. The revenues of the country, which formerly amounted to 90 lacs, have now declined to between 40 and 50, but with good management this might be increased to three times that sum. The Ameers are as ignorant as the people: their time is spent in the harem, or in hunting, and the latter is pursued with such eagerness that the country is thereby daily more and more depopulated. In order to enlarge their preserves, which consist of Babul trees, a species of Mimosa Arabica, tamarinds and tamarisks, they have recourse to the most arbitrary measures. Thus Meer Futteh Ali expelled the inhabitants from one of the most fertile districts of the Indus, near Hyderabad, which produced a revenue of nearly two lacs, because it was the favourite haunt of the Babiroussa; and Meer Murad Ali caused a large village to be totally destroyed, in order that the lowing of the cattle and crowing of the cocks, might not disturb the game in an adjoining preserve belonging to his brother. In the middle of this preserve is a small isolated building with a pond in front of it; thither the game is driven and killed by the Ameers who are stationed behind the wall. When Lord Keane entered the country with the army, three of his officers took possession of a building of this kind, which was closely surrounded with trunks of trees: here they intended to pass the night, and to enjoy the pleasures of the chase on the following morning; but the wood, which was dried up by the sun, was set on fire, probably by design, and all three perished in the flames.

Each of the Ameers has his own preserve, which they visit in great style, attended by their chiefs and a number of servants, with dogs and falcons. They are either mounted on camels or horses, or go in their large state barges along the river. The people along the road thither are compelled to provide for the numerous train, and the inhabitants of the villages in the immediate vicinity of the preserves are forced to beat up the game; and it not unfrequently happens that some of them are shot instead of the game, or torn to pieces by the Barbiroussas. In hunting, the Ameers use long muskets, inlaid with gold and jewels, to which the locks of the guns presented by the English are fixed, though they do not esteem them as they ought. It is considered a great honour to a stranger if he is invited to one of their hunting parties.

The language of Sinde, both oral and written, differs very much from that of the rest of India, but the princes and people are so ignorant, that very few Mahometans are able to write it. The characters are called Khada-wadi, and are found in the letters of the merchants. Compared with most of the alphabets of Hindostan, that of Sinde is very poor: there are but two characters which designate vowels, and these are only used as initials. Hence the written language is used merely in letter-writing, and the few books in Sinde are written in Persian characters. The pronunciation of the Belooches is so uncouth, that the Sindians say they learnt it from their goats, when they were herdsmen in the mountains of Kelat! There are two different dialects; that of Lar, which is used in Hyderabad and the environs, and that of Sar, spoken in Upper Sinde.

The first British settlement in Sinde appears to have been formed in the year 1758, when the demand for woollen and other manufactures, for which the countries, watered by the Indus were celebrated, invited the English to open a trade with them; and the profitable sale of these goods seemed to promise a favourable result. These connections were, however, broken off again in the year 1775, because the government in Sinde threw great obstacles in the way of the trade. But repeated attempts to pass through the channel of the Indus induced the East India Company to renew the commercial connection with Sinde in 1799. Mr. Crow was accordingly sent thither, and succeeded in establishing a factory, and in obtaining from the government of Sinde permission to fix his residence in Tatta, or in Kurrachee. On this occasion, too, the Ameers manifested great repugnance to the introduction of a factory in the latter place, and were urgent that the settlements of the English should be confined to the harbours of Shah Bunder and Tatta. Mr. Crow had scarcely established himself in Kurrachee when, in August 1800, he suddenly received orders, probably at the instigation of the native merchants, to repair immediately to to Tatta, and to confine his factory to that place. The goods had been formerly sent to Dehra-Jamka or Aurungabunder, and thence to Shah Bunder, distant twenty miles to the west. There must have been at that time a pretty brisk trade with Mooltan and Lahore, for the factory of Shah Bunder had twelve boats, each of 30 or 40 tons, and two vessels for travelling merchants.

At length, on the 22d August 1808, a formal treaty was concluded with the Ameers of Sinde, and, on the 19th November 1820, it was renewed, with the additional clause that neither any other European nation, nor the Americans, should be allowed to trade there. It was stipulated, at the same time, that no encouragement should be given to the robberies of the Khosas, and other tribes in Cutch. It is well known that the British government sent Captain Alexander Burnes, in 1821, to the Indus, to obtain a knowledge of the country, and especially of the navigation on that river. His accounts made the Indian government still more desirous to secure the free navigation of the Indus. Accordingly, Sir Henry Pottinger was sent by Lord Bentinck, the Governor-General, with proposals to the Ameers to place the navigation and trade on the Indus on a secure foundation. Sir H. Pottinger succeeded in concluding, on the 19th June 1832, a treaty with Ameer Morad Ali of Hyderabad, and Rustum of Khyrpoor, in which continued friendship was promised, and the merchants of India assured of undisturbed trade on the Indus; the Ameers, however, reserving to themselves the right of granting passes to merchants for a moderate toll, with the condition that no armed vessel should navigate the river, and that no person should settle in the country. This treaty was modified in 1839 by a stipulation that the English should be allowed to have garrisons in Tatta, or at some other points, while they engaged, on the other hand, to defend Sinde against foreign invasion of every kind. When Lord Keane advanced towards Affghanistan, he was induced, for the security of his rear and of the navigation, to put garrisons into Kurrachee, Sukkur, and Shikarpoor. The necessity of making the Indus the frontier of the vast empire of British India, became more and more important. In the conclusion of all these treaties, the Ameers manifested more compliance with the British government than their Belooche chiefs, who very clearly perceived that the establishment of so great a power as that of the English would put an end to their influence and their extortions. The Belooches, therefore, on several occasions, acted in a hostile manner, in opposition to the will of the Ameers. Since that day, the princes of Sinde have been dependent on the British government, and are directed and watched by a political agent at their court.

Sukkur, October 10. 1842.

The preparations for my journey to this place, and the difficulties I encountered, obliged me to break up my communications, and the fresh orders to depart for Ferospoor prevented me from resuming my letter till to-day.

On the 13th September my effects were sent on before to Tatta, laden on four camels, under the care of my servants. Two days later, at four in the afternoon, my palanquin-bearers brought me to Gisry Creek, three miles from Kurrachee, where I found a boat waiting for me in the Garrah Creek, which here empties itself into the sea. There is no doubt that the main arm of the Indus, once flowed in the present bed of the Garrah; and may we not suppose that the few ruins on Gisry Creek indicate the site of the ancient Pattala? My travelling companions had preceded me in another boat. The tide carried us on the Garrah, which is here some hundred paces broad, and winds through a desert country, between tamarisk bushes and acacias; an ancient round tower was the only building visible on its banks. Two miles below Garrah the breadth of the river was diminished to one hundred paces, and it gradually became so narrow, and, as the ebb set in, so shallow, that we were obliged to leave our boat at a short distance before we reached Garrah, and to walk to the village. The soil on both sides is alternately the most fertile mould, and sand covered with salt.

Before I reached Garrah, I was joined by my fellow-travellers: we proceeded together through the dirty village, built on a gentle declivity, to a caravansary at the eastern end. Our way led by the house of a tanner, and I accordingly stopped to examine his operations. The hides are sewed together in the shape of the body of the animal, and suspended to three stakes, over a small bricked basin, with the neck upwards; a constant flow of water and some bark of the Babul tree (Mimosa) is then poured through the neck of the skin, and gradually forces its way through the small apertures. From time to time the hide is let down into the basin to be made more pliable, and the hair is scraped off with a long knife. As soon as the hide is properly tanned and oiled, it is dried in the shade; the leather of Sinde is some of the best in India, and not inferior in softness and durability to that of Europe.

All the houses here are built of clay; they are scarcely twenty feet high, have flat roofs, from which a kind of ventilator sometimes rises, and air-holes supply the place of windows. Long-continued rain would destroy these huts, and sweep away entire villages. The caravansary is a small open apartment, with a court-yard enclosed by a mud wall, and is kept by a Parsee, who is commissioned by the British government to provide for the accommodation of travellers. We resolved to wait here till the afternoon: carpets were accordingly spread in the hall, and, while we took some repose, the servants prepared a repast, consisting of tea, rice, and fish. When the sun was near setting, our little caravan commenced its march to Tatta, some on camels, some on horseback. Our road lay through a desolate tract, first by the side of a dried-up branch of the Indus, then through a fertile district between high tamarisk bushes, and over numerous ditches, partly dry, partly full of water. After riding two hours we found the landscape more diversified by lofty trees and detached farm houses, round which the land was cultivated. We saw a jackal standing by the road-side, behind a tamarisk bush; his large eyes were directed towards us, and he was so bold, that we might have shot him with a pistol.

It was 10 o'clock when we arrived at the village of Gongah, but having the advantage of the bright moonlight, we were enabled securely to traverse the country, which was more and more intersected with ditches. It is a large place, with several brick houses, situated in a very fertile plain. We found the officers who had set out the day before, encamped by the side of a pond, under tamarisk and mango trees; and we took up our quarters next to them. At 3 o'clock in the morning we resumed our march through a plain traversed by deep ditches, between corn fields of Jowaree (*Holcus sorghum*) twelve feet high, and Bajeera (*Panicum spicatum*). Three miles further on, we found ourselves on a broad road in an impenetrable jungle of tamarisks and stunted tamarinds, only now and then relieved by a babul or banyan (*Ficus Indicus*) tree rising above it. Half way there was a small caravansary by the side of a pond, under the care of a priest and some fakirs. The ground about it was cultivated, and a small garden with bananas and mangoes, and a few tamarinds, overshadowing the water, afforded a refreshing and agreeable object in this wilderness.

At 7 o'clock we approached a rocky chain about 150 feet high, on which an extensive town appeared to be situated, but it was a mass of numerous large and small sepulchres, with lofty vaulted roofs like cupolas, covered with glazed tiles, chiefly blue, and adorned within and without, with mosaic work, made of china. Some of them were in perfect preservation; others had suffered by violence, or by the lapse of time, for they are said to be 200 years old. As we rode past them we met the first Belooches I had seen; they were handsome, vigorous men, with dark, fiery eyes, and long beards; wore a shield on their back, a sabre by their side, and a long gun over their shoulder. One of them had a boy, about eight years old, on the horse behind him, and looked at us with an air of defiance. We asked if they were Belooches? "Yes, fighting Belooches," was his insolent reply.

From this elevation we suddenly came in sight of the ruins of Kulan Cote, Tatta, and the Indus in its broad channel, flowing through a boundless fertile valley. Tatta, whether it is the ancient Patala, or Minagara, is uncertain, lies three miles from the Indus, on an eminence slightly elevated above the valley, and affording a surprisingly beautiful prospect from a distance: the streets are narrow, irregular, and very dirty; the houses, which are built of clay, wood, or brick, are from twenty to thirty feet high, and resemble square towers with flat roofs, on which the inhabitants are accustomed to sleep, in the open air, during the warm nights. Cakes of dung, used for firing, and prepared by the women and children, are piled up against the walls.

There are only a few mosques in the place, which are built of stone and painted white, but they have the same dirty and ruinous appearance as the town; and there are no traces of the extensive trade which was formerly carried on. The silk and cotton manufactures of the Lundshis, wrought with gold and silver, which were formerly so much in request, are now nearly exploded by those of Mooltan, and the few that are still manufactured here, are usually taken by the Ameers, who pay barely sufficient to enable the weavers to live. The inhabitants are about 10,000 in number; they wear wide garments, Sinde caps, or turbans, and the women long cotton dresses reaching to the ground; poverty and dirt everywhere prevail. We traversed the town in its whole length, passed through the valley, which is irrigated by water wheels driven by oxen or camels, is highly cultivated, and produces corn and cotton.

We reached the place of embarkation, four miles to the east, at ten o'clock. Here we found our servants, who had already arrived and pitched our tents; but we were unable to obtain any repose, as they did not protect us against the scorching rays of the sun, and the thermometer was 110° of Fahrenheit (in my tent it rose to 118°). Indeed in Sinde the sun is fierce enough to dye white men black, and is sufficiently powerful to roast an egg; an experiment which has been tried with success. The British government has four iron steamers on the Indus, which are 120 feet long, 35 broad, and of 70 horse power: they draw only three or four feet water, and are armed with guns (three pounders) and wall-pieces. Along the coast are depôts of tamarisk wood for fuel, which consumes rapidly, but gives very great heat.

In the afternoon some boats arrived to convey us, and our effects to the steamers, two of which were to

PERSIAN WATER-WHEEL WORKED BY A CAMEL.

start for Sukkur the next day. We were obliged to send the horses by land, by way of Hyderabad. I embarked with four officers on board the Satellite, the others on board the Planet. The captain undertakes to supply the passengers with provisions at four rupees a day, but the table on board was so indifferent, that I was obliged to content myself with rice, biscuit and tea.

We set out at day-break on Saturday the 17th September. The river, which was 600 feet in breadth at the place of embarkation, soon became twice as wide. The sun emerged from its wide watery expanse, and illumined once more the shining summit of the city of the sepulchres. On both sides groves of babul and tamarind, alternated with corn-fields and villages. In the middle of these corn-fields is a high scaffolding, on which a poor fellow is stationed all day long, without any protection against the sun, to scare away the birds, by continued hallooing, and throwing missiles at them with a sling. It is extremely amusing to see how the inhabitants of the opposite banks visit each other, supported by a goat's skin, filled with air, which they fasten to their waist and neck, and swim across from one side to the other: it is very rare indeed that any one is drowned in doing this, or falls a prey to the alligators.

The navigation of the Indus, is very difficult on account of its shifting bed and violent current, which runs four miles an hour: we were therefore obliged to cast anchor every evening, and every day to take on board a new pilot. The slimy and dirty water of the river, when clarified by alum, becomes as clear as crystal, and very pleasant; but the cook on board the steamer would not take this trifling trouble, which would have added so greatly to our comfort. On the 18th, in the forenoon, the thermometer being at 98° Fahrenheit, we proceeded along the right bank; beautiful woods diversify the monotony of the country, and the fresh verdure of the meadows covered with yellow flowers enlivens the eye. We passed a preserve three miles in length, ornamented with the finest babul trees, and surrounded with hedges and a clay wall. This preserve abounds with barbiroussas, antelopes, jackals, hyenas, black and red partridges, parrots and other birds.

On this day we twice stuck upon a sand bank, from which however our engine, and the strong current, soon set us free. In the evening we anchored in a beautiful wooded inlet; the moon behind the shadowy trees, between Jupiter and Venus, pouring her silver light through the foliage, while a cooling breeze wafted the perfume of the babul flowers towards us. Our Hindoos soon made a fire under the trees, to cook their food, while we rambled through the thickets, gun in hand, in search of game, but were soon obliged to give up our intention, as the ground was excessively damp and marshy.

On the 19th, at ten in the morning, we landed opposite Hyderabad, near a mango grove, in which the house of Mr. Mylne, the political agent, is situated. He received me in the kindest manner, and promised to further my wishes to pay my respects to the Ameers, and immediately sent his moonshee with a message to that effect to the palace. Meantime I proceeded to the dwelling of Dr. Leith, some hundred paces distant, to whose lady I had a letter of introduction. Here too I met with a cordial welcome. The time passed away in conversation and music, and on the banks of the Indus I heard the accomplished Mrs. Leith sing to the piano, "Herz, mein Herz, warum so traurig;" which pretty little song, though already forgotten in Germany, awakened in me the liveliest recollections of home. Then came an interesting group of Myrcasis or Luris, the Minnesingers of Sinde, who, in the neighbourhood of the capital, sung an eulogium on Lord Keane's expedition to Affghanistan, and the might of the English. Their instruments consisted of guitars and small drums; their singing was monotonous and mournful, much resembling the noise of water wheels; and where the voice was insufficient, the defect was made up by pantomimic gesticulations.

The moonshee brought word that the Ameers would be happy to receive me at six o'clock. An hour before that time their Highnesses sent four horses, richly caparisoned, their bridles adorned with gold and silver, and their Delhi housings finely embroidered; while the girths were torn and in part mended with dirty ropes. I rode Dr. Leith's horse, while my companions mounted those sent by the Ameers, and, accompanied by an escort of irregular cavalry, we proceeded to Hyderabad, which is more than five miles distant. The sun was already setting, and the moon was high above the horizon, when we obtained a clear view of the city.

On our arrival at the decayed fort, a small, square, clay building, with semicircular towers in the middle of the lines, and surrounded by a moat eight feet broad, we were received by the moonshee of the Ameers, Meer Nasseer Khan, and sixteen of the principal chiefs. These handsome men, in their picturesque costume, and armed with matchlocks, pistols,

MYRCASIS.

sabres, and shields, saluted me in the name of their masters, touching their forehead with the right hand, and said that they were commanded to conduct me to the palace. One after the other approached me, addressing me courteously, and making a number of inquiries; the moonshee was particularly talkative, and repeatedly expressed his regret that I did not understand the Persian language.

Hyderabad, which has 35,000 inhabitants, is situated on a gentle, rocky, eminence, 200 feet high, which here bounds the valley of the Indus, and like all the other towns in Sinde, is built of clay, wood and brick. The streets are narrow and dirty, the bazars very animated, and hundreds of people were standing by the roadside to look at us as we passed by. The Great Fort likewise forms a quadrangle, with circular projecting towers: in the angles it has clay walls, forty feet in height, with a moat eight feet broad and five deep, which however is dry. Here our escort halted. Such an immense crowd of people was assembled at the huge gates, that the chiefs and the guard had some trouble to keep them back when the gates were opened. Though I rode very slowly in order to get some notion of the interior of the fort, I soon perceived that it was quite impossible, because the whole, consisting of huts and small houses, appeared to be an irregular mass of confusion. In a few minutes we stopped at an iron grating, the entrance to the palace of the Ameer Meer Nasseer Khan, and alighted from our horses. This palace is a square brick building, inlaid with coloured porcelain tiles; it rises above the platform of a massy high tower, the repository of their treasure. From this platform is a bird's eye view of the beautiful Indus, which is 900 paces broad, meandering through a lovely country of forests and groves, interspersed with corn-fields and hamlets, while the city of Hyderabad lies on one side, and the circumjacent country, as far as the eye can reach, is spread out before the spectator.

After we had passed through the gate and ascended the platform, the Ameers, headed by Meer Nasseer Khan, surrounded by many of his chiefs, came out to meet us. When Mr. Mylne presented me to them, they all shook hands with me, and Nasseer Khan invited me to take a seat, which was placed opposite to him. The Ameers had taken their places on a long silk divan, around which were ranged the chiefs in picturesque groups, either standing, or sitting cross-legged upon carpets, each with his sword or gun before him, and all eyes turned upon us; the moon shed a magic splendour over this scene, every object, even in the far distance, was perfectly distinguishable.

Meer Nasseer Khan, the eldest of the Ameers, who has a revenue of eleven lacs, is so extremely corpulent, that he is incapable of any bodily exertion, and even on the chase prefers the slow camel to the fleet horse. His Highness is, however, considered by his Belooches to be the handsomest man in the country. Meer Mahomet, an elderly man with a long, flowing, grey beard, is somewhat disfigured by a harelip: he is the same who boasted to Sir Alexander Burns that he had promoted his journey through Sinde, and vaunted himself upon being a great friend of the English. He carried in his hand a magnificent sword, richly adorned with jewels, and a snuff-box which was in constant requisition. Meer Shadad and Meer Hussin Ali are brothers, the former is distinguished by remarkable beauty of person, and highly polished manners. He was leaning on a blue velvet cushion, adorned with brilliants; and when he passed his hand over his carefully trimmed black beard, and raised his dark, flashing eye, I felt involuntarily drawn towards him. His younger brother, who is only seventeen years of age, is shy and mistrustful. Meer Sobdar Khan was not present; he is not on good terms with his colleagues, and desired to receive me alone. They all wore velvet Sinde caps embroided with gold; coloured silk garments, pantaloons and red shoes; pearl necklaces and valuable rings were their only ornaments.

After having for some minutes reciprocally expressed our extreme satisfaction at meeting, his Highness asked my name, which I was obliged to repeat several times: he then inquired about my king and my country. Nasseer Khan candidly confessed that he had never heard of that kingdom, which however must, he thought, be very powerful, as it was on such friendly terms with England. An expression of surprise ran through the whole circle, when on Meer Shadad's inquiring what was the strength of the Prussian army, one of the officers replied that it consisted of above 500,000 well disciplined troops.

His Highness, at my request, sent for his arms; they were long damasked guns, richly inlaid with gold. While I was admiring them, Abas Ali, Meer Assad's favourite son, a handsome youth of sixteen years of age, was introduced; his Highness observed, when he entered, that he was well acquainted with the English language, in which I might converse with him; but the prince addressed me in a jargon which neither Mr. Mylne nor I could understand;

and when his Highness inquired what I thought of the prince's pronunciation, somebody, observing my embarrassment, replied for me, assuring his Highness that I was quite astonished at the prince's progress, which seemed to give his father much pleasure! His tutor, it appears, is a subaltern officer, a deserter, and now commander of the artillery of the Ameers.

After having conversed about half an hour, we took leave of their Highnesses, shaking hands, and embracing each other; and then rode to the residence of Sobdar Khan, a few hundred paces distant. At the entrance of the gate of his palace, we had to pass through a dirty puddle; which, however, is nothing extraordinary here, where dirt and splendour go hand in hand. His Highness received us under the verandah, attended by his two sons and about twenty chiefs. Meer Sobdar is about fifty years of age, his manners are polished, he is chivalrous and of a warlike spirit. He is the only one of the Ameers who loves the military profession, and endeavours to improve himself in it. Here the same questions and salutations were repeated; but I could not forbear expressing to his Highness how much I was struck with the fine appearance of his sons, with which Fatteh Ali, the eldest, was so delighted, that he repeatedly embraced me on our departure.

We set out on our return, again surrounded by the chiefs; as soon as we reached our escort, I thanked each of them for their company, and begged them to recommend me to the favourable regard of their Highnesses. It was already eight o'clock when we arrived at Dr. Leith's residence; we had scarcely sat down to dinner when the moonshee of the Ameer, Meer Mahomet, arrived, and brought to me with his master's compliments several large dishes, with fruits, confectionary, some plain Cashmere shawls, and silks of Tatta, requesting me to accept these trifling presents as a remembrance of him. However, as I am travelling here in the character and enjoy the privileges of the English officers, who are not permitted to accept any present from Indian princes, it appeared to me to be necessary to decline accepting them. Mr. Mylne was of the same opinion, which he endeavoured to make intelligible to the moonshee, who, however, was not satisfied, and laid them down at my feet. To avoid the kindness of the other Ameers, from whom similar presents were said to be on the way, I immediately took leave of Dr. Leith and his lady and went to our steamboat, which was lying on the opposite bank.

At daybreak on the 20th we were already on the way to Sehwan, but the rudder chain breaking, we were detained an hour, and overtaken by the Planet; scarcely were we in motion again when we heard the lamentable cries of a poor Dhoby, whose son, a boy eight years of age, had fallen into the Indus. We saw him rise several times, and then disappear. Werner was going to leap into the river, to save him, but the captain would not permit him, because the current of the stream is so strong, that the best swimmer must have perished; and before the long-boat could have been put out, he must have been carried down several miles. The unhappy parents stood mute and thoughtful the whole day on the deck, with their eyes turned towards the direction where their boy had sunk.

In the evening both the vessels anchored off the village of Becah. We took our fowling-pieces and rambled through plantations of indigo, cotton, and sugar-cane, but shot only a few birds. There must have been plenty of jackals, for we heard them howling all the night through. We had scarcely set out on the following day, when we stuck fast upon a sand-bank, and all our attempts to get off were fruitless; while we were in this predicament a large boat, under full sail, passed us, but all our calling for assistance was to no purpose, till the captain, in order to frighten the uncivil pilot, fired a wall piece in the direction of the mast, on which the boat immediately made towards us; we fastened our anchor chains to its stern, spread the sails, and thus by aid of the wind, got afloat again in four hours. On this day we for the first time saw an alligator on a sand-bank, at which some of our party fired in vain.

On the 22d we were frequently only three steps from the bank, passing by beautiful preserves and richly cultivated fields: at the outskirts of the preserves we saw some jackals, one of which was fired at, and killed; and also several alligators, which however plunged into the water before we got within shot of them. In the afternoon we passed Batchan and Kotiah, which lie close to the foot of the bare Lukkee mountains, and are so washed by the Indus, that nothing is now to be seen of the road which Lord Keane caused to be made for the army. Two miles below Sehwan, the Indus, which had hitherto flowed in a bed 5000 paces in breadth, assumes a totally different appearance; it divides into several branches, the most navigable of which, scarcely 200 paces broad, runs to the town of Sehwan, which we reached at sunset, and landed under some tamarind trees.

This town is situated on an eminence about 100

feet high, and would have been already swept away by the river, were it not protected by its rocky soil. We immediately proceeded to view the town and the old fort, which lies to the north-east, close to the bank, on an elevation 160 feet in height, which is separated from the town by a deep ravine. Its natural position is so favourable that we may well take it for granted that Alexander the Great formed a settlement here; the ruins of the fort are of a later period; they fully resemble in their construction, particularly in the form of the bulwarks, that at Hyderabad, and are probably of the time of the Moguls. The vaults, the strong walls, and the well-shaped bricks indicate the hand of a master. It is not easy to ascertain its shape, which however appears to have been an oval, with broken lines about 2000 paces in circumference.

We proceeded from the fort, through the dirty, noisome town, to the tomb of Lal Shah Baz, a saint from Khorasan, who is said to have been buried here 600 years ago; and whose sanctity and miracles are in such high repute, that pilgrims flock from Afghanistan and India, and even the princes of those countries pay homage to him. The priests assure the superstitious multitude that even the Indus obeys the saint, and therefore no ship dares to pass by without making an expiatory offering. The entrance is bedizened with ostrich feathers and bells; when we came into the paved forecourt, we saw some hundred men and boys dancing to the sound of a drum and pipe, running confusedly about, and throwing up skyrockets amidst songs and shouts. We were soon surrounded by the crowd, who in a very insolent manner insisted that we should pull off our boots;

but my companions would not submit to this, alleging that the Mahometans were not required to take off their turban. As most of these fanatics were in a state of intoxication, we preferred giving up our intention of seeing the tomb, and in the darkness of the evening returned to our vessel.

On the 23d we again got on a sandbank, but were afloat in an hour. At times the current was so strong that our boat could scarcely move on; the navigation became every hour more difficult, because the water had suddenly fallen four feet. The thermometer at noon was usually 103° F., and seldom fell below 89. Our captain and lieutenant were seized with a violent fever, accompanied with frightful retching; which, however, providentially did not prove fatal. In the following days we passed tracts of country which were well cultivated, and sprinkled with villages consisting of wooden houses, built on stakes to secure them against inundations. The district seemed very populous, for the inhabitants flocked in hundreds to the banks to see us pass. The men were handsome and muscular, and wore a garment round their waist; the women were uncommonly tall and slender, and by no means ungraceful, and generally carried pitchers of water on their heads. In the river we saw large flocks of pelicans, geese and ducks, and herds of buffaloes wading in the water; on the banks, stags, jackals, foxes, and several tame bears, which in the evening come from the preserves to slake their thirst. At length, on Tuesday the 27th, at half past eight in the morning, we came in sight of the minaret and graves of Sukkur. The landscape here suddenly assumes a totally different aspect: both the banks are bordered by luxuriant forests of date palms, among which the towns of Sukkur, Bukkur, and Roree, successively appear, surrounded by small rocky islands, covered with tombs of the most various descriptions. After the monotonous countries through which we had passed, they had an exceedingly pleasing appearance.

A WOMAN OF SINDE.

Sukkur, which only eighty years ago was a populous town, but is now covered with the ruins of sepulchres and temples, is built on a rocky calcareous spot which rises 100 feet above the river, and is totally barren. It contains scarcely 6000 inhabitants, and, properly speaking, consists of two towns — the bazar, built by the English close to the bank, and the old town. Between the two towns lie numerous bungalows and the barracks of the regiments stationed here, also erected by the English within the last three years. A minaret about 70 feet high, from which there is an extensive and noble prospect, is situated among tombs on a small eminence at the western end. The mighty stream meanders through the boundless arid plain, becoming narrower and narrower the nearer it approaches Sukkur; and small calcareous rocks rise on its banks, which are suddenly converted into a smiling landscape, by a forest of date palms, extending for several miles on both sides. Bukkur and the Island of the Tombs, lie in manifold groups, under the shade of ancient fig and tamarind trees; while on the bare hills of Sukkur the ruins of temples and sepulchres alternate with pretty bungalows.

If the eye is attracted here by the bustle of military life, it is equally gratified by the prospect of the Meannee, and the white sails of the boats, which may be discovered at a great distance glistening in the sun. To the north of the town the ground becomes level and fertile, and, on that side, the place with its environs might be easily converted into an island, by the windings of the Indus. Bukkur lies opposite to Sukkur, on a limestone rocky island, only 200 feet above the level of the sea, and twenty feet above that of the Indus. It is enclosed by a decayed wall two feet thick, and contains only a few houses besides the barracks and magazines. Roree, the largest of the three towns, is situated on gentle eminences on the left bank: it is built of clay and stone, and has 8000 inhabitants. Between the two towns are some small rocky islets, covered with sepulchres, fig-trees, and tamarinds. The number of different sea-shells inclosed in the calcareous rock, especially near Roree, is very remarkable; there are also great masses of flint, agate, and jasper. At this place, where Lord Keane had a bridge thrown over the Indus, the river is only 1800 feet broad and 30 feet deep. Immediately beyond Sukkur it makes a bend to the north, so that this place is nearly surrounded by water, like a peninsula.

We anchored by the side of the Planet, which had arrived the day before, without accident. Captain Nott, the commander of the flotilla on the Indus, had the kindness to send me his boat, and I received an invitation from Major Clibborn to take up my abode in his bungalow. I am indebted to the hospitality and kindness of these two officers for the agreeable manner in which I spent my time here. The house of the major, an enthusiastic tiger hunter, lies close to the Indus, on a promontory 20 feet high, connected with an ancient sepulchre. There is a charming prospect from the verandah over the three towns and the banks of the Indus. The silence of the whole scene was interrupted only by the continued creaking of the water-wheels, the falling in of the bank, or by the thunder of the cannon of the Ameers of Khyrpoor, who were at this time at variance.

The heat is so great and oppressive, being every day above 100, that it is impossible to take exercise except in the early part of the morning, or after sunset. During my stay here, although the sky was every evening covered with thunder clouds, and flashes of lightning illumined all around, yet not a drop of rain fell; only dense clouds of dust were driven through the air. In order to enjoy the coolness and to be protected against the water-gnats, troublesome little insects with a long sting, the wound of which is very painful, I sleep at night, lulled by the howling jackals, in the open air on the platform of the house. Bathing in the Indus is not refreshing, the warmth of the water being 70°, and it is besides dangerous to Europeans on account of the alligators. Colonel Booth, who is passionately fond of swimming, plunges, notwithstanding, every morning into the waves, surrounded by a crowd of his servants, who, by their cries and shouts, keep these animals at bay. At the hour of noon when all is quiet on the river, the alligators come to the surface to bask in the sun, and we take advantage of this moment to fire upon them. Sometimes we amuse ourselves with the Pula fisheries of the Meannees.

PULA FISHERY.

The fisherman first of all lays a large, oval, iron vessel in the river, commends himself to the protection of Allah, and places himself on it in such a manner that his body covers the opening at the top; he then by the aid of his hands and feet works his way on the stream. He carries in his girdle a small spear, and in his right hand a fork nearly fifteen feet long, to which a wide net with a running knot is fastened, and which closes as soon as the fish is caught: the fish is then killed with the spear and thrown into the vessel. We likewise saw some fishermen with a large net thrown over their left shoulder. Before the Meannee goes into the river, he will wander for miles along the banks, and then let himself be driven by the current, because the Pula swims against it.

Excursions on the Indus in the cool of the evening are very delightful, for in no country are the mornings and evenings so pleasant, or the sunsets so beautiful and sublime, as here. Captain Nott sends me his boat daily, and I need not say that I diligently avail myself of his kindness. One evening when the sun was setting behind dark thunder-clouds, and flashes of lightning illumined the landscape on every side, we visited the Island of Tombs. These monuments, which are supposed to be 800 years old, are under the charge of fakirs. When they saw us approach they lighted the lamps in the dirty sanctuary, but were very much displeased that we contented ourselves with looking at them from the entrance, and did not make them any present. " You will split upon the rocks," cried they menacingly. We smiled at their prophecy, and proceeded to the seven sepulchral towers, built of coloured porcelain tiles. Here, under the shade of poplar-fig and tamarind trees, are said to repose seven daughters of one of the ancient princes, who are regarded as saints, on account of their beauty and virtues; indeed they are so venerated that the Indians affirm that even the fish, as they swim past the spot, invariably turn their heads, and never their tail towards them. Next to these tombs, the lofty vaulted sepulchre, situated at the entrance of the old town, in which the sister of the saint at Sehwan is buried, is the most remarkable. Small bells, feathers, and ribbons, deck the gaily-painted sarcophagus or tombstone. Several persons were praying before it as I entered, and in the piazzas of the court-yard, children, under the direction of a priest, were singing religious songs. An uncommonly large tiger is maintained here by the people in honour of the saint.

Three days before my departure, Sir Charles Napier arrived, not indeed recovered from the effects of his accident, but with the prospect of being so very shortly. He gave me no hopes of witnessing here any military events; and likewise doubted whether any thing decisive would take place on the Sutlej, though he thought it more probable, and advised me to proceed thither. The people in the country are persuaded that the assembling of the army of reserve, is intended for the occupation of the Punjab, and whatever a man wishes, that he hopes to see realised. Thus, encouraged by a letter from the Governor-General Lord Ellenborough, and by the advice of my friends, I have resolved to join the officers, who are ordered to the army in that quarter. Three of my companions proceed to Bhawulpoor by water. Lord Altamont, Captains West and Bennett, and myself, prefer going by land.

LETTER IV.

TO ALEXANDER VON HUMBOLDT.

Preparations for the journey to Ferozpoor.— Departure for Roree.— Ruins of Allore.— Wedding fête near Sangeram.— March through the desert.— Celebration of the 15th October in the village of Retee.— Passing the boundary of Bhawulpoor.— Ahmedpoor.— Hospitality of the inhabitants.— Khaunpoor.— Welcome of the Khan by an escort.— Entry into Ahmedpoor.— Audience of Bhawulkhan at his country-seat in the desert.— Bhawulpoor.— Journey to Memdot.— The Khan of Memdot.— Dangerous illness of one of our party.— Arrival at Ferozpoor.

Ferozpoor, November 13. 1842.

I ARRIVED here safely yesterday at sunrise; and make use of this day to describe to you my fatiguing, but most interesting journey of 440 miles.

Our little caravan consisted of twenty-four camels, five horses, twenty-eight servants, one camel-leader, four camel-drivers, and an escort of one subaltern officer and twelve sepoys. Each of my companions had a large tent; I had only two small ones, such as are used by the servants. We had to pay forty rupees for the hire of each camel, by which we are relieved from all care, because it too often happens that the drivers neglect the animals, or that they are stolen. The British authorities at Sukkur had given us an open Perwannah *, bearing the official seal, and

* Notice is hereby given to the chiefs of the towns and the guards along the river, from Sukkur to Ferozpoor, that four

two Belooches to the frontiers of Bhawulpoor. On the morning of the 9th of October, our camels, horses, and effects were sent across the river Roree, and in the afternoon we went thither ourselves in a gondola. Our arrangement is always to send on two tents, with the culinary department, and an escort, under Werner's superintendence, to the new station, on the preceding evening, so that, on our arrival, we may have protection against the sun, and find breakfast ready. We encamped here for the night, by the side of a brick wall, under tamarinds and acacias: the owner of the camels took leave of us, cordially shaking hands, commending us and his camels to the protection of Rama.

The manner in which the European is obliged to travel in India very much resembles a nomadic life. As the climate does not allow him to expose himself to the sun by day, or to the open air by night, and as he cannot find in the villages either a lodging or the necessaries of life to which he has been accustomed, he must carry every thing with him. Even our caravan, though we were but a small party, looked like a little wandering village. The time of our setting out, was regulated according to the distance we had to go. As soon as the signal was given every thing was made ready for the journey; the tents packed up; the confused talking of the people, and the moaning of the camels, announced the moment

English gentlemen of rank are going by the high road from this place to Ferozpoor. It is expected that no one will molest them, but, on the contrary, to the utmost of their power, to provide for their progress, convenience, and security, and will most strictly conform to this order. Dated Sukkur, October 7. In the year of our Lord Jesus Christ 1842.

of loading them, and in half an hour we were already on our way.

Our Belooches informed us that we could not take the usual road by Subzulkote, as the bridges had been destroyed by the inundations, and that we must therefore go along the edge of the desert, through its whole length. At four o'clock on the morning of the 10th, we set out for the village of Barra, a distance of thirteen miles. The first few miles lay along a steep, stony road, through a bare and desert tract. We then passed two handsome sepulchral, vaulted towers, forty feet high. From this eminence is a view of the ruins of Allore, formerly the capital of the Musikanus; few traces of it remain, but the ground is every where covered with hewn stones and fragments. In the valley, through which a branch of the Indus once flowed, is now a pond, and on the side of an eminence declining towards it, is a small village. An arched bridge is thrown over a canal above fifteen paces broad, which runs from this pond, in a north-west direction to the Indus. The form of the stones and the excellency of the workmanship, seem to indicate, that this bridge belongs to a very remote period. It is however in such a decayed state, and so full of holes, that we were obliged to be very careful in crossing it. From this spot the country is level, intersected by ditches and small canals, with plantations of millet and cotton.

We pitched our tents in the midst of tombs, under some fine tamarind trees behind the village. Two fakirs, who dwelt here in clay huts, offered their services; but their civility degenerated into importunity, when one of our party gave them some arrack, and we had much difficulty in getting rid of them. Soon afterwards several musicians came to amuse us, and celebrated the power of the Queen of England, and the deeds of her ancestors, accompanied by a guitar made of a dry gourd. We sent the Belooches into the village to buy fowls, which our servants dressed for dinner, with which we had shipatos or aaps instead of bread.*

On the following day we were only six miles from the little town of Sangeram; this place is enclosed with clay walls, has 2000 inhabitants, and lies on the border of the desert; the road to it led through a richly-watered and cultivated low tract of land. A little beyond the town, where we pitched our tents, we found an encampment of several hundred persons, who had come from a great distance to be present at the celebration of a marriage. We were told that a little girl, only six years old, a near relation of the Ameers of Khyrpoor, was to be betrothed to a boy fourteen years of age, the son of an eminent Belooche chief. The father of the bridegroom, a handsome, elderly man, was seated smoking his pipe under a large tent, surrounded by his attendants, while dancing girls and musicians, were exhibiting their performances before him; and outside the tents the people likewise amused themselves with dancing. Above twenty men, with wooden staves in their hands, went round in a circle, jumped and leaped in the air, and when they met in the centre, turned backwards and forwards, both parties touching their staves, and beating time to the music with their feet. There was something wild and original in this dance, which was continued for nearly an hour, under the

* The flour is kneaded with water, and the dough pressed into a flat cake between the hands, and roasted in an iron pan.

scorching rays of the sun, till they were quite exhausted. In the afternoon the bride, closely veiled, appeared, seated on a camel under a red palanquin, which was completely covered, in order to thank the company and to take leave. As soon as she retired, the chief made an address to the persons assembled, mounted his horse, and all hastened homewards. Our tents were surrounded the whole day by people, who assured us that they had never seen white men before, and gazed with wonder and amazement at our watches, arms, and other things.

On the 12th, we had to travel eighteen miles to Moobarekpoor; a very fatiguing journey indeed. Our way led through a tract mostly covered with tamarisk jungle, and intersected with numerous ditches and channels; we had to cross the river Narra, which is eighty paces broad, and, in one place, so deep that my horse was obliged to swim across. After a ride of five hours, we reached the place of destination; but our camels did not arrive till several hours later. Some had fallen into the water, with our luggage, and others were so weary that the drivers were obliged to pack them afresh. Moobarekpoor is a large village, at the eastern entrance of which is a square fort, built of clay. Close to our encampment was a band of gypsies: I was quite surprised to find them sheltered under moveable huts made of reeds, as in Europe, and that they gained their livelihood by basket-making. All day long we were pestered by hawkers, beggars, and musicians, and at night we were disturbed, as usual, by the howling of dogs, jackals, and hyenas. On the 13th, the Belooches conducted us through unbeaten paths along the borders of the desert; we every where saw traces of former civilisation, abandoned villages, dry ditches, and decayed walls. An hour after sunset, we met several Belooches armed to the teeth, with their servants, mounted on camels and horses; our guides told us that they were hastening to Khyrpoor to assist the youngest of the Ameers.

A BELOOCHE ON A CAMEL.

We did not reach the village of Ghara-Kakote, which was nineteen miles distant, till nine o'clock. It lies on the edge of the desert, consists of wooden and reed huts, and was first inhabited, only a few years ago, by some Belooches who preferred agricultural pursuits, to their former predatory habits. We had pitched our tents under a shady plane-tree, close to a channel full of good water. Towards evening, when our camels were about to be sent on, the leader of the camels came running up in great alarm, and informed us that our Belooches having been affronted by the subaltern officer, had inflamed the inhabitants of the village, and that there was every prospect of our being attacked. Soon afterwards we heard a great noise in the village, upon which we ordered our guard to load their pieces, and made every preparation to defend ourselves. We were told that we should have to encounter more than a hundred well-armed men; but happily for us, just at this juncture, the news of the taking and destruction of Cabool reached the village, and the chief succeeded in quieting the people, by prophesying that they might expect the same fate. He subsequently came to us, with several of the oldest inhabitants, and promised to furnish us with a guide the next morning, as the Belooches had deserted us. For the sake of security, we deferred our journey through the desert, till after sunrise on the following day. It was ten o'clock when we reached the twelve huts of Heyet-Kekote. The village, which is built on a sandy eminence, is separated by a pond from a marshy jungle, near to which we encamped. In the evening, on entering my tent, such a sudden weakness overcame me, that I sunk down on the carpet. Werner covered me with my cloak and blankets, and I soon fell into a sound sleep. A profuse perspiration relieved me from this attack of fever, and on the following day I felt quite vigorous.

On the 15th of October we started for the village of Retee, sixteen miles distant; our way led through thick and luxuriant tamarisk bushes, and a country abounding in antelopes, hares, and black and grey partridges. We found our tents pitched in an open field near the village. This being the birthday of our sovereign, I invited my fellow-travellers to dinner, and gave a goat to my servants. A sheep and two fowls were prepared for the festivity, and a few bottles of hock and champagne, which I had carefully brought from Kurrachee for this purpose, gave a zest to the repast. It was certainly the first time that a Prussian kept the birthday of his king between the Indus and the great Indian desert. My companions participated in my pleasure, and cordially joined in the toasts proposed.

The village of Dandee, for which we set out on the following day, was only twelve miles distant. The scenery became more variegated and luxuriant; we passed through three pretty large villages and several fields of holcus sorghum, which were so flourishing that some stems were fifteen and sixteen feet high. The stalks are almost as thick as the sugar-cane; the sap has a juicy, sweet taste; it is eaten by the inhabitants, and is a nourishing and wholesome food for horses and oxen. Dandee is a large village, but is built of clay, and the walls of the houses are disgustingly covered with cakes of dung of the cow or camel, to harden in the sun for fuel. Our guide, a handsome young Belooche, was the first who, on our giving him two rupees, pronounced the blessing of Allah upon us.

Favoured by the finest weather, the thermometer being only at 73° Fahrenheit (whereas yesterday before sunset it was at 82°), we crossed on the 17th the frontiers of Bhawulpoor. The territory of the

Khan begins three miles beyond Dandee. The soil is better cultivated; the villages, though built in a similar manner, more cleanly, and the inhabitants more friendly and hospitable. We here, for the first time, met a letter carrier; he bore the letters in a leathern bag on his head, and in his right hand carried a long stick, painted yellow and black, with an iron head, to which coloured ribbons and bells were fastened, by means of which he not only announces his approach from a distance, but frightens away the wild beasts by the sound of his bells. The stations are seldom more than six miles apart, a distance which these people accomplish, in a constant trot, in an hour and a half. At seven o'clock in the morning we reached the town of Ahmedpoor-Barra, which is surrounded with a clay rampart and rude towers, as a means of defence; but the rampart is decayed in many places, and would ill stand a siege. On the platform of each of the towers was a gun. An officer, with a guard of fifty men, was stationed at the entrance gate; as soon as he saw us approach, he rose and gave us a friendly salam. A citadel, with projecting towers, stands at the north-eastern end of the town, which contains some large brick buildings, and is said to have a population of 6000 inhabitants, and a garrison of one thousand men. It is situated in a very fertile, low valley, planted with corn, cotton, indigo, and sugar-cane; a few lofty tamarinds, acacias, and poplar figs flourished in the greatest luxuriance; but the landscape was otherwise entirely destitute of trees. Towards nine o'clock we completed our day's journey of eighteen miles, at the village of Katta-Ke-Basta.

We had scarcely alighted, when the Kemda (the

chief of the village), with the principal inhabitants dressed in their best costume, came to welcome us. Our perwannah was read by the barber, a handsome man with a long beard, to his companions; and when they had assured themselves by its contents, and a few questions which they addressed to us, that we were the parties whom they expected, the Kemda told us that his Highness had given orders that we should be treated with the greatest attention; that nine men should keep guard at night before our encampment, and that six horsemen should accompany us from place to place. They supplied us with fowls, eggs, milk, and butter, and did their utmost to comply with our wishes. A village watch is the surest safeguard for a traveller in the East against robbery, for the village thereby engages to pay in money the value of the stolen goods. It is, however, very singular, that if a traveller is robbed in countries governed by Indian princes, the British government insists on an indemnity, which must be paid by the place near which the robbery was committed, or by the government interested; but that if a robbery is committed in the British territory, the person robbed obtains no indemnity.

The promised watch appeared in the evening—miserable-looking men, some armed with sabres, some with sticks. A guard was placed at each corner of the camp, who, according to the custom of the natives, crouched upon the ground; to keep themselves awake and to frighten the thieves they called to each other by name all night long, adding, "Are you not happy?" "What an honour!" &c. &c. You may easily suppose that with all this noise and the howling of the jackals, sleep was out of the question. Our escort arrived early on the following morning. Two of the horsemen armed with shield, sword, and a long gun formed the vanguard; the others armed partly in the same manner, partly with long spears, bows, and arrows, followed at some distance. These long-bearded men in turbans and ample upper garments were extremely attentive to us. Travellers whom we met were informed in a few words of the rank of the strangers, and a respectful salam was offered us by everybody. We were received in the same hospitable manner at Nowshuhur (14 miles and a half), a large, neat village, which contained some houses of two stories, with glass windows, the first we had met with since we had left Sukkur.

Throughout the whole of our journey, we were struck with the large number of dogs, and here we were equally astonished at the immense number of asses, which the inhabitants use, both for carrying burdens and for riding. Our tents were pitched under tamarisk trees to the east of the village; the people brought us the customary provisions at reasonable prices, such as fowls, eggs, milk, and a goat; but we refused the latter, having observed that these animals were excessively dirty feeders. The weather was, as usual, bright and clear; the heat before sunrise was 65°, at noon 92°, but in my tent 106°. The beautiful moonlight night invited a pious priest to watch, and he broke the profound silence, by crying in a shrill tone of voice without intermission till the morning dawned, "Allah is great!"

On the 19th we travelled along a broad road to Sumaboo-Kote (13 miles and a half). This village is distinguished by a far better style of building, and greater cleanliness. Surrounded by flourishing fields of millet, and under the shade of poplar figs and tamarinds, it has a comfortable rural appearance. On the following day we proceeded to Khaunpoor (14 miles and a half). The road thither lay through a more cultivated country; the corn fields were surrounded by small woods abounding in game; but the villages were hid in a complete mist, occasioned by the smoke of the morning fires, for when the cool season sets in (we had 55° Fahr. before sunrise) the inhabitants kindle a fire in their houses very early in the morning, round which they sit, the women grinding corn between two stones, while the men are idly smoking their pipe. These handmills are used every where in India, and are unquestionably of the most remote origin. Of equal antiquity are the oil-mills worked by oxen; a large rammer crushes the seed, which is placed in a stone vessel, or in the hollow trunk of a tree. Coffee, spices, &c. are pounded in a mortar made of stone or metal, generally the former.

At seven o'clock we skirted the north end of the town to our tents, which were pitched beyond it. Khaunpoor is a town containing 8000* inhabitants, but, with the exception of a few brick buildings two stories high, all the houses are built of clay; the streets narrow, unpaved, and very dirty. The most remarkable building is a lofty and beautiful mosque in the centre of the town. A channel fifteen paces broad, the last which issues from the Indus, waters the ground, which produces various kinds of corn, cotton, indigo, sugar cane, melons, and some culinary vegetables. Towards the south, not far from our encampment, is a vaulted powder magazine, with two brass six-pounders in front of it. Nearly opposite is a

* Mr. Edward Thornton says 20,000.

mosque, lately built by the Khans, and behind it a hunting-seat of his Highness, lying in a small garden. Immediately after our arrival, the postmaster came with his messengers to receive our commands, and to request our names, which he had orders to send to the Khan. In the afternoon we took a walk in the environs, and he accompanied us to his Highness's country-seat, a small brick building two stories high, with a verandah. We, however, saw only the outside, for the keeper refused to show us the interior, because a favourite lady of the Khan resides in it. The garden is very prettily laid out in flower beds, interspersed with bananas, figs, and oranges. The Khan resides here several days in every year, when he enjoys the pleasures of the chase in the neighbouring jungles, which abound in game, and receives the petitions and complaints of the people.

In the town we remarked some traces of an illumination which had taken place the preceding evening by order of the Khan, to celebrate the storming of Cabool; for his Highness, who is a faithful adherent and admirer of the English, neglects no opportunity of manifesting his amicable sentiments. We were every where saluted with a respectful salam by the people, who touch their forehead with the right hand. In the evening some Bayaderes and musicians came to our tents, to amuse us with singing and dancing. Their movements were graceful and animated, and their fine bright eyes, and expressive countenances, corresponded with the feelings expressed by the dance.

From Khaunpoor the road leads along the desert, through tamarisk bushes, to the desolate village of Mamoo-Kote (fifteen miles). It was formerly a considerable village, but it now consists of only a few wretched huts; the ground is covered with an incrustation of salt, and is but little cultivated. We could obtain neither provisions for ourselves, nor fodder for the horses, and were obliged to send our servants to a considerable distance to purchase some. On the twenty-second we passed through a fine hunting ground to the village of Choudurree (eleven miles). Nothing remains of the once large town but some clay huts, and the ruins of deserted houses; a former hunting seat of the Khan, built of clay, surrounded by a wall, with circular towers, lies completely in ruins, and is covered in part with the sand of the desert. The very simple apartments of the Khan, the harem, the audience chamber, in which he received the people, the apartments for his servants, and his attendants, and the stabling, may be easily distinguished. While all around spoke of ruin and decay, some lofty tamarisks and poplars were growing in the court yard in the greatest luxuriance. We had an extensive view from one of the towers which is twenty feet high: on the one side lay the rich verdant valley of the Indus and the Sutlej, while on the other was stretched the boundless desert. These decided contrasts of contiguous barrenness and fertility produce a strange effect on the mind.

The following day, which was particularly fine, we continued our route to Chan-Khan-Digot (thirteen miles): we were within a mile of that place when we met an officer of the Khan accompanied by twenty-five horsemen, who greeted us in the name of his prince, by whom he had been sent to meet us and to conduct us to his residence. He assured us that his Highness was much rejoiced at our arrival, and at the prospect of seeing us. He was mounted on a fine chestnut stallion, whose bridle was richly ornamented with silver. His upper garment bordered with gold lace, and his coloured silk turban distinguished him from his attendants, who were dressed in very gay apparel, and were armed with guns, spears, shields, and bows and arrows, and showed much dexterity in discharging their arrows, firing their guns at full gallop, and throwing their spears.

Channi-Khan-Digot is bounded by the desert on one side, and on the other by the richly cultivated valley of the Sutlej, and is a large village; the houses are of brick, and many are two stories high. When we arrived at our tents we found ten dishes of confectionery, which his Highness had sent us from his harem, together with a present of sheep, fowls, eggs, and milk. It was his Highness's desire that we and our servants, should consider ourselves his guests.

Surrounded by the escort provided by the Khan, we made our entrance next day into Ahmedpoor, the residence of Bhawulpoor Khan. We set out by moonlight under a temperature of 64°, first along the borders of the desert, then, as we approached Ahmedpoor, through a more and more cultivated country, till we at length reached the fertile plain which surrounds the capital. The town was veiled in a transparent mist, environed by gardens, in which poplar figs, tamarinds, bananas, and vegetables flourished in luxuriance. The first object that struck us was the stone house of the former British resident, but it is quite dilapidated: of the garden nothing remains but the ruins of the outer walls; and the house itself is in a state of decay and uninhabited. Our tents were pitched just at the outskirts of the town in a plantation of indigo: a crowd of people were here assembled to see us arrive. We had scarcely entered the tents, when Moossa Khan, one of the chief nobles of his Highness, arrived, escorted by several soldiers in scarlet uniforms, to bid us welcome in the name of the Khan. Moossa is a corpulent man, and has the most good-natured countenance in the world: he was dressed in a red tunic embroidered with flowers of gold, wore a crimson turban, and red and white striped pantaloons, and a sabre at his side. He addressed us in the highly poetical language of the East. On our invitation that he would enter our tent he did not omit taking off his shoes, in acknowledgment of his inferiority. His first questions concerned our health, he next congratulated us on having made so rapid and safe a journey, and then very dexterously turned the conversation on politics and news, making inquiries respecting my king, my country, and myself. After we had amply satisfied his curiosity, I asked him what was the strength of his Highness's army. "His warriors," said he, "are more numerous than the grains of sand in the desert."—"And how many guns?" continued I.—"Oh, they cannot be counted: the power of the Khan obscures the sun." Meantime, more presents arrived from the Khan, consisting of five bottles of rosewater, twenty large dishes of confectionary, goats, sheep, fowls, &c., which were laid at our feet. This was a glorious feast day for our servants! On taking leave, Moossa repeatedly expressed the wish of the Khan to receive us at his palace in the desert: this we gratefully accepted, leaving it to the pleasure of the Khan to fix the hour.

Our tents were surrounded the whole day by visiters from the town; most of them attired in their gala dresses, and all conducted themselves with the greatest respect. An aged man expressed his gratitude that we permitted them to approach us, as former travellers would never allow it. After breakfast, Lord Altamont and I rode into the town: it is pretty large, containing above 15,000 inhabitants; but it is confined and dirty, and nearly all the houses are built of clay. The bazars are very extensive and exceedingly animated, though but poorly supplied. The most considerable buildings are a fort with round towers at the west end of the town, within which the residence of the Khan is situated, and likewise a mosque with four small minarets. On the south of the town we passed a large court yard, surrounded with a wall, where we saw several carriages and some handsome horses and oxen. On our riding into it, the people met us, crying out that we must instantly turn back, and we subsequently heard that the wives of the Khans alighted at this place, and that some of them had just arrived, to make purchases in the town.

On our return we found Bayaderes and musicians; but their external appearance was so very unpleasant that we declined their performance. At two o'clock the moonshee of his Highness brought us word that two of the Khan's carriages should be in waiting at about four o'clock, to convey us to his palace. Accordingly, at the appointed time, Moossa appeared at the head of thirty horsemen and the carriages: one of them was drawn by horses, and the other by two uncommonly large snow-white bulls. The carriage rested on two wheels, and was covered with a vaulted canopy of red cloth, and profusely adorned with fringes and little bells. The horses and bulls were likewise

CARRIAGE OF BHAWULKHAN.

hung with scarlet trappings, and were guided by a coachman, who sat on the pole. The equipages were of a very antique form, and so contrived, that it was only possible to lie down in them. Captain West and myself chose the carriage drawn by bulls. When we set out, Moossa with a part of the escort rode before, while the others followed or surrounded the carriages; two men ran by the side of each carriage to guide the beasts or to support the vehicle, where the road was rough.

The palace of his Highness is situated seven miles to the south of Ahmedpoor, in a fertile, pleasant Oasis of the desert, which is planted with corn, cotton, and sugar-cane. We rode at a very brisk trot around the town, on a very bad road, which was sometimes rugged, sometimes deeply covered with sand, and generally intersected with ditches, and then crossed a handsome arched bridge across a small channel. Here we passed the stabling for the Khan's camels, which consists of several plain buildings and a spacious court-yard surrounded by a high clay wall. The palace of his Highness now came in sight; for its situation was pointed out at a great distance by lofty tamarinds, acacias, and poplar figs. The approach is by a drawbridge about 10 paces broad: this leads into a forecourt 100 paces long and 50 broad, surrounded by a wall, at the four corners of which rise very neat wooden towers. Crossing this court-yard we entered a quadrangle 300 paces long and nearly as broad, at the north end of which stands the palace. A wooden building raised above the platform, with a projecting roof, and an elegantly carved verandah, appears to be the residence of the women, because I perceived several female figures in white veils behind the lattice. A verandah runs round the palace, which on the side towards the east is 30 paces broad. The lodgings for the domestics and the stabling, which are made of clay, lay on one side, and had red curtains. The whole is surrounded by a high wall and a moat.

Three of the Khan's regular regiments, about 1800 strong, were drawn up along both sides from the entrance into the quadrangle to the verandah; they were clothed in white, brown, and red, and armed with old unserviceable guns of the East India Company. On our approach they fired a salute, and the music struck up. The red regiment was commanded by a youth not more than sixteen years of age, a favourite of his Highness. We were received at the steps of the verandah, by three of the principal ministers, who conducted us to the Khan. As we turned the corner of the verandah, to the east side, the most striking image of an Indian Court presented itself to our view. The Khan was seated in the centre of the verandah, on a pure white, silk carpet, supported by large cushions, and surrounded by a semicircle of more than 200 of his chiefs and officers, whose picturesque costume and various groupings and different arms realised a scene of the Arabian Nights. His sword, guns, and pistols lay before him. On our approach he rose, with his attendants, embraced us, shook hands, and invited us to sit down by him. His Highness is a tall, handsome man, between forty and fifty years of age; but the expression of his large dark eye is faint and languid in consequence, it is said, of his free indulgence in the harem. He had a long, dark brown, silky beard, and his hair fell partially curled upon his shoulders. He was dressed in a white muslin garment trimmed with gold lace, wide silk pantaloons, and a rose-coloured turban, with a handsome dagger in his red silk scarf. He wore no jewels except a few rings, and a necklace of large pearls which were fastened by a diamond clasp.

As soon as we were seated, a servant with an immensely large fan approached to cool us. The conversation commenced with inquiries respecting our journey, its object, and my country; we next spoke of the chase: his Highness regretted that he could not get up a hunting party for us, but gave us permission to hunt at pleasure in his territory, adding that we should find lions and tigers in the jungles beyond Bhawulpoor, but that the first were merely a small race, and not numerous. Politics too were touched upon, but only slightly; we then spoke of the troops of his Highness, which seemed to give him pleasure, for he smiled with much complacency when I told him that I had been greatly surprised at the good appearance and discipline of the regiments we had just seen. After having conversed about half an hour we rose to depart, but his Highness requested us to prolong our visit, and probably another hour elapsed ere we took leave, when we repeatedly expressed our gratitude to the hospitable prince, who embraced us and cordially pressed our hands. The ministers accompanied us to the first gate, while the troops saluted as before. Moossa conducted us to the carriages, and escorted us back to our encampment with his cavalry.

At a short distance from the town we saw a number of Syedees (religious women) standing by the road side; these females pretend to be descendants of the Prophet, and were closely veiled in dirty white garments, with no other aperture than a net-work inserted in it over the eyes. They approached us, importunately demanding alms, but we had no money about us to entitle us to receive the benefit of their benedictions.

A SYEDEE.

When we reached our tents I found a bay horse, caparisoned with a bridle and saddle richly studded with silver, and its feet and tail partly painted red, which his Highness sent to me as a token of remembrance; however, as there is a law which forbids English officers from accepting gifts from the native princes, I thought myself bound to decline this handsome present.

Bhawulpoor is bounded on the east and west by Sinde and the territory of the Sikhs, on the north by the Indus and the Sutlej, and on the south by the desert, and contains a population of scarcely half a million of inhabitants. The soil is fertile in the vicinity of the river, but in the interior of the country it is sandy and incrusted with salt. Its productiveness depends on the inundations and on irrigation, as there is often no rain for two years together. As soon as the snow melts in the Himalaya mountains in May and June, the water of the river flows into many canals, and from these into smaller channels, whence it is conducted, by means of water-wheels, over the fields and pastures. At this season of the year the country is nearly impassable. There are two harvests in this part; wheat and barley are sown in November; and rice, jowary, bajree, cotton, indigo, sugar-cane, melons, and vegetables, are planted in March. Besides tamarisks, tamarinds, and figs, bananas and oranges flourish; and the date palm, the fruit, wood, foliage, and fibres of which are invaluable to the inhabitants, begins to spread its bounties over the neighbourhood of Bhawulpoor. The climate is dry; in December the thermometer falls before day-break to freezing point. On the other hand, the hot season is beyond all conception oppressive; clouds of dust fill the air, and the eyes are dazzled by the white sand of the desert.

The Bhawulkhan has two wives and six sons; but he is said to have above a hundred concubines and their forty sons lodged in his harem. Though his revenue does not exceed twelve lacs per annum, he maintains an army of 5000 men, under the command of Captain M——, an Englishman, a fugitive from his native land, who took up his residence here. His treasure is said to consist of above thirty lacs, and his jewels to be of immense value; but he is tenacious of being seen in them. Since Rundjeet Sing deprived him of the fertile Mooltan, he adheres more and more closely to the English. He spends much of his time in his harem and on the chase, without however being neglectful of the government of his kingdom; and he may be classed among the best of the Indian princes.

The inhabitants of Bhawulpoor are chiefly Mussulmans; they are superstitious and immoral; they revere the Khan because he does not oppress them, reserves to himself only twenty-five per cent. of their produce, and exercises a patriarchal authority over them. Many of them are persons of considerable affluence, and I frequently saw the chief magistrate of the villages decked with costly jewels. In saluting their friends they touch first, the right shoulder, then the left, cover their brow with their right hand, and stretching out their hands repeat the usual salam. While the Mussulman, after the first salute, examines the weapons of his friends, the Hindoo, on the other hand, invariably inquires the price of provisions, especially of ghee, his favourite dish. Besides being occupied with agriculture they pay much attention to the breeding of camels, horses, and asses: large flocks of goats and sheep abound here.

On the 25th of October, we rode to the villages of Khyrpoor and Noorpoor, through a narrow road intersected by ditches and running between cornfields. We pitched our tents on the outskirts of the villages; and immediately on our arrival, the 9th Bengal Cavalry regiment entered, on its route to Sukkur. It consisted of 590 horse, in admirable discipline. According to the custom of the natives, one of their trumpeters had gone on before, to station himself at the place of encampment, and, by the sound of his little trumpet, to intimate their halting-place to his comrades.

Our own Hindoos had hitherto been rather remiss in the performance of their various rigorous observances; but after they had encountered so many of their co-religionists to-day, and among them several Brahmins, each one drew a circle round his fireplace, and incessantly rang a little bell, while he was cooking his victuals, to scare away the evil spirit. If an uninitiated person happens accidentally to cross the circle, the food is considered to be unclean, and the Hindoo, be he ever so hungry, throws it all away. Above 1200 persons were attached to this regiment —servants, grass-cutters, water-carriers, and camel-drivers; besides 138 camels, 50 ponies, and 12 carts for transporting the tents and baggage; the greater part of their things having been sent by water. Colonel William Pattle, the commander of the regiment, had an elephant, the first animal of the kind which I saw in active employ in India.

We spent the evening with the officers of the corps, who had every comfort around them; even bread, which we had not tasted since we left Sukkur, was served at table. It was rather singular that the Colonel spoke to us in the highest terms of the faithfulness and integrity of his confidential domestic, who had been in his service above sixteen years;—but experience unhappily proves that the natives are not to be depended upon, and this sad lesson the Colonel too was taught, for, that very same night, the man decamped, carrying off with him several hundred rupees, the property of his master.

On the following morning we were on the wing as early as three o'clock, as we were anxious to reach Bhawulpoor, a distance of 15 miles, without loss of time. At first, the country was barren and sandy, but, as we approached the town, it became more fruitful and cultivated. Three miles before reaching Bhawulpoor we saw, on our left hand, a very handsome stone monument, erected by his brother officers to the memory of an English colonel, who had died here of fever. Immediately behind it is a dry stream twenty feet in width, with some deserted villages lying along its banks. From this point commences the richest and most luxuriant tract, cultivated with various kinds of corn, indigo, cotton and sugar, above which rises the date palm in graceful pride, imparting to the whole scene the character of a tropical landscape.

The town, which contains 40,000 inhabitants, is surrounded by an immense wall, nearly four miles in length, and has six gates: the streets are narrow and dirty, and very few of the houses are built of brick; but, in every place, in every street, as well as in every garden, the palm spreads her beauteous branches, and flocks of pigeons build in the turrets of the minarets and the old walls. Bhawulpoor carries on a trade in silk and cotton stuffs, which, like those of Mooltan, are distinguished by the richness of their colours and the beauty of the patterns.

As our tents were pitched on the other side of the gate, we were obliged to traverse the city in its entire extent. Soon after our arrival we were welcomed by Meer Ibrahim Khan, the political agent of the British government; a very handsome Mahometan, who, besides being conversant with the Persian and Arabic languages, is likewise master of the Hindostanee. On our interrogating him respecting the news of the day, and especially the reserve army, he assumed the character of a cunning diplomatist, who is acquainted with every circumstance, but is not at liberty to converse of any. Ibrahim is one of the very few natives who has some knowledge of Europe; yet he could not form any conception of Prussia, till my companion, Captain Bennet, informed him that I belonged to that kingdom which, under Blucher, had contributed to the downfal of the great Napoleon. He had heard of both, and his interest was so strongly excited in what he heard, that he seized pen and paper, in order at once to take down the replies to some of his many questions. From the ardour and the manner in which Ibrahim sought to obtain instruction, it was evident that he was a very uncommon specimen of his countrymen. We thankfully availed ourselves of his proffered services; for we had lost three camels on our march, and were obliged to let our servants and cattle have a complete day's rest. We learnt from him that our comrades, who had come by water, had preceded us by three days, and were already on their march to Ferozpoor.

Ibrahim invited us to visit him in the afternoon at his own house, which lay in the middle of the town. Passing through a lofty gate, we first entered the court for the caravans, then into a smaller one surrounded by a wall, which led to his dwelling. In front of this were several flower beds, a fountain, and a basin for bathing. His dwelling consisted of only four apartments, furnished with carpets, a table, and a few chairs, but no other furniture of any kind whatever. Carpets were spread in the court, and chairs placed for us and a few other guests, the most respectable persons in the town, and three Persian merchants, who had just arrived from Lahore and Mooltan, and intended returning to their own country by way of Herat. Tea and sherbet were handed round, and the merchants showed us carpets and silks of Mooltan; the former were made of cotton, woven in the most beautiful patterns and colours, and seemed almost imperishable; the silks had for the most part only a slight mixture of cotton, and were wrought with gold and silver, but they are neither as beautiful nor as durable, and are used by the natives for tunics and turbans. We returned to our tents through the bazar of the town in the evening: this is the time when the activity and trade of the inhabitants is the greatest: the sellers light up their booths, the Bayaderes appear in their gayest dress, music is heard, and the crowd presses forward in quest of barter or amusement.

During the night the thermometer fell to 52° F.; and my porous water-vessels were covered with a hoar frost in the morning: we felt these changes in the temperature the more sensibly, as we still had a heat of 90° in the morning. In the evening the sky was overcast, heavy clouds of dust were carried through the air, and single drops of rain began to fall. Ibrahim, however, came to take leave of us, and requested us to give him a certificate of his readiness to serve us, a request with which we had much pleasure in complying.

On Friday the 28th we continued our march through a very sandy country to Bakkedera, about 13½ miles distant. An envoy from Bhawulpoor entered it at the same time; he was seated on an elephant, and was surrounded by about twenty horsemen, falconers, and many servants on foot. He was the bearer of presents to the Governor-General then at Ferozpoor, and was deputed to investigate the state of the country on his route thither. About three o'clock in the afternoon the sky suddenly became obscure, and a fearful storm arose above the Sutlej, clouds of dust, as dense as masses of earth, were carried through the air, and such Egyptian darkness succeeded, that we could not see four steps before us: at the same time a violent rushing and roaring sounded in the air, and the masses of dust were as thick and continued as if the whole desert were in motion. This storm, unaccompanied by rain, continued till an hour after sunset, and appeared to have been confined to a narrow slip of land, inasmuch as the servants, who had been despatched an hour before it arose, had entirely escaped it. As it was, we were thankful that our tent was not overthrown by it.

From this time the heat abated during the day: at night the thermometer sank to 54 °; and at mid-day, on the 29th, it was only 82° F. Got-Nur-Mahomed is very prettily situated, surrounded by date palms, tamarinds, and tamarisks. On our road thither, we met a man coming from the village howling and screaming; we inquired the cause of his distress. "Ah!" exclaimed he, "my brother has just died, and I must bemoan him to-day." In the evening the funeral obsequies were celebrated in the wildest manner, with dancing and singing; old as well as young were intoxicated with liquor, and rioted till break of day round a fire, near the corpse.

On a lovely morning we wandered through the fertile, richly cultivated valley of the Sutlej to Khyrpoor. This town, which contains about 8000 inhabitants, lies embosomed in a forest of palms, tamarinds, pipala, and plums, about three miles from the Sutlej. To judge by the ruins of deserted dwellings, it must formerly have been a considerable place; indeed, there are even now many handsome, though dirty, mosques with cupolas, and several lofty structures. The road to the village Kemry-Kekote (fourteen miles), whither we marched on the 31st, leads through steppes rather than through cultivated land; every thing indicated our near approach to the desert. After traversing eleven miles, we reached the village of Khanghurh, where a number of priests have shut themselves up within four walls, and lead a sort of monastic life, and stand high in the estimation of the people for their sanctity. The Bhawulkhan has a residence within the citadel of this enclosure, where he annually spends several days to perform his devotions and to follow the chase; and at that season many valuable presents are made to the monastery by the wealthy. In the village of Kekote, I saw the remains of an ancient castle, constructed of bricks, and surrounded by high walls, but it is completely in ruins. The village itself is extensive, and contains a mosque, with three cupolas and two minarets.

On the 1st of November we made a march of twenty-one miles from Hajeepoor to Bhauda, and although we were only four miles from the Sutlej, the ground was covered with jungle and steppes; and the fruitful, cultivated fields gradually disappeared. A gypsy band had encamped under their reed huts in the outskirts of the village; they busied themselves during the day with platting, but were playing the livelong night on their wretched musical instruments, to the great enjoyment of the villagers, who were all up, dancing and singing. The next night, which we spent in Kassimkee, was an equally turbulent one. As usual, we entered the jungle in the afternoon, gun in hand, but we shot only some hares, partridges, and parrots.

Our Mussulmans celebrated the feast of the new moon with dance and song, in the village of Macdoom. Here we were forcibly reminded of the state of our country in the middle ages, by the appearance of a nobleman and his suite, who seemed to be a knight of those days of bygone chivalry. He was seated on horseback in a coat of mail; his son, riding on a pony at his side, bore a shield and sword, while before and around him were servants and attendants carrying falcons and guns; his lady, closely veiled, was seated on a camel with her child, followed by camels laden with tents and baggage. On the following day, the 5th of November, we reached the village Sczacki-Ky (*Sikunka?*), the hospitable inhabitants of which were most anxious to forward our wishes; nay, an aged man approached me as I was walking in his *jowary* fields, and begged me to pluck as much corn as I liked, adding that he should esteem it a real pleasure to show kindness to the stranger! Next day we pitched at Remmuk, about 400 paces from the Sutlej. The chief of this village brought his son, a fine boy about ten years of age, and begged that we would cure him of a wound, caused by the bite of a horse; we sent him to Dr. Christie, who, with two officers, was a day's march in advance, assuring the distressed parent that we thought his child would soon be restored. The district lying between this village, Tuwukkul and Lukeeke, is the favourite resort of lions and tigers: a few days previous to our arrival the inhabitants killed a very large tiger; and on the 7th we saw the recent traces of a lion, in a tamarisk jungle, on our way to Lukeeke, but we soon lost sight of it. This village consists of only a few mud huts, and lies close to the Sutlej. Here we had the pleasure of rejoining our comrades: we partook of a cheerful repast in Dr. Christie's tent, and drank our last bottle of wine to the weal of our country. Towards evening we went to the Sutlej on an alligator hunt, and saw many of these animals on the sandy downs, but our aim took effect on only two of them: they turned over several times, and then plunged into the water.

On Tuesday, the 8th of November, we had crossed the boundary of Bhawulpoor, and, after proceeding five miles, entered the little territory of the Khan of Memdot, which is under the protection of the English. Issuing from a thick tamarind jungle, we entered a cultivated country, where we for the first time saw corn magazines belonging to the natives: they are built of clay, and their shape is like those of the Kirghis, from 10 to 15 feet in height, and 4 to 6 in diameter; they have an opening on one side towards the top, which is closed with clay, so soon as the magazine is filled; others look like a large clay chest, either round or square, furnished with a lid or cover.

About half way, we passed the extensive village of Bahee, which lies on the highest point of the valley of the Sutlej, and from the plateau, which is 80 feet in height, the eye ranged over boundless tracts of jungle spread before it on every side. At the village of Bodlah we were received by the brother of the Khan, who said that information of our expected arrival had reached him some days previously; that the Khan was delighted to hear we had had a safe journey; that he was to provide for our accommodation, and attend us to Memdot. But the Khan's professions and promises did not correspond with their performance, and we had much difficulty in procuring food for ourselves or provender for our horses, for either love or money.

Here we dismissed the escort that had accompanied us from Ahmedpoor, with thanks and presents; we gave the officer a very ample testimonial, and requested him to repeat to his prince, in our names, our most grateful thanks for his Highness's hospitality and friendship.

We passed the 10th of November in the village of Pajaike, where two of our party, Dr. Christie and Captain Nicholson, fell sick; the doctor, however, soon recovered, while the illness of Captain Nicholson assumed a very unsatisfactory character. Passing through Mohunke, we arrived, on the 11th, at the little town of Memdot. The country round is well cultivated; the town small and dirty; but the citadel is by far the best which we have seen throughout our journey. It is situated on the north side, and built of clay and brick, surrounded by a wall 40 feet high, with round projecting towers.

The Khan's residence, a simple dwelling with glass windows, lies within the walls of the citadel. My comrades here received bread and provisions, which had been sent by their friends at Ferozpoor. To our extreme regret, Captain Nicholson was now so severely ill from brain fever that we were obliged to have him carried next day to Ferozpoor.

Impatient to reach our destination, we set out the following morning, at 3 o'clock; at sunrise we came in sight of the fort and the cantonments lying three miles to the south of it, and in an hour after we arrived at our tents, which were pitched among the bungalows. Here have I been engaged since yesterday in writing to you. What may next take place is not known; many conjecture that the army of reserve, which is to be assembled here in the course of three weeks, is destined to enter the Punjab, and support the Maharaja Sheer Singh, against his rebellious minister, Dheean Singh. On this my hopes and wishes depend,—but "man proposes, God disposes!" Therefore I will fearlessly leave those things, which are concealed from my mortal sight, to the unerring guidance of that Almighty hand, which has hitherto so wonderfully led and protected me.

LETTER V.

TO ALEXANDER VON HUMBOLDT.

The Punjab.—The Sikhs.—Runjeet Singh.—His government and position relative to the English.—Suttees.—Burning of the corpse of Runjeet Singh with eleven of his wives.—Dheean Singh and the Fakir Uzeezoodeen.—Maharaja Kurruck Singh and the Rani-Chand-Kour.—Sheer Singh.—Ferozpoor.—Entry of the commanding general into the camp.—Hospitality.—Elephants.—Arrival of the Governor General, Lord Ellenborough.—His camp and baggage.—The army of reserve.—General Sale passes the Sutlej.—Generals Pollock and Nott.—Present from the Indian government of one of the cannon taken at Kabool to the King of Prussia.—Camp at Ferozpoor.—Entrance of the Rajah Heera Singh, and on the 10*th December of the crown prince, Perthaub Singh, accompanied by Dheean Singh.—Grand review and festivities.—Departure of an extraordinary embassage to Lahore under Mr. Maddock, Member of the Supreme Council.—Journey thither.—The city, and reception by the Maharaja.—Festivities in Lahore.—Mausoleum of Shah Dura.—Grand review of* 60,000 *men and* 200 *pieces of artillery.—Chase.—Farewell audience at Shahlimar.*

Lahore, Jan. 12. 1843.

FROM the land of the ancient Cathays, the former Sangala, I will give you a description of reviews, military festivities, processions, elephants, and Indian tales. When the last few weeks, with their rich and ever-varying scenes, pass before my mind, it seems as though I had dwelt for months in another land: I feel as if just awakened from a lovely dream, which transported me into the early ages of the world, with all their golden fairy tales and legends.

In no country on the globe, except in China, have the people retained their ancient usages and manners, their ancient customs and habits, so unaltered as in India. Here we behold a state of things which has been recorded by the history of the earliest ages; — living pictures so antique, that one might fancy they were the revivified images of the days of old. Before, however, giving you an account descriptive of my journey to Ferozpoor, I must conduct you into the Punjab, the land of the Sikhs, the dominions of the Maharaja Sheer Singh.

The Punjab, or country of "five waters" (*punj*, five; *ab*, waters), covering an area of 6000 geographical square miles, lies between the Indus, the Sutlej, and the Himalaya mountains. The four streams which rise in these mountains, intersect the country, and divide it with the Indus into four distinct doabs. The first district, lying between the Indus and the Jailum (Hydaspes), is 147 miles in breadth. The Jailum, a clear stream, from 300 to 400 yards across, flows in a sandy bed, at the rate of two miles an hour. Its temperature in December was 45° Fahrenheit at sunrise, and rose during the day to 51°. It is the most sterile, the least cultivated, and the least populous part of the country; it is covered with undulating, bare eminences, which rise considerably towards the centre, and is intersected by rugged declivities. The waters flow in deep beds, enclosed by high steep banks, and consequently cannot be employed in irrigation.

The numerous defiles and eminences present great obstacles to the traveller in this country, and we rarely find any large towns. The greater part of the ground is covered with thickets, and among the few fertile tracts is a most lovely valley, near the Indus, once the favourite abode of the emperors of Delhi. The splendid ruins of their palace lie towards the south, near several sources, which rush impetuously from the rocks, and flow into the little river Tombra. In December, when the temperature of the atmosphere was at 69° Fahrenheit, that of these springs was 71°, and of the Indus 63°. The most remarkable places in this doab, are Rotas, situated on gigantic rocks on the banks of a small affluent of the Jailum; it is a large, extensive fortress, with lofty walls and towers; Jailum, which is half a day's march from it, is still larger, and is situated on the river of the same name, across which there is a ford, above the town.

The rivers Jailum and Chenaub (Ascisines) enclose the second of these divisions, growing narrower till its breadth is only forty-six miles. This district is entirely level, with the exception of a low range of hills, the termination of the beds of rock salt, which run through the Jailum, and for a short distance are parallel with its left bank. It is, for the most part, covered with jungle of *Scirpus lacustris*, *Ziziphus Jujuba*, *Capparis aphylla*, and *Erogrostes cynosuroides*. Among these tracts of jungle lie dirty villages, under the shade of tamarinds and acacias, surrounded by fields of wheat, grain, jowary, cotton, and sugar-cane.

The soil is in general light and sandy, but so overgrown with grass and weeds, that numerous herds of oxen, camels, sheep, and goats subsist upon it. The inhabitants have bestowed much pains in the construction of the wells in the centre of this doab: they run to a depth of fifty feet; and, as the fertility of the soil depends mainly on them, Persian wheels are placed near them, for raising the water and irrigating the land. The country, in its entire extent, might be easily converted into a most fertile garden by means of large canals; but this is not to be expected from the present government. The Chenaub is a clear, gentle stream, attains the breadth of 100 yards, and a depth of 10 feet; in December, when the temperature of the air was 60° Fahrenheit, that of its water was 48°.

The third doab, which is enclosed between the Chenaub and the Ravee, or Hydraotes, is 76½ miles in breadth at its widest part; the Ravee is the smallest of these rivers, and is not navigable till within a short distance of Lahore: till it reaches that place it is only 200 feet broad, with a depth of 3½ feet, so that it is fordable at many places. This doab consists of an arid plain, of which only a third part is cultivated. The remainder is overgrown with wild indigo, sirky (*Saccharum munja*), tamarisks, and kedchra. This country, also, might be converted into a most fertile tract, if the mountain springs were conveyed in canals; but, unhappily, the land is cultivated only in the immediate vicinity of the towns and villages. The large neglected canal proves that cultivation was formerly more extensive than it now is. Besides the Mimosa, the poplar-leaved fig, and tamarind tree, the date palm flourishes here in all its luxuriance and beauty. There are several considerable towns on the main road from Lahore to Attock, the largest of which is Rhamneghur, on the left bank of the Chenaub, which is inhabited by Mussulmans.

The narrowest and most neglected of these four doabs is only 44½ miles broad, and is bounded by the Ravee and the Sutlej, or Hyphasis. Here, too, nature has done all to produce the most luxuriant vegetation, with very little help from the hand of man; but, as in the two above-mentioned districts, this is wanting, and only small tracts are cultivated. Here are the largest towns — Lahore, Amritsir (Amritasara, *essence of Ambrosia*), and Kussoor. The Sutlej is the most considerable of the tributaries of the Indus. It is from 250 to 400 feet broad, and in the rainy season overflows its banks to a great distance, and fertilizes the surrounding country. In December, when the temperature was 74° Fahrenheit, that of its water was 55°.

Besides this country, so highly favoured by nature, but so neglected by man, the empire of the Sikhs extends over the fine and rich province of Mooltan, a tract seventy miles wide, along the right bank of the Indus, beyond Mettun-Kote and the province of Peshawar. The territory under the dominion of the Maharaja may be estimated at 8000 geographical square miles, with five million inhabitants and a revenue of between two and three millions sterling. It is divided into provinces and districts, the administration of which is committed to governors and sirdars, who pay a certain sum to the prince; and of course, each of them endeavours to extort as much more as he possibly can from the country under his charge. Mooltan, which is governed by a Hindoo, enjoys the best administration, and Kashmir is the most plundered and desolated.

At the end of the fifteenth century, there arose in the country of the Kingless tribe (as Arrian designates the inhabitants of the Punjab) a religious sect, that of the Sikhs, at the head of whom was Nanick, who was soon joined by thousands of fanatics and enthusiasts. He was a scholar of Kahir, consequently a kind of Hindoo deist, who asserted the principle of universal toleration; for he affirmed that God was pleased when men worshipped Him, but that He was indifferent under what form they did so.

This tolerant religious spirit, was an abomination to the bigoted Mahometans; and after this sect had flourished during a century, their spiritual chief was killed by them in 1606. This tyrannical proceeding changed the peaceable Sikhs into fanatical warriors, and under Har-Govind, the son of their priest who had been so cruelly sacrificed, they took up arms, as declared enemies and avengers against their oppressors. Being however too weak to oppose the troops that were sent against them, and still more enfeebled by internal dissensions, the Sikhs were driven from the vicinity of Lahore, into the mountainous districts of the north.

In the year 1675, Ghooroo-Govind, their tenth spiritual chief, grandson of Har-Govind, succeeded, with the spirit of a Grecian lawgiver, in inspiring the adherents of the Sikhs to unite in a religious and military association. He abolished caste among his adherents, accorded equal rights to every convert, whatever might have been his previous profession, and, that there might be more harmony and uniformity among his followers, he commanded the adoption of a peculiar dress and manners. All were obliged to serve as warriors and to carry some weapon, to wear a blue garment, and suffer the hair and beard to grow. They despised tobacco because it defiled the body, and, like the Hindoos, they considered the bull sacred.

This spirit of moderation and tolerance, is however

not possessed by the Ghooroos, their present priests, or by the Acalees, their fanatic fakirs, and the Mussulmans are compelled to perform their religious observances in secret and retirement. The Acalees acknowledge no superior governor, and merely tolerate their reigning prince, whom they traduce in every possible way, and even openly seek his life, if he opposes their views. They are generally provided with a round quoit, which they wear either round their pointed turban, or at their side. The quoit is a flat iron ring, from eight to fourteen inches in diameter, the outer edge of which is ground extremely sharp; they twirl this weapon round their finger, or on a stick, and throw it to a distance, with such dexterity and force, that the head of the person aimed at is often severed from the body. Many of these Acalees form a special troop in the army of the Maharaja.

From this nation, Runjeet Singh, the son of an obscure Sikh Sirdar, named Maha Singh, rose to be paramount chief, by means of his wisdom and valour. In India, a bold determined character, has less difficulty than in any other country to gather a host of military enthusiasts round his banner, and this is especially the case with so warlike a people as the Sikhs. Runjeet Singh was born in Gujuru Walla, a village twenty-five miles from Lahore, on the 2d November 1780 : at the age of twenty he obtained possession of the wealthy kingdom of Lahore, and successively expelled the three chiefs, Ischet Singh, Muhuc Singh, and Sahib Singh, who opposed him.

In the year 1805, he penetrated into the doab between the Chenaub and the Indus, to subject a Mussulman chief; and here, by means of the Maharattas, whom Lord Lake had driven beyond the Sutlej, he first came into contact with the English. Holkar, the Maharatta chief, expected to find an ally in Runjeet, but the crafty conqueror felt that it would be wiser to be a friend of the British.

In the year 1800 the news of an invasion by Napoleon, spread like wild-fire throughout India, which induced the British government to ascertain the sentiments of the independent princes. Among these, Runjeet Singh held an important rank, and Sir Charles Metcalfe was accordingly sent as British agent to Lahore. Runjeet Singh was at that time engaged in the subjection of the several petty independent Sikh princes; he indeed received the envoy at Kussoor, but broke off the negotiation, and penetrated to the left bank of the Sutlej. On this the British government declared to him, through Sir Charles Metcalfe, that the whole country, from the Jumna to the Sutlej, was under its protection, and that it would not tolerate any superior authority there. A corps under Colonel Ochterlony, and an army of reserve under General St. Leger, the first of whom advanced without opposition to the Sutlej, succeeded in inducing the valorous Runjeet Singh to conclude a treaty.

An accidental circumstance favoured the demand of the envoy, and convinced the Maharaja that he had to do with an adversary superior to himself in every respect, especially in the excellence and discipline of the troops. At the end of February, 1801, Sir Charles Metcalfe, with an escort of only two companies of native troops and sixteen cavalry, was in the camp of the Sikhs at Amritsir. His Mahometans celebrated the festival of Moharrem in honour of the death of Hussein and Hassan. The Acalees considered this an insult to their religion, and tumultuously collected a large body of Sikhs, who, led by the bigoted and fanatic Phula-Singh, attacked the camp of the envoy, with a fire of musketry. The small escort immediately seized their arms, and repulsed their tenfold more numerous adversaries, with great loss.

Runjeet Singh, attracted by the uproar, appeared just as the disciplined sepoys had obtained the victory. The bravery of this little band made a great impression on him: he expressed his admiration at the discipline and resolution of the British troops, offered an apology, and declared himself ready to conclude a treaty. It was signed on the 25th of April, 1809, in four articles, by which a permanent friendship was to exist between the English and the state of Lahore; and the Maharaja gave up the tract of country which he occupied on the left bank of the Sutlej. In order however fully to secure the position of the Sikh princes, it was agreed that the British government should renounce a tribute from these princes; and that they on the other hand, should engage to afford the British troops every facility on any expedition, or march which they might undertake, and in case of war should join their forces. Colonel Ochterlony, as superintendent of the affairs of the Sikhs, was only once obliged to act against the Rajah of Pattiallah, who oppressed his subjects most cruelly, and was consequently placed under strict guardianship.

From this time, till the year 1830, we find Runjeet Singh without any direct connection with the English, but unceasingly engaged in aggrandizing his dominions and increasing his army. He conquered Mooltan and Kashmir, sword in hand, and was continually engaged in contests with the Afghans, the most violent enemies of the Sikhs, till he at length succeeded in getting possession of Peshawar, through the treachery of the brother of Dost Mahomed, whom he bribed with the promise of an annual pension of two lacs.

Two French officers, Captains Ventura and Allard, who, after the fall of Napoleon, had in vain sought an honourable employment in Persia, repaired to the court of Lahore, in the year 1822. They met with a friendly and brilliant reception, and were employed by Runjeet to organize his army on the French footing. Four years afterwards they were followed by Generals Court and Avitabile. By the aid of these officers, on whom Runjeet Singh conferred the rank of generals, the Maharaja succeeded in forming a well-armed and tolerably disciplined army of 50,000 men, besides 100,000 irregular troops; cannon founderies, powder magazines, and manufactories of arms are established in Lahore and Amritsir.

Runjeet Singh required the Europeans, who entered his service, to engage not to eat beef, not to shave their beards, and not to smoke tobacco. The latter, however, was allowed them, on their declaring themselves ready to comply with the first two conditions. These officers were respectively placed at the head of a brigade or division; Ventura and Allard were the founders of his regular cavalry; General Avitabile was distinguished as an infantry officer, and to the chivalrous General Court, Runjeet is indebted for his artillery. But notwithstanding this great confidence which the Maharaja placed in them, with this honourable and extensive sphere of action and princely recompenses in lands and money, they were not applied to in any affair relative to the court and the government; they were not allowed to sit down in the presence of the Maharaja, and were often obliged to petition for their high pay, from 2000 to 3000 rupees a month.

When Sir Alexander Burnes, the bearer of presents from the King of England to Runjeet Singh, arrived in Lahore, in July 1831, he found the Maharaja at the height of his power, dreaded by his enemies, and respected by the British. The veteran hero was flattered by so distinguished a mark of honour from a nation which he highly venerated, and whose superiority he acknowledged in every respect. The splendid reception which he gave to Sir Alexander Burnes, as well as the high esteem which he then manifested for the English, led to an interview between him and Lord William Bentinck, then Governor-General of India, at Roopoor, 1835. In consequence of this interview a treaty of navigation and commerce between Runjeet Singh and the English was concluded; by which it was stipulated that the merchants should pay a certain duty, in order to put an end to the arbitrary exactions which had hitherto taken place.

A short time before the opening of the campaign against Afghanistan, in 1838, another interview took place between the Governor-General, Lord Auckland, and Runjeet Singh; on which occasion the Maharaja promised to give the British some assistance, and granted them a free passage through his territory. But Runjeet Singh was at this time in an enfeebled state of health; his dissolute mode of life brought on dropsy, and he died on the 27th of June, 1839, of paralysis, in the fifty-ninth year of his age and the fortieth of his reign.

The Suttee, or the custom of burning the women on the death of their husband, is extremely ancient in India, though no mention is made of it in the laws of Menu; but Diodorus gives a description of it, which is quite correct, even at this day. Though the English have never interfered to hinder the religious usages of the Indians, they, however, permitted neither the Suttee, nor the crushing of the devotees under the wheels of the sacred car of Juggernaut, in the countries subject to their government; and, according to the assurances which I have received from well-informed persons, it appears that as far as control is possible, no Suttee has taken place within the last ten years in Bengal and in the Presidency of Bombay; this cruel custom does not prevail to the south of the river Kishna. Even the relations themselves, now often endeavour to prevent the burning of the widows; and in families of high rank, the prince of the country, in person, undertakes to offer consolation, and, while he is endeavouring to dissuade the widow from her purpose, the corpse is hastily carried away and consumed.

In Bengal it was customary to bind the dead and the living together with ropes to a stake, and to pile up bamboo canes so high around them, that escape was impossible. The widow was led by a string to the pile, accompanied in solemn procession by the nearest relations of her late husband, with a band of music, and attended by young women and relatives, her male descendants going before. In Orissa the pile is made in a pit, into which the wife throws herself as soon as the flames arise; and in the Deccan the woman sits upon the pile, with the head of her husband in her lap, till she is either suffocated, or crushed by the heavy wooden covering which is placed over it.

When a woman intends to burn herself with her husband, her grief assumes a sublime character; she sheds no tear, she makes no lamentation, she lays aside her veil, and no longer conceals her person from the eyes of men; the thought of entering with her beloved into the blissful state beyond the grave—nay, by this expiatory sacrifice, to have facilitated and prepared the way for him, gives her the incredible energy to dedicate herself to such a martyrdom. Women have been seen to pray and wring their hands in the flames; others overcome by their sufferings, have rushed out of the fire, but were immediately driven back by those around them. An Englishman who was witness of such a scene, took the part of the unhappy woman, and stopped the awful sacrifice; but, what was his surprise, when on the following day she overwhelmed him with the most virulent reproaches, saying that he had robbed her of her salvation, and that she must now be an outcast and a wanderer, neglected and despised by all.

According to the custom of the Sikhs, the dead body of the Maharaja was burnt on the day following his decease, before the gates of the palace Hasuree-Bagh, in the presence of all the great men and the assembled troops. Four of his wives, and seven of his female slaves committed themselves to the flames with his body. An eye-witness told me that nothing had made so deep and lasting an impression on him, as the moment when these female figures issued, in solemn procession, from the palace gate, amid the sound of music and the thunder of the artillery. Almost all the inhabitants of Lahore were present at this fearful solemnity. The corpse was placed in a sitting posture, between high piles of wood; and as soon as the flames were at their height, the unhappy victims prepared for death.

Two of the wives, who were only sixteen years of age, and possessed of extraordinary beauty, looked as if they were happy in being able, for the first time, to show their charms to the multitude; they took off their most precious jewels, gave them to their relations and friends, asked for a looking-glass, and with a slow and measured step walked towards the pile, sometimes gazing at the glass in their hand, then at the assembly, and anxiously asking if any change were observable in their countenance. They entered the glowing furnace, and in an instant were caught by the flames, and suffocated by the heat and smoke.

The other women seemed less resigned and cheerful; and, when they caught sight of the frightful element, horror was depicted on their countenances; but they knew that escape was impossible, and patiently submitted to their cruel fate. The minister, Dheean Singh, appeared to be about to throw himself into the flames, but the descendants of the Maharaja, particularly Sheer Singh, held him back.

Runjeet Singh, who has not unaptly been called the Porus of our days, was a small, mean-looking, deformed man, and blind with his left eye, in consequence of the small-pox. With all the magnificence which prevailed at his court, he was himself very simple in his attire, and wore but few ornaments; but he loved to see show and splendour in every thing about him. In battle, he was always seen at the head of his troops, and foremost in combat; he twice crossed the Indus with his cavalry, in the very face of the enemy, and gained the victory. In energy of will, endurance, and craftiness, he was unequalled by any of his people; and though he was a tyrant, in the full extent of the word, he was not destitute of feelings of compassion. When Runjeet Singh conceived a thought, he never delayed carrying it into effect. Thus, having heard of a fine horse, which was in the possession of an Afghan prince, he offered to the owner an ample remuneration, if he would give up this valuable animal; but as this was refused, he suddenly fell upon him with his cavalry, and triumphantly carried off the coveted prize. The want of education was covered by the splendid mental powers with which nature had endowed him; and prudence and knowledge of mankind enabled him to maintain himself in his high station. Even at the latest period of his life, he endeavoured to acquire instruction, loved to speak of his campaigns and plans, and when a happy thought or some pleasure animated him, he uttered, with youthful enthusiasm, his favourite expression, "Barra tamasha," fine fun.

By means of excessive liberality, he attached faithful servants and brave warriors to himself; and, with equally royal munificence, he gave presents to strangers, but could never conceive why the English were obliged to deliver them up to their government. To prevent this he once caused a valuable gift to be carried during the night, into the house of an English general for whom he had conceived a high esteem. His interest in every thing European went so far, that when, on the accession of Queen Victoria, several colonels in the British army were raised to the rank of generals, he nominated an equal number in his army; and to console one who was passed over, assured him that at some future time he would make him a lord! The character of this great man is darkened by his dissolute life, especially the vice of drunkenness, which, at last increased to such a degree that, in his latter years, he could not exist without the strongest spirituous liquors.

At the beginning of his course, he once saw a common lancer by the side of his elephant, breaking in a vicious horse; the beauty of this young man struck him, and his bold carriage, skill, and courage, made a favourable impression on Runjeet Singh, and the courteous reply to a question put by the Maharaja decided the fate of the impoverished young nobleman. This was the handsome Meer Dheean Singh, who was at that time five-and-twenty years of age, and was the descendant of a noble family in the lower regions of the Himalaya. From the post of porter in the royal palace, he rose to that of minister and first vizier, but with all his apparent submissiveness he attempted to kill his own son, Heera Singh (Diamond Lion), the handsomest boy in the country, because the Maharaja appeared to take a liking to him. Dheean Singh, now the all-powerful minister of the kingdom, is almost the unlimited master of the mountainous country, and has his own troops and his own artillery. In his little forts, built on high rocks, he feels himself secure and independent, and bids defiance to every person or power that attempts to rival him.

No less remarkable and important a person is the Fakir Uzeezoodeen, the chief physician and political adviser of Runjeet Singh; the best encomium that can be pronounced upon him is, that he has been able to maintain his high position, for a period of thirty years. Every embassage to the British Government was accompanied by Uzeezoodeen; without him no resolution is formed, and every party seeks his counsel or assistance. He is descended from the Ansaris Arabs of the desert, between Bagdad, Damascus, and Aleppo, and, like the whole of his family, belongs to the fakirs of the country.

The fakirs lead a very retired life, quite shut out from the rest of the world; their women are never visible, and but little is known of their domestic arrangements. They intermarry only among each other, and, under a servile and fawning exterior, they make a semblance of extreme poverty, though they have amassed immense riches. Runjeet Singh extorted large sums from them when his coffers were empty.

The younger brother of Uzeezoodeen, Halifi Nuredden, the owner of Gulabhana, where the distilled waters, essences, and medicines are manufactured, is a man of no less influence at court, and has free access to the Maharaja both morning and evening. He has also the superintendence of the buildings, manufactories, and royal magazines. A third brother, the Fakir Imameddin, is blind, and lives in Amritsir. He is represented at court by his son Tageddin, to whom, as commander of the fortress of Goorindgher, the treasure deposited there, to the value of six million sterling, in jewels, gold, silver, and Cashmere shawls, is intrusted. The second son of Uzeezoodeen, the Fakir Errikeddin, is agent of the Maharaja at Ferozpoor.

Runjeet Singh was succeeded by his only son, who was then thirty-seven years of age, by the title of Maharaja Kurruck Singh. Not favoured by nature, grown up without education, intemperate and effeminate, he sought only his pleasures and the harem; and left the affairs of government to the cruel Ceth Singh. But the latter, having formed the plan of putting Dheean Singh to death at a Durbar, he was cut in pieces at the side of the Maharaja by Dheean Singh and the crown prince, Nou Nehal Singh, who had been sent for from Peshawar. Kurruck Singh was seized with a severe illness soon after his accession, and, it is reported that his only son, the favourite of his grandfather, was not unconcerned in his premature death; for he died, after languishing seven months, of a neglected and improperly treated intermittent fever, on the 6th of November, 1840, and was burnt the same day with one of his wives and two female slaves.

Nou Nehal Singh, a youth of nineteen years of age, ambitious, expert in all warlike exercises, spirited, energetic, and full of great plans, was resolved to show the world what he was capable of. He was a sworn enemy to the English, and formed the bold project of declaring against them on the first favourable opportunity. He could scarcely conceal his joy, even at the immolation of his father's corpse, at finding himself the actual possessor of the throne. Guided by Rajah Meer Udum Singh, his friend and counsellor, he resolved, after the completion of that mournful ceremony, to wash away his sins in the Ravee, but as he was riding through the outer gate of Hasuree-Bagh, a large piece of the archway fell upon them both, from a height of thirty feet, killed his friend on the spot, and wounded the young prince so severely in the head, that he expired in three hours, while only a few of the great men, who accompanied them, were wounded. His death was concealed in the fortress for three days, in order to give time to his absent mother, the Ranee Chandkaur, and to Prince Shere Singh, who was residing at his country house, to secure the throne. The body was burnt early in the morning of the third day, on the same spot where he was killed, with his two wives in the bloom of youth and beauty. The Ranee Chandkaur arrived in the fortress an hour before Sheer Singh, and occupied the inner part of it, upon which the latter with his adherents took possession of the garden Hasuree-Bagh. The great men of the kingdom, spent several weeks in deliberating which of the two should ascend the throne; till at length on the 30th of November the thunders of the artillery announced to Sheer Singh the painful intelligence, that Chandkaur had been chosen queen. He himself was obliged, according to the custom of the country, to repair to the palace of the sovereign, and, conducted by the ministers, to make the first present of 101 pieces of gold coin, but he left Lahore immediately after.

Chandkaur was the first wife of Kurruck Singh : she was at this time between forty and fifty years of age, rather corpulent, but of a pleasing exterior. She governed the kingdom under the guidance of twenty of the principal men, who called themselves counsellors. She showed herself only to her confidants, among whom the Rajah Gulab Singh, Dheean Singh's elder brother, and the Jemedar Koshal Singh, had the pre-eminence. Full of jealousy and distrust of the dictatorial, imperious Dheean Singh, these two took advantage of his absence, while he was enjoying the diversion of the chase in the forest of Merlebele, to supplant him. They accused him to the sovereign, in the presence of the counsellors, of having issued orders of his own authority, and obtained a decision, that all ordinances, to be valid, must henceforward be signed by Chandkaur's own hand. Two letters (haha sasa) indicated the royal pleasure: but if they related to grants of money, the seals of the three deceased princes and of the minister were to be added.

This proceeding spread discontent through the country: insurrections broke out in various parts of the kingdom, and there was reason to fear, that there would be a rebellion in the chief city, Lahore. To take advantage of this state of things, Dheean Singh, under pretext of going to hunt in the mountains, repaired, with his younger brother, the Rajah Soochet Singh, to Shere Singh, inviting him to put himself at the head of the movement, and to take possession of the throne. Shere Singh acceded to this proposal; and they advanced with some thousand men against Lahore, and besieged the queen in Hasuree-Bagh. She had shut herself up here with the Rajahs Goolab Singh, Heera Singh, the brothers Itter Singh, and Achet Singh, (sirdars of the Sendooal family, who, as the nearest relations of Rundjeet Singh, had also pretensions to the throne,) and with 4000 men, chiefly mountain troops. The besieged gave up the fortress in five days, on the 28th of January, 1841. The Rajahs Goolab Singh and Heera Singh were allowed to retire with their troops to Chauduree, on the other bank of the river Ravee: the two sirdars fled across the Sutlej to the British possessions, and the queen was guarded as a prisoner in the fortress.

Thus Shere Singh ascended the throne. During his temporary residence at his summer palace, the ex-queen was found in her apartment, mortally wounded. Four of her female slaves had broken her skull with tiles, and she survived this barbarous treatment only three days. The murderers were sentenced to have their hands, noses, and ears cut off; and were exiled beyond the Ravee. On the day of his coronation, January 27. 1841, Shere Singh, at the intercession of Dheean Singh, pardoned his brother and son, who were invited to be witnesses of the ceremony of the coronation.

The Maharaja was born in the little town of Velateh, in 1807, and, according to the assertion of his reputed father, is said to be the son of a dhoby. Although educated in warlike, stirring times, at the most splendid court in India, he has never been able to attain to personal importance, and, being effeminate, and utterly devoid of firmness of character, he has been led by the current of events and by the most resolute men of the time. Among the latter, Dheean Singh occupies the most prominent position; for Shere Singh, independently of a sense of deference for this extraordinary man, is bound to him by the strongest ties of gratitude, inasmuch as he is indebted to him, not only for the throne but also for his life. A plot had been laid by Chandkaur that he should be murdered in the palace: Dheean Singh gave him timely warning, and defeated the plot. This, together with the immense influence which Dheean Singh possesses in the country, has however made Shere Singh so utterly dependent upon him, that he does not venture to act, even in the smallest matter, without his approbation; nay, he, the Maharaja, the monarch of the land, rises and folds his hands in the presence of his minister! — a token of the deepest submission among the natives! Dheean Singh has nominated creatures of his own to all the highest posts, both in the country and at court. His son Heera Singh, commander-in-chief of the army, is a vain ignorant young man, twenty-five years of age, who, properly speaking, belongs to no party, but is carried away by the impulse of the moment, and would be quite capable of betraying his own father; he is, besides, disliked by the army on account of his overbearing, tyrannical conduct. It is true that the Maharaja has some adherents, both in the country and in the army; but, like their master, they have not the courage to give vent to their sentiments.

Shere Singh has three wives, but only one son, the crown-prince Perthaub Singh, an intelligent boy twelve years of age, full of life and energy; and, much might be hoped for from him, were he not educated according to the custom of the country. He has been placed with the Generalissimo Heera Singh, in order that he may have the opportunity of ingratiating himself with the army; but his guardian has neither the ability nor the inclination to act the part of tutor assigned to him by the court. The other most influential men about the court of Lahore are Soochet Singh, the sirdars Achet Singh, Sham Singh, Tej Singh, and Itter Singh: Goolab Singh still remains in the mountains, notwithstanding the numerous invitations he has received to appear at court.

So much for this remarkable kingdom, which must soon become a question of life and death for the British power in India. Unless possessed of this, there is no security:—the Indus above Attock, with the mountain chain beyond Peshawur, and the Himalaya mountains, form the true and natural frontier of the immense dominions of the British empire in India.* When once this has been attained, all her powers can

* See note, p. 235.

be concentrated in the interior, and civilisation take root and flourish.

You must now return with me to Ferozpoor. The town itself is a small cheerful place, built of bricks, and surrounded by a wall: it is about two miles from the Sutlej, and lies on an eminence, in a boundless plain. At the north-west end, is the square, old citadel, which commands the town and the environs: it is defended by four pieces, and is occupied by an officer and sixty-eight men. At the northern issue from the town is a very fine bricked pond, with a flight of steps, close to which a small pagoda is embosomed in fig-trees (*Ficus religiosa*) and acacias.

Before the English settled here, Ferozpoor and its environs were desolate and ruinous: now the town increases daily, and the plain is every where brought under cultivation; and, where only a short time ago desolation reigned, and jungle covered the soil, the most luxuriant fields of corn are now flourishing. A dry arm of the Sutlej runs to the south, in many windings, between the town and the cantonment; and many ditches intersect the country, which, as numerous closed wells indicate, must have been formerly highly cultivated. Nothing is here wanted but wells, which, at the depth of thirty feet, supply an abundance of water for irrigation, and the fertile soil yields the richest harvest without manure.

A road planted with trees leads from the town to the cantonments, which are three miles distant to the south, and are divided into streets, which cross each other at right angles. Here are the magazines, which are built of stone, and the barracks of the Europeans, those of the native regiments, and the bungalows of the officers, surrounded by gardens, in which tamarinds, oranges, bananas, all kinds of flowers, pinks, roses, mignionette, and European vegetables, flourish in abundance.

Lord Altamont and myself have been obliged to hire a bungalow for 100 rupees a month — for my tent was not calculated to be set up in the magnificent camp of an Indian army. Here we keep house for ourselves, which is expensive enough, as you will see, when I tell you that a fowl costs one rupee, a bottle of wine, five rupees, and a small ham, weighing scarcely eight pounds, thirty-six rupees: other necessaries of life are in the same proportion.

When the gun announces the dawn of day, we mount our horses and ride to the camp, to be present at the exercising of the troops, or to witness the entrance of the fresh regiments. Our time is then taken up in visits, in which Captain Ewart's advice and assistance are of great service to me. I pass many cheerful hours in the society of this intelligent officer and his accomplished lady, who possesses great musical talent. But, this interesting course of life has been sadly clouded by the death of two of my fellow-travellers. Captain Nicholson died in consequence of the exertions attending his removal, three days after our arrival. He was an excellent officer, beloved by every one, and the third son of whom his mother had been deprived by the destructive climate of India. I was no less affected by the loss of Captain West, who fell a victim to the cholera; and, already foreboding his fate at Sukkur, said to me that he should never see his country again.

On the 20th of November, the Commander-in-Chief, Sir Jasper Nicolls, arrived at the camp, with 80 elephants, 300 camels, 136 draught oxen, and above 1000 servants. This immense retinue was merely for his service; and for attendance on the animals, but did not include those domestics and animals which are required for his own person and those of his suite. Sir Jasper Nicolls has two tents, each fifty-six feet long and thirty-two broad; and several smaller ones, enclosed in a linen fence, in which he and his family reside. Opposite to them is the Durbar tent, which consists of several apartments. The floors are covered with shawls and carpets, and the tent is provided with a canopy, tables, chairs,

and furniture of every kind; nay, chandeliers are not wanting, so that in these canvass houses, he is as comfortable as at home. A band of one of the regiments performs every evening in the principal street of the camp.

Sir Jasper Nicolls and his lady render my abode at Ferozpoor very agreeable by their hospitality, and Lady Nicolls has had the goodness to lend me her elephant several times. I felt a singular mixture of curiosity and anxiety when I mounted one of these animals for the first time. A hair cushion is laid upon his back, for this is the most tender part of the animal, and the greatest care must be taken by his keeper to protect it from injury, because any wound there is very difficult to heal. Over this cushion is spread a covering of red cloth, embroidered with gold, which hangs down on both sides; on this rests the howdah, which is fastened by cords and girths round the body of the elephant. The howdah is very much like our sledges, and has seats for two persons and their servants. The Mahout, who guides the elephant with an iron prong, one point of which is bent outwards, sits on the animal's neck, while the driver, with a large club in his hand, runs by his side, inciting him to proceed by words and blows. A ladder is suspended at the side of the elephant to enable the riders to ascend and descend.

As soon as the rider is ready to mount this majestic creature, the Mahout cries, *Beit! beit!* (*Beittna*, *i.e.* to lie down,) upon which the elephant kneels down; the ladder is set up, and the rider mounts and takes his seat. The motion of some of these sagacious animals is most agreeable, and that of others very fatiguing, for it depends entirely upon his gait. When he is driven, his step is so long and quick, that a horseman must trot to keep pace with him; but he soon relaxes in his exertion, and I should think could probably not travel more than twenty-four miles in the course of a day. When much heated and covered with dust, he sprinkles himself from time to time, with the water, which he carries in his trunk, for this seeming purpose.

An ordinary elephant costs 1000 rupees, and his keep is about 40 rupees a month; however, the quantity of food which he consumes depends on his size: he receives twice as many seers of baked flour (a seer = 2 lbs.) as he measures feet in height, besides leaves, corn, and hay. This remarkable animal supplies the place of carriages; and here, where the ground is covered with ditches and holes*, I find him most serviceable, for it seems to be an impossibility that an elephant should fall.

On the arrival of the General-in-chief the army of reserve begun to assemble: the cavalry regiments were the last to arrive, because there was a scarcity of grass for the horses. The morning always found me amid the bustle of the camp, or attending the exercises of the troops; and, as most of the corps of officers had invited me to their tables, I generally passed the evenings in the camp. At one of these dinners given by the 16th regiment of Lancers, I met Hindoo Row, the brother of Bacza Baee, the favourite wife of the Maharaja Dowlah Row Scindia: he headed his brother-in-law's army fifteen years ago, and on his death was greatly inclined to possess himself of

* There is a sect of the natives who grovel after a large species of lizard, of which they are very fond, on account of its fat; and it is in consequence of their digging for these reptiles, that the ground is so full of holes.

the vacant throne. He now lives at Delhi, on a pension guaranteed to him by the British government from the state of Gwalior. He is passionately fond of tiger hunting, and a great admirer of the English. He amused himself with sitting in perfect silence at table, admiring our appetite, without touching any thing himself. Not long ago he had addicted himself to drinking; but, happening one day to meet a European soldier in a state of intoxication, and being told by his friends that he conducted himself in a precisely similar manner whenever he had indulged too freely, Hindoo Row vowed that he would never more touch spirituous liquors; and he has kept his word.

At the entertainments given by the General-in-chief, we frequently met the officers who were on their way from Afghanistan, as well as some of the prisoners. Among the former I was especially pleased with making the acquaintance of one of my countrymen, Baron Meyer: this brave young officer was wounded in an action at the Khyber Pass, and has not yet recovered from it. We have passed many an hour in talking over events connected with our beloved country. The camp daily assumed a more motley and lively appearance, by the concourse of persons congregated from different parts of India. Yet we were not without scenes of melancholy and distress: we saw numerous sepoys who had just returned from the scene of slaughter, and who were mutilated, more by the cold than by the enemy, and who had lost not only their limbs, but their caste, the most dreadful loss which a Hindoo can suffer.

On the 4th December, the temperature before sunrise was 44°, and at noon 77½°, Fahrenheit. I rode down to the Sutlej to look at the bridges of boats erected there. They are 290 feet (yards ?) in length, and are built of Dundy-boats, as is usual, both here and on the Indus, with flat bottoms and broad ends. One of these bridges consists of fifty-nine, and the other of forty-seven, such boats; and they are so strong that the heaviest weights can be borne over in perfect safety.

On my road thither the mountain chain of the Himalayas, for the first time, rose before me. The impression produced by these snow-clad masses, surrounded by a tropical nature and appearing to cleave the clouds, is quite indescribable. Man in vain seeks for words to give vent to the sensations which such a scene produces on his soul — they are thoughts of its inmost recesses — for which no expression can be found!

Lord Ellenborough, the Governor General, made his entry into Ferozpoor on the 9th of December, with 120 elephants, 700 camels, and numerous waggons. The whole army marched out to receive him, and was drawn up in lines on the road to Lodiana. I rode with my friend Lord Altamont to welcome his Lordship. We met first an endless train of elephants, camels, carriages, palanquins, waggons, horsemen, and servants of all descriptions; next the escort of the Governor General, the 3d Bengal regiment of cavalry which trotted before him, wearing the Ghuznee medals with which they had been presented the day previously; and then the king of the country dressed in a civil costume, riding on a splendid Arab, surrounded by his staff. Mr. George Clarke had the kindness to present us to him: we were most kindly received, and invited by his Lordship to reside in the camp as his guests—an offer which we of course very gladly accepted.

In front of the tent of the Governor General is a

road 150 paces broad, along which are pitched tents of the superior civil and military officers, and aide-de-camps, composing the administration: above forty clerks belong to the department of the Secretary of Government alone. At the end of this road or street is the tent which has been put up for me: it is divided into three compartments, with double walls and roofs, thirty feet long, and twenty broad. The Governor General has a body guard of two officers and 120 cavalry soldiers, and hundreds of servants. A regiment of cavalry, another of infantry, and a brigade of artillery, do duty in the camp.

THE CHOWREE BURDAR.

Lord Ellenborough's Durbar tent, consists of three large tents, and is 168 feet long, thirty-two broad, and twenty-eight high. The apartments are covered with the most costly carpets, and are lighted up in the evening with chandeliers; iron stoves impart warmth and cheerfulness; and a canopy, in front of which the standard of England floats on a lofty pole, marks the entrance. From this Durbar tent, a glass door leads through a covered passage to the dwelling and sleeping tents. When we sat down to dinner, which was served on silver, the band of the Governor General struck up "God save the Queen:" a servant in a scarlet livery stood behind the chair of each guest, while two stately Hindoo attendants fanned his Lordship with a chowree, made of the tufted tail of the Hindoo ox, in a slow and measured movement.

A few days after the arrival of Lord Ellenborough, the irregular cavalry made trial of their skill in the presence of his Lordship. The Governor General, as well as all the superior officers, and the ladies, were seated on a long row of elephants, while a number of spectators were ranged on horseback. The riders, dressed in red and yellow, first riding at full gallop, fired their matchlocks at glass bottles, nine of which were struck; then, continuing at their utmost speed, they thrust at the tent pins with the lance—a feat which required great dexterity and bodily strength: all sorts of equestrian exercises concluded the interesting spectacle. Lord Ellenborough presented the victors with handsome arms; such as guns, sabres, and bows.

I looked forward with the greatest possible interest to the entrance of the troops returning home from the war, as these valiant defenders of Jellalabad were to cross the Sutlej, and were to be received with peculiar honours. General Sale and his brigade had encamped, on the 16th, on the right bank of the river close to the bridges. At an early hour in the morning Lord Altamont and I rode to his camp. We met a number of Afghans, with their wives and children, who had left their native home and had joined the English; many British officers, and interspersed among them, several Afghan prisoners, with their attendants and followers. Nearly all the people wore the Afghan dress, which is the most picturesque, and at the same time the most convenient costume which I have ever seen.

We found Jan Fishan Khan, one of the principal Afghan chiefs, a member of the royal family, and a descendant of the Prophet, in his circular, gaily-striped tent. He is a handsome man, about forty-five years of age, and was sitting without the tent, dressed in a red Shoba*, embroidered with gold, attended by his two little sons, and surrounded by his servants. These were employed in repairing articles of dress, while he was amusing himself in playing with the lively children. His wives were in an adjoining tent; but one of them stood by his side, completely veiled with a long white garment, which concealed not only her face, but her entire person. He spoke with the highest esteem of the English, among whom he said he hoped to find a second country; he, however, seemed much concerned about his wife, who had been robbed of her jewels a few days before; though the loss itself did not appear to affect him.

On the following day General Sale crossed the

* A wide garment falling to the ankles, with full sleeves, a low collar, and wrought with a great diversity of patterns.

Sutlej, and advanced to the camp of the army of reserve: Lord Ellenborough had invited me to ride thither with him upon his elephant. It was perfectly dark when our cavalcade of elephants left the camp; we were, therefore, preceded by torch bearers, while the body-guard followed. The army of reserve lined the road on both sides, and close to the bridges stood 200 elephants richly trapped and painted. On Lord Ellenborough's approach, these sagacious animals saluted him, by kneeling down and raising their trunks in the air, a mark of respect which they had been taught by their Mahouts. The bridges were adorned with flags and streamers; and at the side of one of them a gallery was erected, under which we took our places. Several Indian princes, and many ladies on elephants and on horseback, imparted a picturesque and poetic charm to the scene.

At 8 o'clock General Sale's brigade defiled, the bands playing "God save the Queen," amid the thunder of the artillery and the enthusiastic cheers of the army. A joyous, yet affecting, sensation pervaded the whole assembly, when the officers and soldiers, led by the heroine of the day, Lady Sale, mounted on a magnificent elephant, saluted their friends. The brave warriors who followed showed not a trace either of the privations of a protracted siege, or of the fatigues of a long march. In the rear of the troops came the baggage, the whole presenting the most strange, but most faithful picture, of a march of crusaders. Invalids mounted on elephants and camels, and others, more seriously ill, in palanquins or doolees; camels, oxen, and asses heavily laden; here an Afghan female closely veiled, with trellis embroidery before her eyes, and wrapped in a white robe, which merely exposed her small feet, covered with gold-embroidered slippers; there a mother with her child on a camel; children on ponies, fondling a cat or a dog, or watching pigeons and fowls in baskets; fettered game-cocks and fighting rams; men, women, and children in the strangest costumes; Afghan chiefs with their families; merchants and servants of the most diverse nations and professions, flocks of sheep and goats, and waggons drawn slowly by oxen.

The passage of this motley train of one brigade, across both the bridges lasted full four hours! We were never tired of looking at this diminutive emigration of the nations, and remained nearly an hour longer lost in contemplation and reflection. We afterwards assembled at breakfast, in a tent, pitched near one of the bridges, where these varied scenes were again brought before us.

In the evening the Governor General gave a most splendid entertainment in his tent to the valiant defenders of Jellalabad, and, according to the English fashion, there was no lack of fine speeches and toasts. Lady Sale was present at this feast: she has passed nearly the whole of her life in India, and is a soldier's wife in every sense of the word; but she has the appearance of a worthy matron rather than of the bold determined heroine of the day.

General Pollock defiled with his corps on the following day; his baggage train was, of course, much more considerable, and it was evening before it reached the camp. Of the cannon which the troops captured at the storming of the Bala-Hissar of Cabool, the Indian government has committed to my charge a large nine-pounder cast under Dost Mahomet, for his Majesty the King of Prussia.* The gun will travel by the Indus to Bombay, whence it will be sent by the first opportunity to Europe.

General Nott crossed the Sutlej with his corps on the 23d of December, the anniversary of the murder of Sir William M'Naughten. He brought with him the famous sandle-wood gates of Somnauth, which were covered with red cloth, embroidered with gold, and drawn by twenty-four oxen. It is said that Mahmood the Ghuznevide took these gates with him to Ghuznee, when he destroyèd the temple of Somnauth, in 1025; but this splendid Hindoo temple, to which they are to be restored, retains scarcely a trace of its former magnificence, and its remains have been converted into a mosque. The Maharaja, Shere Singh, had not only sent a body guard to receive the gates on British territory, but had given a present of a sum of money to the escort. When I went to examine the gates more closely the next day, I found a number of

* "Camp, Ferozpoor, Dec. 19. 1842.

"The Governor General of India requests L. von Orlich will have the goodness to take measures for the conveyance to Berlin of one of the Afghan guns, brought by the British army from the Bala-Hissar of Cabool, and to express to his Majesty the King of Prussia the earnest hope of the government of India that his Majesty will be pleased to accept the gun as an acknowledgment of his Majesty's friendship for the British nation, and of the gratifying mark of that friendship which his Majesty has given in sending Captain Von Orlich to serve with the British army in Afghanistan.[1]

"Capt. L. Von Orlich, of his Majesty's Guards."

---

[1] This gun was forwarded to Bombay, through the kindness of Major Fraser, but had not reached its destination in October, 1844.

Brahmins, strewing flowers upon them, who assured me there was not the slightest doubt that they were genuine. They are most skilfully carved with stars and arabesques, and bordered with Kufic characters, but unfortunately the gates are so much injured, that scarcely the half of the beautiful work has been preserved.*

* So much interest has been excited by the circumstances relative to these celebrated gates, that the reader will doubtless be gratified by the following extract from the Archæologia, vol. xxx. 1844 : —

" Letter from C. J. Richardson, Esq., F. S. A. to Sir Henry Ellis, K. H., F. R. S., Secretary, accompanying a drawing, with details of the sandal-wood gates of Somnauth.

" I have the honour of laying before the Society of Antiquaries a drawing of the celebrated sandal-wood gates of Somnauth : it has been made from some elaborate sketches taken by Lieut.-Col. Luard, in the camp of Loodiana, in January last. Independently of the historical interest which these gates possess, they merit consideration from the beauty of their design and execution, proving the high state of art among the Hindoos at the remote period of their construction : they are probably one thousand years old.

" The temple of Somnauth in Guzerat was considered by the Hindoos as the holiest in India, and 'it was frequented,' says Vigne, quoting Ferishta, 'in the time of the eclipses by from 200,000 to 300,000 people.' The idol was supplied twice daily, with fresh water from the Ganges, though that river was about a thousand miles distant. The temple is described as being a superb edifice, built of hewn stone, its lofty roof supported by fifty-six pillars, curiously carved, and set with precious stones. In the centre of the hall was the great idol Somnauth, a stone figure five yards in height, two of which were sunk in the ground.

" The temple was destroyed by Mahmood of Ghuzni, A. D. 1025. He ordered two pieces of the idol to be broken off, and sent to Ghuzni, that one might be laid at the threshold of the principal mosque, and the other at the gate of his own palace. These identical fragments are mentioned by Mr. Vigne, who visited Ghuzni in 1836, as still to be seen there. Two more fragments

During the night both the bridges were destroyed either by the swelling of the river, or, as was generally suspected, by the unhappy Sikhs who are hovering about. From this day there were 53,000 men in arms, and above 100,000 servants of all descriptions

were reserved to be sent to Mecca and Medina. It is a well-authenticated fact, that when Mahmood was employed in destroying the idol, a crowd of Brahmins petitioned his attendants, and offered a quantity of gold if the king would desist from further mutilation. His officers endeavoured to persuade him to accept of the money; for they said that breaking one idol would not do away with idolatry altogether, but that such a sum given in charity among true believers would be a meritorious act. The king acknowledged there might be reason in what they said, but replied, if he should consent to such a measure his name would be handed down to posterity as 'Mahmood, the idol-seller,' whereas he was desirous of being known as 'Mahmood, the destroyer of idols:' he therefore directed the troops to proceed in their work. The next blow broke open the body of the statue, which was hollow, and discovered a quantity of diamonds, rubies, and pearls, of much greater value than the amount of money offered by the Brahmins.

"After the destruction of the temple, the gates were carried by Mahmood to Ghuzni, where for 800 years they adorned the entrance to his tomb. In October, 1842, they were removed and carried away by Major-General Nott, and crossed the Sutlej with the army on the 23d December; and Lieutenant-Colonel Luard, who writes January 17th, says, 'They are now moving in procession, to be restored to the temple of Somnauth.'

"The gates are eleven feet in height and nine feet in width; the upper portion is still perfect. Surrounding them is the door-case, torn from the tomb of Mahmood. On this portion is an inscription in the Kufic character, which may be thus translated:— 'In the name of the merciful and compassionate God, there is mercy from the habitation of God for the most illustrious Ameer and Surdar (whose ancestors were kings), the right hand of the state, the defender of the faith, and the father of Casim Mahmood, son of Subuktugeen: may the merciful God be with him, and if God have pardoned, there is mercy for him!'"

in the camp: thousands, however, were laid up with the cholera, small-pox, and fevers. Independently of this, Ferozpoor and its environs were incapable of supplying provisions for the countless multitude of elephants, camels, horses, oxen, and mules, so that nearly 200 of these animals perished in a day; and, on the road leading to Lodiana, twenty dead camels might be seen lying in one spot, infecting the air to an immense distance.

In the distinguished society which surrounded me, I had frequent opportunities of coming into contact with many eminent men, among whom I was particularly interested with Generals Pollock, Nott, and Sale. General Nott reminded me, in his personal appearance, of a French marshal of the school of Napoleon. I am indebted to him for many interesting communications respecting the war in Afghanistan. Equally instructive was the acquaintance of several highly accomplished statesmen; for instance, Mr. Maddock of the Supreme Council, and Mr. George Clarke. Both have lived in such important spheres of action, and have rendered such eminent services to their country, that I scarcely know whether most to admire their unassuming manner, or their deep penetration and correct conception of all existing relations.

I have also had the pleasure of becoming acquainted with Captain Boileau, who superintends the Magnetic Observatory at Simla. He entirely coincides with you respecting the snow-line on the Himalaya, namely, that it extends lower on the southern declivity than on the northern. I have proposed to him to open a correspondence with you, since no one can have a stronger claim to be informed of the latest discoveries in the field of natural history than yourself, and I only hope that he may fulfil his intention.

Among my daily associates are Colonel Ashburnham, Captain Durand, and Captain Hay. With the former I take long walks every day, even at the risk of being looked upon by our Hindoos, on account of this vulgar enjoyment, as belonging to an inferior caste. Our usual walk was to the village of Khanga, where a fakir has fixed his abode among old decayed tombs, under acacias and tamarinds. He resembles a skeleton rather than a living being, and depends on the alms of the pious for his subsistence: his only society consists of three monkies and a dog.

The setting sun is an object of unceasing astonishment and admiration to us; perhaps in no other country in the world does it diffuse such an indescribable magic, and such splendour of colouring over the firmament as in India. This effect is the most beautiful and diversified when light clouds traverse the deep blue sky, for as soon as the sun begins to decline, the beams become fainter and fainter, while the sky in the west is covered with a sea of liquid gold, which glows in ever-varying colours, sometimes changing into purple, then again to crimson and violet, or shining in all the beautiful tints of the rainbow. The little clouds beam like rubies, and the east glitters in a roseate hue from the reflection of the evening red, above which the snowy masses of the Himalaya rise in silver light.

We have also horse races here, an amusement of which the English seem as fond as of billiards. There is a race course and a large stand, as at Ascot; but the chief attraction of that place, namely, the great assemblage of people, was wanting; and, as I have never taken any pleasure in horse races, I can give you no account of those at Ferozpoor. I must however not forget to tell you that our servants adorned the tents on Christmas day with flowers, and in the morning presented us with cakes and nuts for breakfast: of course in this delicate attention they had an eye to our liberality.

During this military and festive life there were continual negotiations with the court at Lahore. The Maharaja Shere Singh, and more especially his ambitious minister, Dheean Singh, were so fully convinced that this army was destined to take possession of the Punjab, that they assembled an army of 80,000 men and 200 pieces of cannon between Lahore and Amritsir. They appeared to be the more confirmed in this notion, when the Governor-General refused to receive an envoy of Shere Singh in Lodiana, because he had suffered the troops appointed to escort him to wait two hours beyond the time agreed upon, which, as afterwards appeared, had arisen from a mistake. I looked with anxious expectation for the end of these negotiations, which were conducted by Mr. George Clarke, for it depended upon their issue whether I should become acquainted with this remarkable country and people, and visit Kashmir.

The court of Lahore held out the hand of reconciliation. Accordingly the handsome Heera Singh arrived at Ferozpoor on the 28th of December, in the character of ambassador extraordinary, and was invited to an audience at two o'clock in the afternoon in Lord Ellenborough's tent, which, on this occasion, was decorated with the standards taken in China, and with those which were to immortalise the victories of

Afghanistan; and beneath them was placed the silver chair of state for the Governor-General.

The embassy arrived on richly adorned elephants, with gold and silver howdahs, accompanied by an escort, which presented a most strange medley in their costume and arms. They were all lean, muscular men, with long beards, deep set dark eyes, slightly aquiline noses, and oval countenances. There is something so prominent and marked in the expression of the countenance of a sikh, that, like a Jew, he cannot deny his race.

Heera Singh has a fine countenance, which may almost be pronounced as perfectly noble, yet his features are more expressive of mildness and effeminacy than of gravity and dignity. He wore a rich green shoga, embroidered with gold; and a red turban, entwined with strings of pearls, and an azure ornament on the forehead, surmounted by a feather fastened by an agraffe of rubies, became him extremely well, and gave him a dashing and coquettish appearance. His companions, the Rajahs Soochet Singh, and Kesry Singh, and the Jemedar Kooshal Singh, were dressed in a similar style; the latter, who was a Hindoo, and originally a cook to a private soldier, had already become a sikh and an eminent commander in the time of Runjeet Singh.

The cunning old fakir Uzeezoodeen accompanied the ambassador as his counsellor, and, faithful to his order, appeared in a plain and dirty dress. He always calls himself the poor fakir, but everybody knows that he has amassed great treasures. Heera Singh was attended by about thirty officers, each with a shield on his shoulder and a sabre in his hand; some of them stood, others sat cross-legged at the feet of their master, and formed the most picturesque groups.

The conversation had scarcely begun, when, according to custom, some bags of money were laid at the feet of the Governor-General: each of the chiefs presented in his open hand some pieces of gold coin, which Lord Ellenborough touched, and his interpreter, Mr. Maddock, received; then the presents sent by Shere Singh to the Governor-General were brought in, consisting of a magnificent sabre set with pearls and diamonds, bows and arrows, precious stones, pearls, Kashmir shawls, silks, and carpets.

These presents, as well as all others of the kind, belong, by law, to the East India Company; the Baboo receives them for the Toshakana*, from which they are afterwards sent to be sold by auction. In less than an hour the Governor-General gave the signal for breaking up, by presenting the betel nut wrapped in gilt leaves, and the ottar of roses. Heera Singh had announced that the Maharaja was prevented by indisposition from offering his salutation in person, but that he would send his son accompanied by Dheean Singh.

Purthaub Singh had passed the Sutlej with 5000 men, and pitched his tents on the banks, four miles from our camp, on the 30th of December. He was invited by the Governor-General to the grand review

* The Toshakana is the collection of all the presents received, and all the valuable articles which the Indian Government buys up for presents in return. It is under the Secretary of the Government, and is superintended by a Baboo, by which name a native is understood who must be acquainted with the English language, and has raised himself by his education and official position above the inferior class.

which was to take place on the following day. Some gentlemen of Lord Ellenborough's suite rode out on elephants to welcome the new guests, who, accompanied by some hundred officers, a body guard of 200 cuirassiers and 500 infantry, appeared in our camp at 10 o'clock, on 25 elephants. Prince Purthaub Singh is a pretty boy; but weak and delicate, and rather disfigured by a very crooked set of teeth. He carried a shield on his shoulder, and a sabre in his hand; he was dressed in yellow silk, and his turban, neck, and ears were lavishly ornamented with pearls and diamonds. Dheean Singh, who led him by the hand into the tent, wore under a blue silk vest a shirt of mail, over that a silver cuirass, light brown leather pantaloons sitting very tight to the leg, and red shoes embroidered with gold, which, according to custom, he put off at the entrance. His silver helmet, wound about with pearls, and yellow and blue silk shawls which floated over his shoulder, was ornamented with a feather, which was fastened by an agraffe of rubies, and gave him an appearance of great haughtiness. When I saw him, who is the handsomest man of his nation, galloping at full speed on his bay horse, with a golden bridle and a panther skin, with a staff in his right hand, I could have fancied that I saw one of the heroes of antiquity. The attendants were dressed in the same style of magnificence, and looked extremely elegant and picturesque; and the Durbar exhibited a scene which carried us all back to remote ages: it seemed as if the warriors had come to life again who had fought under the banner of Porus.

During the audience the band played "God save

the Queen," six bags of money were laid at the feet of the Governor-General, and the chief men presented gold coin; while the cunning fakir, with his dirty turban, acted as usual as the spokesman, and delivered an address in flowery language. In half an hour Lord Ellenborough gave the signal for breaking up; and all pressed forward to obtain a drop of ottar of roses. Most of the company mounted their horses; some of them, however, among whom was the effeminate Shere Singh, chose elephants. As the noble Indians never appear in public without their falconers, grooms, and other attendants, we were surrounded by a motley irregular crowd, which the Governor-General's body guard were obliged to keep at bay with their whips. The young prince, more taken up with his fine ornaments and jewels than with what was passing around him, began to be tired, and twice sent a message to Dheean Singh, requesting permission to change a horse for an elephant; but his request was very positively refused.

The defiling of 22,500 men, and 102 pieces of cannon, (the rest of the troops having remained to guard the camp, or being laid up by sickness,) afforded a very uncommon scene. Behind us was ranged a line of 100 elephants, on which the gayest groups of European ladies and noble Indians were seated enjoying the scene: while many Indians who had not taken their places along this line were mounted on horseback. Among the latter Hindoo Row was an object of great interest: he is said to have made the remarkable observation to an officer, "It is not long since I was in a distinguished situation: and these men, who are now glittering in honour and splendour, will, in a few years, be in the same situation as I am; but thus it must be — the progress of civilisation demands it."

In the evening, Lord Ellenborough gave a ball in his tent, to which 800 officers were invited; but there were only between 30 and 40 ladies. Several of the Indian princes were present, but none of the Sikhs, because their notions of European manners are still so obscure, that the ladies might easily have experienced some unpleasant treatment. It was a carpet dance; two bands of music played alternately, and the splendid circle was so animated that they did not break up till the morning. Who would have believed, after the unhappy catastrophe at Afghanistan, that within only a twelvemonth such a fête as this would have followed! so closely allied in the history, both of nations and individuals, are mourning and joy.

Lord Ellenborough promised to return the visit of Prince Purthaub Singh on the 2d of January. Accompanied by the body guard and a squadron of Hussars, we repaired thither, on richly ornamented elephants, at two o'clock in the afternoon. Heera Singh, with some persons of distinction, came to fetch us; and his father met us half way, accompanied by several Indians of rank mounted on elephants. The Prince's camp consisted of two large and several small tents, surrounded by a canvass wall six feet high. The body guard of the Maharaja, consisting of distinguished veteran soldiers, in shirts of mail and helmets, lined the avenue leading to the tents. In front of the tent of reception there was a handsome canopy elegantly embroidered with flowers and birds, and supported on silver pillars, and the most costly

Kashmir carpets were spread upon the ground. A salute of artillery announced our approach. The Prince awaited the arrival of the Governor-General, at the entrance of the tent, and conducted him to his seat. His Highness and Lord Ellenborough sat down under the canopy, upon golden arm-chairs, and we upon silver seats; opposite to us several hundreds of the principal chiefs and officers were ranged in a semicircle. They were most picturesquely grouped, and their elegant costume, their various arms, their striking countenances, and long beards, formed a most unique picture.

After the customary salutations, the gentlemen accompanying the Governor-General were introduced to the Prince. My uniform, being so different to that of the English, attracted much notice; and Dheean Singh, and his son especially, made many inquiries respecting my king and country. Meanwhile the chief persons brought gold coins in their open hands to the Governor-General. On these occasions the offering of presents is a matter of great importance: it is a formal act of the state, on which every thing depends. With this, too, the old fakir was busying himself, holding a long list in his hand, and reading aloud the names of those who were so fortunate as to be entitled to receive them.

The presents of the Indian princes always consist of horses, sabres, jewels, shawls, and silks. Lord Ellenborough was first presented with a beautiful string of pearls, rings, and bracelets of jewels, and a sabre richly ornamented with pearls and diamonds, and sixteen large salvers, containing Kashmir shawls and silks of every kind: the young prince insisted upon throwing the pearls round his Lordship's neck, and placing a ring on his finger. The gentlemen about Lord Ellenborough and General Sale next received each a handsome sabre: the attentive fakir seemed also to have included me, but his obsequiousness resulted only in good wishes. However, the whole thing is a mere matter of form. No one can enjoy his handsome present; for the Baboo and his associates lay embargo on it, in the name of the East India Government. All the presents are afterwards sold, and the money pays for the gifts which must be made in return. However necessary such an arrangement may be, there is something extremely disagreeable in it, for it degenerates into a mere barter.

We were then conducted into the large tent, where Champagne, Madeira, and the fruits of Cabool and Kashmir (apples, pears, and grapes), were placed in silver vessels upon a long table. The Prince and Dheean Singh did the honours of the table to admiration; they helped their guests to wine, and requested some of them to accept the silver goblets and vessels, in token of remembrance. A present intended for the Queen of England was next exhibited: it was a perfectly beautiful green Kashmir tent, embroidered with silk, containing a silver bed and morning dresses for ladies, with pearls, jewels, and other ornaments; while the floor was covered with the finest Kashmir shawls. But the Prince seemed to think a great deal more of a wretched portrait of Runjeet Singh, daubed on paper with water colours, which was to accompany the present. The entertainment was concluded by the entrance of about twenty Bayadères, among whom were several Kashmerians. All of them were overladen with jewels, and some of them had painted, not only their eyelids, but had even dotted their cheeks with antimony. Very few of them had a pleasing exterior: indeed some of them were positively ugly; and we were astonished that the court of Lahore should have retrograded so much in this particular. They were to have entertained us with singing and dancing; but as we were still to witness a review of the Sikh's brigade, Lord Ellenborough remained only a short time, and presented them with 1000 rupees: they, however, seemed very much disappointed at being so summarily dismissed.

We mounted our elephants, and Lord Ellenborough invited the young prince to a seat in his howdah. Dheean Singh, with his son at his side, followed close, in order to give a report to the Maharaja of all that had occurred. The weather had become so cool, being only 57° Fahrenheit, that Dheean Singh very considerately took off his shoba and wrapped it round the Prince.

The Sikh brigade, consisting of two regiments of infantry, one of cavalry, and two batteries, manœuvred with great precision, under the command of General Court: the manœuvres were evidently executed on a preconceived plan, and the movements of the artillery and cavalry were as rapid as could be desired. The infantry first formed in line, then divided into two bodies with sharpshooters in advance, and then formed columns of attack, supported by the cavalry, which advanced round the wings and attacked. When repulsed, it rallied behind its infantry and artillery, which had formed in squares, and opened a brisk fire. It was quite dark when we took leave, highly gratified by the courtesy and attention of our exalted host.

The Governor-General presented 11,000 rupees to the troops, who had been six hours under arms: this being the custom of India.

The scenes I had witnessed to-day made me wish, more ardently than ever, to become acquainted with the court of Lahore, and the army of the Sikhs; I was, therefore, highly gratified, when Lord Ellenborough proposed to me that I should join the extraordinary embassage, which was going thither under Mr. Maddock; but before setting out, his Lordship invited me to be present at an audience of leave, given to Prince Purthaub and several other princes and ambassadors. With the pomp and magnificence of an Eastern monarch, Prince Purthaub Singh, surrounded by his grandees and officers, and a train of thirty elephants, appeared in our camp on the following day. He, as well as his followers, were to receive the splendid presents from Lord Ellenborough: a star of brilliants, a pearl necklace, and many shawls and silks, borne on twenty-six large salvers, were the gifts of the government; to these Lord Ellenborough added three silver gilt tankards of the time of Henry VIII. Dheean Singh, his son, and sixteen officers, among whom was General Court, likewise received handsome presents; but the gloomy and discontented countenance of the former betrayed that all was not right; nor did it assume a cheerful and animated expression, till the Governor-General presented him with a handsome silver sabre.

On occasions of this kind, it is customary for the Indian nobles to bring the artist attached to the court, to take the portraits of those present: the painter of Shere Singh was, therefore, incessantly occupied in sketching with a black lead pencil those likenesses which were afterwards to be copied in water colours, in order that they might adorn the walls of the royal palace; and some of them were admirably executed. I was among the honoured few, and the artist was very particular in making a faithful representation of my uniform, and hat and feathers.

Immediately after the reception given to the Sikhs, the ambassador of the Bhawulkhan was admitted. He was a good-humoured, corpulent Mussulman, attended, as counsellor, by an elderly man wearing spectacles, who stood in a most humble attitude, with his hands folded, before the king of the country, and assisted his master in the conversation, by furnishing him with replies. The ambassador delivered a writing and presents from the Bhawulkhan, which consisted chiefly of wrought silks of Bhawulpoor, and received in return, rich gifts of jewels and shawls. Lastly appeared the four Afghan princes,—Jan Fishan Khan, Narib Shurif Kuzzilbash, Saleh Mahomet Azahudeen, and Saleh Mahomet Kuzzilbash: the latter, who is the keeper of the prisoners, has a mean hypocritical countenance; he first deserted from the English, and then defrauded Akbar Khan of a year's pension, which had been promised him, by delivering up his prisoners to Sir Richmond Shakspeare.

The Governor-General, attended by his body guard, one regiment of cavalry, two of infantry, and six pieces of artillery, broke up on the 5th of January for Delhi; and within a few hours after the extraordinary embassage, consisting of Mr. Maddock, Lord Ellenborough's military secretary, Captain Somerset, myself (I name the persons according to the prescribed etiquette), Lord Altamont, General Churchill, the Secretary of Legation, Mr. Greathead, and several other gentlemen, crossed the Sutlej.

Our escort, under Major Skinner, consisting of a squadron of lancers, a squadron of light cavalry, and two pieces of artillery, together with our attendants, elephants, and baggage, had been sent forward two days in advance. The escort had orders to wait for us ten miles south of Lahore. Two carriages, several officers, and some cavalry of the Maharaja, were in waiting on the opposite bank of the river, to conduct us to Lahore. Both the carriages, each drawn by four horses, were presents from the British government; but they were in such a wretched condition, that we lost one of the doors half way, and were obliged to leave it at a village.

The country immediately adjoining the Sutlej, consists of corn fields, and resembles a luxuriant valley without trees; the fresh young green crops, contrasted with the incomparable blue of the sky, had a most soothing, yet enlivening, effect upon my mind. But this fine cultivation continued for about three miles only; the soil soon presented immense tracts of jungle, interspersed with tamarinds, stunted tamarisks, and bushes, amid the ruins of old mosques and tombs, till the eye became perfectly wearied of the monotony of the scene.

A short distance before Kussoor, we crossed the ridge that encloses the valley of the Sutlej, where the ruins of a large city lie scattered about in wild confusion. Some mosques, with handsome domes and a few columns, indicate that they belonged to an age when the arts flourished. The road led between the citadel and the town; the former, which is about 500 feet distant, lies to the left of the road, on a small eminence, and commands the place; it consists of a low wall, narrow ditches, and projecting bulwarks, and is not capable of making much defence. The town is surrounded by high walls and towers, and is closely built of brick. A salute was fired from the citadel, to which the attending officer particularly directed our attention. As we had to change horses here, crowds of people had collected in the streets, and upon the walls and houses, and we were assailed by numbers of beggars, who implored our compassion with loud cries, and to whom the ambassador threw some handfuls of rupees.

At four o'clock we had reached Lulleeana, thirty-four miles from Ferozpoor, where our tents were already pitched. Lulleeana is a large village, surrounded with clay walls; on one side lie corn fields, and on the other jungle. The Maharaja had caused a splendid tent, of richly embroidered green Kashmir, to be prepared for the ambassador. A lofty canopy of the same material, resting upon silver columns, was placed in front of the entrance, and most valuable Kashmir carpets were spread on the ground. Within the tent was a handsome silver bedstead with silk bedding. The following morning the sun poured down its invigorating rays, and we, therefore, breakfasted under this canopy. Our little circle was extremely cheerful, and we were all in anxious expectation of seeing the celebrated Lahore, the most brilliant court in India, before the evening set in.

We found our escort and our elephants at Lakpatery Kakote, ten miles from Lahore. We were scarcely mounted when we were welcomed by a handsome old man, the Raja Fateringh Khan, attended by fifty horsemen, who were to form our body guard. We passed several ruins, and our road lay between the most luxuriant corn fields: we had soon the delight of beholding Lahore, which extended far from east to west, and the camp of the army covered the ground on our right hand. At some distance from the camp, we struck across to the west end of the city; and, near the ruins of a large mosque, quite undermined by an arm of the Ravee, and of which nothing remained but three high octagonal columns, we were received by Dheean Singh, who was accompanied by a squadron of cuirassiers and several great men, who escorted us to the house of General Ventura, which the Maharaja had caused to be prepared for our reception.

This house lies without the city on an arm of the Ravee: it is connected with an ancient sepulchral tower, and is built in the French style, though due regard has been paid both to the climate and to the manners of the country. It is surrounded by a small flower-garden: there is a harem attached to the villa! and the tower not very long since was assigned to a celebrated beauty of Kashmir. In front of the house is a large court-yard, on the east side of which were the one-storied barracks, built by Runjeet Singh.

This court-yard was appropriated to the camp of our escort, and five large tents, which were furnished with silk beds, had been put up by command of the Maharaja. The apartments were very luxuriously furnished with carpets and beds; and it was the first time since I quitted Bombay that I again slept in a house, and in a silver bedstead with silken hangings.

The balcony and platform were likewise covered with valuable carpets, and a sleeping tent, hung with Kashmir shawls, was erected on the latter.

We had a fine view of the city and its environs from the platform; the minarets, the winter palace, and the glittering blue domes of some mosques, of the time of the Emperor Jehangir, were particularly striking, bounded in the far distance by the bold outline of the snow-capped mountains of the Himalaya. To the south of the city are hills of débris, formed of the ruins of the ancient Lahore; and these again are joined by a town lying in ruins, interspersed with decayed caravansaries, sepulchral towers and mosques, of which I counted no less than forty. These once splendid mosques call to mind a wealthy and religious age, fond of the arts! A few buildings, surrounded with beautiful gardens and overshadowed by the crowns of the date palm, impart increased charms to this image of the past.

A melancholy impression was made on my mind by the sight of a red striped tent at the extreme south corner of the barracks, in which the once mighty, dreaded Afghan princes, King Fateh Khan, and the unfortunate blinded Zeman Shah, are now residing, and in consequence of the withdrawal of their pension are reduced to extreme poverty. There is probably no country in the world which can produce such sudden changes of fortune as India. A fence of linen fastened between two of the barracks concealed their harem and their children.

After Dheean Singh had made us acquainted with the various localities, and endeavoured to ascertain the wishes of the ambassador, he took leave in order to inform his master of our safe arrival. Shere Singh had already sent us several hundred baskets, filled with the fruits of Kashmir and Cabool, and sweetmeats of every kind; likewise 1500 gold coins (of four rupees each) for the ambassador, 800 rupees for the military secretary and General Churchill, and 500 rupees for me and each of the other gentlemen. Similar presents in money were sent several times during our stay here. From the moment of our arrival, not only we, but our escort and all our attendants, amounting to about 5000 men, were his Highness's guests. The steward of the household of the Maharaja had great difficulty in procuring a sufficient supply of fowls; his assistants were sent about in the neighbourhood, to lay their hands on all they could find, and even the Europeans in the service of the Maharaja were dealt with in the same summary manner, except, indeed, that they received payment for what was taken away; but the provisions which were daily sent, and which consisted of rice, confectionary, and game, served in China-silvered dishes and in leaves, were not suited to our European palates, and we merely tasted them from curiosity.

The presentation audience was fixed to take place as early as the following morning at ten o'clock, because, as it was said, "his Highness could scarcely await the moment to salute his exalted guests." Accordingly, on the 7th of January, an hour before the appointed time, the Rajah Soohet Singh, the Sirdars, Fateh Singh and Ghanda Singh, the Khiladar (commandant of Lahore) Mur Singh, and the Kalifa Nur-eddin, seated on elephants, came to fetch us. The moment of our mounting the elephants was announced by a salute of artillery, and the squadron of lancers placed itself at the head of the procession.

We rode round the walls on the west side of the town and then turned towards the banks of the Ravee on the north side. On the opposite bank was a battery and regiment of regular cavalry, who presented arms and fired a salute.

Immediately outside the gate of the Hasuree Bagh the spot was pointed out to us where Runjeet Singh, his son, and his grandson, together with their wives and slaves, were burnt on the funeral pyre; a marble monument in the Arabic style, erected by Shere Singh, covers their ashes, and priests were standing about it with flowers, tapers, and fans. We then rode through two colossal arched gates into the Hasuree Bagh; through the innermost of which Nehal Singh was passing intoxicated with joy, when he was killed by the falling of a ponderous mass.

Hasuree Bagh was formerly the residence of the Mogul emperors, and consists of three large quadrangles; the first is 500 paces in length, and is surrounded by vaulted buildings, which are now used as magazines; the western side is occupied by a red sandstone mosque, built by the Emperor Aurungzebe, while a minaret 150 feet in height towers above each of the four angles. This quadrangle leads to the garden court, or the Hasuree Bagh, likewise surrounded by vaulted, though decayed, open halls, with a pavilion of white marble in the centre. A ponderous gate leads to the third quadrangle or citadel, which is surrounded by numerous buildings, among which the winter palace of the Maharaja, on its northern side, with a winding staircase rising above the highest platform, has a very original appearance. Every where we saw traces of the destruction caused by the cannonade of Shere Singh, when he ascended the throne.

His Highness received us in the garden of the Hasuree Bagh, on the west side of which a broad white marble flight of steps led to a large open gallery. The approach was most tastefully draped with carpets, and the gallery with Kashmir shawls. Shere Singh, surrounded by several hundred of his great men, had taken his place in this gallery. Prince Perthaub Singh and Dheean Singh received the ambassador at the marble pavilion, and conducted us between a line of cuirassiers and officers to the Maharaja, who, on our being presented to him, shook hands, and cordially saluting us, invited us to be seated. Shere Singh, the prince, and the ambassador took their seats on gold arm-chairs, and we on silver ones; the grandees standing behind us, and Dheean Singh behind the Maharaja.

Shere Singh is rather above the middle height; he is very corpulent and strongly built, but is light in all his movements; his features are expressive of good-nature and a love of pleasure, and his fine dark eye beamed with kindness and affection; his black beard was very carefully dressed. He was attired in a yellow silk garment and turban, which was ornamented with pearls and jewels. Nearly all the attendants were dressed in a similar manner, yellow being the favourite colour of the court. After the delivery of the credentials*,

* From the Right Honourable the Governor-General of India to his Highness the Maharaja Shere Singh.

Dated Camp, Ferozpoor, 4th Jan. 1843.

MAHARAJA,

IT has been a subject of much regret to me that circumstances should have prevented my having the interview with your with which his Highness touched his forehead, and then handed them to his minister, 11,000 rupees were laid down for the Perwannah.

During the conversation, which was almost confined to interrogations and questions of etiquette, and inquiries respecting ourselves, Dheean Singh always took the lead, and when we could not understand each other (for the Sikhs speak only a corruption of the Hindoostanee), the Fakir Uzeezoodeen came to our assistance. We broke up in the course of half an hour, and his Highness conducted us to the lowest step; a salute of nineteen guns was at the same time

Highness, so much desired by us both. Hereafter circumstances will be more favourable. In the mean time, I have had much satisfaction in becoming acquainted with Koonwur Perthaub Singh. I congratulate your Highness on having a son so amiable and well disposed. I shall transmit by the hands of an officer of the garrison of Jellalabad the splendid presents your Highness has tendered for the acceptance of the Queen, my most gracious mistress. I doubt not that this proof of your Highness's attention will be grateful to her Majesty. I have directed Mr. Maddock, the secretary of the government of India, who will soon have a seat in the Supreme Council of India, to wait upon your Highness and express the true sentiments of friendship personally, as well as on the part of the British Government, I shall continue to entertain towards your Highness. He will be accompanied by Captain Somerset, my military secretary, and other gentlemen, and likewise by Captain Von Orlich, of the guards of his Majesty the King of Prussia, whom his Majesty had sent to witness the campaign in Afghanistan; but by God's aid, the war was finished gloriously before he reached India, and he has only witnessed the victorious return of the armies. He has been a witness also to the recent evidences of the mutual friendship of the two allied governments; and I rejoice that he will be enabled to report to his sovereign that our alliance endures for ever. I pray for your Highness's welfare, and the prosperity of your government.

(Signed) Ellenborough.

AKALEES.

fired by the troops stationed on the other side of the river.

On our return several Akalees jeered at us, at the same time giving us a specimen of their dexterity in the use of their quoit. We were received in front of our house by a band of Bayaderes and musicians from Kashmir, who displayed great adroitness in the Derwish dance.

An unceasing communication was kept up between our residence and the palace; sometimes mutual inquiries respecting health were made, and sometimes desires to be informed of our wishes. Nay, writers were actually seated in the vestibule, who sent never-ending reports to court, detailing all that we said and did; and whoever was the happy bearer of some agreeable message was rewarded by the Maharaja with a shawl or a present of money!

As Shere Singh had prepared daily festivities for us, I made use of the intermediate time to visit the town and its environs. According to etiquette I could only go to the former on an elephant. Lahore lies close to the Ravee, and contains 80,000 inhabitants; it is about eight miles in circumference, and is surrounded by a rampart with indifferent bastions, and a broad moat. Besides Hasuree Bagh, the tomb of Semat, and the handsome, but dirty and decayed, mosques of Padshah and Vizier Khan, the city contains nothing worth seeing. The streets are narrow and dirty; the houses are high and built of brick, with flat roofs. They have a mean appearance, and the only thing that attracts the eye is the very elegant carving of the wood balconies and low windows. A kennel runs down the middle of the unpaved streets, and renders them almost impassable in rainy weather.

The bazars are the most animated part of the city, though nothing remarkable is to be found there; they furnish little beyond eatables, to which our elephant very unceremoniously helped himself with his trunk as he went along. The people ran to the windows and the platforms to look at the strangers; even the women and girls appeared without their veils, so that we could readily distinguish the women of Kashmir, by their fair complexion, from the natives of India. Very few of them could be called pretty, but they all had fine bright eyes; they had, however, blackened their eye-brows, and had even painted little patches of antimony on their cheeks, and were covered with a superfluity of jewels and rings. They laughed and made sportive remarks upon us, which seemed to be provoked by my friend's eye-glass, held fast by the eyelid.

Next morning we again proceeded to Hasuree Bagh, where the ambassador intended to deliver to the Maharaja the presents which he had brought. His Highness received us surrounded by an equally numerous circle of civil and military officers, but the Prince and Heera Singh were absent; we were told that they were with the troops in the camp. The Maharaja was dressed in red and white, and still more richly adorned with jewels than yesterday, and strings of most costly and rare pearls were twisted round his yellow silk turban.

Immediately after the first salutation, the presents were delivered; they consisted, as usual, of jewels, Kashmir shawls, silks, weapons, chandeliers, telescopes, and, lastly, a costly sabre and a silver shield, on which the Goddess of Victory, surrounded by sunbeams, was displayed in high relief. This was so greatly admired, that Dheean Singh gave orders that it should be shown to every person present. We then went into the quadrangle, where the four horses which we had brought were led out. His Highness then showed us 20 horses of his stud, all with the most costly bridles, and some so richly adorned with gold and jewels that they might be estimated at 90,000 rupees. The horses themselves, with the exception of one Afghan horse, were of ordinary breed, large, bony, and too well fed.

On the same afternoon General Churchill, Captain Somerset, and myself rode to the camp of the Sikh army. The way led us through the ruined city I have before spoken of, past old castles, mosques, and a large caravansary. The camp was pitched at right angles, and perfect order was every where observable, and the discipline was so over strict, that they would not even allow us to ride along the front. In the evening, while we were at table, some Bayaderes were announced, who danced and sung for an hour in front of our tents.

On the following day his Highness was to give an evening fête at his winter palace. We therefore employed the forenoon in visiting the tomb of Shah-Dura, beyond the Ravee, where the Emperor Jehangir (*i.e.* the hand of the world) reposes. The morning proved very misty, but at eight o'clock, accompanied by an escort under Colonel Seth Singh, we quitted our encampment on elephants: almost immediately a crowd of Akalees, who were standing by the road side, so grossly insulted us, that the anxious Colonel and his horsemen were obliged to disperse these fanatics in order to make way for us to pass. Our elephants were taken over the Ravee:

we were rowed across in a small boat to Shah-Dura. The fog had dispersed, and the sun-beams illumined the fertile valley and Lahore, which presents a strikingly fine appearance from this place. In a quarter of an hour we landed near the garden walls which are already undermined by the Ravee.

Shah-Dura consists, properly speaking, of three large buildings, the principal of which is the tomb, which is built of white marble and red sandstone, and lies in the middle of a garden which is traversed by four bricked canals proceeding from the centre, and in which innumerable fountains were introduced; but the whole is in ruins. The tomb itself is a large square building, surrounded with a piazza, and ornamented with the most elegant mosaic, of precious stones, in white marble, of which the rosettes and arabesques over the arches, which are executed with extraordinary skill and taste, and are in a perfect state of preservation, are particularly striking. Two rows of black letters inlaid in white marble, over the entrance, contain the name and titles of the emperor, and in many places the word "Allah!" is inscribed in Persian and Arabic characters. The white marble sarcophagus with Arabic and Persian inscriptions stands in the centre, under a dome which Shah Bahadur caused to be destroyed in order that the rain and dew might fall on the tomb of his ancestor.

Salthyn Mahomet Khan, brother of Dost Mahomet, has taken up his quarters with his Afghans in the apartments of this fine monument, and has so completely ruined it, by kindling fires in the halls, that in many places the colour of the stone cannot be distinguished. Salthyn Mahomet sent one of his servants, expressing his wish to pay his respects to us, to which we agreed, on condition that it should be without any ceremony and without delay. On quitting the tomb, we found Mahomet under the verandah on the side next the water. His Afghans had hastily spread some Kashmir shawls on the floor, on which he and his attendants awaited our arrival. He had been afflicted with fever for two months and looked very ill, but had a very striking resemblance to his brother Dost Mahomet, who, as I was informed, has never forgiven him for surrendering Peshawar.

Adjoining the garden is the caravansary which is attached to every grave of an emperor; it is a quadrangular building 500 paces in length, with an interior court of 400 paces, containing 400 dwellings. This caravansary is joined by an equally large quadrangular court, surrounded by an immense wall twenty feet high, and contains a mosque and dwellings for the priests. Near it is the tomb of Nourjehan (*i. e.* the light of the world), the consort of Jehangir, whose life is equally romantic and eventful.

Nourjehan was the nursling of poverty, born in misfortune and under the most melancholy circumstance. Her grandfather, a Persian of Teheran, filled an eminent post in that country; but his son Meerza Gheis was induced by the deepest poverty to emigrate with his wife and children to India. Followed by misfortune on this long journey, he had parted with the last remains of his property, when the caravan, which he had joined, reached Candahar. Immediately after his arrival his wife gave birth to the celebrated Nourjehan; but, in their destitution, the parents despairing of being able to bring up the infant, exposed it early in the morning on the road by which the caravan must pass. One of the richest merchants in the caravan was the first who saw the abandoned child; full of compassion, and struck by the beauty of the little babe, he took it up and resolved to bring it up as his own. There is a tradition that her own mother filled the place of nurse, and that thus an interest in the infant's family was excited in the breast of the rich merchant. He befriended them, and recommended them to the Emperor Akbar. Meerza and his sons obtained place, and by their wisdom and prudence soon rose to a higher station.

Meantime Nourjehan arrived at womanhood, and by her beauty, grace, and loveliness, caused a great sensation at court; for she was the constant companion of her mother, who had free access to the harem of the emperor. On one occasion she was seen by Prince Selim, afterwards the Emperor Jehangir, who appeared so struck by her beauty that the anxious mother opened her heart to the princess who was used to permit her visits. The affair came to the ears of Akbar, who hastened to remove the dangerous beauty from the sight of his son, and immediately married her to Shere Afghan Khan, a young Persian, who had lately entered his service; at the same time presenting her with a jaghire in Bengal.

Jehangir had, however, scarcely been a year upon the throne, when he commissioned his foster-brother, who went as viceroy to Bengal, to procure for him the object of his affection. Jehangir seems to have entertained a latent hope that he might accomplish his end by an amicable arrangement; but Shere

Afghan was most deeply offended and mortified: when compelled to appear before the viceroy, he drew his dagger and stabbed him, and was himself instantly cut to pieces by the swords of the attendants.

Nourjehan was brought as a prisoner to Delhi, where the emperor, with the most tender respect, offered her marriage; but as she was a noble-minded and highly-gifted woman, she rejected his offer, and remained as the companion of the empress-mother. But the passion of Jehangir became more and more ardent, and his attention and love at length awakened kindlier feelings in the bosom of Nourjehan, and she consented to the marriage. Nourjehan attained a position never before enjoyed by the wife of a prince in India. Her beauty and her virtues went hand in hand with her talents and prudence, and procured her great and lasting influence over the emperor and his counsellors.

At the death of Jehangir, this extraordinary woman disappeared from public life. Though she was treated with the profoundest respect and an annual income of 250,000*l.* sterling was assigned to her, she lived in silent retirement, devoted to works of charity, and to the memory of her husband. It is related in the Khafi-Khan, that from the day of her husband's death, she never put on a coloured dress, but always wore white. She died in 1646; and the tomb which she erected for herself, next to that of her husband, now lies entirely in ruins, only the marble sarcophagus is preserved; and the beautiful vaulted rooms are now the abode of cows and oxen!

At five o'clock in the afternoon, one of the chief courtiers arrived, to escort us to the winter palace. We went as usual on our elephants, rode through

Hasuree Bagh, turned to the left through a large double gate into the quadrangle of the citadel, through a passage twenty feet high, northwards through a second gate into a small court-yard, and thence through a third gate into the garden-court. We now alighted from our elephants, and were led by the prince, by a short flight of steps, into a small apartment surrounded by piazzas and covered with carpets and Kashmir shawls.

Here, surrounded by his courtiers, the Maharaja was awaiting our arrival, and invited us to rest ourselves. It was already quite dark, and, from the bright reflection of light, which increased more and more at one side, we inferred that some extraordinary festivity was being prepared for us. A messenger soon announced that all was ready for our reception, and the Maharaja conducted us by a flight of marble steps to the fountain and the state apartments: here a fairy scene, admirably described in the Thousand-and-One-Nights, burst upon our view.

A square marble reservoir, containing numerous fountains, in the centre of which stood a colossal silver peacock with outspread tail, and surrounded by parterres of the choicest flowers, formed the refrigeratory. It was enclosed on two sides by lofty walls ornamented with little turrets, while the two others displayed open vaulted marble chambers, supported by angular columns and decorated with draperies of the most splendid and costly Kashmir. The whole was illuminated with innumerable lamps and lights, interspersed with devices, burning suns, mills, wheels, &c. &c., and the most brilliant fireworks.

His Highness was much delighted to see the surprise which we manifested, and then led us through all the apartments. In some of them were ranged the presents which had been sent to Runjeet Singh and the Maharaja by foreign princes; services of silver, porcelain, and beautiful cut crystal, and a collection of arms, which is probably the most select and the most valuable in India.

While Shere Singh was explaining every thing to the ambassador, Heera Singh joined me; he speaks so much English, that we could readily understand each other. He appeared to take great interest in Europe, but could not form any clear idea of the military power of Prussia, and only expressed his astonishment how it was possible to keep so many soldiers fit for service. He said that he had a great desire to become acquainted with Europe, upon which I offered to accompany him thither if he liked to go, under my protection. "Alas! alas!" replied he, "I dare not leave my country; I am undone if I turn my back upon it."

We were then invited to sit down with his Highness at a long table, which was covered with fruit and champagne. The Maharaja here set us a good example, and showed such dexterity in emptying his glass at one draught that we naturally inferred that this was his daily practice: his Highness was most richly adorned with jewels; he wore on each arm three large golden bracelets: among those on the left arm was the "kohinoor" or "mountain of light," the largest diamond in the world, and round his neck three rows of pearls hanging down to a great length, perhaps the most beautiful and rarest ornament of the kind. While we expressed our admiration of all these treasures, Shere Singh took off all his jewels and made them pass from hand to hand.

The "mountain of light" once adorned the peacock throne of the great Moguls at Delhi, whence it passed into the possession of the Afghan kings, and was at length extorted by Runjeet Singh from Shah Shooja, the ex-king of Cabool, when he was in great distress. It is beautifully cut, of the size of a walnut, and, with the exception of a scarcely perceptible dent on one side, perfectly faultless. It is set between two large diamonds, and this armlet is estimated at a million rupees. While we were admiring this treasure, highly amused at the childish joy of the Maharaja, who made his treasurer bring several caskets of jewels, the cup-bearers took the opportunity of emptying one bottle after another on our account.

At length several Bayaderes appeared, some of a very pleasing exterior, but, for the most part, they were very plain, and one of them so extremely corpulent, that as soon as we heard her voice we could not refrain from laughing. His Highness observed, that indeed she was not pretty, but that she was the best singer at his court. We could not coincide in this opinion, for we thought her voice as disagreeable as her person. In the science of music, however, the taste of the Indians differs very much from ours, for they affirm that the Europeans are superior to them in every thing except in music. These Bayaderes formed, under Runjeet Singh, a special corps of Amazons, but are now replaced in their original position, and are maintained for the amusement of distinguished guests. They are generally the first present that is sent to visitors, at this as well as all the other courts of India; and, accordingly, when one of our party spoke of the beauty of one of them Shere Singh immediately requested that he would consider her as his property! Attended by many torchbearers, and saluted by a fire of artillery, we returned home at nine o'clock in the evening.

The grand review was fixed for the 10th of January. About two o'clock his Highness appeared before our house to conduct us to the camp, and was dressed entirely in white muslin trimmed with gold lace. Dheean Singh was seated in the howdah behind him, holding an umbrella over his head, a matter of some difficulty, as it was six miles to the place where the troops were assembled. After a full hour's ride we reached the camp, where the Maharaja and the ambassador mounted another elephant, richly caparisoned, and carrying a gold howdah on his back.

The troops, amounting to 60,000 men with 200 pieces of cannon (of which, however, only the half had horses affixed to them), occupied a line of eight miles, and had passed the whole time, from five o'clock in the morning till now, before they could be arranged in this manner. In spite of the remonstrances of the European officers in Shere Singh's service, Heera Singh had chosen this position, in order, as he said, the more clearly to exhibit the great number of the warriors.

The procession was opened by the three carriages of his Highness, among which was the large state carriage, built by Runjeet Singh, drawn by six horses, and surrounded by a verandah in which there is room for twenty Bayaderes, who were obliged to amuse the one-eyed hero during his journies. The turbaned coachmen were dressed in the manner of English grooms, and looked more like the outriders of troops of equestrian performers than the Whips of a state carriage. Next followed the riding horses, with gold bridles and saddles and velvet trappings, embroidered in beautiful patterns, with pearls and rubies. Before the elephant of the Maharaja rode the provost of the army, in the uniform of an English officer of the general staff, except that a huge turban took the place of a hat and feathers.

Something more than a third part of the army which was assembled here consisted of regular troops, and of these about 5000 were cavalry. They are divided into divisions and brigades, and are under the immediate command of the European officers. The command is given in the French language, but the tactics differ in the various brigades; those which are under French officers being trained on the French system, while those under British officers, according to the English tactics. Thus unity is wanting, and discipline is defective. A single mishap would cause a complete disruption of these troops, and endanger the lives of their commanders. This, in fact, happened to General Court, who, on the accession of Shere Singh, faithful to his oath, refused to do homage till the ex-regent had absolved him from his allegiance to her; on this, the general was attacked in his house by his own soldiers, and had a most miraculous escape.

These troops are better paid than those of the East India Company, but not so regularly, and two rupees per month are besides deducted from their pay for their maintenance. Their uniform is red and blue: some regiments wear chakos, but most of them turbans; they are armed in the same manner as the English. The cavalry is in general well mounted, and consists of cuirassiers and dragoons. With respect to the artillery, the guns are scarcely inferior to those of the English, but their horses are very indifferent. Their movements are rapid; their firing very unskilful, for of six shot from six-pounders only one hit the mark at a distance of 800 paces.

The irregular troops consist chiefly of cavalry, who are obliged to furnish their own horses, weapons, and clothing; some are armed with spears, shields, and bows, and the greater part of them have matchlock guns; they are excellent soldiers, brave and vigilant, and are quickly rallied after a defeat. The irregular infantry, armed with guns and spears, can make no resistance in the open field. The most distinguished among them are the Chagaris, led by the Akalees; they are clothed in black and have black standards, with a lion embroidered on them.

We were a party of between forty and fifty elephants, and rode along the front. Generals Ventura's and Court's division was on the right wing; each regiment had its own band of music, and presented arms as we approached. Almost every one of the Sikh officers of these regular troops was dressed according to his own taste; some in English, others in French uniform, or in a mixture of both; some wore turbans, or caps with shawls wrapped round them, and others helmets and chakos: some had high boots with coloured tops, others shoes; some wore white, and others coloured pantaloons. It was altogether a strange medley; General Court wore a French general's uniform, and joined us on his elephant. The irregular cavalry, about 10,000 strong, looked very picturesque,—nay, antique.

As we approached the Akalees, those savage hordes set up a scornful shout; some gallopped out of the ranks and, with uplifted hands, abused the Maharaja;

his Highness, however, who appeared quite used to this sort of thing, took no notice whatever, and said he was glad that they had not pelted him with mud, as they had frequently done to Runjeet Singh on similar occasions. My elephant, unfortunately, became tired just at this juncture, which afforded these ruthless clamourers a welcome opportunity to manifest their insolence. I sent my servant to Major Skinner, with the request that he would let me join him on his, but I had scarcely seated myself when the strength of that animal likewise failed. Dheean Singh observed our embarrassment, and immediately despatched an officer to fetch the state carriage, in which we took our seats, and were joined by General Churchill and Captain Somerset. As the review was over, and nothing remained but for the artillery to fire a salute, we returned in Runjeet Singh's Bayadere coach, to our camp.

In the evening the ambassador had invited all the Europeans in Shere Singh's service to dinner: those present on this occasion were General Court, Colonel Munton, Colonel Lefaieux and his son, Colonel Steineck, Captain de la Roche, and Dr. Honigberger, &c.; General Ventura was expected to return from his furlough in Europe, and General Avitabile with Colonel Van Corthaud, and Captains Argoud and Quilette, were in Peshawar. My countryman, Dr. Honigberger, told me that the Maharaja had been very busy this morning in looking out the presents, and had said that he was happy to be able to give them at least to one person who was permitted to retain them.

On the following day, Shere Singh sent in the afternoon to fetch us to the winter palace. We had to pass through the mews, an open piazza supported by marble pillars, and up a narrow, dark staircase to the apartments looking into the court-yard. We were received, at the entrance, by his Highness, Dheean Singh, Heera Singh, and several great men. We took our seats upon a platform, from which we had a most noble prospect; the city, in its entire extent, lay at our feet, and beyond it the extensive ruins situated amid green corn fields; on the opposite side was the wide-spread fertile valley of the Ravee, with its ruins, villages, and luxuriant fields, while the snow-crowned masses of the Himalaya towering above the clouds, formed a noble background. This incomparable panorama indemnified us for our long and tedious conversation with his Highness and his great men; and we were glad to be able to take our leave at sunset.

Our audience of leave was fixed for the 12th, when the Maharaja contrived a further gratification for his guests. We proceeded at noon on elephants to Hoosuree Bagh, but to our great surprise found him waiting to receive us at the very entrance, opposite the marble sepulchre of Semal. The ambassador had expressed a desire to visit the tomb of the three kings whose remains are interred here. The tombs are situated upon a high, exposed platform, under marble cupolas, which are supported by angular pillars in the Arabic style. As we ascended the flight of steps, priests in white garments came to meet us, with flowers and garlands; others stood before the tomb with censers, praying, singing, and strewing flowers on the marble sarcophagi. We took some of the flowers from the baskets which they presented to us, and followed their example, in honour of the memory of Runjeet Singh.

This ceremony produced a comic, rather than a

solemn impression on the unprejudiced observer; for as we did not wish to detain the Maharaja, who was watching us from his elephant, we, as well as the priests, proceeded with such undue haste that we completely jostled each other in trying to get first, and the priests had neither time nor room to exhibit their performances. An old greybearded priest, who held in his hands a book, and a cow's tail, which he kept waving before him backwards and forwards, was the only one of the party who did not suffer himself to be disturbed in his devotions. The ambassador rewarded the priests with a present of 1000 rupees.

We next went to the hunt which his Highness had prepared for us, near the Ravee. We tried to force a passage with above forty elephants, through a thick jungle, surrounded by drivers or beaters mounted on horseback, cuirassiers with shields, and lancers, falconers, and other attendants, who could scarcely be seen among the reeds, which were sixteen feet high. So original and attractive a hunting scene could only be produced in the country of the Sikhs. The Maharaja and Dheean Singh possess a cabinet of the finest English fowling-pieces, which we were permitted to use. The chase, however, was very unproductive; we only met with partridges, hares, foxes, and a few jackals; Shere Singh and his minister proving the most able sportsmen. The chase ended in an open plain near a battery, which practised in our presence with balls, but for the most part missed the mark.

At sunset we arrived at the summer palace of Shalihmar. A regiment which was stationed before the garden-gate, with two pieces of artillery, presented arms and fired a salute. Shalibagh or Shalihmar, the garden of the Emperor Shah Jehan, who reigned from 1627 to 1656, bears this inscription: "House of Joy:" and is built in the same style as the Shalihmar in Kashmir. It is an oblong parallelogram, surrounded by a high wall, 1200 paces in length, and 800 in breadth, with three terraces of equal size rising successively ten feet above each other. A canal brought from a great distance crosses this delightful garden, and discharges itself in the middle terrace, in to a large marble basin: nearly 500 fountains rise from this basin and from the canal, and cool the air most delightfully.

In the centre of the garden is a small palace of white marble, and other pavilions and structures are scattered about in various places; but they are all going to decay. The garden is full of tall magnificent trees, but we were especially struck with some avenues of oranges which were richly laden with such an abundance of large fruit, that the branches seemed ready to break under the weight. The whole garden, even to the remotest parts, was most tastefully and splendidly illuminated with thousands of small lamps, gay paper lanterns, torches and wheels of fire, and from time to time fireworks diffused the most singular lights and colours by which the garden seemed to float in an ocean of flame.

After strolling about in this magic scene, we assembled in the marble villa round a long table, when we were regaled with fruits and champagne, and some Bayaderes were also there, with the vain hope that they would afford amusement: they were the first handsome women whom his Highness had introduced, and two of them especially were exceedingly beautiful.

They sat at the feet of the Maharaja, caressing sometimes him and sometimes the young Prince, and even extended that favour to any one who looked complacently at them. A person present making a remark on their gracefulness, his Highness requested that they might be courted at pleasure!

The Maharaja rose on a sudden and proposed the health of the Queen of England, a compliment which the ambassador returned by proposing the health of the Maharaja. The presents were now brought. Mine consisted of a horse with a golden bridle and saddle, a sabre, a costly pearl necklace, gold bracelets set with brilliants, an agraffe of rubies, six shawls, Kashmir and silk stuffs, and a robe of honour. I committed them to the decision of the Indian government, which they gave in favour of the Toshakana. His Highness himself girded on my sabre, attached the agraffe to my cap, and hung the pearls round my neck, saying, "May the friendship between the Queen of England and me be as permanent and as blessed, as it is between her Majesty and your Master and King!" At nine o'clock we took leave, amid the most cordial greetings of his Highness and his whole court; and the Maharaja was sensibly affected when he bade Mr. Maddock farewell. Heera Singh likewise seemed to feel very much at parting, and even on the following day sent a few kind words in English to the ambassador. It was nearly ten o'clock before we reached our tent; and midnight has passed while I have endeavoured to delineate a faint sketch of what I have seen within the last few days.

NOTE to p. 179.

THE question, "What is the best boundary for the British empire in India?" is so important and interesting, that it will perhaps be acceptable to the reader to learn the opinion of another German traveller, Baron von Hügel, on this subject. He says,

"This seems to be a proper place to introduce some observations on the western frontier of British India. This splendid inheritance of the English nation, which was founded by bold adventurers, has natural frontiers in all directions, and only the western boundary is the subject of some doubts. Surrounded towards the south by the ocean, enclosed on the east and north by impenetrable forests and chains of lofty mountains, bounded on the west by the Thuor, or Great Indian desert, there remains only a comparatively narrow stripe in the north-west, which is liable to some difficulties. England, by its perseverance, has acquired such an extensive territory that, in determining its boundaries in Asia, one or two thousand square miles are of little account.

"Any person who glances at the map will at once point out the Indus as the proper boundary. It is certainly very convenient for geographers to take a river for a boundary; but the case is different with respect to a frontier between two nations, and especially with a line of defence (such as the north-western frontier of British India must be) on the only side which is open to the approach of an enemy. A river is undoubtedly a good frontier as a line of defence: whereas between two nations it is not a line of separation, but rather a means of communication; for all over the world, as far as is known, the two banks of a river are inhabited by the same race of men, and the same language is always spoken on both banks. It may, therefore, be worth while to discuss more minutely, the question whether the Indus answers or not, to our preconceived idea as the boundary of the Anglo-Indian empire.

"From the moment when the Attock or the Indus penetrates into the mountains, it rushes, like the Jailum, in continual cataracts over rocks, till it reaches the plain of Cutch, at the end of which, near the confluence of the Kabool with the Indus, Attock is situated. From this point it again enters the mountains, and, after it has broken through the salt mountains, traverses a sandy desert: it flows towards its Delta through a more or less fertile country. From the mountains to the sea, the Indus gives life to the country on its banks — even in the desert there is a narrow slip of land fit for cultivation; but the Indus alone animates the country: on its right bank begins the sandy desert which extends far to the west: on the left bank the cultivated slip is rather broader; but from the Ran, which is itself 150 miles wide, the desert rapidly increases, till, under the 28th degree of latitude, it almost entirely covers a tract 360 miles in breadth.

"It would be useless to discuss at length, why from its mouth to the junction with the rivers of the Punjab, the Indus cannot be a line of defence nor a military frontier; because it may be stated in a few words, that an army cannot fall back on its line of operations, which must be beyond the desert, and because an army posted here would leave all Hindoostan exposed to the enemy; besides, an enemy would scarcely be expected from this side, though the first Mahometans, coming from Kandahar and Ghuznee, penetrated into Guzerat by this route: they, however, came only in detached bodies, while the great armies always cross the Indus at Attock.

"From the junction of the rivers of the Punjab upwards, the right bank is the last slope, of a rude and steep mountain chain with scanty cultivation, which is inhabited by savage tribes of Afghans, through which solitary caravans made deep paths, but which are scarcely practicable for an army. Here, too, the Indus would be the very worst frontier, because it must be immediately abandoned, in order to unite the troops at the point where the enemy would appear, which must be Attock, 300 miles distant from the confluence of the rivers of the Punjab.

"The fact that the enemy must appear at Attock is what makes the Indus so inviting as a frontier; but a frontier is good only when it is difficult for an enemy, and easy for your own troops to reach it. Now it would be easier for a marauding party to approach the Indus from the west than from the east; that is, from its mouth to Attock: on the Indian side the Indus is, in fact, as good as inaccessible to troops, and, a military force stationed there could maintain its communications with Bombay by means of steam-boats, whence the Indus might certainly be used to make a diversion on the enemy's line of communication; but a General would hardly send his troops in steam-boats up and down the Indus, and deprive himself of their co-operation in Hindoostan.

"It is recorded in history as something astonishing, that Alexander the Great, found the way to India, and even the most intelligent modern historians admire his sagacity, in having entered it at the very point where it was most easy to be assailed. Others wonder how Vasco de Gama found the way from Mozambique on the east coast of Africa to Calicut, on the coast of Malabar. There is, however, nothing more wonderful in this, than in a plain journeyman mechanic finding his way from Vienna to Paris; for even in the time of Alexander, the productions of India were brought to Persia and Greece, and the merchants chose, not merely the easiest, but the only road : in the same manner Vasco de Gama met with a pilot who conducted him from Mozambique to the well known commercial city of Calicut. * * * * * * All the subsequent conquerors, Timour, Baber, Nadir Shah, and Achmet Shah, took the same road to India as Alexander. The cause is simply this, — that this is the only road for an army.

"But supposing the Indus to be the frontier of India, it would be extremely rash in a General to risk a decisive engagement there. A finer field of battle than the plain near Attock, which is like a parade, extending 15 or 20 miles in every direction, could hardly be chosen; but what would be the consequence of a victory to the defenders of India? that the enemy would retire to the strong positions in his rear, through a country which cannot easily be exhausted, and where the roads are not rendered impassable by the rain, and where the invading army might remain if it pleased a whole year unmolested, while the rainy season would entirely hinder the arrival of supplies on the other side of the Indus. But if the battle should be lost, what would be the consequence to the English troops? It would be this; the defeated army would be obliged to retreat through a most difficult and barren country, in which a shower of rain would make it impossible to bring the artillery, and even the beasts of burden through the endless ravines : the army would not be able to rally, till it reached the Jailum, and from thence the rivers are so close together, and subject to such dreadful, irregular inundations, that there would be imminent danger, in case of a second disaster, of losing the remainder of the artillery. From the Indus to the Sutlej, all the disadvantages are on the side of the retreating army, and every position may be turned, while the retreat can be only in one direction. What an undertaking it is to cross a river with an Indian army is manifest from the fact, that for every fighting man there are ten unarmed followers.

"Now, compare with this highly extolled natural line of defence of the Indus, the artificial decried line of the Sutlej. The broad tract of the Indian desert extends along the Indus and the Sutlej to Ferozpoor, which makes it almost impossible for an army to pass through it, and in which small Rajapoot States form advanced posts, Rajapoots, who have been, at all times, distinguished by unequalled bravery and love of liberty, and who are fully equal to oppose any corps that might find it possible to penetrate on this side through the desert. From the end of the desert and arid tract near Ferozpoor to the Himmalaya, the distance is not much more than 100 miles, and an army stationed behind the Sutlej can more easily move from one place to the other, than can be effected by the enemy on the right bank, who cannot turn the position, either through the Himmalaya or through the desert. Whatever may be the frontier of India, the great battle must be fought on the plain of Sirhind, where all the advantages are on the side of the defenders, and where a defeat, exposes the invaders to the same destruction which awaits the former, in case of their losing a battle on the Indus. The most evident proof of this, is afforded by Achmet Shah, who, after losing a battle in the plain of Sirhind, on his first invasion of India, fled, without stopping any where, across the Attock. * * * * *

"Should events (and they will do so) extend the English frontier to the Indus, they must necessarily advance their line of defence further to the west, into the mountains between Kabool and Herat, perhaps as far as Herat itself." — TRANSLATOR.

LETTER VI.

TO CARL RITTER.

The Anglo-Indian army.—The Sepoys.—The Hindoo and Mussulman.—The European soldier.—Strength and divisions of the army.—Pay.—The corps of officers.

Karnoul, January 25. 1843.

KEPT close prisoner in my tent by increasing torrents of rain, I will employ myself in complying with your request to give you some particulars relative to the Anglo-Indian army: but you must consider these communications merely as a sketch, and not be surprised if many of your questions remain unanswered.

The Anglo-Indian army is unquestionably one of the most experienced in the art of war, because war is its proper and true vocation. Impressed with the recollection of the glorious actions already accomplished, it looks forward, after a short repose, to new combats, full of hope and expectation of performing new deeds of chivalry, and of reaping fresh laurels. The British army in India has never been without opportunities in which soldiers were formed, who, in endurance and resolution, are not exceeded by any army in Europe.

The Hindoos, of whom the greater part of the army is composed, have no *national* basis, either in themselves or in their history. India, under its Hindoo dynasties, was split into a thousand petty states, each of which contended with the others for the supreme power, and in which some individuals indeed founded kingdoms which were equal to the largest in Europe, but their existence was too transitory to have any influence on the present generation. Those days are entirely forgotten;—the Hindoo of the present day neither knows nor cares to what dynasty his ancestors belonged. He considers himself merely as a part of the great race of the Hindoos.

Religion and the privileges of his caste, on the other hand, are sacred in the estimation of the Hindoo; in them alone lies a separate political existence, with which the British government has never interfered. The tribes, too, which belong to the military profession, are neither original nor particularly distinct from the great body of the Hindoo nation. We find in the ranks of the soldiers, the brahmin, as well as the merchant, the peasant, and the artisan.

They are totally ignorant of the manner in which the country is governed: their life passes away, for the most part, in the camp or in barracks, separated from the great mass of the people. A portion of the Hindoos in the Bengal army belongs to petty tributary states, which might certainly make them accessible to political influence.

The Hindoo sepoy of the Madras army, is still more alien to the great body of the Hindoo people than the sepoy of Bengal: he is in general of very low caste, born and brought up in the field. Thus every regiment is, as it were, a little wandering colony, isolated from the rest of the world: but a large proportion of the soldiers are Mahometans. Hence it has hitherto been easy to send troops of this army beyond sea, which was done some years ago, to Egypt, and lately to China. The Hindoo of a higher caste would consider this, as a neglect of the precepts of his religion, and he is not permitted to dress any provisions on board a ship.

The greatest punishment that can be inflicted on the sepoy of the Bengal army is to expel him from the ranks. The Hindoo and the Jew of the Bombay army are, on the other hand, nearer to civil life than the Madras soldier; but even here they are often entirely separated by position, from the greater part of their countrymen. Like the Madras sepoy, he is content with his situation in the army, because advantages are offered him there, which he would not enjoy in any other position.

The Mahometans of India, both in the army and in towns and villages under the British dominion, as well as those of foreign states, are every where the same. They belong to one great family, united by the same religion and the same interests, and will always be ready to defend their national cause with their services and their money. Religion and government are never divided in the mind of the Mahometan, and he will never forget that his supremacy in India has been totally overturned by the English.

The eyes of the whole Mahometan population of India, will be turned upon him who preaches a crusade against the infidels, and the result will be followed and supported with as much anxious expectation and interest in the remotest village of the Deccan, as in Calcutta or Delhi. Symptoms of such a disposition have frequently appeared, even in the army. Yet it is difficult to determine the impression which it would make on the Mahometans in the ranks of the British army. They are more observed by their officers and their Hindoo comrades, than the inhabitants of the towns can be, and we may be certain that they would be the last of the Mahometan population, to join in any such movements.

At present this is not to be apprehended, nay, it is almost impossible that a general rising of the Mahometans in India can take place; they have lost all hopes of it; and if the Mahometan does not acknowledge it, yet he feels most sensibly that there is now no existing power to which he could attach himself. Besides, the Mahometans of India are already so infected with Hindooism, the customs and manners of which they have imbibed from their childhood, that they have neither energy nor decision enough to divest themselves of it.

The war against the Afghans (the preceding, as well as all the latest combats,) has amply proved the efficiency and capability of the native soldier. The Mussulman is not so effeminate, yet as brave, trustworthy, and enduring as the Hindoo: but he is not so temperate. Both, however, require to be led by an European officer; if they lose their confidence in him, they give themselves up for lost. They are ready to risk their lives for their officers, of which I have been told many instances: and are filially attached to them.

During our march, officers and privates of the native troops frequently came from the distance of many miles to see their European officer, and to recall the good old times. On these occasions there is no important moment which they do not recall:

no circumstance is forgotten, and they part from their officers like children from their parents. They even exchange letters with them, for the native is very fond of corresponding by letter.

Ornaments and distinctions are highly valued by the natives; their officers are rewarded with gold neck chains and medals; the latter are also given to private soldiers, who never lay them aside, and even fasten them to their white national dress. With still more pride and satisfaction they look upon their well-earned standards, and many a regiment has three such tokens of honourable distinction, inscribed with the name of the battle in which the victory was obtained.

With cries of "Ram, Ram-Mahadeo!" the Hindoo rushes to the battle; "Jai, Jaii-Kar!" they cry, encouraging each other in the combat; and return from the victory in a cheerful, though serious mood, singing "Ramchandre-Kee-jai!"

Soldiers are raised partly by recruiting, for which purpose officers are sent to the districts, or by voluntary application, or by the enlistment of soldiers, children above the age of sixteen. When the native distinguishes himself, he may be promoted to the rank of officer, there being in each company two native officers, a subedar (captain), and a jemedar (lieutenant), and in every regiment a subedar-major (staff officer).

In general, the native serves as long as his bodily strength permits, and many grey-headed officers and subalterns are found among them. Wounds, sickness, and twenty years' service, entitle him to a pension, or to be provided for as an invalid. Corporal punishment is not used towards the native soldier;

if his crime is dishonourable, he is expelled from the ranks. In other cases it is sufficient to maintain discipline among them by a strict enforcement of the duties of the service ; for it may justly be affirmed, that there is no soldier more docile than the Hindoo.

Having said thus much of the native soldier, I will add a few words respecting the European — the English soldier. He forms the real basis of the army in India; he is the instrument by which the immense power of India has been founded, and by which it is supported. Only 45,000 Europeans! a mixture of all the lowest classes of Great Britain, but hardy, adventurous men who, in hope of a better situation, have sold their lives for twenty years.

The English soldier knows that he is in a foreign land, that on decisive occasions he must depend upon himself alone: "to conquer or to die," is his motto, which is so deeply rooted in him, that it seems to him incredible that he should ever be conquered; coolness and presence of mind are combined in his character with boldness and perseverance.

In battle the English soldier is generally employed where the hottest combat is expected, and the native takes courage from his valour. On such occasions, there is no want of reciprocal sacrifices, in which no one will be behind the other: and the Hindoo values chivalrous deeds as much as he is grateful for sacrifices made for himself. Thus in the last war, some soldiers of the 13th, or Queen's regiment, rescued some soldiers of the 34th Bengal regiment from the hands of the Afghans, at the hazard of their lives, for which that regiment was saluted by the other on their meeting, and the privates of the 34th regiment prepared a festive entertainment at Ferozpoor for their

European comrades, in the most affectionate manner, which was afterwards returned by them, with a corresponding feeling.

Unhappily, however, the English soldiers are not temperate; they are addicted to spirituous liquors, by which in this climate, so dangerous to Europeans, death makes fearful ravages among them. It may be assumed, that most of the European regiments lose ten per cent. of their men in the first year of their being here. Thus, to mention only a few examples, 132 men of the 22d regiment died of cholera and fever in the first two months; the 86th lost in eight days, 1 officer and 23 men; the 28th in three weeks, 1 officer and 80 men; the 41st lost in the first three years, 11 officers and 235 men; and the 1st European Bengal regiment of grenadiers was so fearfully visited by fever on its march from Karnoul to Ferozpoor, that of 1000 men not the half were under arms, and 800 palanquins were employed in carrying the sick.

The government does all that is possible to preserve the soldier, the loss of whom is of great importance to them as a pecuniary consideration alone, for the Company loses 1000 rupees for every one that dies. In Bengal only two or three regiments generally remain, exposed to the hot climate; the others are stationed in the northern provinces, or in the mountains; but before they have completed the long march thither, death, in spite of all warning and care, has already thinned their ranks.

The strict maintenance of discipline in the British army is proverbial, but it by no means degenerates into despotism. It has often been contemplated to abolish flogging: but it is affirmed that discipline would suffer by it; we must not however believe that this is an ordinary punishment, or executed in a summary manner; it cannot be inflicted, except after sentence of a court-martial.

The Company's army consists, according to the presidencies, of three divisions—the Bengal, the Madras, and the Bombay army.

The Bengal army consists of 2 regiments of European light infantry (2000 men); 74 native regiments (81,400 men); 1 Ghurka battalion (1000 men); 11 regiments of cavalry (6600 men); 7 brigades of artillery (7000 men); 1 corps of engineers (without men); 2 divisions of pioneers (1000 men); and 1 regiment of invalids (1000 men).

The Madras army consists of 2 regiments of European light infantry (2000 men); 52 native regiments (52,000 men); 8 regiments of cavalry (2400 men); 4 brigades of artillery (4000 men); 1 corps of engineers (without men); 2 divisions of pioneers (1000 men); and 1 regiment of invalids (1000 men).

The Bombay army consists of 2 European regiments of light infantry (2000 men); 26 native regiments (26,000 men); 3 regiments of cavalry (1800 men); 2 brigades of artillery (2000 men); 1 corps of engineers; 1 division of pioneers (500 men); and 1 regiment of invalids (1000 men).

Besides these, there are, under British officers,—the corps at Hyderabad, the Deccan, Mysore, Oude, Shekawatte, and the Bheel troops in Kandeish and Malwa. There likewise are in Bengal, Mysore, Guzzerat, and Sinde, 18 regiments of irregular cavalry.

Of royal troops there are in India 30,000 men, of whom one seventh are cavalry.

Thus it may be assumed that the Anglo-Indian

army is 264,000 men strong, commanded by 820 British general and staff officers, and 5500 subaltern officers, who, according to Major Everest's map, are spread over a kingdom of 1,076,590 square miles, and are to defend a boundary of 707 geographical miles. This includes four Mahometan states:— Hyderabad, 8887 geographical square miles, and ten millions of inhabitants; Oude, 2392 square miles, and 3,000,000 of inhabitants; Bhopal, 677 square miles; and Tonk, 110½ square miles. Eight Maharatta states: —Satarah, 794 square miles; Gwalior, 3294 square miles; Berar, 5673 square miles; Indore, 424½ square miles; Baroda, 552 square miles; Kolapoor, 318 square miles; Dhar, 146½ square miles, and the little Dewas. Nineteen Rajpoot states:—Odeypoor, 1178 square miles; Jyepoor, 1342½ square miles; Jodhpore 3413 square miles; Kotah, 438¾ square miles; Bunda, 229 square miles; Alwar, 323 square miles; Beekaneer, 1806 square miles; Jaysulmeer, 978 square miles; Kishungurh, 72½ square miles; Banswara, 144 square miles; Purtaubgur, 145¾ square miles; Dongurpur, 200 square miles; Karouly, 187¾ square miles; Sirohi, 302 square miles; Cutch, 739½ square miles; Rewah, 1031 square miles, and Dhatten Jhansi. Maharatta and Turrah, 1617 square miles. Six other Hindoo states:—Mysore, 2800 square miles; Travancore, 457 square miles; Cochin, 197¾ square miles; Bhurtpoor, 194½ square miles; Dhoolpoor, 162½ square miles; and Sanjore, 93½ square miles. The Sikh states under British protection, 1662 square miles; and those in many small states and jaghires, among which those in Samblepoor and Bundelcund, are the chief. Lastly, the mountain chiefs of Sikkim, Manicpoor, Singboom, Chota Nagpoor, Sirgoojah,

Sumbhulpoor, Oudepore, Tanjore, Curg, the Bareitsh family, Ferozpoor, and the jaghires in the southern Maharatta country. The area of all these states under British protection, is about 45,000 geographical square miles; whereas the countries belonging to the English, comprehend about 62,648 square miles.

There are besides, quite distinct from the regular army, about 300,000 men, who are furnished with matchlocks and shields, and employed in the finance, police, and judicial departments. The greater part of this force is regularly organised and trained, and one twentieth is mounted and armed like the irregular cavalry.

The pay of the officers, as well as that of the privates, is very high, in comparison with that of the European armies; but the considerable expenses to which the European is liable in this country requires such high salaries. The pay of the general in chief is 10,000 rupees per month, that of a lieutenant-general 6000 rupees; of a colonel of infantry in the field 1280, and of a colonel of cavalry 1467; of a captain of infantry 411, and of cavalry 560 rupees; of a lieutenant 254, and of an ensign 200 rupees. The sepoy receives nine rupees monthly, of which one rupee and a half is deducted for his clothing.

The clothing is provided for, under the superintendence of Clothing Boards, for each army. From the surplus funds, each full colonel of a regiment derives an annual revenue of 500*l.* sterling.

A European regiment of cavalry costs, in Bengal, 73,778*l.* sterling per annum; a European regiment of infantry, 51,754*l.*, a native regiment of cavalry, 35,784*l.* sterling, a native regiment of infantry, 24,492*l.* The Bengal army cost in the year 1841, 4,000,000*l.*

sterling (at 40*l.* per man); the Madras army, 2,859,927*l.* sterling (at 45*l.* sterling per man); and the Bombay army 1,547,640*l.* sterling (at 47*l.* sterling per man); consequently the whole army 8,407,567*l.* sterling.

You are aware that the corps of officers decides the value and the capability of an army; that it is the chain which gives unity and character to the great moveable body, and that it gives the stamp to the whole army. Through its medium the general directs the instruments which determine the fate of states, and gives a new bias to the events of the world.

It is the sound vigorous good sense, and the chivalrous spirit of the corps of officers, which has raised to such a height the power of England in India. High spirits, thirst for glory, conscious independence, self-confidence, a practical mind, and the ability of quickly accommodating himself to every circumstance, are the peculiar characteristics of the English officer, more perhaps than of any corps of officers of the European armies. But these noble qualities are not merely gifts of his nationality — no, he is indebted for them to the manifold important vicissitudes of his life, which lead him to almost every country in the world, whereby he becomes acquainted with the most diverse nations, and is initiated into the most complex of relations.

India is justly considered as the school for English officers. Though the wars in that country may differ in many particulars from those in Europe, yet in the most essential points they are nearly, if not quite, the same, and in other respects they are more difficult. Almost all the distinguished generals of Great Britain have been trained, and have gathered their experience in India. The Duke of Wellington came from that country to the Spanish peninsula, as an accomplished commander.

The political position of England in India requires, more than any other country in the world, an army inured to war and ready for combat. Ten years' peace might be more detrimental there, than thirty years' peace to an European army, because it might be forgotten that India must be governed on military principles; and, in order to save expense, the unhappy thought might be conceived of reducing the army, diminishing its pay, or otherwise neglecting it.

Though the military officer is sensible that the sphere of action of the civil officer is more extensively important, and his task more difficult, yet, as he feels that the latter works and acts under his protection, a degree of ill-will must ensue. In a government like that of India, the whole cannot prosper, unless both act hand in hand, and both enjoy equal privileges and equal honours. It therefore appears inconceivable how power could have been given to political agents to dispose of the troops at their discretion — nay, even to direct their operations. We have seen times when men, without any experience in the art of war, laid commands upon generals: in such cases the agent should be responsible, but the general was judged according to the result.

A peculiar institution, which, with all its other advantages, is very injurious, is what are called the "staff appointments," *i. e.* appointments for the service of the general staff. These are not merely confined to the troops, but are also appointments in the country. They, indeed, place officers in the most important and most instructive spheres of action, but they deprive the regiments of their services, and thus draw the officer entirely away from the troops, a system which cannot fail to have an injurious effect upon the regiments which are so scantily provided with European officers. I became acquainted with a captain, who, in twenty years' service, had been only two years with the troops, had left his regiment ever since, had always resided in one spot, and never yet seen the cavalry or artillery! Three years ago Bengal had 406 such staff appointments, Bombay 189, and Madras 301. I must, however, observe that, every one who aims at such an appointment, must first be examined, by a committee, in Persian and Hindostanee.

On the other hand, the association of the officers has great advantages, and has a very beneficial influence. I have had the good fortune to be acquainted with most of the European armies, but I have found in none more genuine cordiality and self-denial than in the English. In this no one will be behind another; in this they consider themselves all as equals; the superior officer is not distant from the younger, whose interests are his own—in joy and in sorrow they are one.

A corps of officers in India is, in the true sense of the word, a large family. There is something hearty, confidential in the manner in which the youngest officer at table challenges the general to drink a glass of wine with him. At the same time, there is the strictest regard to duty in the service, and never a neglect of that respect which the younger owes to the elder.

But the British army in India requires, like most other armies, the vigour and energy of youth at the head of the troops. Most of the generals and staff officers are too advanced in age, and never find opportunity to arrange and to move great masses. They have passed the greater part of their lives in India; some have not visited their native country since they were seventeen years of age; others, perhaps, only for a short time; the Indian mode of life has become a second nature to them. Even among the captains, young men are seldom found, most of them not having attained that rank till after eighteen years' service, though they obtain the rank of brevet captain after fifteen years' service.

The difficulties with which the general of an Indian army has to contend, exceed all our notions of the mode of making war. He has to provide for the maintenance of two armies: the combatants and the train; the latter being the most numerous, the most irregular, and the most burdensome; not only, because all must live under tents, but, on account of the large number of servants required for attendance, and for conveying all the necessaries of life, and the strict adherence of the Hindoo to his customs. Each sepoy carries his kitchen utensils with him when he goes into camp, erects his own little hearth, surrounds it with a circle, to keep the uninitiated from the food which he prepares for himself alone, and, in this, no caste may mingle with the other.

In a European regiment of infantry, one serjeant, one corporal, and fourteen privates form a society under one tent, served by a clashy (tent-striker), a behitshy (water-carrier), and a dhoby (washerman), and require four camels: in a sepoy regiment, two serjeants, two corporals, and twenty-eight men belong to one tent, with two clashys and two behitshys. In the cavalry, each soldier has a groom, who dresses and feeds the horses; two soldiers have a water-carrier, and, two horses, have always one grass-cutter. The tents and other necessaries follow on camels and waggons.

To every piece of artillery there are four water-carriers, four grass-cutters, four grooms, two washer-men, and a tent-striker. The army of reserve, consisting of five regiments of cavalry, twelve regiments of infantry, and forty-eight guns, was supplied for the conveyance of its baggage, &c., with 164 elephants, 1745 camels, 2000 draught oxen, and 5422 baggage servants.

When the troops, returning from Afghanistan, had joined it at Ferozpoor, there were 36,000 men under arms, with 102 pieces of cannon, 400 elephants, 25,000 camels, 6000 draught oxen, and nearly 100,000 servants of every description. This army, when in camp, occupied a space of about ten miles, and, on an accurate calculation, extended, on its march, along a line of eighty miles!

That relish, for the comfort of life, which the Englishman so greatly enjoys in his own country, accompanies him to India; but here, where nature is so lavish of her bounties, where enjoyments are so various, where the climate, the manners, and the customs provide so profusely for the conveniences of life, these comforts are found in a much higher degree.

The great number of servants required, — a lieutenant having seldom fewer than ten, a captain generally fourteen, and a general above twenty; and, the separation from the natives, with respect to whom he is obliged to conduct himself like a superior being, — compels every one to form his own establishment. Hence, in the cantonments there are as many country houses, called bungalows, as there are officers, and where new stations are established, the handsomest residences, surrounded with lovely gardens, arise within a short time. Behind the bungalows are the clay-built barracks of the natives, looking like huts, rather than regular buildings, while the barracks of the European regiments, on the contrary, are built with comparative grandeur, and with every possible attention to climate.

Every corps of officers has its own mess bungalow, which consists of a drawing-room, dining-room, billiard-room, and library; a garden supplies the table with the necessary vegetables, fruits, and flowers. The dinners seldom consist of less than ten dishes, served in silver and rich porcelain, which is all carried with them when they travel in this extensive country. The mess alone, costs each officer 60 rupees per month; yet, we must do the English officer the justice to say, that, when called to use the utmost exertion, he also readily submits to the greatest privations; he will not renounce these comforts where they are to be had, but he cheerfully dispenses with them when necessity requires it.

I think I cannot do better than conclude this sketch by briefly describing the life of an English officer in India. If he is born in India, his parents send him to England before he is eight years old, lest he should fall a prey to the climate. Here we find him in the college at Addiscombe, where he is educated for his profession, and, in his eighteenth year, returns to his parents in India. For a few years he is occupied in the service, in learning the native languages; the new sphere of action, the novel impressions made on him by the natural scenery and the inhabitants, are very attractive to him. But, when this novelty has worn off, his interest in it has disappeared; it becomes indifferent to him, and the more disagreeable, when he is bound to a station, and the climate becomes unsuited to his constitution.

In the morning before sunrise, the troops are exercised, or he takes a ride on horseback, but this must be terminated before the beams of the sun become too powerful. A bath refreshes him after this exertion, and, at nine o'clock, he meets his comrades at breakfast. After this he passes his time till two o'clock at the billiard-table, in reading, working, smoking the hookah, or in a *dolce far niente.* At this hour he is again in the mess-room, to take a second warm breakfast, tiffin as the English here call it. After this the time glides away as before; and it is not till the sun is near setting, that the service again calls upon him, or that he takes bodily exercise, in riding, playing at tennis, or cricket. At eight o'clock dinner is served, which is rarely finished before ten o'clock.

The only interruptions to this monotonous life, are horse-races and hunting parties, especially the chase of the tiger and wild boar; a recreation, and at the same time a danger, which every one desires to enjoy, and spares neither expense nor pains to procure. The Duke of Wellington always looked for such bold lovers of the chase, when some decisive blow was to be struck.

Ten years' service entitles the officer to three years' leave of absence, of which he seldom neglects to avail himself, because in general his health and attachment to his native country lead him to return to Europe; or he seeks for the restoration of his health at one of the five sanatory stations of Mahabaleshwur mountains, Neilgherries, Simla, Cherra-Punjy (in the Cosseah mountains), and in Darjyling. If he is married and has a family, he probably purchases an estate, and considers India as his second country. Very few of the officers feel themselves actually happy in this extraordinary country: most of them withdraw after five and twenty years' service, hoping to lead a more congenial life at home, but find that they have become estranged from their relations and friends, and cannot attain the sought-for happiness.

LETTER VII.

TO ALEXANDER VON HUMBOLDT.

Return from Lahore to Ferozpoor.—Journey through the protected Sikh states to Samanah.—Chase of the antelope with a leopard.—March with the Governor General to Dathal; Saqun, Keythul, and Karnaul.—Visit to Paniput and view of the town and of the field of battle.—Haunt of elephants.

Delhi, 14th February, 1843.

I SALUTE you and all my dear friends at home from the renowned Delhi, formerly the capital of the Kuru and of the great Moguls. You have, I hope, received my letter from Lahore, and, if so, you will remember that I mentioned that I purposed visiting Kashmir. The British government, and especially Mr. George Clarke, the ambassador at the court of Lahore, were ready to make the necessary arrangements with the Maharaja, but Mr. Maddock seriously urged me to give up my cherished plan. He told me he considered that the state of things in that country was extremely insecure, that the government was very weak, and that if a revolution were to break out while I was in those parts my life would be exposed to the greatest danger. Though the counsel of so judicious a friend would, of itself, have sufficed to induce me to give up my plan, I was still more influenced by the apprehension, that my intention might be disapproved, and it was my first duty to act accordingly. The expense, besides, is so considerable, that I feared it would far exceed my ability, and not be compensated by the advantages.

In my last letter I took leave of you at midnight, when I had just returned from Shalimar, and had had a parting audience of leave of the Maharaja. On the following morning, the 13th January, we set out on our return to Ferozpoor, in the same coaches, and attended by the same escort which had accompanied us hither. We breakfasted at Lulleeana, under a tent that had been sent before, and then, while the horses were being changed, we were again saluted at Kussore by the guns of the fortress. Our escort, commanded by Colonel Sheth Singh, kept constantly at our side; and the appearance of some of the horsemen was so highly picturesque, that I very much regret not having taken a sketch of them. My attention was particularly attracted by a grey-bearded life-guardsman, who continually kept watching us with his piercing eyes, and, without changing his horse, arrived at the same time with us on the Sutlej. Here we found boats ready to take us across, and on the opposite bank carriage and elephants were in waiting, to convey us to the cantonments at Ferozpoor.

I found the usual hospitable reception in the bungalow of my friend Captain Ewart; we chatted away the evening hours in the company of his amiable wife and of Captain Hay, who listened with much interest to my account of the remarkable court at Lahore. The following day was passed in making preparations for my journey through the protected Sikh states to Sunam, and it was arranged that the same men who had carried Mr. Maddock and Captain

Somerset should convey me thither the next evening. Mr. G. Clarke had the kindness to lend us a dawk, by means of which we were able to overtake the Governor General at that place.

The Sikh states (14,000 square miles in extent) are governed by 150 Rajahs and Sirdars, of whom those of Patialah, Keythul, Naba, and Jheend are the most considerable, and are under the protection of the British government. With the exception of fifteen, they are Sikhs, and the conquerors of the countries belonging to them; their subjects are chiefly Mussulmans and Hindoos, whom they govern with great despotism. The revenue of all these petty principalities and jaghires is estimated at about fifty lacs per annum, and, it is believed, that they could muster 5000 cavalry and 20,000 infantry.

Favoured by the finest weather and bright moonlight, with a temperature of 56° Fahrenheit, I set out at 9 o'clock in the evening. Eight men bore my palanquin alternately, a torchbearer went by my side, and a man mounted on a camel, armed with a sabre and a gun, trotted on before. Till we reached the first station, we proceeded principally through jungles, and the road, which the army had taken, was but too plainly indicated by the immense number of dead camels, which were surrounded by the ravenous jackals, which had been attracted to the spots. This road is never used by palanquin travellers; and the bearers were wholly unaccustomed to this kind of service, for they had been taken from the villages, but we promised to pay them well, on account of the insecurity of the roads, which do not enjoy the best reputation. English officers have often been attacked here, and a few days before an officer had been robbed in the night of his horses, camels, and part of his effects. This induced Mr. George Clarke to appoint Suwars (riders on camels) for our protection, to whom the superintendence over the bearers was also entrusted. After passing the village of Malwal, I accordingly found two armed riders, and, in lieu of eight bearers, eighteen. But the men, with all their good-will, found the unusual work very fatiguing, and, instead of three miles in an hour, they scarcely carried me two; when the Suwars, therefore, proposed to me, at Mudkee, to mount one of their horses, and to let my palanquin follow, I joyfully accepted this offer.

We now proceeded by way of Bhaga-Parana, Patokee, Bhadaur, Ugaikee, Hudaya, and Sangawal to Sunam. The country was more or less cultivated; the soil extremely fruitful; and I was more than once reminded of the middle ages of my own country by the many small forts which lay on the side of the road, like knights' castles.

In four-and-twenty hours I had travelled a hundred miles, and at nine in the evening came in sight of the little town of Sunam, surrounded with walls, and the camp of the Governor General beyond it. Having taken no nourishment, and being much fatigued by the heavy motion of the horses, and the inconvenient saddles, I was so exhausted that I was scarcely able to reach the tent of my friend Durand, to beg him to procure me some refreshment. Colonel Ashburnham, who had taken care of my faithful Werner during my absence, immediately had a bed made up for me in his tent, where I soon fell into a sound sleep, from which I rose quite refreshed the following morning.

On the 17th January we set out for the village of Deerbah. We followed in the rear of the troops and the camp, who covered the whole road of thirteen miles in extent, and we had considerable difficulty, and were obliged to go a good deal about, before we could wend our way amid this vast multitude. We were accompanied by some of the Sikh rajahs, one of whom had an elephant with him, which was only six months old, and which was born in a domestic state; another of the rajahs had a leopard, which had been trained to the chase of antelopes, and we arranged for a hunting party with it immediately after our arrival. On these occasions the leopard is hoodwinked as the falcons are; as soon as the huntsman is near enough to the game, the cap is taken off from the leopard, the leader strokes his hands several times over the eyes of the animal, and turns his head towards the antelope. Scarcely does the leopard perceive it, when he immediately springs forward, but, if he does not succeed in overtaking the antelope in two or three leaps, he desists and quietly lies down. His leader again takes him up into the cart and gives him some meat and water to strengthen him. The attempt is then renewed, but, if he fails a second time, he is quite discouraged, and is unfit for the chase for some days. The antelope possesses such elasticity that it makes leaps of thirty to forty paces, and, therefore, easily escapes from the leopard, and hence it is indispensable to get as near to the game as possible. But if the leopard succeeds in catching the antelope, he leaps upon its back, clings to it with his paws; it falls down; he thrusts his fangs into the neck of his hapless victim, and sucks the blood, and then quietly follows his leader.

A CART WITH A LEOPARD FOR THE CHASE.

We were on two carts, drawn by oxen, and the leopard with its leader was on a third. The weather was clear and cool, for we had only 69½° F. at noon. Two miles from the camp we perceived a herd of antelopes, and we succeeded in getting within fifty paces of them. The leader feared that the antelopes would not stand still any longer, and let the leopard loose, but the ground was too much covered with thorns, and the antelopes made such tremendous leaps, that the leopard, after making two bounds, gave over and lay down. A second attempt was equally fruitless, and we were obliged to return unsuccessful.

On the following morning I joined the Governor General, who is always the first that sets out for the new camp; he is followed by the troops and the baggage, and a gun is fired as the signal of his departure. Accompanied by his staff and a part of his body-guard, Lord Ellenborough generally leaves the camp an hour before sunrise (the temperature to-day was 47½°), and has torch-bearers to light him on the way till day-break; he is usually joined by Hindoo Row and the Afghan chiefs. At a short distance from the new camp, there are always numerous beggars and fakirs standing along the road-side, who seek to excite the compassion of the passers by, by singing, and thumping on little drums; an old fakir, who had made it his business to remain as a protector at the side of the king of the country, had followed Lord Ellenborough from Calcutta.

The road to Dathal, which is eleven miles distant, leads through a plain, but the country is fertile and richly cultivated, and the scenery is rendered very picturesque by numerous small woods, which lie embosomed among the corn-fields. My palanquin, which contained many of my effects, pistols, and money, had not yet arrived here, and Mr. Clarke, therefore, had the goodness to send a messenger on horseback to make inquiries respecting it. I had given up all hopes of ever recovering my property, when, to my no small surprise, the palanquin was brought to me, perfectly safe, a couple of days afterwards; even some money, which was lying loose in it, had not been touched, so great is the influence of the English, and particularly the respect paid to Mr. Clarke in these protected states.

On the 19th January, I rode on an elephant to Sagun, which is ten miles distant. The country is rather overgrown with low bushes, and not well cultivated, but the road is excellent. Shortly before reaching this place, we passed through the Gagger river, which is enclosed by steep banks twenty feet high. At this time it was scarcely two feet deep, but after heavy rains it is so much swollen that it is impossible to cross it, and Lord Auckland was compelled to stop on the bank three days, till the water had subsided. On the following day, on the way to the last Sikh town, Keythul (twelve miles distant), we crossed the Sursetee, an affluent of the Gagger. It was a cool foggy morning, the temperature was only 42½° F., and the road was generally cultivated and very fertile.

Near the entrance of Keythul, the brother of the Rajah was waiting to receive the Governor General; four small mortars were placed by the roadside, and he was attended by several hundred Suwars on camels and on horseback, who were all dressed in yellow garments. The Rajah himself had been confined for years by illness. I had gone in advance of Lord Ellenborough on my elephant, and had, therefore, the opportunity of witnessing the ceremony of his reception. The gunners in their zeal mistook us for their exalted guests, and instantly discharged their mortars, but they soon perceived their error, and stopped after firing two shots. According to the custom of the country, the Rajah sent to the Governor General, flowers, fruits, confectionary, and provisions of all kinds, and his Suwars remained near our camp the whole day.

Keythul is one of the most beautiful localities in these states. A very pretty piece of water, resembling a lake rather than a pond, for such it is, lies in a semicircle, from south to south-east, round the base of the gentle eminence on which the town is built. At the eastern end is a stone citadel, with two round bulwarks fifty feet in height, which project into the water. The palace of the Rajah lies on the same side, and a bridge is thrown across to the other bank, to his summer villa, which is built in the pure Italian style; the palace and the villa are surrounded by beautiful gardens, full of flowers, fruits, and palm trees, which stretch along the banks of the pond: and lofty tamarinds, mango, neems (*Melia azediracta*) and fig-trees, bend over the water, and their graceful boughs, which were laden with blossom, were agitated by the slightest breeze, and were reflected on the smooth mirror. Under the shade of the luxuriant foliage of these trees, are walled tanks, with a gradation of steps, for the convenience of bathing. From some spots, especially the platform of the villa, the eye comprehends at one view the magic charm which is diffused over this delicious landscape. The palace and the harem of the Rajah is on one of the bulwarks, and we observed several female figures, in white dresses, toying with flowers, but they instantly disappeared, when we directed our telescopes towards them. We rode through the town on elephants: the streets are narrow and the houses are built of clay and brick; the bazars were full of animation; silks and shawls from Mooltan and Kashmir were exposed for sale in them, but the latter were of very inferior quality.

As I observed before, the Rajah is extremely ill, and, he sent a message to the Governor General, begging for a physician, a proof that he thought his end was approaching. When he dies, his beautiful little country, with a revenue of five lacs, falls to the British government, because he has no children, nor relations that have any title to it. We were told that his wives look forward to this painful event with much anxiety.

From the charming and richly cultivated Keythul, we came, on the 21st, to Futtehpoor (11½ miles), through a country mostly covered with thickets, for we saw only one village on the road. Futtehpoor is a large but dirty village, and is surrounded with ponds and fine bananas and tamarinds. Our Hindoos were bathing all day long in the dirty green sedgy water, and they even drank of it. There are, perhaps, no people more cleanly, and at the same time more dirty, than the Indians. They perform continual ablutions, always dress in neat white garments, but, the very same water in which they have bathed, frequently serves them for drinking and cooking.

The road to Nisang (fifteen miles) led us on the following day through a fertile country. Towards the east we beheld, in all their magnificence and beauty, the mighty masses of the Himalaya mountains, whose snowy summits (six peaks about 20,000 * feet high), seemed to reach the vault of heaven. The Jamnotri peak was especially distinguished. It is a place of pilgrimage for the Hindoos, from which, however, no one dares to return, because the Brahmins say, that, whoever undertakes a journey thither, is conducted by the gods, into the paradise beyond, but if he returns he loses his caste and is looked upon as a reprobate. Of course it stands to reason that every one who undertakes the pilgrimage perishes with hunger and cold. An immoral and artful Hindoo, whose course of life had given great offence, resolved to clear himself from reproach, and to obtain the reputation of sanctity. He took leave of his wife and children, received the benediction of the Brahmins, and, was accompanied by some of them, to the height of 5000 feet, where they left him, and he proceeded alone. But he found the cold intolerable, and his friends were not a little surprised to see him return a few days after. Full of indignation the Brahmins asked how he had dared to return. "I had pursued my way," he replied, "and was preparing myself to go into the presence of God, when he appeared to me and commanded me to turn back. The more I implored him to allow me to execute my purpose, the more earnestly did he command me to give it up. 'Thou hast a wife and children,' said God, 'who require thy assistance; announce my decrée to the Brahmins, and they will take the will for the deed.'" The Brahmins were completely foiled; they could not

* The cone is 21,178 feet high; the Jamnotri peak, 21,155; the Gangotri, 22,798; the Budrinath, 23,441; the Moira, 22,062; and the Lewahir, 25,749.

answer this address, and the cunning Hindoo obtained his object.

On the 23d we encamped four miles from Karnaul; on the way thither we met a great many antelopes in the jungle: they were so tame that they were not alarmed at the unusual sight of an elephant, and even accompanied us for a long time. In the afternoon the western sky (77° Fahr.) was covered with black thunder clouds, and, while on that side, the landscape was illuminated by flashes of lightning, on the other the beams of the sun silvered the snowy mountains of the Himalaya. A slight indisposition obliged me to drive to Karnaul on the following morning; before we reached it, we were overtaken by the thunder clouds, and a tropical rain fell without interruption the whole day, by which not only we and the troops were wet through and through, but our tents, too, were so completely soaked, that we were compelled to halt for five days. When the ground is thoroughly saturated the camels can scarcely move, and in such weather the weakest animals are often lost, for in falling their hinder feet slip sideways, by which they break the sinews and cannot rise again. It is most melancholy to see these useful, patient animals perish in this manner.

Our camp lay to the east of the cantonments, on a plain, near the church; several tents, and mine among the rest, were so surrounded with rain water, that they stood as in an island, and we could only get to them by means of small dams. The cantonments extend in a semicircle three miles about the town; besides the barracks they include hundreds of villas and bungalows, many constructed with much skill and taste, and all surrounded by pretty gardens or little parks.

Karnaul has unfortunately ceased to be a sanatory

station for the English, for, within the last half year the most destructive fevers have raged among the European troops, and it was found necessary to abandon a great portion of the villas and bungalows. It is still uncertain whether this is to be attributed to the clearing of the canal, which extends from this place towards Delhi, to the Jumna; or whether, as is the opinion of good judges, it is a transitory evil, confined to a certain locality, precisely where the barracks of the European troops are situated. The town itself is built for the most part of bricks, and is surrounded by an old wall; it is confined and dirty, and contains scarcely 8000 inhabitants. The cantonments are traversed in all directions by roads planted with trees.

The sky did not clear up till the evening of the 26th, till which time we were kept close prisoners in our tents. We now indemnified ourselves by making excursions on every side, and by contemplating the sublime prospect of the Himalaya, whose colossal, mighty forms, had never appeared so clearly relieved by the dark blue of the sky. Lord Ellenborough gave entertainments in his tent almost every day, and likewise a ball, which, however, from want of ladies was not very animated, and obliged the gentlemen who loved dancing to enjoy it among themselves. On Sunday divine service was performed in the church; hitherto we had assembled to thank and praise God in the tent of the Governor General. This was the first church with a belfry that I saw in India, and it forcibly reminded me of my own country. The puncas (hanging fans) rather interrupt one's devotions in the church, but the climate renders them indispensable.

On Monday the 30th, the camp broke up to proceed to Garaunda (twelve miles). The road thither was, however, so soaked, that several waggons and camels fell, and evening approached before we had collected all our baggage. On the road from Karnaul the minarets which Akbar the Great caused to be erected, instead of milestones, from Delhi to Kashmir, at the distance of a coss (a coss is two miles) from each other, are still preserved. They are tapering, round, stone towers, twenty feet high, and some of them had been repaired by the inhabitants as an act of devotion. Half way to Garaunda there was a handsome, lofty arched bridge, built by the Emperor Humaioon over the canal to Delhi; a remarkably large cotton tree near it seems to be also of that age.

Garaunda is a small place with an old caravansary, the best preserved parts of which are the large, handsome, turreted gates, on the north and south sides. Taking a walk in the evening through the camp with Mr. Maddock, we saw a woman performing the most singular feats. She had suspended herself to a high tree, by her hair, and thus hanging in the air she executed all possible manœuvres with her body and limbs. Though this spectacle was any thing but attractive to us, it very much delighted the crowd, who were kept in good-humour by the comical explanations of a buffoon, who succeeded in extracting a few coppers from their pockets, by no means an easy matter with the natives, and supposes the receiver to be possessed of great powers of persuasion.

On the following day we marched to Paniput (ten miles). The country is in a high state of cultivation, and the wheat and barley were extremely fine. Paniput is a small cheerful place: it is built of brick, is environed by a wall, and contains 6000 inhabitants; the bazars are clean and spacious, and are well supplied with goods from Delhi. On the western side there are small hills, formed by the ruins of deserted houses, mosques, and caravansaries; indeed, throughout India, and especially in the northern parts, the towns and even the villages are encompassed by such ruins.

The town is in some repute among the Mahometans, inasmuch as it contains the tomb of one of their saints, Shah Ali Callandas; and in the history of India those fields which lie towards the south have been the scenes of bloodshed and victory. Three battles have here been fought; in the last (in 1761) no less than 200,000 of the Maharatta cavalry are said to have combated here.

The Governor General, accompanied by his staff, &c., went thither on elephants, attended by an old Mussulman, who acted as our guide, and gave his explanations according to the information which he had received from his father, who at that time was actively employed on the scene of action. Men, women, and children, dressed in their holyday clothes, crowded the streets and the platforms of the houses, and very respectfully saluted the great lord as he passed along; but, in front of the tomb of Callandas, and in the marble court-yard, which is enclosed with a wall, there was so dense a throng that we had great difficulty in passing through it. The people shouted and cried for joy, and drums and pipes resounded as soon as the Governor General appeared. The saint lies in a white marble sarcophagus, with Arabic inscriptions, surrounded by a curiously carved wooden lattice-work. As Lord Ellenborough returned from the sepulchre, an old fakir threw himself on the ground, and stroked his feet in token of his gratitude.

From the tomb we proceeded, through the bazar, and around the town to the battle-field. It is an immense plain, admirably adapted for cavalry; a well overshadowed by trees is said to mark the spot where the artillery gave a decisive turn to the issue of the battle. Our guide affirmed that 100,000 men perished here!! For several days the temperature has been pretty equal, not below 47° F. before sunrise, at noon not above 74° F., and in the evening generally 63° F.

On the first of February, we marched fourteen miles to Sumalka, on a fine broad road, through a cultivated country, every where sprinkled with hamlets and villages. The peasantry formed the most picturesque groups, as they stood along the road-side and in the villages, to see us pass; in the early part of the morning, when it was still chilly, they had thrown their gay-coloured covering about the upper part of the body, or wrapped it round their head, while the lower part of the body was enveloped in the usual white garments, and the feet were bare. Sumalka lies under the shade of fine umbrageous tamarinds, fig-trees, and acacias.

At no great distance from Sumalka is the camp of our 120 elephants, which I am very fond of visiting, for the purpose of observing this sagacious animal. In consequence of the persecution it has suffered from man, especially by the chase and by taming him, either for the purpose of adding to the splendours of the courts, as a beast of burden, or as an instrument of war, the elephant has almost entirely disappeared from the interior of India, and is now to be found wild only in the lower ranges of the Himalaya, namely, in the Dshemna forest, in Nepaul, in some parts of the Ghauts, in Tarrai, in the kingdom of Ava, and in Ceylon. On the Upper Indus near Attock, where Alexander the Great first chased the elephant, in the Punjab, and on the banks of the Jumna, near Kalpy, where the Emperor Baber annually enjoyed the pleasures of the chase, no trace of that royal animal is now to be found.

The first taming of the elephant is not recorded either in the mythology, or in the sculptured representations at Allora; like all the commencements of Indian civilisation, it is assumed to be already existing: however, the manner of taming it, appears to have differed in different places, for, when Jumaway, the king of the Avacenses (1306—1330 B. C.), was driven into Hindostan, he is said to have taught the Hindoos the best method of catching the elephant. Though this one-handed animal (Hastin or Karin, as it is called in Sanscrit from Hasta or Kara, the hand), was employed in war, in the most early times, and rendered thorough obedience, yet it was not possible to rear it in a domestic state. There have certainly been some instances, where the animals have had young ones in a tame state, and we in fact saw an elephant ten months old which belonged to a Sikh Rajah; but I will not pretend to say whether it is feared that the animal will become degenerate, or whether it is thought preferable to be satisfied with those that are taken in a wild state.

It is said that the elephant in its natural state attains the age of 200 years, and, when tamed, 120 years and upwards. Those of Ceylon and of Tarrai are of the smaller races, and seldom have tusks: a very experienced elephant hunter assured me, that in Ceylon scarcely two elephants in a hundred have tusks. If they catch one of the latter, they saw off his tusks within one or two feet, and the extremity is tipped with gold or silver. The largest I have seen belonged to the Governor General, the Maharaja of Lahore, the King of Oude, and the Rajahs of Bhurtpoor and Alwar, and were scarcely eleven feet high, but they were more lively, quick, hardy, and sagacious, than the generality. Such an elephant costs 5000 rupees or more, whereas an elephant of middling size, about seven feet high, may be had for 1000 rupees. In general the elephant can carry five times as much as the camel, and is employed in the army, not only to carry the principal persons and the sick, but likewise to convey the large tents and carpets. The elephant might be employed for draught, with equal, if not greater advantage, for he draws, with the utmost ease, burdens which ten horses can scarcely move; hence he has lately been employed by the English with the greatest success in the artillery. On the other hand, there is some difficulty in employing him in passing large rivers, because he resolves upon it with so much reluctance; it is difficult to guide him when in it, and he sinks so deep in the water, that only the extremity of his trunk, which he then holds aloft, is visible. Whenever he passes over a pontoon bridge, or over a marshy soil, or crosses the river in a boat, he tries its firmness with his trunk, and then steps carefully with one foot, to examine the ground that is to bear his weight.

It is a sign of joy and satisfaction, when the elephant raises his trunk perpendicularly in the air, and his Mahout takes advantage of this, and teaches him to show this demonstration of joy and respect, by dropping on his knees at the same time, on the approach of his master or superior. The Hindoos affirm that on moonlight nights he turns towards that luminary, which probably has given rise to the notion that he worships it.

The elephant is particularly useful in hunting the tiger, both to carry and to protect the sportsman. This chase is generally in the thick intricate jungle, where a person on foot or on horseback would scarcely make his way upon the marshy ground, among thickets and reeds, which are sixteen feet high. The months of April and May are the most favourable for tiger hunting, because at this season the tiger goes out more frequently in search of food, approaches the villages, plunders the flocks, and is then far more easily captured. The huntsman has generally two tiger guns of larger calibre than ordinary in his houdah, and his assistant takes the place of the driver who usually sits there. Several hunters usually join in the chase, and they always endeavour to manage that some of the elephants whom they employ are experienced and accustomed to the exertion.

As soon as the tiger is traced, he endeavours to slink away, but on the first shot puts himself on his defence, and, if wounded, raises a dreadful howl, and gnashes his teeth. In this moment of excitement all depends on the elephant; if he turns his back on his enemy, all is lost; but if he give the huntsman time to fire a second shot, by keeping the tiger at bay with his trunk, in which most elephants show great dexterity, the huntsman makes sure of his prize. As soon as the tiger is killed, the elephant expresses his joy; and, experienced sportsmen have assured me that he becomes bolder and more persevering with every new victory. But should it happen that the huntsman must fly from his elephant, and leave him to maintain the combat with the tiger alone, it is difficult ever to induce him to go upon another expedition of the same kind.

As soon as the elephant is freed from his load, a stake is driven into the ground, to which he is fastened by a chain attached to one of his forelegs; and though it would be easy for him to free himself, he never attempts it except in the rutting season. On festive occasions the Mahouts take great pains in painting his head and trunk with arabesques, in white, red, yellow, or blue. The sort of reason which he shows in his actions has caused the Indians to choose him as the symbol of the highest knowledge; Ganesa, the god of the arts and sciences, being represented with an elephant's head. But this animal is especially honoured by the Hindoos, because they consider him the companion of the gods, the guardian of the vestibules of the temples, and the caryatide and ornament of their architecture. They believe, that the souls of penitent princes and brahmins are in the bodies of elephants, and a Hindoo of the lower caste may perhaps even consider him as superior to himself. According to the law of Menu a bride is to have the graceful step of a flamingo, or of a young elephant; therefore even now the princes and princesses of the ancient Hindoo dynasties are instructed in the paces of the elephant!

The Mahouts take the greatest possible care of the animals entrusted to their charge, and it is remarkable that they are themselves extremely dull and stupid.

A Mahout will not venture to defraud an elephant of his food, and still less to starve him. His tent, in which he resides with his wife and children, is close to the elephant, so that the animal lives as it were with the family. First of all the Mahout roasts, on an iron plate, the kneaded flour for the elephant, and the animal stands by, and waits very patiently till the chipatos or cakes laid before him are cooled, and then he receives his food from the hands of the Mahout and of the family. The elephant is passionately fond of sugar-cane and millet. While the elephants were being fed with it to-day, one of them lost his patience because he saw his neighbour enjoying this favourite food, while his Mahout seemed to have forgotten him. Like a froward child, who stamps with his foot when his wishes are not attended to, this creature vehemently struck the earth with his trunk, but was perfectly quiet as soon as ever he saw the Mahout bringing his food. The elephant is very fond of throwing earth and leaves on his back with his trunk, and this he is constantly amusing himself with, when he is at leisure; but he takes greater pleasure still in splashing about for hours in the water. When his keeper washes him, he lies quietly down on his knees, or on his side.

Near the village of Burke-Choky, where we encamped the following day, we saw a *Ficus indica* near a well, which spread its luxuriant dark foliage over a grave; its descending branches had struck root, and again formed new stems. This wonderfully beautiful tree was more than eighty feet in circumference, and forms such a thick and extensive arbour, that several hundred persons can take shelter under it. On the road to Barota, we passed the little town of Sompath, which lies on hills eighty feet high, which are formed of the débris of decayed buildings, and we saw on every side the ruins of mosques and caravansaries, among which we could recognise the grand style and the beautiful arches of the gates and cupolas. The nearer we approached Delhi, the more numerous were the ruins; we were especially struck with the picturesque appearance of a mosque, close by the road leading to Near-Allipur, which was most gracefully interwoven and encircled with the roots and branches of a banyan tree.

END OF THE FIRST VOLUME.

TRAVELS IN INDIA, INCLUDING SINDE AND THE PUNJAB

TRAVELS IN INDIA,

INCLUDING

SINDE AND THE PUNJAB

BY

CAPTAIN LEOPOLD VON ORLICH.

TRANSLATED FROM THE GERMAN,
BY

H. EVANS LLOYD, ESQ

IN TWO VOLUMES.

VOL. II.

GYAN

Published by

GYAN

Gyan Publishing House
5, Ansari Road
Daryaganj, New Delhi-110002
Phone: 011-47034999, 9811692060
E-mail: books@gyanbooks.com

Distribution Network
gyanbooks.com
India, USA, Canada, UK, Australia, France

ISBN : 978-81-212-4148-9 (Set)
ISBN : 978-81-212-4720-7 (HB)
First Published, London, 1845

2nd Impression 2020

Printed at: Gyan Press, Delhi.

Travels in India, including Sinde and the Punjab
Author: Captain Leopold Von Orlich

CONTENTS

OF

THE SECOND VOLUME.

LETTER VIII.

ADDRESSED TO ALEXANDER VON HUMBOLDT.

LETTER IX.

ADDRESSED TO CARL RITTER.

LETTER X.

ADDRESSED TO ALEXANDER VON HUMBOLDT.

LETTER XI.

ADDRESSED TO CARL RITTER.

LETTER XII.

ADDRESSED TO ALEXANDER VON HUMBOLDT.

LETTER XIII.

ADDRESSED TO ALEXANDER VON HUMBOLDT.

TRAVELS IN INDIA.

LETTER VIII.

TO ALEXANDER VON HUMBOLDT.

Entrance into Delhi.—Description of Delhi.—The Jamma mosque.—Arrival of several rajahs.—Their audience of the Governor General.—The Rajah of Bickaneer and the Rajah of Bhurtpoor.—Audience of the Rajahs of Bhurtpoor and of Alwar.—The feast of Moharram.—The Feroze-Cotelah.—The observatory.—The palace of Delhi or Jehun-Abad and the present king.—The peacock throne.—The Cootteb-Minar.—The tomb of Safdir.—Junge.—The Emperor Hoomaioons.—Council at the Rajah of Bickaneer.—Preparations for our departure.

Delhi, 14th February, 1843.

On a lovely morning, the 5th of February, we rode to Delhi, the ancient Indraprast'ha, the capital of the Great Moguls: we were all mounted on elephants, because, according to etiquette, the Governor General could only approach on this noble animal. Luxuriant fields of wheat, already in ear, lay extended before us, interspersed with the most fantastic ruins, the arches, domes, and columns of which rose above the thick foliage of the trees, or were covered with their branches as with a magic veil. Behind these ruins we saw the sun rise in all its glory and beauty: a sunrise more magnificent and striking I have never seen.

Near a ruined caravansary, about a mile before our camp, the chief men of Delhi, mounted on about fifty elephants, were ranged in a line close by the road side, waiting for the approach of the Governor General. It was really very imposing to see so many richly-adorned elephants, with silver houdahs, in which sat the first men of the ancient Mogul empire, richly dressed, decked with jewels, and wearing a Kashmir shawl, thrown like a toga over the right shoulder, bowing with great reverence to Lord Ellenborough, and, touching their forehead with their right hand, thus saluting us with their salam.

Accompanied by them we made our entry into the camp: on our road thither the principal persons were introduced to his Lordship. A petty Rajah, surrounded by a disorderly troop, armed with lances, guns, bows, and arrows, availed himself of this opportunity to present, on a white handkerchief in his open hand, some pieces of gold coin, in token of submission.

Our camp was pitched to the north of the city, near the cantonments. Immediately after breakfast my friend Captain West and I rode on horseback to the city—for we could not restrain our eagerness to see the celebrated Delhi, and to enjoy the first impression. A road, constructed of canear, led through the cantonments, past some handsome bungalows, to an eminence about a mile distant. Here, on the right of the road, is a bare, rocky height, the last offset of the range, descending from the ghauts, which traverses India from east to west in its whole breadth, and here gradually declines with an inclination of four hundred feet towards the Jumna. On the highest summit the flag of England is displayed on a watch-tower, from which there is one of the finest prospects that can be conceived. The road now gradually descends for about two miles to the Kashmir gate; it is skirted by beautiful villas, among which that of Mr. Macduff, lying in a fine large park, is conspicuous by its handsome colonnade.

Delhi (in 28° 40′ N. lat. and 77° 16′ E. lon.) was before the time of Sultan Mahomed Tagluk (1325—1351) called the envy of the world: it is described by the learned traveller Ibn Batuta, ere the tyrant in his anger ravaged it, as a grand and splendid city, combining both strength and beauty. He says that its walls were unequalled in the whole world — that it was the largest city of Hindostan and of Islamism in the East. It, in fact, consisted of four cities, which, joining each other, formed but one, and were surrounded by walls twenty-two feet thick. There were corn-magazines in the city, in which the grain could be preserved for a long time: rice and kodru, a kind of millet, had been known to be preserved in them, uninjured, for ninety years. The mosque was far superior in size and beauty to any other: it had previously been a temple of Boodha, which was by the Mahometans called Butkana: it had such a lofty tower, that, looking down from its summit, the people below seemed like little children. Immense stone pillars, composed of seven different pieces, stood in the court of the temple; and, without the city was a basin for rain-water, a league and a half in length, and a league in breadth, from which the inhabitants obtained water for drinking: in the vicinity of the city lay the gardens of the great men.

The present city of Delhi, built on the ruins of this decayed splendour, surrounded on the south by ruins, which cover a space of twenty square miles, is now only seven square miles in extent. It is seven miles in circumference, is surrounded by walls of red sandstone, thirty feet high, and from three to five feet thick, with a moat twenty feet broad, and has seven colossal arched gates, which are defended by round bulwarks. It is said that under the Emperor Aurengzebe there were two million inhabitants in this city; a hundred years ago half a million; but, at the present day there are not more than 250,000, of whom the Mahometans are to the Hindoos in the proportion of two to seven.

It was from the before-mentioned eminence that we had the first view of the city, above which the cupolas and elegant white marble minarets of the Jamma mosque rose into the air. As soon as we had passed the Kashmir gate the first object that struck our sight was a Protestant church; we then rode through many narrow animated streets, by the side of high garden-walls, to the silver market. It begins at the palace of the Great Mogul, is forty paces broad, and divides the city from east to west into two parts; a walled canal flows through the middle of it, and in hot weather cools and refreshes the air. Here are the richest bazars, which are the scene of the most active trade, and are constantly filled with a busy crowd. For this day we contented ourselves with a cursory glance of this little world, our visit being intended solely for the Jamma mosque, which the Mahometans consider the wonder of the world. They come from great distances to visit this temple: the Mahometan in Egypt and in Afghanistan inquires after this mosque, and congratulates him who has been so happy as to behold it.

Riding from the silver market, through a narrow street, we suddenly found the Jamma mosque before us. We were greatly struck by this magnificent work, in which the Byzantine-Arabic style is carried to the highest perfection. Shah Jehan employed on the building, several thousand men for six successive years (1631—1637). It stands upon an equilateral foundation, which is 450 feet in breadth, and 30 feet in height, and is composed of blocks of red sandstone. The mosque is situated on the west side; the three other sides are enclosed by high walls, ornamented with small turrets: from the north, east, and west, broad flights of steps lead through large gates into the court-yard, which is paved with sandstone. When you enter through the eastern gate the magnificent building faces you, in all its grandeur and beauty. It is built of white marble and red sandstone, which is inlaid, like mosaic, in lines and arabesques, or alternately with the marble in large, elegantly-carved blocks.

A massive portico, flanked by two minarets, ornamented with Arabic inscriptions from the Koran, leads to the marble halls, supported by angular columns, and, of course, under the principal cupola. At the two extreme corners rise minarets 150 feet high, between which and the principal gate two lofty domes project over the halls; ever-burning lamps adorn these halls, and in the middle of the court is a small marble basin for the ablutions of the worshippers. We were soon joined by a priest, who conducted us, by a winding staircase, to the summit of one of the minarets.

From this elevated position we had a view of the city and the boundless tract of the ruins of this Indian Rome, once graced by the mosques, palaces, pavilions, baths, gardens, and mausoleums of the emperors, their consorts, and the great men of the empire. The spirit of destruction and cruelty of Nadir Shah is impressed on this scene of desolation. This tyrant, in 1737, beheld with fiendish pleasure, from the mosque Roushen ud Doulah, the dreadful massacre perpetrated by his hordes, who, in a few hours, murdered 30,000 people, and carried off booty to the amount of 28,000,000*l*. sterling.

I retained, for a long time, the impression of

this sight, and, lost in thoughts and contemplations on that time and the present, I did not arrive at our camp till late in the afternoon. Here, on the following day, I witnessed a scene which is certainly very uncommon in India, namely, a religious discussion. A Brahmin, who had embraced the Christian religion, met with a Mahometan priest in the tent of one of our party. Both equally enthusiastic, and, penetrated with the truth of their belief, were solicitous to prove that theirs was the only true faith. Their conversation grew more and more animated; the Christian seemed superior to his opponent both in spirit and conversational powers, and was frequently so impressed with the truth of his words that he cast round a triumphant look, believing himself to be the victor: but the Mussulman would not admit the validity of his adversary's proofs; and their discussion might have degenerated into acrimony, had not the by-standers interfered. I much regretted my inability closely to follow this learned religious controversy.

My excursions were interrupted by the arrival of several Indian princes, who came from a great distance, with their court and their troops, to pay their respects to the Governor General. Their arrival was announced by salutes, such as are due to reigning princes, from the bulwarks of Delhi. We have already the Rajah of Bhurtpoor, with 5000 men; the Rao Rajah of Alwar, with 4000 men; the Rajah of Bickaneer, with 10,000 men; the Rajah of Dhoolpoor, with 5000 men; the Rajah of Shapoorah, with 600 men. The Rajah of Jeypoor would have greeted the Governor General in person, but, he imagines that he should lower himself, if he were to come to Delhi, because he considers the King of Delhi as of inferior descent, and thinks that the latter might, perhaps, fancy that the visit was intended for him.

The camps of these rajahs are all pitched on the field of ruins, and present the most singular and motley scene of Indian manners and customs. Journeys of this kind, which the princes undertake with great numbers of servants and cattle, sometimes exhaust their pecuniary resources, and they are obliged to remain stationary for several months after, or else to borrow money at high interest, whereby their subjects are afterwards the more oppressed.

The Rajah of Bickaneer appeared on the 8th of February: he was the first who came to our camp to attend the Durbar. His family, a younger branch of the house of Joudpoor, is one of the most ancient in India, and, as the Rajah informed us, was driven with its tribe, consisting of above 90,000 persons, by the Moguls from the fertile plains of the Jumna into the wilderness. His country is, indeed, 18,059 square miles in extent, but it contains only half a million of inhabitants. The revenues amount to more than thirty lacs, of which, however, only five lacs come to the Rajah's share, while the chiefs and Jaghidars receive the rest. His force consists of about 2000 cavalry, 8000 infantry, and 35 pieces of cannon.

The situation of his country, which lies on the

border, and in the interior of the great Indian desert, the nature of the soil, where water fit to drink cannot be obtained at less than 200 or 300 feet below the surface, have protected it from the incursions of the Mahrattas; but, on the other hand, the Rajah has often been brought into difficulties by his rebellious subjects, particularly by the predatory Takoors. Rajah Kour Rattan Singh had been three months upon the journey, attended by 10,000 men, of whom 2000 were armed.

The entry of his Highness had a rather antique appearance, but it was very mean. His suwars, mounted on camels, rode on before; he was carried in a richly-gilt takt-i-rawan, attended by his son and successor, his brother and nephew, twenty-two barons, twenty-two ministers and chief officers, and several hundred men armed with lances, shields, and swords. The Rajah and his attendants were all dressed in full white robes, and wore red conical turbans; they carried a shield on their backs, and sabres in their hands. Their appearance very much resembled the pictorial representations of the ancient Egyptians.

The Rajah, who, conformably with the ancient Indian etiquette, had been well instructed in the paces of the elephant, entered the tent with this heavy step, and was received by Lord Ellenborough, who shook him cordially by the hand. His Highness was free, communicative, and animated in conversation. His minister took the liberty, in describing the dominions of his sovereign, to make some witty remarks on its natural poverty and desolation, at which the Rajah smiled. "We have," said he, "neither lions nor tigers, because water is scarce, only hares and feathered game, and after a continuance of rain, wild boars; but rain is as scarce with us as gold!" His Highness left us in the course of half an hour, loaded with rich presents.

Soon afterwards the Rajah of Bhurtpoor appeared, on a handsome, splendidly adorned and painted elephant, on whose head was a golden peacock. He was preceded by his suwars on camels; then came his horses, coaches, and his palanquins; his relations, sirdars, and principal officers were mounted on elephants; his troops were partly on horseback and partly on foot. His Highness has been educated under the care of the English; he is only twenty-five years of age, tall and robust, but, he is disfigured by the small pox, and has no advantages of person; he has, however, the virtues which distinguish a good Indian prince, among which that of gratitude to his benefactors, the English government, is not wanting. This young Rajah was dressed in a long blue silk robe, trimmed with gold lace, and richly adorned with jewels; his two cousins wore green silk, and his nineteen barons and ministers were arrayed in divers-coloured garments. As the Rajah is naturally very reserved and silent, his visit was but short; the presents were brought, ottar of roses was distributed, and he took his departure.

Hindoo Row, who lives here in a very charmingly-situated villa, had also requested the favour of paying his respects to Lord Ellenborough. He was received in a particularly friendly manner, and presented with a sabre, a watch, a gold chain, and a handsome gun. After him came the Thakoor of Khurwa, who possesses a small jaghire in the province of Ajmeer, under the protection of the British, and addressed the Governor-General in the English language. Both of them left our camp highly gratified with their reception.

Colonel Sutherland, who, as resident at Ajmeer, is ambassador to most of the Rajahs now here, proposed to me that I should pay my respects to some of these princes, which of course I gratefully acceded to. It was agreed that we should first visit the Rajah of Bhurtpoor, who received me in the small circle of his court, his Highness being descended from the Juts, the cast of the peasants, has not those refined manners which generally distinguish the Indian princes, but he was exceedingly openhearted and friendly. The Rajah and his soldiers occupy a large encampment, and his own tents, which are enclosed in canvass fences, are unusually spacious. He is exceedingly interested in making preparations for an entertainment for the Governor-General, when four hundred persons are to dine in the European fashion. Though the Rajah will not himself partake of the good cheer provided for his guests, it is a remarkable phenomenon that a Hindoo prince should interest himself in such matters.

After many inquiries respecting my king, my country, and myself, the Rajah invited me to visit

Bhurtpoor and Deeg. "I will furnish you with horses and an escort," said he, "and do my utmost to provide for your entertainment; and I only regret that I cannot personally receive you in my residence." As these places are not far out of my way, and Colonel Sutherland advised me not to reject such a courteous offer, I shall hope to visit them after seeing Agra.

Unwilling to intrude any longer on his Highness' time, we took our leave and hastened to the Rajah of Alwar, who had already sent one of his relations with an escort to meet us. The Rajah received me with all honours, a salute was fired on our arrival, a guard of honour drawn up, and his little court was assembled in all its splendour. His Highness is a tall, handsome man, his fine open eye expressive of goodness and sincerity; but his beautiful teeth were unfortunately tinged red from chewing the areka. "I consider it a great honour," said he, "that you, who belong to so great a king, come from such a distance to visit me." There was something noble and princely in his address and conversation; and he was so animated and untiring in his questions that we staid nearly an hour with him.

His Highness said he was very fond of the chase, of the army, and of fine gardens, and wished I would come and amuse myself in his country, where I should have the best opportunity possible for shooting tigers, wild boars, and antelopes. The Rajah has dogs which will attack and kill a tiger, and had brought a tiger and dog with him in order to exhibit such a combat; but as this might be attended with some danger, and Lord Ellenborough is no friend to such sports, it is probable that the matter will be dropped.

For our diversion, and to make our reception complete, a very pretty and richly-dressed Bayadere entered. Her petticoat was very full and wide, and she wore ample silk pantaloons; she was covered with jewels, and her ankles were adorned with silver rings and bells; her movements were not without grace, but too uniform to attract attention for any length of time. Lastly, I was sprinkled with ottar of roses, received the betel-nut wrapped in leaves of the betel-vine, and we most cordially took leave, amid a salute of artillery, accompanied by the escort to the extremity of the camp.

As the Rajah of Alwar was invited by the Governor General to the Durbar on the following day, I resolved to join the gentlemen who rode on elephants to receive him. We met first several hundred men on camels, who every now and then fired their long guns, in token of rejoicing; then came the general of the troops, on an elephant, and after him a battalion of regular infantry. The Rajah followed on an elephant adorned with gold and silver, two fowling-pieces were placed before him in the houdah, and several hundred irregular cavalry, in every variety of dress and arms, closed the procession.

The Rajah, as soon as he saw me, waved his right hand, and very kindly saluted me with his salam, assuring me he was not a little pleased to find me among those who came to greet him. Though the Rajah has only a revenue of ten lacs, there was nearly as much splendour in his procession as in that of the Rajah of Bhurtpoor, and his suite was not inferior, for he was accompanied by thirty of his captains, officers, and ministers. The conversation between him and the Governor-General lasted full half an hour. He spoke of his journey, and of his country, and, on receiving his presents, repeatedly expressed his joy at being so liberally supplied with arms.

After him came the Rajah of Shapoorah, a branch of the house of Odeypoor, whose possessions are partly in this state and partly in the British territory; his equipage was very simple, for his revenue is only one lac; he was in a takt-i-rawan, and his attendants on foot and on horseback.

So much for the present, respecting the princes who are here. You must now accompany me on my excursions. The Mahometans are at this time celebrating the feast of Moharram, in honour of the death of Hussein and Hassan. During this festival the people indulge in amusements of every kind. In front of some shops and mosques little towers, most elegantly made of coloured paper called tabut (*i. e.* coffin), are illuminated with small lamps, which on the last day of this festival are carried in solemn procession to a piece of holy water, into which they are thrown, and, as it were, buried.

The evening is the best time for getting an

insight into the ways and manners of the people; I therefore gladly accepted the offer of Captain Bowen to ride with him on his elephant through the streets of Delhi, his surwar, mounted on a camel, trotting on before to make way for us. We proceeded to the silver market, the broad street which intersects Delhi from east to west. When we turned into it, at the extreme west end, the most interesting scene of Indian common life met our eyes. The houses in this street are of two and three stories, built of sandstone and brick. On the ground-floor are the open bazars, from which innumerable lamps diffused a light, equal to that of the finest illumination; the upper stories are the residence of the merchants, where, at the open windows, or in the balconies or verandas, the women and girls, gaily dressed, were gazing upon the multitude below.

The people passed in crowds from shop to shop; elephants and camels endeavoured carefully to make their way through this living mass;—here were the merchants praising their goods, there were handsome female figures, in their airy white garments, giving vent to their joy in laughing and jesting: bands of music were playing, while female dancers and buffoons collected a little circle around them, who expressed their admiration more by gestures than by words. A cunning fruitseller offered his hookah to every passer-by, to entice customers. Jewellers now and then opened their caskets and displayed their beautiful ornaments of gold, silver, precious stones, and pearls; for the work of the goldsmiths of Delhi, especially in filigree, are more ingenious, tasteful, and inexpensive than any where in India, and far excel those of Genoa. Paintings on ivory, portraits, as well as buildings and processions, are executed here in the greatest perfection, and would do honour even to our best artists. Not merely is the likeness admirable, but the delicacy and fidelity of the execution are very great. We rode about for a couple of hours through this busy world, and it was late in the evening before we reached the camp.

One morning I breakfasted with Captain Dyke, who has the care of the arsenal, and where I was introduced to the editor of the Delhi Gazette. His fine house possesses, like many of those inhabited by the Europeans, subterranean apartments, in which, during the prevalence of the hot winds, he is protected against the dry, sultry heat, and enjoys a temperature lower by 10°. Not far distant is the garden Shalihmar, formed by the Emperor Shah Jehan, where the mansion of the British resident is situated: at present it is uninhabited, and the extensive garden, full of the finest trees, is rather neglected.

We afterwards visited the printing office, in which there is also a lithographic press. The greater part of the men employed in this office are natives. But what especially interested me was the arsenal, which is situated on the water side: it contains 110 guns of various calibre, arms for every kind of troops, arranged with great care and taste, and two powder-magazines, in one of which there are

200 barrels of powder. Though all the magazines are perfectly adapted to their purpose, many objections might be made to such an accumulation of warlike stores in the city, at a distance of three miles from the troops.

Late in the afternoon of the same day I rode through the city, to the ruins of the palace of the Sultan Feroze, situated a few hundred steps without the south gate. On the plateau of this palace is the celebrated Feroze-Cotelah, or column. It is one of those columns which the pious Fabian speaks of, in his travels 1400 years ago, and of which there is still one in the fort at Allahabad, and three others in North Behar, one in Terai, near to the frontiers of Nepaul, the second not far from Bettiah, and the third on the river Gaudaki. They have all the same inscriptions, in the ancient Pali, or Deva-Magalhi language, and the Feroze-Cotelah has, also, inscriptions in Persian and Sanscrit. The learned James Princep succeeded in deciphering that in the Pali language. It is an edict of As-ò-ko, the Bhoodist king of all India, who lived from 325 to 288 B.C., forbidding the destruction of living animals, and enforcing the observance of Bhoodism.

The Feroze-Cotelah consists of one piece of brown granite; it is ten feet in circumference, and, gradually tapering towards the summit, rises to the height of 42 feet. It is embedded in the platform of the completely ruined palace. The sun was nearly setting when I arrived before these extensive ruins: I tied my horse to a portion of the standing wall, and clambered over ponderous arches and porticoes up to the plateau. On this spot, standing before a monument more than two thousand years old, which reminded me of three great epochs of the history of India, that of the Bhoodists, of the Brahmins, and of the Moguls, surrounded by ruins, extending further than the eye could reach, with a view of Delhi, whose minarets and domes were gilded by the setting sun, — those times and nations could not fail to rise in a magic picture before my mind.

A solemn silence reigned around; only now and then the busy hum of life, scarcely audible, fell dull and distant on the ear from Delhi; and, amid the abodes, where life and splendour once held their sway, I saw a jackal prowl about in search of food. In such solitude man feels and acknowledges more than ever how perishable and transitory are his works; how nations rise and pass away, and how the most exalted works of human invention sink into desolation. I involuntarily repeated —

> Was ist denn dauerend in der Welt zu sehen?
> Was steht denn fest, wenn Rom nicht konnte stehen?*

I reached the camp just in time to accompany some friends to the city, where the last day of the Moharram (10th of February) was to be celebrated. The houses of the principal inhabitants are open at this time to every body, and strangers are received with much pleasure. The well-lighted

* Can aught on earth's vast space e'er hope to stand,
Since Rome has sunk beneath Time's conquering hand?
TRANSLATOR.

apartments are ornamented with flowers, and laid with carpets. The master of the house, surrounded by his family, sits upon an ottoman, salutes the company as they enter; Bayaderes and musicians make their appearance, and sherbet and comfits are handed round; while visiters come in and go out at pleasure.

In the streets the people — men, women, and children, in large processions — carry and accompany the tabats, preceded by musicians, elephants, torch-bearers, and a crowd with painted paper lanterns, images, flowers, and palm-branches. Wherever the tabat passes, the people sing and shout, and fireworks are let off. This bustle continues till midnight, when perfect silence at once succeeds.

On the following morning I took a ride as usual before sunrise, and now bent my course towards the observatory, in the western part of the city. It was built in 1724, under Mahomet Shah, by his minister and favourite, Jeysingh, Rajah of Jeypoor, who was celebrated for his love of astronomy. This observatory is about two miles west of the city; it lies in the midst of many ruins; but it was never completed, and has been, unhappily, so wantonly dilapidated by the Juts that the shattered ruins alone are to be seen. However, enough remains to show the plan of this fine building: the colossal sun-dials and quadrants, which rest upon large arches, are formed of red sandstone and bricks, and the ascent to them is by handsome winding marble staircases. Besides this observatory, Jeysingh erected four others in his Rajahpoot. His astronomical tables, which he completed in 1728, he called, in honour of his imperial patron, "The Tables of Mahomet Shah."

On my return, through the Delhi gate, I met my friend Captain West, who invited me to view the palace of the Great Mogul, Captain Angelo, the commandant, having offered to show it to us. The present king is the twenty-sixth prince of his house since Timour (1413) raised his dynasty to the throne of Delhi, but whose sovereign power, in fact, ceased at the death of Aurungzebe, in 1707. When the English delivered Shah Allum, the grandfather of the present king, from the power of the Mahrattas, in 1803, he possessed nothing more than the palace and the lands around it, and an annual sum of two lacs of rupees. The British government declared that, although it was under no obligation to provide for his Majesty, it would not only leave him in possession of his palace and his family estate, but grant him an annual pension of twelve lacs, or 120,000*l*. Shah Allum, a worthy old man, who had been blinded by Gholam Khadir, enjoyed the love of the inhabitants of Delhi, and all the Mahometan princes of India manifested the same reverence for him that his powerful ancestors had possessed. He died in 1806, aged eighty-seven. Akbar Shah, his successor, died on the 28th of September, 1837, at the age of eighty-two.

The present king (whose title is Abul Mozuffer Sarajuddyn Mahomed Bahadur Shah Badsha-i-Ghazie) is the mere shadow of a prince, and has lost the affection of his people by his dissolute life and his quarrelsome temper: he is not on good terms with his family, and is constantly at variance with his ministers. A few days before our arrival, he was obliged to ask the assistance of the British residents to expel the minister of his household from his palace, which he would not leave of his own accord. He has also had some vexation, attended with public scandal, in his harem, caused by one of the keepers, who had been bought as an eunuch. The enraged king could not take vengeance on the slave-merchant, and he dared not inflict capital punishment on the pretended eunuch; the only chastisement with which he could visit him was to have him flogged, and expelled from the palace.

To the great regret of his family, the King, who is in his sixty-ninth year, contracted a new marriage a few months ago, and lately had much correspondence with Scindia, as he is very anxious that he should send him a physician who, as his Majesty expresses it, possesses the invaluable art of exciting an appetite, which may enable a person to consume twenty pounds of provisions in a day! It was still uncertain whether the Rajah of Gwalior will spare this wonderful man for any time.

Whoever wishes to wait on the King must apply to the minister of the household, and has to pay seventy or eighty rupees, for which he receives a sabre which he cannot use, and a robe of honour which he cannot wear. The King appears in public only twice a year, when he visits the Jamma mosque and the grave of Hoomaioon. He then rides on an elephant, most singularly painted and ornamented, surrounded by his ministers, the chief men of Delhi, and his suwars. Akbar Shah used sometimes to appear in this manner, smoking his hookah, which rested on the head of the elephant, and was held by the mahout. He then required, even from Europeans, that those who were in carriages should alight, those on horseback dismount, and pay their obeisance to him; but it was intimated to him, as well as to the present king, that he could make no claim to such honours.

The King's palace, which is all that remains to him of the splendour of his ancestors, was built by Shah Jehun, who reigned from 1627 to 1656. It is built on the low quartz cliffs of the right bank of the Jumna; it was commenced in 1631, and finished in ten years. An irregular quadrangle, comprising the residence of the Great Mogul, is enclosed by a wall of red sandstone, forty feet high, with small bulwarks and towers, and a deep moat, 4000 paces, or nearly 10,000 feet, in circumference. Two colossal double gates, with small fore courts, one on the west, the other on the south, lead into this little town. The eastern side is washed by the Jumna, which, however, is so far from the wall as to allow room for a small garden; the north side is separated by a canal from the old palace, which is situated on an island. It is a complete ruin; it was once used as a state prison, and is connected by a bridge with the new palace.

We saw the palace, through the kindness of Captain Angelo, who resides over the west gate. Entering by this gate, we proceeded through a high vaulted passage, which is lighted from above, and is furnished with niches on both sides; then, passing under a gateway, we entered the first court, which is 300 paces in length, and is enclosed by walls. This court is crossed from north to south by a narrow canal, which passes under the southern gate, and runs into the large moat. We traversed this court, and passed, through the large eastern portal, into a quadrangle 200 paces in breadth.

In this quadrangle is a pillared hall of white marble, within which the exterior throne is placed; the façade of the hall is formed by a double row of twenty columns, in the Arabic-Byzantine style, and the sides by eight columns. The throne itself is a marble seat, the back of which is adorned with arabesques in Florentine mosaic, amongst which an Orpheus, of precious stones, immediately above the throne, attracted our special attention. It is a picture eight feet high, and appears to be a copy of some celebrated master-piece of the Italian school. Before this throne the Great Moguls used to give audience to ambassadors and the principal men of the empire, who, upon such occasion, were always commanded to appear on elephants. The elephants had to march in a particular order, and were drawn up behind a barrier, where there was room for about 200 elephants.

From this court we passed, through a small door on the north side, into another court, which was paved with white marble, and led to the Dewan

Khas, the chief hall of audience: this hall is also of white marble, and the vaulted ceiling is supported by thirty-two marble pillars in double files. In the centre of the Dewan Khas once stood the celebrated peacock throne: it was composed of massive plates of gold, covered with diamonds, rubies, emeralds, and pearls; on either side was placed a golden peacock, whose expanded tails were composed of jewels; and above this most splendid throne in the world was a parrot, as large as life, cut out of a single emerald. Tavernier, the jeweller, who saw the throne immediately after it was completed, valued it at six millions and a half sterling. Timour the Tartar carried off the most precious of the stones, a ruby of extraordinary size and beauty, and all the other jewels were taken by Nadir Shah to Persia. At present there is only a simple seat, standing on a high base; thin plates of gold, adorned with worthless stones and pearls, cover this throne, above which there is a canopy supported by silver pillars. On the sides are inscribed, in Arabic characters, the following words: "If a paradise ever existed on earth, it is here, it is here, it is here!"

Three very elegantly-wrought latticed marble windows look out upon the Jumna: in the centre window there is an opening, at which the Great Moguls used to sit, and from which they alone had the privilege of enjoying the prospect over the fertile valley below.

The marble palaces of the king and of his wives, lie along the river, to the south of the Dewan Khas; and the residences of the princes, the baths and the gardens, and a small mosque, lie to the north. All these buildings are of white marble, and are inlaid with mosaic, composed of precious stones: the whole presents a combination of splendour and elegance; the manifold variety of patterns on the pillars, balconies, and halls display the most admirable skill and taste; several parts are, however, so decayed that some of the apartments and baths cannot be used. The garden too, in the centre of which are a basin and several fountains, has been deprived of all its original beauty by tasteless additions and alterations.

Before the entrance to the residence of the Great Mogul a pair of scales are suspended over a stone seat, to indicate that justice alone is administered in these apartments. As we entered the halls which lead to the king's apartments we saw a rhapsodist, who was sitting before the bedchamber of the Great Mogul, and relating tales in a loud voice. A simple curtain was hung between him and the king, who was lying on a couch, and whom these tales were to lull to sleep. We descended by a flight of steps into the garden, which lies on the banks of the Jumna, and is adorned by every variety of flowers, and some large tamarind and banyan trees; doves also are kept here for the special amusement of the aged king, who enjoys the pleasure of an excursion on the Jumna (which is here 900 feet in breadth) every morning and evening.

We concluded our interesting inspection of this remarkable palace by visiting the residence of Captain Angelo. We ascended the tower, which rises above it, whence we enjoyed a complete panorama of Delhi and its environs, with a view of the Chunderi Choak. The Jamma mosque glittered high above the dense mass of houses, and beyond it lay a boundless barren tract, covered with innumerable ruins; to the north were several villages interspersed with green corn-fields, and the cantonments surrounded by a small grove, while the view over the valley of the Jumna was perfectly enchanting. The palace itself, in which nearly 7000 persons dwell, has indeed a magnificent appearance, but the impression is sadly marred by numerous clay huts which are erected on the outer side of the courts.

One of the greatest curiosities of Delhi is the Coottub-Minar, which is fifteen miles from the city, and is a conspicuous object at a great distance. This celebrated pillar was erected in 1193 by Coottub-ud-Deen, the founder of the Ghoorides, who overthrew the throne of the Brahmins in Delhi, in commemoration of the triumph of Mahometanism over Brahminism.

I was of course anxious to obtain a closer view of this monument, and accordingly started from our camp at daybreak on the 13th, accompanied by a camel suwar. The morning was bright and cool, the thermometer being only at 49° Fahrenheit before sunrise. I rode round the west side of the city, past the camp of the Rajahs, and then traversed the tract of ruins and desolation in their entire extent, the Coottub-Minar rising nobly in the back-ground.

I halted at the mausoleum of Sefdar Jung, in order to view this handsome monument, which contains the mortal remains of a near relation of the royal house of Oude. The sepulchre is built of white marble and red sandstone, placed in alternate parallel perpendicular stripes; it consists of a large dome, surrounded by arcades, in the centre of which is an octagon: here the marble sarcophagus containing the corpse is placed; the whole is covered with a second story, which projects and covers the splendid coffin. The cornices of the building beyond the platform are ornamented with small towers, the domes of which are supported by angular pillars, and finished with delicate minarets. The garden is pretty well kept up, and was full of beautiful aromatic flowers; but the basins and the fountains, which once jetted their cool waters into the air, have fallen into decay.

The sun was just rising when I stood on one of the highest towers, with the garden and its rich pastures at my feet; wild peacocks were sporting amid the flower-beds, and beyond the garden lay an endless succession of ruins, with Delhi in the back-ground. Profound and solemn repose rested over this quiet and solitary scene, which seemed formed by nature for the resting-place of the mortal remains of man; but it is to be lamented that the living pay so little respect to the memory of the dead, and deny them this repose. Every where the finest monuments exhibit traces of sacrilege, and this sacrilege is not committed by the Hindoos, but by the Mahometans themselves, who perpetrate the greatest ravages, and do not show the slightest regard to the memory of their ancestors; indeed they leave it to the English to protect and repair their mosques, tombs, and palaces.

About eight o'clock I stood before the lofty Coottub-Minar: it is built of very fine, hard red sandstone, is 62 feet in diameter at the base, and rises to the height of 265 feet; it is divided into three stories, and the upper gallery is elevated 242 feet 6 inches above the ground. This column, which is the highest in the world, was intended by Coottub-ud-Deen to mark the entrance to a mosque which he purposed building. The lower story is about 90 feet high, and is built in alternate angular and concave channelings, on which sentences from the Koran are inscribed in raised Arabic characters; the other two stories consist of concave flutings only, and diminish gradually to the summit. The whole is crowned by a small dome, which is supported by eight square pillars: this dome was shattered by an earthquake in the year 1803, but has been restored by the English in its original form.

The column stands in the midst of some very ancient Bhoodist and Hindoo buildings and Mahometan ruins. The colossal gates and columns, and the bold vaults of the former, still indicate an age of great prosperity, which intended to immortalise its faith and its history by the grandest works of art. On the cornices are sculptures, representing the processions of their kings, similar to those of the princes of our times. The pilasters are ornamented with elephants' heads; and a careful observer might here trace some isolated moments of the history of an age long since past, and of which so little is known. A longer stay than I was enabled to make is however indispensable to an investigation of this kind, and I was forced to content myself with a cursory view. In one of the courts is an ancient iron pillar thirty feet high, with Sanscrit and Arabic inscriptions, on which the tyrant Nadir Shah, in a passion, struck a violent blow with a hatchet, the mark of which still remains.

After I had spent some hours among these remarkable ruins, my guide conducted me, by a winding staircase of 383 steps, to the summit of the Coottub-Minar, which is surrounded by an iron gallery. But how shall I describe the prospect that now lay before me, for all that I had hitherto seen of Delhi and its environs in distinct portions now appeared in one grand panorama. There lay the ruins of palaces, villas, mosques, sepulchres, caravansaries, and gardens of bygone ages, among the remains of which 160 cupolas and towers may still be distinguished! Delhi, with its dazzling white marble domes and minarets, and the river Jumna flowing in the verdant valley, bounded the sombre picture. I sat for a full hour gazing on the scene where there is so much to engage the mind of man, and where thousands of years speak the language of warning and instruction. My guide, a handsome Hindoo, stood as lost in contemplation as myself, and at length interrupted the solemn silence, by saying, " Sahib, here nothing is durable; much tribulation and little joy: the living thought only of reposing after death in splendid sepulchres, and their descendants have thought only of destroying what was intended for eternity."

I arrived at our camp just in time to witness some interesting Durbars held by the Governor General. Two pieces of cannon and a battalion of infantry were stationed as usual in the principal street to do honour to the princes on their entry. The first who appeared was the Rajah of Dhoolpoor Bary; he was attended by a train resembling that of the Rajah of Bhurtpoor, and like him is a Jut prince, but he has a revenue of only five or six lacs. He was accompanied by his only son, an infant of eighteen months, and twenty-six sirdars and ministers. After him the nobles of Delhi arrived on elephants and in palanquins; among them were ancient ministers of the Great Moguls, some sirdars, and the principal bankers: most of them were very aged men, and so infirm that they were obliged to be supported by their sons. They paid their respects severally, bowing very low, and were presented with gold chains, strings of pearls, or shawls, and received ottar of roses and betel-nut.

The most interesting ceremony of the day was the investiture of the new Rajah of Jhytpoor, a tall, handsome man, in the prime of life. He was to be invested with the little principality of that name in Bundlecund, because the late Rajah had rebelled against the English, and fled, and was subsequently deposed. When called to the throne he was in extreme poverty, and some friends had even lent him elephants and suwars for to-day's ceremony. He listened with great attention to the document of this investiture, which was read to him by a Baboo in the presence of the Governor-General. At the moment when he affixed it to his turban, as a sign that he would engage to perform what it required of him, the first gun was fired, announcing his new dignity, and the band struck up "God save the Queen." A valuable sabre, shield, and armlets were presented to him, and a pearl chain was hung about his neck. This investiture with the princely dignity, or rather this creation of an Indian Rajah, was equally novel and solemn, and seemed to make a considerable impression on the new sovereign.

The last day which I spent at Delhi (the 14th of February) I went with Colonel Ashburnham, on a fine bright morning, to visit the tomb of the Emperor Hoomaioon. It is the mausoleum of the father of Akbar the Great, and lies five miles to the south of the city. We proceeded along a dusty road, bordered with acacias, past the Feroze-Cotelah, to the old fort: nothing remains of this but a decayed mosque and the ruins of the walls, which were forty feet high, and have projecting round towers: several small mean huts have been erected by the peasants within these walls.

Proceeding two miles beyond the fort, we reached the tomb of Hoomaioon, which lies on the left side of the road, at the entrance of a village; it is the largest and handsomest of the sepulchral monuments of Delhi. A tall gate of red sandstone leads to the garden, in the centre of which this immense building is situated. There are but few traces of the choice flowers formerly cultivated here, or of the fountains which used to cool the air.

The mausoleum is built of red sandstone and white marble, and is two stories high, with a large, lofty, vaulted hall, and many niches in the lower story and in several apartments of the upper story. The exterior of this magnificent edifice is adorned with domes, supported by square pillars, with arabesques and sculptures. Here, too, the Byzantine-Arabic style prevails, though the arches and vaulted roofs approximate to the Moorish. The sarcophagi of the emperor and his consort are of white marble, with arabesques and Arabic inscriptions, and stand in the centre of the large hall; those of his family are in the smaller apartments, and some of his ministers have had the honour of being allowed to have their mortal remains deposited on the outer platform of the building.

Hoomaioon's tomb is on a small eminence, commanding the surrounding country. We walked a long time about the decayed, desolate apartments, and were much pleased with the prospect from one of the niches, comprising, in the foreground, the tract covered with ruins, and beyond it the remarkable city, washed by the broad stream of the Jumna. Some hundred paces from this mausoleum, overshadowed by tamarind and fig trees, are the marble tombs of several saints, of which that of

Nizam-ud-Deen is the most remarkable, and is especially distinguished by its very elegant arabesques and filagree work, executed in beautiful white marble.

Several fakirs and idlers had taken up their abode near these tombs: some did not suffer themselves to be disturbed in their devotions, while others came forward and offered themselves as guides. There is a walled tank fifty feet deep, in which the boys of the neighbouring villages exhibit their skill in diving. On our arrival they begged us to throw a piece of money into the pond, into which they plunged, head-foremost, and in a few moments brought it up again out of the dirty water.

Soon after our return to the camp, the Governor General went to visit the Rajah of Bickanree, and we joined in his suite. As the Rajah had encamped several miles to the west, our elephants were sent on before, and we drove to the place of meeting. When we had passed the cantonments, and were climbing over the bare, rocky eminence, we were shown the place where Shamshoudin, Nawab of Ferozpoor, caused the universally esteemed Mr. Frazer to be murdered, fifteen years before, by hired assassins. Whether jealousy was the cause of this crime, as some affirm, or whether it arose from Frazer's having often very seriously and imperatively warned the Nawab to refrain from unjust proceedings, is not ascertained: however, Shamshoudin and his accomplices were brought to trial, and the great nobles of Delhi witnessed the unheard of event, of seeing the Nawab, with the assassins, hanged on the city walls. Shamshoudin's own brother is said to have passed sentence of death upon him, declaring that his brother deserved no better fate, because he had committed to others the vengeance which it was his duty to have executed himself.

The nearer we approached the Rajah's camp, the more animated the road became ; at a short distance before it the Rajah, borne in a takt-i-rawan, surrounded by his nobles and many of his people, came to meet the Governor General, and a salute of artillery announced the moment of their meeting. There was something very original and wild in this reception, for the Rajah being carried in a takt-i-rawan, while we were mounted upon elephants, his bearers were obliged to exert themselves to the utmost to keep up with Lord Ellenborough; and the crowding, running, and shouting of innumerable Suwars and servants, presented a most novel scene.

We alighted from our elephants before the canopy of the reception tent; beautiful carpets covered the ground, and various draperies adorned the large tent. We sat in arm-chairs on the right hand of the Rajah, and his nobles on the left. The presents intended for the Governor General were brought at the commencement of the conversation; they consisted of shawls, silks, and jewels—very rich gifts from so poor a prince. After this, several Bayaderes came in, accompanied by a dancer, the first man whom I have seen dance in India. They wore the usual dress of these women: their ornaments were very valuable; and their dance, though rather graceful, was, however, a very monotonous and springing movement: the man was by no means attractive, and his leaps approached the burlesque. While his Highness presented Lord Ellenborough with the ottar of roses and betel nut, his brother, with much ceremony, did us the same honour. We took leave at sunset; and our return home was rendered extremely unpleasant by thick clouds of dust, which so completely enveloped us, that we could not distinguish each other, and our elephants, in order to refresh themselves, kept constantly sprinkling their bodies with water, of which we received a due share.

The preparations for my departure to Agra now occupy every spare moment, so that I can only send you a few particulars respecting the temperature. I have attempted here, according to Boussingault's method, to ascertain the mean temperature of Delhi, and, with all precautions to prevent the pressure of external air, bored a hole eighteen inches deep in the ground, into which I sunk the thermometer. At the expiration of half an hour, the mercury was at 67½° Fahrenheit, which seems to testify in favour of the correctness of Boussingault's assertion. I intend to repeat this experiment at Calcutta, which is much nearer to the tropic. During the last fortnight of my residence here, the mercury has risen very regularly nearly one degree every day: for, on the 4th February we had in the morning 48°, at noon 75°, and in the evening 64° Fahrenheit; whereas, on the 15th, it was in the morning 56°, at noon 80½°, and in the evening 71°.

LETTER IX.

TO CARL RITTER.

Journey in a palanquin to Agra.— The scenery between Delhi and Agra.—Description of Agra.— The Tauje Mahal.— The tomb of Etimaud-ud-Dowlah.— The gardens on the Jumna, and the Ram Baugh.— The fort of Agra, or Acberabad.— The Mootee Mosque.— Secundra. The tomb of Akbar the Great.— The orphan asylum.— The police in the district of Agra.—Marriages, and marriage customs of the Indians.— Journey to Futtihpoor. —Sikra.—The runis of the palace of Akbar the Great.— History of Bhurtpoor.— The city and our reception there. — Chase of antelopes with leopards.—Journey to Deeg and Mathura.—Return to Agra.

Agra, 21st February, 1843.

You have accompanied me in my wanderings to the moment when returning from the camp of the Rajah at Bickanree: I was obliged to break off in my letter from Delhi to make preparations to continue my journey. The many proofs of kindness and friendship which I received from all quarters made it painful to take leave of such dear friends; but it is a happy feature in the character of the Englishman, that he preserves an attachment, which he has once conceived, during his whole life. To his practical good sense, his desire to acquire solid knowledge, and his elevated moral standard, England is indebted for her greatness and her power. I have never seen these virtues so predominant as in this country.

The more I learn of England's mode of government here, the more I am compelled to admire the talent of the English for colonisation. It is an error to suppose that the British power in India has attained its meridian height; on the contrary, there are every where indications of a further development, founded on duration and stability; but it may be affirmed, with equal confidence, that this immense empire is very far from having attained its concentrated form, and reached its extreme boundary. It is not in the power of the English to say, So far we will go, and no further—the necessity of securing their own existence will compel them to make the Indus, or rather the Soliman mountains and the chain of the Himalaya, their boundary, and entirely to subdue the kingdoms in the interior.

Want of nationality among the Indians, the despotic government of their princes, and the degenerate morals of their courts, will favour the attainment of this end, and the more gradually it is done, the less will be the sacrifices and the more inconsiderable the dangers.

As travelling in India when the hot winds blow, is dangerous to the health, and attended with great privations, I was obliged to hasten, in order to reach Calcutta before that season set in: I therefore, sold my horses, tents, and other effects here, discharged my servants, and resolved to travel by dawk.* This is the usual mode of travelling in India; but this seems the more inconceivable, because there is a road from this city to Calcutta which may compete with the best in Europe. With some sacrifices on the part of the government, it would be easy to establish a waggon post, drawn by oxen or horses; it is alleged, however, that for some years it would be used only by the English, the natives being very unwilling to deviate from the customs which have prevailed from the most ancient times. Thus, then, persons and letters, with the exception of short distances, are forwarded only by men.

On these dawk roads, are small houses (dawk bungalows) at intervals of every twenty miles, in which the traveller, for a rupee per day, finds accommodation and attendance, and may refresh himself with a bath; but some necessaries, such as tea, sugar, wine, and bread, he must take with him in his palanquin. As there are no inns whatever, the traveller in India is compelled to have recourse to the hospitality of the English, which, in truth, cannot have been exercised to a greater extent in the earliest times of our ancestors than it is here in the present day. Every where, even without letters of recommendation, you find the most hearty welcome, and the most hospitable reception. The longer the guest is pleased to remain, the greater is the satisfaction which he gives to his host.

* Dawk, pronounced dork, is the name given to travelling in a palanquin. The Indian government has now had palanquin carriages made, which are drawn by men.

Yet I have often thought, however unwillingly it might be owned, that it must be a great burden upon those who are particularly noted for their hospitality.

I had engaged eight bearers to carry my palanquin, and six for the doolee of my attendant Werner. Besides these, I had four Banghybürdars (men who are each obliged to carry forty-pound weight, in small wooden or tin boxes, called Petaros, with the help of a long bamboo cane, resting on the shoulder,) and two Massalchies or torch-bearers. For my journey to Agra, 137 miles, I had to pay 140 rupees, which is equal to the expense of travelling post with six horses in our country.

On the 15th, at 3 o'clock in the afternoon, I left our camp, attended with the good wishes and blessings of all my friends. There are two roads to Agra, the shortest, which is the worst, by way of Mathura, and the better one by way of Alighur. I, of course, chose the latter: my bearers carried me at a rapid pace, through the Cashmire gate, and past the palace, immediately behind which a bridge of boats, which is taken up in the rainy season, is laid across the Jumna. After crossing this bridge, we proceeded a full mile when we reached a road bordered with trees. This road is made of Cancar, a compost of gravel, loom, and clay, which is found in most parts of India, from three to four feet below the surface of the ground; it gradually becomes hard, and is the best material that can be employed for this purpose. From

TRAVELLING IN A PALANQUIN.

Agra to Delhi there are twelve stages, the longest fourteen, the shortest ten miles. An express acquaints the post-masters beforehand of the approach of travellers, so that the new bearers are always found ready. I was, however, advised not to give any gratuity when the palanquin was set down to change the bearers: this is said to be the best means of preventing a delay; for if any such occurs, the traveller must pay the bearers at all the following stages for their lost time.

The country between Delhi and Agra is perfectly level, and for the most part cultivated: at this time the sight of luxuriant fields of wheat and barley, was very refreshing to the eye, and an unclouded sky with bright moonlight favoured my journey. When we met with any travellers we saluted each other, calling out *Ram, ram!* and whenever we approached a new stage all the bearers set up a shrill cry to announce that they were coming. After the usual salutations, and a few questions, the bearers, panting and blowing, proceeded rapidly: the torch-bearer runs by the side, occasionally feeding his cotton torch with oil, which he carries with him in a wooden bottle, or a bamboo cane, and the oldest of this indefatigable crew, on taking leave, adds a petition for money; "*Sahib, bakshich*" (sir, a present, a gift), is the petition reiterated at every stage.

It may be easily conceived that travelling in a palanquin is most disagreeable, however luxurious it may appear to be. At the little town of Alighur, which is surrounded by a wall, and in the middle of which rise the minarets and cupolas of a mosque, I took some refreshments in the bungalow. Pipul, tamarinds, and Neem trees, and the gardens of the bungalows, to the north of the place, give a picturesque appearance to the flat country. After stopping for nearly an hour, I was again on my journey; the landscape was every where the same; a level ground, the uniformity of which was only broken by groups of fine trees. Some miles from Agra there is another bridge of boats, leading to the right bank of the Jumna, and at six in the morning of the 17th of February, I was in the bungalow of Mr. Riddle; I had therefore travelled this long distance, carried by men, in thirty-nine hours, being nearly three miles and a half an hour.

Before I give you an account of my proceedings here, permit me, in the first place, to prefix a general sketch of the former residence of Akbar the Great. Agra is built on the right bank of the Jumna, which here makes a bend towards the west, in 27° 12′ N. L. and 78° 17′ E. L. from Greenwich: viewed from the river-side it presents a very picturesque appearance, and towards the fort itself it has an imposing effect. Low, calcareous hills form a semicircle round the town: on the south side are the bungalows and barracks of the military; on the opposite side those of the civil officers, and the government buildings. The numerous gardens in which banyan trees, fig trees, tamarinds, mimosas, and acacias, with their various foliage, form a thick shade, and the roads planted with trees, which traverse the cantonments round the town, give the whole place the appearance of a tract covered with small groves.

The city itself, which numbers 65,250 inhabitants, (of whom 47,300 are Hindoos, and 17,950 are Mahometans,) and 10,000 troops with their servants, is four miles in length and three in breadth. The houses are for the most part built of red sandstone, some are painted white, and others of various colours, and are three or four stories high. A handsome broad street, paved with flags, crosses the city from north to south, beginning at the fort, and ending at the Mathura gate; the other streets are narrow indeed, but they possess the unwonted luxury of being very clean. The bazars, most of which are only eight feet wide, are in the principal street, and here is constantly a busy crowd, and much bustle from morning till night, just as in the Chandrie Choak in Delhi.

The trade, however, is not so great as it appears to be; the inhabitants are in general poor, and only a few merchants and bankers carry on a more extensive business. The merchants reside chiefly on the banks of the Jumna near the custom house, where there are considerable magazines of cotton and salt: the latter article is not allowed to be manufactured on the left bank of the Jumna, and the duty on it produces nearly six lacs every year, whereas the duty on cotton, most of which comes from Gwalior, Jeypoor, and Bhurtpoor, produces scarcely three lacs, nay, in 1839–40 only one lac and 300 rupees. The total revenue of the custom house is between nine and ten lacs annually. Agra carries on also a pretty considerable trade in kalabatum, a kind of gold lace, which is much in favour with the Indians.

The gardens of the bungalows, some of which are laid out with much care and taste, are a great ornament to the environs; but as they must be kept constantly watered, it is difficult to preserve the flowers in perfection: and a team of oxen required for this purpose, costs twelve rupees per month. Good water, too, is scarce, that of most of the wells being brackish. In the time of the hot winds from April to the end of June, the climate is almost intolerable to Europeans; as soon, however, as the rainy season sets in, the air becomes more pleasant; and in October, when refreshing dew or mist rises in the morning, the colder season gradually comes on. All nature then appears in the most luxuriant splendour and freshness; the country is adorned with the most lovely verdure, and the most beautiful flowers, and the air is filled with the balsamic perfume of roses, violets, and myrtles. In this season, when the deep azure sky is always clear and serene, the European feels himself inspired with new life and vigour; and in December, when friends assemble in social converse in the evening around the fire, they are more than ever reminded of their native land.

My first excursion was to the Tauje Mahal, or the Diamond of Seraglios, the most beautiful edifice in India. It is situated a mile to the south of the city, close to the Jumna, and was built by the emperor Shah Jehan, in honour of his beloved consort Mumtaz Mahal. Mumtaz Mahal is indebted to her virtue and to her beauty, for this splendid monument; for when she died at the birth of her only child, the emperor vowed that he would erect a monument to her which should proclaim to all ages his devoted affection, and her incomparable renown.

We rode along the bank of the river by a road made during the famine in 1838, and passed the ruins of the palaces in which the nobles resided during the reign of Akbar the Great. Here are walls so colossal and solid, that they are preserved in spite of all the violence which they have suffered: we saw pieces ten feet thick united by a cement which nothing but gunpowder can break up.

We perceived at a considerable distance this diamond of the buildings of the world, which from the dazzling whiteness of the marble, of which this magnificent sepulchre is built, looks like an enchanted castle of burnished silver. It is a lofty dome, surrounded by four minarets 120 feet in height, and of such admirable workmanship, that the whole is in perfect preservation; except that a few crevices were caused by the earthquake in 1803, which have, however, been carefully filled up with cement. We entered on the east side through a lofty vaulted gate, adorned with mosaics, into the exterior court, which is enclosed by a high wall of red sandstone with four bronze doors: the four corners are flanked by bastions, which serve as the bases of octagon buildings, which are crowned by lofty domes supported by angular pillars. Here were the dwellings of the keepers, and the apartments assigned to the reception of travellers who visited this wonderful edifice. On the south side is a second gate, still more beautiful and massive, and leading to the garden, which is enclosed by high walls.

An avenue of ancient cypresses, between which are marble basins, fountains, and flower-beds, leads in a direct line to a broad flight of marble steps; by this we ascended to a spacious platform; above which rises the noble dome, with its elegant slender minarets. The garden is always filled with fragrant flowers, and is intended to represent eternal spring; and the wanderer finds protection against the scorching rays of the sun, under the shade of the tamarinds, banyan, fig, and mango trees.

The Tauje Mahal forms an octagon which supports a cupola seventy feet in diameter, adorned with arabesques and garlands of flowers, in the style of Florentine mosaic. The interior consists of an immense vault, which is lighted from above, by marble windows of lattice work, and is surrounded on the four principal sides by as many vaulted vestibules. It is covered with mosaic of the most splendid precious stones, which, conformably to the idea of paradise in the Koran, ornaments the walls like an arbour of the most tasteful and manifold festoons of flowers and fruits of every kind; even sounds, as they gradually die away in these magic halls, resemble the music of an expiring echo. In one of the most beautiful of these flowers there are seventy-two precious stones: in the mosaic, twelve kinds of stone are chiefly employed; among which are lapis lazuli, agate, cornelian, blood-red jasper, chalcedony, sardonyx, &c. The first, not found in India, is said to have been brought from Tibet.

The hallowed corpse, enclosed in a plain marble sarcophagus, lies in the lower vaults, and the state sarcophagus, ornamented with the richest mosaic work, with Arabic inscriptions, stands in the centre of the great hall, protected by a marble grating. We do not know who was the architect of this building of magic beauty; but there is much reason to suppose that an Italian was placed by Shah Jehan at the head of the undertaking, and was loaded by him with great honours. Perhaps he was one of those who are buried in the Roman Catholic cemetery, and who, according to the date on the tombstone, lived here at that time. Eleven years were employed in building it, and many more were required for finishing the ornamental parts. All the provinces of the empire contributed, and vied with each other in sending valuable gifts for its adornment. The revenues of thirty towns were assigned to keep the mausoleum in repair; and if there were any surplus the half was given away in alms, and the other deposited in the vault as a treasure. A choir of priests presented the daily offerings; singers and musicians were appointed for the service of the mosque, and it was committed to the care of a noble guard.

The Emperor Jehan intended to build a similar sepulchre, called Mathob Baugh, for himself, on the opposite side of the Jumna, and to connect both by a splendid marble bridge. He had already commenced the building, ruins of which are still to be seen, when a rebellion broke out, and he was deposed at an advanced age by his own son, Aurengzebe. His remains are deposited near those of his consort, in an equally costly and beautiful marble sarcophagus.

From the left side of the principal entrance, sacrilegious hands had stolen a few of the most valuable stones out of the mosaic; but the British government has had the place repaired under the direction of Captain Boileau, and paid 3000 rupees for the restoration of these few arabesques! Keepers and gardeners are now appointed, and on Sundays the fountains play, and hundreds of people visit the spot. The minarets stand detached at each corner, scarcely twenty paces from the main building. They have within, a winding staircase of 162 steps, which leads to the very summit. The eastern and western sides of the platform, which rises fifty feet above the Jumna, and is paved with black and white marble, are occupied by extensive buildings of red sandstone, ornamented with mosaic, and consisting of open-vaulted arcades: the north side is washed by the Jumna, which is 500 paces broad at this place.

The finest prospect is from the upper gallery of the south-east minaret, and from that point I have seen not only the rising and setting of the sun, but also this fairy palace illuminated by the bright light of the moon. At these times, the most solemn silence prevails: the air is more filled than ever with the aromatic perfume of the flowers, and a magic glow is shed over the wondrous building. The Jumna meanders, like a stream of silver, through the verdant landscape; the ruins of palaces and sepulchres cast a mysterious shade; and Agra, with its minarets and elegant marble palaces in the boldly rising citadel, seems to be shrouded in a mystic veil, under which the numerous lights of the strand and the bazars sparkle like little stars. But such solemnity, such profound melancholy is diffused over this scene, that it seems as if man could not attain unmixed happiness, or enjoy the pleasures of the present moment.

The wish of the Indians to be honourably remembered by their descendants is so strong a passion among them, that they wholly forget the duties of the present; the Mussulman endeavours to immortalise himself in colossal mausoleums and caravansaries; and the Hindoo in pagodas and handsome walled tanks. Namkiwasty (*nam*, reputation, name; *ki*, for; *wasty*, object) is a phrase familiar to every ear, and to know that a name will be transmitted to an age when the person has long fallen into oblivion, is often the business and the aim of a whole life! Even some Europeans who have spent and ended their lives in India, have been imbued with this pardonable vanity, or their heirs have thought it their duty to erect such a memorial to them. As an illustration of this, my friend took me to the Roman Catholic cemetery, on the north side of the city, where a Dutchman, named William Hessings, has had a monument of red sandstone, on the model of the Tauje Mahal, erected to his memory by his heirs; but the minarets are wanting. A short sketch of this remarkable man, in the English language, is inscribed on the sarcophagus, which states that he came to India as a common soldier, in his twentieth year, experienced a great variety of fortunes, and concluded his active life as an officer of rank in the service of Scindia. On this side, the city is bounded by a bare, sandy tract, covered with ruins: it is a melancholy, undulating spot, animated only by the gentle stream of the Jumna.

As Agra abounds in remarkable mosques and gardens, I will mention some of the finest in the immediate vicinity. The great men in the times of Akbar and Jehangeer had their palaces, gardens, and sepulchres on the banks of the Jumna: here we see ruins upon ruins, and some remains in a tolerable state of preservation. Immediately beyond the bridge of boats which crosses the Jumna, near the Custom-house, is the tomb of Etimadaula ud Dowlah, in the centre of a garden; he was probably one of the principal men in the court of Akbar. The whole is surrounded by a lofty wall; the entrance is by a magnificent gateway, with small cupolas and alcoves, and similar gigantic portals and erections are in the centre of the northern and southern walls. Basins and fountains formerly cooled the air, and nourished the beds of flowers; but they are now fallen into total decay: rude hands have unhappily stripped the sepulchre of its finest ornaments; for it was built of white marble with the most costly mosaic, and was as beautiful a gem in miniature, as the Tauje Mahal is on a large scale: purity and elegance of style, and delicacy of execution, are seen in the highest perfection. It is likewise an octagon, and contains one large and several smaller apartments, in which many marble sarcophagi are deposited. After long legal proceedings, the British government has lately come into possession of this monument, and workmen were at this time employed in clearing away the rubbish, and putting the garden in order.

Not far from it, and also on the left bank of the Jumna, lies Ram Bagh, one of those charming country seats, in which the great men of Akbar's time passed the hot season on the refreshing banks of the river. It is a very extensive garden, distinguished from all the others by the great variety and beauty of the flowers, and by its fine orange and tamarind trees. The British civil officers are accustomed to reside here for several days after the rainy season, to enjoy, in solitude and quiet, the charms of nature in the picturesque environs of the Jumna.

The fort of Agra, or Akbarabad, is of the time of the Moguls, and one of the greatest architectural works of India. Though it would not be able long to resist the battering cannon of our days, it is undoubtedly the most solid, and the most judiciously constructed fortress of those times. I have viewed it frequently, and have spent an afternoon in examining every part of its interesting details. It is a mile in extent, and is built entirely of red sandstone, with a double wall, the exterior one towards the river being eighty feet high, and the whole is surrounded with small bulwarks, and a moat twenty feet broad.

The interior consists of three courts with galleries, porticoes and towers. The first court has vaulted colonnades, which serve as a shady retreat for the imperial guard, running all round; the second, furnished with similar arcades, was for the ministers, omrahs, and superior civil officers; and is now occupied by the magazines of the English, and a company of sepoys, who constantly keep guard. In the third court, towards the Jumna, are the marble palaces of the emperor and of his son, the baths, the harem, a mosque, the palm groves, and the flower gardens. With the exception of the last-named building, which is of red-sandstone, all are of the most beautiful white marble, the cupolas gilt, or covered with blue enamel.

The apartments of the emperor are small, it is true, but they are extremely airy and pleasant: verandas supported by elegant pillars, and windows with marble lattices, are on the side next the river. One of these delightful balconies, which is in the form of a bow, and is covered with a cupola, supported by pillars, is said to have been a favourite spot of Akbar and his son Jehangeer; for here there is a prospect over the extensive landscape, watered by the Jumna, and of the beautiful Tauje Mahal in all its splendour. At a short distance from this is an open spot, and on the side, two open terraces, where the troops used to exercise, and the combats of elephants and tigers took place. Though these apartments are so very inviting, it is said to be impossible to live in them during the hot season.

Unique of its kind, and a real pearl among the buildings of India, is the Mootee mosque, which is situated next the garden. It is not built in the profusely lavish style of architecture that excites admiration, but, in the noble, pure, and simple style which delights the eye. Colonnades of white marble surround the court, which is paved with marble, and in the centre of which is a small basin for the ablutions of the devotees, and five open portals, supported by angular pillars, lead to the halls.

Returning from Akbarabad to the city, the Jamma mosque, an edifice in a grand style of architecture, resembling the mosque of the same name at Delhi, lies on the outside of the fort. A broad terrace, with numerous small towers and minarets at the sides, leads to the interior, where the people offer their devotions; and three vast domes, nearly of equal size, rise boldly above the whole. But this fine building is every day falling more and more into decay, large blocks of sandstone and marble threaten to fall from their dizzy height; and unless the English undertake to repair it,—for nothing can be expected from the apathetic Mussulmans, —it will speedily become a mass of ruins.

Secundra, the sepulchre of Akbar the Great, the wisest and best of the Mogul princes, is situated eight miles north-west of Agra. In order that I might view it at leisure, and enjoy the rich and fertile landscape in the midst of which it is situated, my friend devoted an entire forenoon to it. Our servants with culinary utensils were sent thither the preceding day that we might breakfast there. On one of those glorious mornings usual here at this season, the thermometer being at 52° Fahr., we set out at the first dawn of day, on an admirable road, to Mathura. We passed many interesting ruins, among which I must not omit to mention a tombstone by the roadside, under which one of the favourite horses of Akbar the Great is buried, the figure of a horse of red sandstone is placed over it: there is another similar monument outside the walls of Akbarabad.

The majestic Secundra burst upon our view from a great distance: we reached it exactly as the sun was rising. It is in the middle of a garden, and forms a regular quadrangle 850 paces in length, surrounded by a high wall, flanked with small projecting bulwarks at the corners. The principal entrance to this mausoleum is on the south side; in the centre of each of the other walls is a high vaulted chamber, which has the appearance of a closed gate. The gateway by which we entered consists of three lofty, arched portals with bronze doors: they are built of sandstone, and are adorned with mosaic work. Above the centre portal is a bastion, adorned with four white marble minarets, which are 120 feet high, and are fluted half way up; and, inside of which, are spiral marble staircases, which lead to the balconies, but the summits of the minarets have unhappily been thrown down by the Juts, as is generally affirmed.

The mausoleum itself is a quandrangular building, the interior side of which is 350 feet, and the exterior 410 feet in length: it is four stories high, which successively diminish; and the entire height is 120 feet, ornamented with many towers and cupolas, supported by fluted pillars up to the very top story. On the outside of the building white marble staircases lead up to the summit. In the centre of the ground-floor is a plain marble sarcophagus, containing the remains of Akbar, above which a bronze lamp of antique form sheds a dim light over the gloomy apartment. The second story consists of four large vaults, which lead to twenty different apartments: these are the vaults of the wives and princes of the family. The third story resembles the second, and is likewise built of red sandstone. The fourth, consisting entirely of white marble, of uncommonly elegant filagree work, contains the state cenotaph, which is composed of one block of white marble, covered with bas reliefs and ornaments of various kinds. This story has no roof. From this point there is a panoramic view, extending above twenty miles round, over a fertile country, every where covered with ruins of ancient splendour; among which Agra, with its sparkling minarets and cupolas, rises majestically with the Jumna in the background.

There are basins in the garden, and small canals issuing from the centre of the four sides, in which numerous fountains formerly played; but these water-works, like so many others of the same kind, are quite dilapidated. On the other hand, the British government bestows great care in keeping the flower garden in order, which flourishes in great perfection, in the shade of the tamarind, orange, and fig trees. While we were admiring the splendid productions of nature, from one of the small towers of the second story, and taking our breakfast amidst the testimonies of departed magnificence, the gardener brought us some elegant nosegays, requesting us to keep them as a remembrance of the great man whose remains are here deposited.

At the distance of some hundred paces from Akbar's mausoleum, there is an orphan asylum in the ruins of an ancient sepulchre. It is for the children of the natives who perished in the famine of 1837–8, and whose education is provided for, as well by the charity of the Christian community, as by the support of government. Of the 2000 children who at that time found an asylum here, 350 remained in the institution, and the others were received by kindred establishments. At present there are 160 boys and 140 girls here: 60 had died, notwithstanding all the care that was taken of them. Each child costs two rupees and a half per month, and the whole establishment 700 rupees per month. Mr. Moore was the founder of this institution, which is now under the direction of Mr. Driberg a German missionary.

The children are educated in the Christian religion, and those who are distinguished by their abilities are trained for the office of teachers:

three hours in the day are employed in instruction, and three more in learning different trades. The boys weave carpets, woollen cloth, and calicoes, or learn mechanical trades and agriculture; the girls are employed in household duties, in the kitchen, and in spinning. A large garden, attached to the establishment, is cultivated entirely by the pupils, and produces the necessary vegetables and fruits. It is intended to found with them a Christian village, for which the government gives the land. Some are already married, and have commenced the establishment of this colony. The teachers are for the most part natives; the children are perfect masters of the English language; they translate readily from English into Hindoostanee, and had made great proficiency in writing and ciphering. Their healthy blooming appearance, and their cheerful countenances, showed that they were contented and happy.

I will now say a few words about the prison in this place. From a population of four millions of people, there are 1000 criminals here; the number in the whole of Bengal is said to be 25,000. They live in airy apartments, surrounded by high walls: murderers are kept in close confinement, and are heavily ironed; the others have iron rings round the ankles, which are connected by a chain, which is fastened to their girdle: they are employed either in work in the prison, or in repairing the highways.

It may be interesting to you to hear how the police is administered in the districts of India. The police is closely connected with the collection of the revenue. Every district has over it a magistrate, before whom all criminal cases are brought in the first instance, and who can pass sentence of imprisonment up to the term of three years; immediately under him is the joint magistrate, with equal authority, who has an assistant magistrate, in whose hands is lodged power to inflict seven months' imprisonment. In every district, according to its population and extent, there are divisions of the police called *Thannahs*, which have a chief police officer called *Thannadar*, a *Moharer* (clerk to the Thannadar), a *Jemadar*, or assistant, and a certain number of Suwars, and *Burkandazes*, or police officers.

The duty of the Thannadar is to inform himself of every thing that passes in his district, and to report it without delay to the magistrate. To support him, there are in every village *Chowkeedars*, or watchmen, who are paid in land, and who are bound to make the necessary communications to the Thannadar. The district of Agra is divided into twelve such Thannahs, (that of Allahabad, with 4000 villages, contains twenty-four Thannahs,) and consists of 47 *Jemadars*, 54 *Duffadars*, 61 *Moharers*, 913 *Burkundazes*, and 48 *Suwars*. Besides this regular police, there are two other branches, with especial regard to the collection of the taxes.

Every district is under the superintendence of a collector of the revenue, who has magisterial powers, under whom there are a *Covenanted Deputy Collector*, and an *Uncovenanted Deputy Collector*, the latter of whom is not in the regular service of the government. The revenue is collected by the *Tehsildars* (natives), who are assisted by native officers and *Chuprassys*. The *Zemindar* of the village, as the owner of the land, is answerable for the due payment of the taxes, and must make his tenants responsible. Two thirds of the rent paid to him comes to the government; and if negligence is the cause of his inability to pay, his land is publicly sold.

In the district of Agra, the Moofussil, the Chowkeedar establishment consists of 1791 Chowkeedars, and 1149 Ballahdars, or assistants of the Chowkeedars, who are paid by the Zemindars, either in money, or in land. The municipal establishment of the Chowkeedars consists of 227 Chowkeedars for the superintendence of the city and environs Agra, and is supported by a tax on the householders. They are under a Cutwal, and supply the place of nightly watchmen.

The Indians are now in what they call the " Rosy month of love: " it is the season when the God Cama, (son of Makia, *i.e.* of seduction, and the husband of Retty, *i.e.* inclination,) the friend of spring, a handsome, roguish youth with a quiver, full of flowers, and surrounded by lovely dancing nymphs, flies through the air, in cool moonlight nights, on a chattering parrot, and discharges his amorous darts at those who pass by. Almost every day, I I see happy individuals, both adults and children, who have been struck by his flowery darts! Thus I one morning met a boy twelve years of age, in a red silk garment richly adorned with jewels, in a Takt-i-rawan: his parents and relations, men, women, and children followed in several waggons drawn by oxen: they were all dressed in fine white garments, and some uncommonly pretty female figures were among those in the waggons, and inquisitively put their heads through the curtains. They were going to a village, where the bride, a little girl eight years of age, was to be betrothed to the pretty boy who was looking around him as joyously as if the whole world were his portion.

It is well known that among the Hindoos, six kinds of marriage are recognised as legal, of which only four are permitted to the Brahmins; but it is a law in all of them that the father shall give away his daughter without any remuneration.

Two of these forms of marriage are allowed to the caste of soldiers, viz. when the warrior after a victory takes a woman, and marries her against her will, and when the two parties pledge themselves to each other, without the performance of any ceremony. On the other hand, marriages are forbidden, if the father receives a present on the occasion, or if the woman through intoxication, or any other cause, is in such a condition that she must be considered as being incapable of giving her consent to the marriage. It is not considered any disgrace to accept means of subsistence from a son-in-law, or a brother-in-law. Men may marry women of an inferior caste, but women are not allowed the same liberty.

In Maharatta, woman is considered the honour of the family: she is the life and soul of her husband, his second self, his best friend, and the source of all his happiness. Woman, with her amiable converse, is the companion of man's solitude, and his comfort, in the journey through the desert of life. According to the laws of Menu, women are to be esteemed and honoured by their fathers, brothers, and husbands, that they may themselves be happy, for the gods rejoice when honour is paid to women.

Girls are generally married in the eighth, and boys in the tenth year of their age: the father choosing for his children; but if he has neglected this duty for three years after his daughter has attained that age, she is at liberty to choose for herself. Among the higher castes, the marriage is celebrated with many ceremonies; but in the lower castes, the hands of the bride and the bridegroom are merely united by a blade of sacred grass. When the daughter of a warrior marries a Brahmin, she holds an arrow in her hand; the daughter of a Visya (the caste of merchants) holds a whip; and the daughter of a Shoodra (caste of shopkeepers) lays hold of the border of a mantle. As soon as the bride has advanced seven steps to meet the bridegroom, and they have both repeated a certain appointed text or sentence, the union is indissoluble at the seventh step. If the young husband dies before he has lived with his wife, she remains a widow for her whole life; at least the Hindoos of a higher caste hesitate to marry a woman who became a widow in her childhood.

The daughters of two rich merchants at Calcutta had lately been placed in this melancholy situation, and I was assured that the fathers had assigned them a large dowry to obtain husbands for them.

The bridegroom proceeds with great pomp to the house of the bride, where he is received with much festivity, accompanied by music and dancing ; the apartments are brilliantly lighted up, and adorned with flowers, and a cow is brought in, apparently for sacrifice, but the bridegroom begs her life, and at his request she is set at liberty. When the father of the bridegroom is a person of distinction, he generally takes the bride to his own house, and has her educated under his own protection, especially if her parents are not in good circumstances. A separate building is erected for the brides of princes, and their parents who come from another country. As soon as the ceremonies and the festivities are over, the youthful husband returns home, or the father of the bride takes her away with him; and when she is of age to marry, she is fetched by her husband with much ceremony.

Persons of distinction, on these occasions lead the procession mounted on richly adorned elephants: the servants follow, in their best attire, surrounded by musicians, some carrying branches of palm, flowers, painted paper lanterns, &c.; and the bridegroom, handsomely dressed, accompanied by his relations, riding on an elephant, a horse, or in a Takt-i-rawan, closes the pageant. Ornaments of all kinds, often to the value of several thousand rupees, are the first and principal gifts which he offers to his bride; for the Hindoo is commanded by his religion constantly to provide his wife with trinkets and handsome clothes, that she may remember his affection and find amusement in her solitude.

As the marriage is to be indissoluble, and he is not permitted, except under certain circumstances, to take a second wife, it seems worthy of notice, that he may legally separate from his wife if they have no children within eight years, or no daughters in eleven years. On the other hand, the wife is obliged to wait for her husband eight years, if he has left her for religious purposes; six years, if desire of wisdom or of glory have called him into the world; and three years, if the pursuit of pleasure is the cause of his absence.

As I already wrote to you from Delhi, I decided on undertaking my proposed journey, by way of Futtehpoor, to Bhurtpoor, Deeg, and Mathura. The resident agent of the Rajah informed me that every thing was ready for my reception, and for facilitating my further progress. On this journey of 150 miles, I have had recourse to all the modes of travelling practised in India: after a buggy I had a horse, then a waggon, an elephant, a palanquin, and, lastly, a camel.

I was accompanied as far as Futtehpoor by Mr. Jackson, who had some business to transact in that place. We set out very early in the morning on the 22d of February, the thermometer being at 51°, in a buggy; the road was, indeed, broad, and in some places lined with trees, but so rough and full of holes, that, as my companion drove very rapidly, I was really apprehensive lest we might meet with some accident. Immediately after sunrise, we halted at the gate of the large ruined city, formerly the residence of Akbar the Great; and here are ruins, so grand and magnificent, that they reminded me of ancient Rome. No description can give so faithful a picture of the taste and mode of life of Akbar as we derive from his numerous palaces, in the remains of which, perhaps twice as many persons might find room as in the colossal imperial palaces of Rome.

Futtehpoor was built partly in the plain, and partly on a mountain ridge of red sandstone 150 feet high, running from south-east to north-east. A high wall of the same stone, and of granite, nearly five miles in extent, enclosed the place. The greater portion of the interior space was occupied by the palaces; the town itself appears to have been insignificant. The wall, the town, and the eastern side of the palaces, are in ruins; a colossal gate, with large round towers, likewise stripped of its ornaments, indicates the entrance. It is said that these fine and very remarkable buildings were destroyed by the Maharattas. Every thing is annihilated, and the masses of stone are thrown about, as if Cyclops had been at work here, or as if an earthquake had shaken the city to its foundations.

We passed from the lodges of the guards, through the palaces of the ministers, and through those of the princes of the family, into those of the Emperor. These consisted of lofty, vaulted apartments, supported by square pillars covered with manifold arabesques and ornaments, and contain three courts of audience, in which small gardens, with basins and fountains, once afforded refreshment both to the mind and body when relaxed by the heat.

The palaces of the three wives of Akbar, a Roman, a Turkish, and a Hindoo female, have suffered the least. The Hindoo was his favourite wife, and was the mother of his first son. A portion of the court-yard of the extensive harem, is paved with slabs of various coloured marbles, and is the table or playboard as it were where the great man had the weakness to play at a game of the natives, called Chaoophar, resembling the German game of mühlspiel (a kind of draughts), with the women of his harem, who represented the pawns: a stone seat still indicates the spot where the emperor used to be seated to enjoy the sight.

There is something very original in the contrivance of Akbar's hall of audience. In the middle of a spacious square apartment is a pedestal ten feet in height, covered with very pretty ornaments, on the top of which was affixed a marble seat for the Emperor; from this centre, narrow passages run to the four corners of the apartment, where stood the seats of his four ministers, with whose aid he governed his large empire. Each of them had his respective place of egress, at which their secretaries and messengers were in waiting for orders, to convey the commands of the sovereign to the four cardinal points. The people stood in the space below, so that the Emperor soared above them like an eagle.

Passing through these palaces, which are built of

a stone resembling porphyry, and proceeding to the south, we came to the mansions of the ambassadors. We then went through a large square court, which is surrounded by a kind of piazza, and formed the stabling for four hundred horses, and then to the stables for the elephants: it is well known that Akbar possessed six thousand of these animals—a thousand of which were accommodated here.

The mosque is preserved nearly entire. It resembles, in the style of its architecture, that of Agra, but it is grander; for the inner side of the quadrangular court, which is surrounded by arcades, towers, and minarets, measures 476 feet. In the middle of it, rather towards the north, the emperor erected a marble sepulchre for his favourite priest Sheikh Selim Tshish, from gratitude for his fervent prayers that Allah would give him a son and successor. It is made of filigree work, adorned in the style of the Florentine mosaic, and resembles an elegant jewel-box.

Behind the mosque is a deep tank for the people to perform their ablutions; and round it are the wretched houses for the inhabitants of the present village. At the north-eastern issue from this former city of palaces there are colossal gates, surrounded with large, round bulwarks, and beyond them are the court-yards for the combats of wild beasts. Between them is a small round tower, forty feet high, from which the emperor viewed the combat, or killed the animals, driven together for his diversion.

The servants of Mr. Jackson had spread carpets,

and prepared our breakfast in the apartments of the Empress, at the north-east end of the highest point of the chain of rocks. This lovely woman could not have selected a finer spot to enjoy the beauties of nature, and to while away her lonely hours of solitude; and Akbar, it is said, was accustomed, after the labours of the day, to indulge in gazing upon the fertile and diversified scenery of the rich province of Bhurtpoor: it is, in the most literal sense of the term, a boundless garden. Luxuriant corn-fields alternate with small groves, in the midst of which, villages and little hamlets lie embosomed, and, in the immediate vicinity, the colossal remains of by-gone splendour. We remained for a long time lost in admiration of the delightful scenery, and in the recollection of those glorious days.

Meantime the sun had risen very high, and neither the promised carriage nor the guard from the Rajah had made their appearance. We accordingly sent some Suwars to make inquiries, one of whom at length brought word that I had been expected to come by the other road; and as it would be near evening before the carriage, which had been sent thither for me, could arrive here, I mounted the horse of the officer on the station, and, accompanied by a Suwar, set off at eleven o'clock for Bhurtpoor, which was eight miles distant. The heat was 83° Fahrenheit, and my umbrella was the only protection I had against the burning rays of the sun.

The state of Bhurtpoor, which is 1945 square miles in extent, and has a revenue of 15 lacs, is the only Jât principality of any consequence in India; the only one which has still retained some traces of national character, and whose princes and nobles are of the same race. The Jâts derive their origin from a peasant named Ramjee, who had thirty-four children, and was reverenced by his numerous descendants as their father and prince. At the beginning of the last century they migrated from Mooltan to northern Hindoostan, and obtained permission from the Mogul emperors to settle in the Doab, on the Ganges and the Jumna.

During the confusion which ensued on the death of Aurengzebe, their chief succeeded in obtaining power and authority. They took possession of the present country of Bhurtpoor, and, by means of the rich booty which they had acquired, built the fortress of the same name. This fortress being constantly more and more strengthened by the addition of new works, became the asylum of the Jâts, and a secure depository for their plunder. Sooraj Mull, one of their chiefs, assumed the title of Rajah; and, though a Jât, he was so vain as to pretend to be descended from the caste of warriors. He was killed in a battle with Nudjiff Khan near Delhi, in 1763.

The first offensive and defensive alliance between the English and Bhurtpoor was concluded on the 14th November, 1803. By this treaty, the Rajah relieved himself from the payment of a tribute, and obtained, besides, possession of considerable territories, of the value of 20 pergunnahs.* But when Holcar, in his flight, took refuge, first in Deeg, and then in the fortress of Bhurtpoor, and incited the Jâts to rise against the English, General Lake advanced to blockade it. After four unsuccessful attempts to take it by storm, which were repulsed with the loss of three thousand men, a fifth attempt was on the point of being made, when the Rajah, Runjeet Singh, abandoned Holcar to his fate, and capitulated. On the conclusion of peace, April 17. 1805, the offensive and defensive alliance was renewed, the Rajah paid twenty lacs of rupees for the expenses of the war, and ceded to the English the territories before conquered from Scindia. The fortress of Deeg, and one of the Rajah's sons, remained in the hands of the English, as securities till the conditions were fulfilled.

In those years, when the Mahrattas ravaged almost all the states of India, Bhurtpoor and Alwar were the only ones, which, being protected by the British alliance, escaped; but though the Rajah was sensible, when he compared his flourishing country with the neighbouring states, that he was indebted for its preservation solely to the protection of the English, enmity and hatred, were, nevertheless, so deeply rooted in his heart, that they completely stifled every feeling of gratitude. The reciprocal distrust was kept up by disputes on the frontiers; and the question whether fugitives

* Hamilton says "these districts yielded a revenue of 754,000 rupees per annum."

were to be given up was a fruitful source of discord.

Runjeet Singh, however, died in 1823, and left four sons, and was succeeded by his eldest son Randir Singh, who died a few weeks after his father, without leaving any issue. The throne was then claimed by Durjan Sal, son of the third son of Runjeet Singh, who rested his claim on the fact, that his uncle had adopted him to the exclusion of his own brother Baldeo Singh. The latter, however, got possession of the Musnud on the 26th February, but he also died within a few months. Civil wars ensued; and the British government was induced to defend the rights of Bulwunt Singh, an adopted son of the last rajah, against Durjan Sal.

General Combermere advanced with 25,000 men to Bhurtpoor, effected a breach by the explosion of a mine, and stormed the fortress, with considerable loss, on the 18th January, 1826. A treasure of 2 millions and a half of rupees was found in the fortress, and taken to defray the expenses of the war. The fortifications of Bhurtpoor were demolished, and the Rajah, a minor, was educated under the protection of the English. When he assumed the government, a few years ago, the debts, amounting to twenty-five lacs, were paid, and the country converted into a flourishing garden. Should the Rajah, as seems probable, die without children, this fine country will fall into the possession of the English.

Thinking of the combats which had rendered

Bhurtpoor so very remarkable a place, I felt a high degree of interest as I approached the town, which is seen at a great distance. As I crossed the plain, I beheld on every side luxuriant fields of wheat and barley in full ear; and I was very much struck with the appearance of the tall, vigorous Juts, who were pursuing their agricultural occupations with their sabres at their sides, and their spears stuck in the ground, apparently for a land-mark. Their wives, too, were working diligently, close by their husbands. They are more robust than the Hindoo women, and were dressed in red garments, very much like shawls.

The agricultural implements of the Indians appear to be rude, heavy, and clumsy; no iron is to be seen about the plough, except the share; its place is supplied by wood or copper. The harrow, or the implement used to break the clods of earth, has wooden teeth, and the field when sown is levelled and rolled with a square, smooth beam. Just before reaching Bhurtpoor, I passed through a little wood, and turned from it towards the eastern gate.

Bhurtpoor is situated in 27° 15′ N. L., and 77° 32′ 61″ E. L., from Greenwich: it has 40,000 inhabitants, is surrounded only by a low wall, and consists of stone houses, which are two or three stories high. It is a very animated, but a closely built and dirty place. It was one o'clock when I passed through the narrow streets to the Char Baugh, that is, the Four Gardens, near the citadel; an uncommonly pleasant villa, surrounded by four small flower-gardens, which the Rajah has caused to be laid out solely for the use of the English who visit him. Flights of steps lead from the gardens to a platform paved with stone, beyond which is the small villa, which is two stories high, with a veranda and a flat roof.

The keeper of this pretty villa is a Castellain, who is paid by the Rajah, and is directed to provide for the maintenance of the guests, and to attend to their wishes. The Rajah could not have found a more obliging man than this servant, in whom humour and wit were agreeably combined, and who saluted me with a friendly salam, as I alighted from my horse. I was much rejoiced to find two young officers from Agra, who had arrived a few hours before me, with the intention of spending some days here to enjoy the pleasures of the chase.

The indefatigable Castellain no sooner learned that I was the expected guest, than messengers were despatched in all directions to announce my arrival. Accordingly, his Highness's treasurer, and the minister of police, with a crowd of servants, appeared soon afterwards, to welcome me, in their master's name; and declared that the Rajah had given orders that every thing should be done to make my residence in his territory as agreeable as possible. I was first presented with a number of baskets, full of flowers, fruits, and vegetables, arranged in the most tasteful manner; then with fowls, sheep, eggs, and other provisions. The treasurer expressed his regret that his Highness had taken all his cooks with him to Delhi, and that it would therefore be impossible to set before me such a repast as he ought: he added, that a carriage and elephants were at my command, to view the citadel and the city, at my convenience.

Close to the Char Baugh is an orchard, in which the Rajah keeps rams, cocks, antelopes, and quails, for fighting; and innumerable favourite birds, for the amusement of his wives. Among the game-cocks, are several for which his Highness had paid 200 rupees for the pair. Near this garden some tigers, and six leopards, trained to hunt antelopes, were kept: each of the latter animals reposed on a bedstead, and had two servants to attend on him, one of whom was constantly engaged in driving away the flies and other insects with a fan! On our return to the villa, a combat of animals was exhibited on the lower platform for my entertainment:— these combats are often the only amusement, and the only employment of Indian princes! The two ministers with their attendants stood round us in picturesque groups, and at every furious attack of the fighting animals asked us, with childish glee, if it was not *tumasha?* (very fine.)

When the sun was near setting, an elephant was brought to carry us to the citadel. It lies at the north-western end of the town, is in the form of a pentagon, and consists of walls of hewn stone sixty feet high, reckoning from the bed of the moat, which is thirty feet deep, and is full of water, in which there are many tortoises. Within the walls, besides, the old palace, which contains the harem, is the Rajah's new palace, surrounded with pretty flower-gardens and fountains. With the exception of some closed apartments, this palace chiefly consists of open colonnades: one in the upper story contains the Rajah's sleeping apartment, in the hot season: the bed is so very large that ten persons might very conveniently lie down on it; costly carpets, chandeliers, some tables and chairs, are the only furniture of these apartments.

A small villa, sheltered by luxuriant trees, situated on an eminence, which rises in terraces, is the residence of the Rajah in the rainy season. The view from the platform commands the whole city, and the beautiful, richly cultivated landscape to a great distance. An extensive palace, built of sandstone and marble, in the Italian style, was nearly finished; and I was told that it was the Rajah's intention to fit it up for distinguished British visiters.

On the following morning, the treasurer of his Highness had arranged an antelope hunt with leopards, on the road to Deeg; and, in order that we might arrive more quickly at the place of rendezvous, relays of elephants were placed at the distance of every ten miles. We rode in the dead of night, that is to say, at three o'clock in the morning, through the solitary streets of the town, and then on a broad road, between a fine avenue of old fig trees to Deeg. When we had passed the gate, the heavens, with their countless hosts of stars, were spread over us in unclouded splendour and brilliancy, and were beginning to be tinged with a rosy hue from the first flush of the morning dawn.

Sunrise, on a fine spring morning, has always

a new and ineffable charm; but here, where the atmosphere is so rare that the colours appear equally tender and defined on the dark blue sky, where the brightest rose-colour gradually deepens into the most beautiful purple, and where at length the glowing orb of the sun rises from an ocean of gold, this sight is always inexpressibly magnificent: this morning we enjoyed this glorious scene in all its splendour. We had just mounted the second elephant, when the warm beams of the sun raised the temperature from 52° Fahrenheit to 63°. A little before seven o'clock we reached the carts on which the two leopards were placed.

The chase continued two hours, amid small woods and luxuriant wheat fields in full ear. The country abounds in game, and troops of antelopes were seen alternately with flamingoes and peacocks: these birds, which are looked upon as sacred, and paraded in great numbers in the fields, must not be pursued on any consideration. They are so tame, that we could have caught them with our hands. After we had let the leopards loose three times, I took leave of my companions and proceeded on the road to Deeg.

If I was already charmed with this lovely country, and astonished by the abundance of game, I was still more delighted as I proceeded on my journey mounted on an elephant, for I counted in one place above 300 antelopes, and great numbers of partridges and peacocks. At a short distance from Deeg, we met the camp of the Rajah, who was returning home to his capital; I, however, avoided an interview, because I knew that it would not be convenient to his Highness.

A handsome, but ruinous gate, of the time of the highest splendour of the Mogul empire, leads into Deeg, which is otherwise quite open, and contains a neglected clay citadel, and some colossal Mogul ruins, which resemble those of Delhi. On the other hand, there is a palace built by Runjeet Singh, which is one of the finest Hindoo edifices of modern date. On my arrival there, I was received by the governor of Deeg, and the principal persons in the town, who offered to show me the palace and the gardens.

The palace, which is situated in a pleasant fruit and flower garden has a very fine façade, and projecting wings. There are several open, vaulted colonnades, in the Mogul Hindoo style, which are closed with curtains. Great care has been bestowed on the waterworks; there are no less than 600 fountains, in the most varied forms; but as eight days are requisite to make them play, I was obliged to content myself with looking at the hundred fountains of the front basin. From the centre arcade of the principal building is a complete view of these waterworks and of the garden in its whole length; and here a seat was placed, that I might enjoy this interesting sight, as well as the splendid show of flowers.

The officers of his Highness behaved with the most delicate attention, and presented me with beautiful baskets of flowers and fruits; making many inquiries respecting my wishes or commands, and were pleased repeatedly to express their regret that I would not spend the night here. When I took leave, the governor requested me to sign a report to the Rajah, that his Highness might be convinced, that I was satisfied with my reception.

After having rested here above an hour, I again mounted my elephant, and rode on to Mathura. In the vicinity of a village, about half way from Deeg to Mathura, is a beautiful Hindoo temple, situated in the middle of a garden, and before it is a large walled tank, with steps descending into it.

A battalion of his Highness's troops was encamped near this temple. Most of the soldiers were bathing in the tank, others were performing their devotions in the pagoda, and gave me a view of Hindoo worship on a large scale; but it was rather a picturesque and original than an elevating scene.

In the last village of the Rajah's dominions I had to change my elephant for a palanquin. While the bearers were preparing for their journey, the chief of the place, with several attendants, paid me a visit, and, to show their hospitality, brought flowers, almonds, raisins, and sugar-candy in plated earthenware vessels, and repeatedly expressed their satisfaction at my tasting some of the sweetmeats. At four o'clock I was already on the classic soil of Mathura.

When Mahmood I. of Ghuznee destroyed this remarkable place in 1017, and gave it up to plunder for twenty days, he was so struck with its splendour and extent, that he wrote to his governor at Ghuznee that, "there were in it a thousand buildings and temples, mostly of marble, as firm as the faith of the faithful; buildings which must have cost many millions sterling, and have required at least two hundred years for their erection."

Mahmood spared the temples, the solidity and beauty of which are said to have restrained him; but part of the city was burnt, and all the idols, the majority of which were of gold and silver, were destroyed or melted down. According to Ferishta, there were five idols of gold here, whose eyes, which were made of rubies, were worth 50,000 denari (22,333*l.*); on another idol there was a sapphire weighing 400 miscal, and the idol itself yielded 98,300 miscal of pure gold. Three hundred camels were loaded with silver alone, and sent to Ghuznee: but there are now scarcely any remains of the ancient capital of the Saracenæ, though some spots indicate that extensive buildings formerly stood there. Mathura having been the birthplace of Krishna, is the resort of pilgrims and of Hindoo princes; among whom, the Rajah of Bhurtpoor comes several times in the year to wash away his sins, and also goes to Bindrabun for the same purpose.

Mathura is built in the form of an arch, on the elevated right bank of the Jumna, hard by the river, where there are numerous flights of steps descending into the water, which is the resort of many hundred persons, who come from far and near to bathe, in this spot which is sacred to Krishna. The town was formerly surrounded by the lofty wall, of which only some fragments and three gates now remain; the old fort, which stands on a high hill, also lies in ruins, but, like the town itself, has an uncommonly picturesque appearance, when viewed from the flat sandy plain on the opposite bank.

The interior of the town is extremely dirty; the streets are narrow, irregular, and dusty, and in some places so ill-contrived, that two persons can scarcely pass without touching each other; where the bazars are situated (of which there are 2350) the houses, which are built of bricks or clay, rise to the height of two or three stories, whereas in all the other parts they are little better than huts. The city is divided into 58 quarters, containing 7000 brick houses with flat roofs, 5000 houses built of clay thatched with grass or reeds, 190 Hindoo mandars or places of prayer, and 19 mosques.

Among the latter is the famous mosque built by the Emperor Aurengzebe, which is called by his name. A magnificent Hindoo temple, erected by Rajah Beer Singh Dro, of Oorcha, at the cost of 36 lacks of rupees, formerly stood here. This temple Aurengzebe caused to be pulled down, and with the materials built the present mosque on its site. The population of Mathura is estimated at 6000 Mussulmans, and 54,000 Hindoos; among the latter there are 15,000 Brahmins and Fakirs, who live about the holy places, and on the Ghauts (open flights of steps), on the banks of the river, and subsist on the alms of the devotees.

Though the Jumna is navigable at all seasons of the year, even for large boats, trade is not considerable, because the surrounding country produces only corn and cotton. In the rainy season the river extends to the breadth of 600 paces, but in the dry season it divides into several arms, and forms sand banks, and, in some places, (for instance, near the cavalry barracks,) is only three feet deep. It is said, that since the canal between Karnaul and Delhi has been restored, the depth of water in the river has decreased two feet at this place: from October to June the communication is kept up by a bridge of boats below the town.

The soil is light, sandy, and mixed with Cankar: it is not, however, favourable to horticulture, because the water of the wells employed in irrigation is for the most part brackish, the earth is saturated with saline particles, and in many places undermined by white ants. Grapes, strawberries, and peaches, which flourish in great perfection at Meerat and Karnaul, are here rare and insipid. There is, however, a great abundance of water-melons, some vegetables, and even potatoes. When the English took possession of this place in 1803, Mathura was made a sanatory station: 10,000 men were formerly quartered here; but at present the garrison consists of only one regiment of sepoys and a troop of artillery: the cantonments are to the south of the town, and are crossed in all directions by roads made of Cankar.

My friend at Agra had given me letters of introduction to Mr. Raikes, his colleague at this place, who had been expecting me for some time, and received me in the kindest manner. After my fatigue and privations, because in the last two days I had in fact lived on fruit and rice, a bath was the first thing that refreshed and reinvigorated me. I was unfortunately obliged to renounce the pleasure of excursions in the neighbourhood, because my dawk from Agra to Cawnpoor had already been provided for, for the following day. I was, however, fully indemnified by making the acquaintance of Mr. Raikes, who, like so many of his countrymen residing in India, is distinguished by his cultivated understanding and his urbane and friendly manner, and possessed the happy art of making the evening pass in the most agreeable way possible.

On the following morning, at 3 o'clock, I proceeded in a palanquin, to a village on the high road, ten miles distant, and twenty-two miles from Agra. It was my intention to go to that city in a buggy, which my friend at Agra was to send to meet me, and Mr. Raikes had furnished me with a Suwar, to provide against any mistakes; but when we reached the village no carriage was to be found, and I had no resource left, but to mount the Suwar's horse, and continue my journey alone, in hopes that I might find some other conveyance on the road. However, I saw neither carriage nor camel for ten miles, when my horse became so tired, that I was obliged to proceed at a very slow pace. Luckily for me, I met with an officer under Mr. Raikes, who was just on the point of returning to Agra in his carriage, in which he very politely offered me a seat, which I gladly accepted, and left the horse under the care of the chief magistrate of the village. We had scarcely set out when we met the camel, and a Suwar sent by my friend from Agra; and it appeared that a misunderstanding had been the cause of the delay. Thus I reached the town in very good time, and quickly making preparations to continue my journey, took leave of my friend, and set out in a palanquin for Cawnpoor.

LETTER X.

TO ALEXANDER VON HUMBOLDT.

Journey to Cawnpoor.— The town and the neighbourhood.— Journey to Lucknow.—Historical notices of the kingdom of Oude.—Lucknow.—House of the British Resident.— Combats of elephants.— The country palaces of the King of Oude. — Nasseeree-Baugh, and Padsha-Baugh. — The Mews.— The palace of Constantia.— The Observatory.— The road from Husan-Abad.— The tombs of Imam-Bara and Husan-Abad. — Rides through the bazar.—Audience of the King of Oude.—His palace and mode of life.— Tomb of the Nabob Saadut-Ali Khan. The King's menagerie.—Ride along the Goomty.—Return to Cawnpoor.—Departure for Allahabad.—Allahabad and its environs.— Tombs of Shah Kusra.— Society at Allahabad.—Journey to Benares.— Benares.—Peregrination through the city, and view of the Hindoo temples.— The village of Durgagund with the sacred monkeys.—Ruins and tower near the village of Saranath.

Benares, March 14. 1843.

I TAKE it for granted that you have read my letter to Mr. Carl Ritter, in which I give an account of my stay at Agra, and of my journey through the country of Bhurtpoor. Resuming my narrative at the point where I broke off, I will now give you an outline of some of my proceedings in the kingdom of Oude, in Allahabad, and Benares. You will probably hear many things, with which you are already acquainted; but an eye-witness is always inclined to be led away by his own personal experience, and to take for new what is already well known.

I left Agra at five o'clock in the afternoon of the 24th, and performed the journey to Cawnpoor, a distance of 130 miles, in twenty-four hours. My bearers took me over the bridge of boats, to the left bank of the Jumna, and proceeded, at a brisk pace, on a road of Cankar, which is partly planted with trees, through the fertile, diversified Doab, to Mynpoore. It is, as Dr. Adams has observed, a light-coloured, slimy soil, consisting of clayey, silicious, and calcareous earth, which, as you approach Allahabad, is more and more mixed with mica, which is not found on the south bank of the Jumna: it is very different from the Bundelcund side, where a black clayey earth, mixed with vegetable substances, predominates.

On the 25th, at eleven in the morning, I reached the town of Mynpoore, which is surrounded by pleasant gardens, and elegant bungalows: here I first met the bearers of water from the Ganges, which is taken by the Brahmins, at certain points of that river, particularly at its confluence with the Jumna: it is sealed by them, or attested by a certificate as the genuine sacred water, and is delivered to the bearers. It is usually put into round brass vessels, with flat lids, which are enclosed between four small bamboos, tied together in a point at the top: two or four such vessels fastened to a bamboo cane, lying over the shoulder, are carried by the bearers to the most distant parts of India, and are sold to the princes and nobles at high prices, or, they are presented as consecrated offerings to temples which enjoy particular celebrity.

In the hours of noon, when the burning heat of the sun renders travelling very fatiguing, I passed many extremely picturesque groups of travellers, who had pitched their tents, or were resting under the shade of bananas and mangoes; merchants with their waggons of goods, families going to weddings or other festivities, bayaderes, water-carriers, and peasants; the men with their sabre in their hand, and a shield at their back; the women enveloped in white garments. In the vicinity of these shady places there is generally a tank or a well, at which the weary travellers refresh themselves by a bath, or by sprinkling themselves with water, while others are preparing the repast, or smoking the hookah in silent contemplation.

I arrived at Cawnpoor on the 26th February, at 1 o'clock, when the heat was 82½° Fahr., which was extremely oppressive. The town itself (situated in 26° 30′ north latitude, and 80° 12′ east longitude from Greenwich) is small, mean-looking, and dirty; but on the right bank of the Ganges many hundred bungalows, the barracks of the troops, and the bazars, extend in a semicircle, for nearly five miles, which imparts to the whole a striking and splendid appearance. Cawnpoor is a principal station of the British, in which there are at present one European regiment of infantry, one European regiment of cavalry, four regiments of native infantry, one regiment of light cavalry, some companies of artillery, and several depôts; in all, above 8000 men.

Several of the bungalows are most picturesquely situated, on the banks of the Ganges, which rise to the height of 100 feet: they are fitted up most luxuriously, and have very extensive gardens, in which tamarinds, mangoes, bananas, neemes, acacias, and fig trees (*F. rel.*), overshadow a rich carpet of flowers which charms the senses by the magnificence of its colours, and the fragrance of its perfume. In the circumjacent country, there are fine fields of wheat and barley in ear, which are succeeded by the crops of maize, rice, sugar-cane, cotton, gram, jowary, and indigo; potatoes, pease, and cauliflower, and many other vegetables, are grown in the gardens, but the former are insipid. This is the time of the birds of passage, some of which, especially the ortolans, are considered a dainty: they are rather larger than our larks, but their taste is more piquant. The climate is very agreeable to the European from October to the end of February, and fires are by no means unwelcome in the morning and evening. On the other hand, the time of the hot winds, from March to July, and the rainy season which succeeds, are equally unhealthy and intolerable. In the former, thick clouds of dust constantly load the dry, glowing atmosphere, against the prejudicial influence of which, even the mats of the verandas, though kept constantly wet, afford no adequate protection; and when the monsoons bring incessant torrents of rain, which cause all the rivers to overflow, the air is filled with very disagreeable dampness which produces fever and cholera.

One of my friends had given me an introduction to his brother-in-law, Lieutenant Anson of the ninth regiment of Lancers; but before I could find his residence in this great city of villas and bungalows, several hours had passed away, and evening would have come on, if that hospitable officer had not sent one of his servants to meet me. I passed only one day at Cawnpoor, chiefly among the officers of the ninth regiment of Lancers, who had the kindness to make me a member of their mess.

On the 27th, at six in the afternoon, I set out by dawk, for Lucknow, which is forty-three miles distant. The day was clear, but extremely warm and oppressive; for the temperature, which had hitherto been, uniformly, not above 58° in the morning, 82½° at the most at noon, and 73½° in the evening, suddenly rose on this day to 60° in the morning, 87° at noon, and 78° in the evening, at which it remained almost unchanged for several days. My palanquin bearers carried me over the bridge of boats thrown across the Ganges, which is 500 paces in length, and subsequently for some miles along the sandy bed of the river. As soon as I passed from the English territory into the kingdom of Oude, — the ancient North Kausala, or "the Happy," — I was struck with the difference in the cultivation of the soil: there, the country was like a garden, here, there are only a few arable fields amidst immense tracts of desert.

The vizirs of Oude, the representatives of the great Moguls, made themselves quite independent of the throne at Delhi after the death of Aurengzebe. They are some of the most ancient allies of the English; for their country was guaranteed to them as far back as the year 1765, in consequence of which, in 1768, the vizir engaged not to maintain more than 35,000 men under arms, of whom only 10,000 were to be disciplined like the British troops. At a later period, the British government having secured to the vizir the possession of some portions of territory, he engaged to pay two lacs and 10,000 rupees per month, in order to subsidise for his protection, a corps of two battalions of Europeans, six battalions of sepoys, and a company of artillery. The vizir being unable sufficiently to protect himself, either in his own country or against attacks from without, became more and more dependent on the English, and was gradually obliged to consent to the cession of larger tracts of territory, and to the payment of more considerable subsidies.

By the offensive and defensive alliance, concluded in the year 1798, Sadat Ali Khan not only agreed to pay a subsidy of 66 lacs per annum, but ceded Allahabad to the English, and consented to receive an auxiliary corps of 10,000 men: it was stipulated at the same time that the vizir should not make any political alliances without the consent of the English. The payments agreed upon being, however, made very irregularly, the British government induced the vizir to cede territories of the annual value of 135 lacs: the English, on their part, promised to protect him on all occasions, and for that purpose stationed a brigade with some artillery at Lucknow.

On the other hand, this shadow of a prince was recognised by the English, in 1819, as King of Oude, and in the following year, on his coronation, he assumed, to his great satisfaction, and to the vexation of the Mahometans, the titles of "Father of Victory, Restorer of Religion, Protector of the Stars, the true Sultan, and King of the Age!"

By this proceeding he put an end to the nominal connection which still subsisted, as vizir and subedar of the King of Delhi, and made himself a prince wholly dependent on the English. In the Burmese war the king lent to the British government 3½ crores of rupees at six per cent.; of which sum, however, the Company retained a part, for which it engaged to pay certain pensions, to the relations and ministers of the king, after his death. For on the death of a king of Oude, not only are his immediate officers changed, but his relations are set aside, and the ministers who were in office disappear from public life.

King Naseer-ud-din Hyder, who is well known as a poet, died on the 7th of July, 1837, and his next surviving uncle on the father's side, Naseer-ud-dowlah succeeded him on the throne, according to the Mahometan law; but the widow of the late king wished that her adopted grandson, Mun Jaun, should be king, and she succeeded in seeing him placed on the throne, for a few hours, in the Baradehri of the palace. Colonel Low, who at that time resided at the court, with his brother-in-law

Captain Shakespeare, was in the palace endeavouring to dissuade the king's widow from this step: but all his remonstrances were fruitless, and he was for a time exposed to the greatest danger from her adherents, from which he and his brother-in-law were not relieved, till the troops burst open the gates of the palace, by means of elephants. The queen-mother, with the pretender and the chief partisan, were taken prisoners and conveyed to Chunar.

Naseer-ud-dowlah, who was constantly confined to a sick bed, by bodily sufferings, reigned only five years. Mohamed Umjud Ali Shah, who has now been on the throne for the last eight months, governs a country 23,922 English square miles in extent, with only three millions of inhabitants, most of whom are Hindoos: he was born and educated in the harem, and is dissolute and fond of pleasure. Yet this ignorant prince, encouraged by unprincipled flatterers and courtiers, fancies that he is able to guide alone, the reins of so extensive a kingdom.

Insurrections take place, alternately, in all parts of the country. The revenue, which formerly amounted to nearly three millions sterling, now scarcely produces half that sum, and must be collected from the great Jaghirdars by military force. Yet the court is still surrounded with incredible splendour, and is rich in gold, in jewels, and elephants, which, however, is chiefly defrayed by means of the treasures amassed by his predecessors, which are said to have amounted in 1804 to 10,000,000*l*. sterling.

The army, consisting of 43,000 men, with more than one hundred pieces of cannon, is ill paid and equipped, with the exception of the few disciplined troops, among which there are many half-castes.

After travelling about twenty miles, I came to the new road which has been made by the King's order, and crossed several small, arched stone bridges. Immediately after midnight, the sky was suddenly overcast, the lightning flashed on all sides, the storm came nearer and nearer, and the lightning was so bright and continued, that the whole country seemed to be in flames. My bearers ran as fast as they could, almost five miles in an hour; but the storm, accompanied with a violent hurricane and rain, overtook us, the torch was extinguished, and the bearers were compelled to set down the palanquin. Surrounded by these half-naked figures, who, seeking protection behind the palanquin, crouched closely together, I was compelled to lie still, for a whole hour: the storm and the lightning then ceased, the thunder died away, a total calm suddenly succeeded, and the starry heavens appeared without a cloud. This storm was followed by an uncommonly fine morning; nature seemed to be revived; the air was purer, and more aromatic than ever, and the verdure of the fields, and the foliage of the trees, glowed in the brightest hues. At a short distance before I reached Lucknow, I met a man upon a camel, who was sent to meet me by Captain Shakespeare, the political agent at that city, to whom I had been introduced by letter, by his brother Sir Richmond.

Lucknow is situated in 26° 53′ north latitude, and 80° 58′ east longitude from Greenwich, on the banks of the river Goomty, on the classic soil of the Lakhsmanavati. The city is very irregular, partly dirty and closely built, partly consisting of handsome, broad, clean, streets, and has a population of 300,000 inhabitants. Splendid buildings and monuments alternate with mosques, fine gardens, and villas, which bear evidence of the lavish profusion of vain and foolish princes, who endeavoured, by means of their treasures, to collect all the curiosities and toys in the world, in order to adorn with them their palaces, and the tombs of their ancestors, in the most childish, ridiculous, and grotesque taste.

As we approached the open city, which, on this side, did not show any thing of its extent and splendour, my guide led me past some large gardens, then through several narrow, insignificant streets, till we reached the fore court of a handsome building, the residence of Captain Shakespeare. I was received by this accomplished officer like an old friend, and found every accommodation in his pleasant abode, which is fitted up in the most convenient manner.

This villa is a strong building, two stories high, with verandas attached to both stories. The lower apartments open into a small, but very elegant fruit and flower-garden, on the side of which there is a walled basin for swimming: the usual bathing apartments are at the four corners of the house, adjoining the bed-chambers. This charming residence, like most of the houses occupied by the English in this city, was built by Europeans, who were in the service of the vizirs and kings of Oude, whose aide-de-camps they were: the King keeps them in repair, and has left them to the English free of expense.

In the immediate vicinity of this house, separated from it only by a wall and garden, is the palace of the British ambassador at this court. It is erected on a small eminence, and consists of two large, handsome buildings, which are opposite to each other, and have a colonnade in front. In one of them, which contains three stories, the apartments under ground are for the hot season, and in the two above ground there are only the sitting rooms and the offices: all the apartments are spacious and handsome, and are fitted up in the most costly and tasteful manner.

From the platform of this house there is a magnificent view of the whole city, which appears like a panorama, and with its many white minarets, gilded cupolas, palaces, sepulchral monuments, and gardens, traversed by the navigable Goomty, has a very grand effect. The life and bustle of the population, which is more Mahometan than Hindoo, may be traced to the most distant point. They have quite a mania for training flocks of pigeons, which swarm about the royal palaces, and almost every house, and are taught, according to signals made with red flags, to rise in the air, to disperse, and to re-assemble.

When the eye returns from the distant prospect to the scene immediately at hand, it is refreshed by the view of a beautiful flower garden, which surrounds this palace on three sides. In the second edifice are the state apartments; spacious saloons, furnished with costly chandeliers, mirrors, and silk divans. It is the custom for the ambassador to return the invitations to breakfasts and dinners which he has received; the King, therefore, is present at these fêtes two or three times in a year, with his sons and the officers of his household, amounting to more than twenty persons; the King, however, always brings his cook with him, and takes nothing but tea. As soon as dancing begins, his Majesty invariably retires.

General Nott, the present ambassador, had made his entry into Lucknow a few days before my arrival. On this occasion the King and the people had received the celebrated General with the greatest honours. His Majesty, surrounded by his sons and courtiers, mounted on 200 richly adorned elephants, and attended by all his regular troops, went out to meet him: almost all the inhabitants in their gala dresses joined the procession; and General Nott assured me that it was a truly fairy scene, exceeding all the pictures which the fancy could form of an enchanted Indian kingdom.

The King had prepared a breakfast for the General, and afterwards the company viewed from the arcades on the Goomty, a combat of elephants which took place on the opposite bank. This is a singular, but for the Mahouts a very dangerous, amusement; for only male animals with tusks are selected for it, which are driven on by the Mahouts till they rush against each other. When the elephants begin to combat, the shock is often so great, that the Mahouts are thrown off and trampled under foot, and the furious animals cannot be separated except by firing: on this occasion, however, the combat was not dangerous; one of the elephants repeatedly ran away, and, when he met his opponent, made but little resistance: he was soon afterwards seized with the Matta, and killed his keeper.

On the first day of my visit, as soon as the sun had partly gone down, and the heat of 89° Fahr. was less oppressive, my kind host drove me to a summer palace of the King. Though two elephants with splendid houdahs stand from morning till evening before the palace of the ambassador, and of the resident, ready for his service, we preferred a light buggy, and drove through broad, well-watered, macadamised roads, round the royal palace, to the Goomty. On the way, I had ample opportunity to observe one of the fancies of the King, which consists in having all the houses of the city painted white, or in colours, and covered with scenes of Indian life.

It is not his object to encourage works of art, but to produce something gay and glaring to strike the eye, and make the spectator laugh.

There are two bridges over the Goomty; one of stone, which is arched, at the north end of the city, and a pontine bridge at the south. An iron bridge of three arches, 200 paces in length, which Saadut Ali caused to be brought from England in 1810, had remained, up to this time, in the cases in which it was brought. Now, however, it was at length resolved to put it up; but, when the workmen came to place it together, they discovered that some of the pieces were broken, and thus the undertaking is necessarily delayed.

We crossed the bridge of boats, which is 240 paces broad, and proceeded, in the first place, to the Nasseeree-Baugh, which is situated near the river. This is a small garden in the French style, with a summer-house, adorned, or rather overladen, in a very tasteless manner, with articles of glass, china, bad paintings, copper-plates, and all sorts of bagatelles. The Padsha Baugh (or King's Garden), which is situated at a short distance, is, on the contrary, a large and beautiful garden, laid out in the English style, and is uncommonly delightful. A basin with many fountains intersects the garden in its whole length. The ground is covered with the greatest variety of beds of flowers, overshadowed by the dark-green foliage of mangoes, and oranges covered with their fragrant flowers. "These are Bombay mangoes," said the gardener, "but they do not produce such fine fruit as in that country." The effect of the natural beauties of this spot is spoiled by the many painted statues, models of sandstone after the antique, &c. which, by the King's orders, have been daubed with a dirty red colour, and produce a most disagreeable impression.

At the further end of the garden are two pretty summer-houses with marble baths, and vapour-baths, connected with a spacious harem, which consists of a quadrangular building, the windows and doors of which are towards the inner court. This edifice is so situated, that the King can see the amusements of the ladies from the colonnade of the palace. His Majesty often spends several days here secluded from all the rest of the world, and gives himself up completely to the pleasures of the harem.

We next visited the King's private mews: a large square court surrounded by the stables. Above 100 horses were led out before us; among which, were several fine Arab and half Arab animals, but they are all so well fed, that they are wholly incapacitated for any great exertion. The Indian horses (without Arab blood), which are seldom more than five feet two inches high, are not so handsome as the European; the head is large, and not so noble; the ears lie too much forward, but nevertheless, the animals are spirited, hardy, and vigorous. The stables are opposite the royal palace, and so near the bank of the river that we resolved to view the King's yacht.

The sovereigns of Oude have arrived at splendour and luxury, in every thing about them. Naseer ud-din Hyder procured, in 1820, the first steam-boat, for excursions on the Ganges; but this did not satisfy him, and he therefore obtained from Calcutta, at a great expense, a yacht built on the model of a man-of-war. On board this handsome vessel the King has his own apartment fitted up in the most costly manner; but which, as well as the vessel itself, is now in a very dirty and neglected state. On our way back we met the King's second son, a stout youth fifteen years of age, in an open palanquin, wearing a head-dress resembling a tiara, and surrounded by a disorderly crowd of dirty lance bearers and attendants on horseback and on camels; elephants and horses closed the rear. His countenance beamed with cheerfulness and contempt, and he repeatedly nodded to us in the most friendly manner.

In a desolate mangoe-garden, four miles to the south of the city, near to the river, is a large, shapeless palace, called Constantia, which was erected by Claude Martin, the Frenchman, at an expense of 150,000*l.* sterling. We rode to it the following morning, before sunrise, accompanied by some horsemen. Constantia, which is five stories high, is built of marble, sandstone, and bricks; it is a medley of the French, Italian, and Greek styles, combined with Hindoo and Mahometan architecture, and has two towers, which stand on either side of the platform: the battlements and towers are adorned with colossal lions. The apartments, which are small and dark, are ornamented with looking-glasses, shells, and various kinds of Italian sculptures, and bas-reliefs, of plaster of Paris and marble. It bears the following inscription: "*Labore et Constantia.*"

Claude Martin was originally a member of the Roman Catholic church, but having disagreed with it, he stigmatises its customs as prejudices, its ordinances as priestcraft. He found, however, no comfort in the other religious creeds which he successively adopted, and, perceiving, as he said, that their ways to heaven were even still more absurd than the faith in which he had been brought up, he subsequently returned to his first belief, and devoted his life to the relief of the poor and helpless. In this spirit, he founded, at the expence of 100,000*l.* sterling, the institution at Calcutta, called *la Martinière*; in which fifty Christian boys and twenty-six girls received education gratis. His body reposes in a marble sarcophagus, in one of the lower apartments of this palace, with the following inscription: "*Here lies Major-General Claude Martin, born at Lyons,* 1735, *arrived in India a common soldier, and died at Lucknow* 13*th of September,* 1800. *Pray for his soul.*" Four statues the size of life carved out of wood, representing grenadiers, with a musket on the shoulder, keep guard in the four niches.

This extensive palace is now in the possession of the King, who allows the English to live in it at their pleasure. From the summit of the towers, there is a very wide and noble prospect: to the south spreads the valley of the Goomty, bordered by corn-fields, jungles, and woods; and to the north lies the large handsome city, to which the minarets, and the gilded and white cupolas of the numerous palaces and sepulchres, give inexpressible splendour. In front of the palace of Constantia, is a reservoir, with a column forty feet high, rising in the centre, and the eye is refreshed by the bright colours of a pretty flower-garden, and the dark green of the mangoes, which flourish all around.

Next to this is an extensive domain, called the Dil-kusha Park, "The king's Delight;" it is an artificial wilderness, well stocked with antelopes, peacocks, and jackals. In this park is a small country-house, belonging to the King, which was built by Mr. Ousley an Englishman, who resided here as aide-de-camp to Naseer ud Dowlah. The apartments are fitted up in the French style, and are ornamented, with indifferent oil paintings. When we had viewed it, we rode home along a fine road lately made through the park.

After having refreshed myself with a bath, and partaken of a good breakfast, I mounted an elephant and rode to the observatory. The kings of Oude have for many years patronised astronomy, more, however, from motives of curiosity and love of astrology, than from any interest in the science itself. The observatory stands in the middle of a garden, at the south end of the city: it is provided with a library and the necessary astronomical instruments, and a new telescope was about to be set up. Major Wilcox, who is a very scientific man, and has the superintendence of this institution, has even introduced a magnetic observatory: he is assisted by several natives who have been educated in the English school, and of whose capacity, and accuracy, both in taking observations, and in making calculations, Major Wilcox spoke in the highest terms. The present king frequently visits the observatory in the hope of learning his fate from the stars. His Majesty has recently entreated

Major Wilcox to contrive some plan, by means of which a gun, which is to be placed before his palace, shall discharge itself, every day, precisely at twelve o'clock.

The last king, though constantly confined to his bed by bodily sufferings, and consequently unable to enjoy the sight of the various buildings, which he caused to be erected, took great interest in the embellishment of the city. He expended large sums in making the Husan Abad, a broad and handsome street, which runs parallel with the river towards the bridge, and traverses a considerable portion of the northern quarter. Thousands of people congregate here in the afternoons, and pass their time in the bazars, and in the fruit, flower, and corn-market. I also frequently resort thither mounted on an elephant, which affords the best possible opportunity of overlooking the whole, as well as of observing the details, and I daily contemplated these scenes of Indian life with increased interest.

In the centre of the Husan Abad is a lofty portal, ornamented with many small towers, and at the further extremity of the street is the Imaum Barree (holy place), where the Vizir Asoph ud Dowlah is buried. A noble gateway leads to the fore-court, which is planted with flowers, and opposite to it is one of the grandest structures in India, containing the mortal remains of the architect who erected the bridge. The façade is fronted by a vaulted veranda, 280 feet in length and 30 in breadth, and at the north end of it there is a silver pulpit. This is the resort of devotees; and whenever the priest chants verses from the Koran, a man with a drawn sword stands at his side. Among his audience, the descendants of the Prophet are distinguished by their green dress, and the priests by their black or blue robes. The veranda communicates with a vaulted hall 160 feet in length, 60 in breadth, and 40 in height, in the middle of which stands the silver tomb of the vizir and his wife; but this noble hall is deprived of all dignity or solemnity, by the mean and trifling ornaments of lamps, chandeliers, bells, pictures, and birds, with which it is bedizened. At either extremity of this hall are two square rooms sixty-two feet in breadth. Close to this colossal edifice stands a large mosque, built of sandstone; it is ornamented with two high minarets, and three bold vaulted cupolas; and, like the mausoleum, is painted white.

Not far distant in Husan Abad, is the sepulchre of Naseer ud Dowlah, which he caused to be erected for himself, and in which he was interred only a short time after it was finished. His principal servant, Asseen Ulla, who is in disgrace with the present King, but is under the protection of the English, has been nominated to the office of keeper of his master's tomb. The good-tempered little man, attired in his state dress, received us at the gate, and led us through a pretty flower-garden, where many fountains were playing: this garden is enclosed on both sides by stone buildings, which are copies of the Tauje Mahal, in miniature. The sepulchre, which is opposite the entrance, is a plain building with a veranda, and contains several apartments, in the centre and largest of which stands the silver sarcophagus. But here, too, there are so many chandeliers, lamps, glasses, and pictures hung, in the most tasteless manner, that it looked more like the show-room of a glass warehouse, than the sepulchre of a king: it is said, that articles of this description to the value of five lacs, or 50,000*l.* sterling, are accumulated here. The sight of these ridiculous absurdities so amused me that I could scarcely preserve my gravity; and when Asseen Ulla asked me whether I did not think it very beautiful and magnificent, I was actually so confused that I could not make any reply. No doubt, the poor fellow thought I was quite overcome by the magnificence of his master's tomb. The lateral buildings contain a menagerie of the rarest birds, and quadrupeds of India; a large gold-coloured, long-haired goat, from Nepaul, with the head of a cow, particularly attracted our notice. On parting, the good man presented us with some beautiful flowers; and after thanking him for his civility, we mounted our elephant, and proceeded to view the buildings in the Husan Abad street, and the old bazars of the city.

The objects which first engaged our attention were a tennis court, a Belvidere, and a menagerie, which lie near the bank of the river, and immediately strike the eye; we likewise saw a large mosque in an unfinished state, and which will probably ere long be a mass of ruins, as the present king is not inclined to grant the vast sums necessary for its completion. We were much amused with our rides through the old bazar, a long, narrow and dirty street, in which the principal business of Lucknow, with all its peculiarities, is centred. The bazars are kept on the ground-floors of the houses, which are three stories high; the two upper stories are furnished with neatly carved verandas, which run like balconies in front of the sitting-rooms. As soon as the sun declines, the inmates of these houses appear in the balconies in a variety of groups, and look at the traffic in the streets; and as most of the bayaderes reside here and appear unveiled, I had ample opportunity of seeing these fair women of Lucknow. They were all bare-headed, and their beautiful black hair fell down in braids, or was interwoven with jewels; most of them wore large nose-rings, which hung over the corners of the mouth, and their long ear-rings touched their shoulders. Very few of them could be called pretty, but they have piercing eyes, which look the more brilliant because their eyelids are blackened with antimony. A coloured scarf was thrown lightly and gracefully across the neck and shoulders, and displayed rather than concealed the fine contour of the upper part of their persons. They did not fail to make many remarks upon us, and sought to draw our attention, by laughing, joking, and tittering, but it is by no means advisable to pay any attention to them, as these bayaderes are extremely importunate.

General Nott had the goodness to obtain me the

privilege of an audience of his Majesty, to whom I was to be presented on the 2d of March. As we were not to go to the palace till 9 o'clock, I first visited the poor-house, which is under the direction of Dr. Logan. It contained 130 inmates, most of whom were blind. They were lodged in healthy, cleanly apartments, and seemed very comfortable. Dr. Logan employs them in spinning, weaving, and other light manual work, though he at first found great difficulty in effecting this; the blind especially being very unwilling to learn, because they considered it as a punishment not to be allowed to pass their lives in indolence. Now, however, the Doctor has the pleasure of seeing them quite happy in this employment, and manifesting their gratitude to him by the greatest diligence. Each of these poor persons costs two and a half rupees per month. During the famine of 1838, above 800 persons were received into this institution. There is an hospital connected with this poor-house, in which above sixty men and women enjoy every attention. Dr. Logan, every morning, receives the indigent poor of the city, who are furnished with medicines gratis. The beneficial influence of this hospital and dispensary may be inferred from the fact that above 6000 persons were relieved here last year, as I myself can bear witness to, from the tables which were shown me.

The appointed hour for my presentation to "The Protector of the Stars" having arrived, General Nott, Captain Shakespeare, and myself, accompanied by a guard on horseback, drove to the

Furrahbaksh, *i.e.* the place of pleasure. The royal palace lies at the south-east of the city, close to the right bank of the Goomty, and has six principal courts. A large portal, with iron gates, leads to the Pateh-Mahalah, in which is the spacious hall Naubut-Khan, where a military band usually performs every morning and evening. From this first court we entered the Baoli, an oblong parallelogram, ornamented with flower beds, in the centre of which is a large marble basin, where little boats were plying for the amusement of the ladies, and many beautiful fountains jetted the cool waters into the air. The Furrahbaksh lies towards the river: it consists of open arcades and many apartments which may be closed with the most costly curtains, and in the hot season are cooled by perfumed matted reeds, which the attendants maintain in a constant state of moisture. Opposite to the Furrahbaksh, flights of marble steps lead to the great throne hall, a splendid saloon, supported by pillars, where stands the golden throne, inlaid with diamonds, pearls, and rubies.

Towards the east, parallel with the Baoli, is Sangi-Dalaun: it is built of hewn stone, and rises from a vaulted terrace. It is surrounded with double arcades, behind which are the apartments of the inmates. The four corners and the principal façade are crowned with cupolas, whose richly silver gilt roofs glistened splendidly. The inner space is covered with a most beautiful bed of flowers, interspersed with fountains and fine shady avenues, and in the middle rises a small mosque, with gilded minarets and pavilions for the ladies. There are four distinct entrances to the apartments; a covered one on the north side for the ladies; one to the south for the king, and two portals on the east and west for strangers. The rooms are crowded with silk divans, works of art, paintings, and engravings. In almost every room there is a portrait of Naseer-ud-din Hyder, who was sometimes taken in the Indian, and sometimes in the European dress. Among the lower apartments, we accidentally discovered a room hung with black cloth, on which skeletons were painted, and where all sorts of instruments of torture were kept. We were afterwards informed that Hyder used here to confine those women of his harem who withstood his orders, and had actually suffered two of them to perish in this horrible chamber.

Adjoining this edifice on the east, is the Zenanah, which contains a mass of irregular buildings, without external windows: they are the palaces termed Shish-Mahal, Khurd-Mahal, and Rung-Mahal, each of which is environed with small flower gardens, and fountains. Towards the north lies another garden, hemmed in by buildings, which contains the public offices; on the opposite side of the road on the bank of the river, there are three bastions with cupolas covered with silver roofs richly gilt. On the centre bastion is an octagon palace in which the king's mother resides.

We left our carriage at the gate of the Baoli, and General Nott was conveyed to Furrahbaksh in a tanjan; and we followed the General, accompanied by the Ameen-ud-dowlah, the King's prime minister. The King, accompanied by a numerous suite of courtiers, came to meet us at the staircase of Furrah-baksh; General Nott presented me to his Majesty, who gave me his hand and addressed some kind words to me. He is a tall, corpulent man, with a good-natured, but very ugly countenance, which is disfigured by a nose of extraordinary size. A green silk choga, embroidered with gold and silver, fell from his shoulders to the ankles; red silk pantaloons and shoes, embroidered with gold, and the points turned up, completed his dress. He wore a high cap like a tiara, covered with jewels, several strings of large handsome pearls hung round his neck, and two costly diamond rings on his finger. His mode of life and the bias of his inclinations were painfully impressed upon his languid countenance. His Majesty has four wives and nearly 200 concubines, and a great number of children. One of the king's wives (if the portrait which was shown me is faithful) must be one of the handsomest women in India. Effeminate, weak, and without character, the King loves neither the dangers and fatigues of the chase, nor the privations of a military life: he fancies he has a taste for building, and, at present, he is possessed with the mania of having all the houses in the city coloured or painted.

The Ameen-ud-dowlah, the king's prime minister and favourite, has been raised from the dregs of the people to his high dignity; but he is totally ignorant of every branch of public business, full of distrust, and always ready to extricate himself by low intrigues. He has no beard, and he is too slightly made to pass in India for a handsome man. When he speaks, an expression of cunning lurks about the corners of his mouth, and his sparkling eyes are constantly in motion.

As the King had some business to transact with General Nott, his Majesty retired with that officer and Captain Shakespeare to an adjoining apartment. Meantime the Ameen-ud-dowlah offered to show me every thing that was worth seeing; and the renowned Derbar Fakeer Meer Hasseen Ali, called Londonney, because he has lived several years in London, acted as interpreter. The Ameen-ud-dowlah made me acquainted with the persons around us, among whom one of the King's physicians, a handsome slender Persian, was distinguished by his rich and elegant dress. His business, and that of his two colleagues, a Mussulman and a Hindoo, is to visit the king twice a day, and to feel his pulse. Before the king gets into the bath in the morning, and when he gets out of it, these learned doctors are at hand, and with grave countenances are prepared to comfort or to counsel their august master: one might almost think, that the King required to be told by his physicians whether he is sick or well. Meer Hasseen said, that the two black eunuchs, who are very richly dressed in silk and costly shawls, and with gold chains and watches, were extremely happy men, for they could visit the ladies as often as they pleased, and were not only lodged and clothed, but received 300 rupees per month!

The Furrahbaksh contains a large saloon with several smaller apartments adjoining, which are fitted up entirely in the European style. The view towards the river, overlooking the broad stream and the gardens on the opposite bank, is extremely beautiful. On one table in the room lay a number of different head-dresses, as his Majesty likes to change his head-gear very frequently. In half an hour I was summoned to the King, and told to sit down opposite to him: he desired me to tell him much about my country, and very naturally made many enquiries respecting my king and his army. The Ameen-ud-dowlah then appeared with the Hara, the chain wrought of silver thread linked with seven shields, on which the royal arms — two swords, a fish, the tiara, and a crown, are stamped in gold. Of this chain of honour, there are, if I may so express myself, two classes, but both are equally tasteless and worthless, for were it otherwise, the receiver would not be permitted to keep them; that of the first class is valued at twenty rupees. The King first hung the chain of the first class round the neck of General Nott, who thanked his Majesty, and his prime minister; I was then honoured with a similar chain, and as there were no more of the first class left, Captain Shakespeare received two of the second class. The distribution of ottar of roses succeeded to this ceremony, and was also the signal for us to take leave. We were accompanied by his Majesty to the lowest step of the Furrahbaksh, and on parting, he embraced us, and cordially shook hands.

The most remarkable things at Lucknow are the sepulchral monuments and gardens on which large sums of money are expended. Among the former is that of Saadut Ali Khan, which lies at the east end of the city; it is a simple but handsome building, surrounded by verandas, resting upon columns, and consists of a lofty vaulted circular hall, in the centre of which stands a silver cenotaph. The Nabob himself reposes in the lower vaults, in a marble sarcophagus, between his daughter and his grand-daughter. The garden, which is entirely neglected, is surrounded by colonnades and small buildings, which are inhabited by some natives of Cashmere, who fled thither twelve years ago. Hukeem Mehdi, the King's minister and the most judicious counsellor that ever lived at this court, not only gave them a settlement here, but plenty of work, for he at once availed himself of their skill in making shawls. They are still employed in this manner, but their work is much inferior to that of Cashmere, and here, too, like their countrymen, they bear the character of liars and swindlers.

Ghazi ud Deen Hyder Shah, the first king of Oude, is buried on the left bank of the Goomty, in a plain vaulted building which is surrounded by a fine garden. The retired situation, and the silence which prevails here, make this a favourite resort of devotees, and we found a priest here reading the Koran to some pious Mussulmans. Not far from it is the King's menagerie, a large, square court, surrounded by piazzas: we were shown thirteen tigers, many monkeys, rabbits, fighting antelopes, and rams, and fighting quails;

the latter bit each other with such fury, that the keeper was obliged to shut up the little enraged creatures before the combat was decided. Their love of fighting is excited by jealousy; and when the King has large entertainments, he has them put upon the table at dessert, for the amusement of himself and his guests.

I here saw the Beejee or Indian Ichneumon, which is very common in the district of Moorshedabad. When taken young it is easily domesticated, and is very much attached to human beings. It possesses the remarkable property of being able to kill the most poisonous serpents, for even the Cobra on seeing the Beejee coils itself up, and remains in a state of stupor. The Beejee meanwhile looks at its intended victim with a piercing eye, and, at the slightest motion, pounces upon it, seizes the serpent by the head, and kills it upon the spot.

I am sorry to say, the value of this menagerie has been very much decreased by the removal of several animals—six Rhinoceroses and several other remarkable animals having been taken to adorn various sepulchral monuments.

In conclusion, I must mention the Shah-Manzil (*i. e.* the King's house), which is situated in a fine garden, and consists of a spacious apartment, supported by columns, furnished with silk divans, and three chandeliers, of the value of 81,000*l.* sterling. A large marble basin in front of it was nearly completed. Though the English residents have many gardens, they have, however, likewise formed a fine large park at the south-west end of the city, where they enjoy the beauties of surrounding nature.

On the morning of the fourth of March, the last that I spent at Lucknow, I took a ride along the left bank of the Goomty. Immediately beyond the bridge of boats, a path leads close to the waterside; luxuriant corn-fields alternate with fine gardens, where the domes and gilded tops of the summer houses appear between the thick foliage of lofty mangoes which were covered with blossom. This beautiful landscape which we enjoyed in the mild temperature of 65° F., reminded us of some of our native scenery; but the picture became quite Oriental when, on our return, we had the city before us, with its innumerable minarets, its gilded and white cupolas, and the elegant little towers of the royal palace, the sepulchres and mosques, whose brilliant colours, contrasted with the bright blue of the sky, produced a wonderful effect. The river exhibited a scene of uncommon activity, traffic boats, small barks, and fishing boats, were rowing backwards and forwards; the King's gondola, adorned at the forepart with two horses leaping from the jaws of a fish, was steering to the Dilkusha Park, in case it might be his Majesty's pleasure to come back by water.

On my return, I found an invitation from the most wealthy Hindoo banker (who was said to be worth a million sterling) to visit his summer house. The heat at noon was so oppressive, being 96° F., that it was impossible to go thither, except upon an elephant, and I accordingly again availed myself of this agreeable mode of conveyance. This country house was situated near the bridge, in a garden, which runs down almost to the river side, and is built and furnished in the ancient French style. The walls of the apartments were hung with indifferent engravings, representing the adventures of Cupid, and, in the gardens, the gods of Greece, made of sandstone, rose between the high hedges, which surrounded the flower beds, in the middle of which stood a cow painted white!

The brigade of English troops stationed here is three miles to the north-west of the city: the officers and men are in bungalows and barracks, erected expressly for their use. The officers are not only invited by the King several times during the year, to breakfast and dinner parties, when they are entertained with combats of animals, but they likewise receive from him all necessary assistance for hunting tigers and other wild beasts in the jungles, which abound in game. Several of these enthusiastic sportsmen were out, during my stay here, with the King's elephants, on a tiger hunt, and returned after three weeks' absence, with a rich booty of no less than forty tigers; so successful a hunt was almost unheard of. Some of the skins were presented to me, the largest of which, measures nine feet from the head to the tail.

With feelings of gratitude to my hospitable friend, to whose kindness I am indebted for the agreeable and instructive hours I spent at Lucknow, I left the city at four o'clock in the afternoon, in a palanquin, to return to Cawnpoor. The rays of the sun darted so fiercely, that my bearers could only proceed very slowly. When we approached the second stage, dark grey clouds came up on all sides, and completely obscured the sun, and, at the evening twilight, I was enveloped in intense darkness, illumined by lightning. The wind soon raged with great fury; a heavy tempest arose, large drops of rain began to fall, the thunder approached nearer and nearer, and the rain at length fell in such torrents, that our torches were extinguished. The soil was so swampy that my bearers could scarcely move onwards, and they frequently slipped, and sometimes even fell down, for the obscurity was so profound, that they were only enabled to see their way, when the dazzling flashes of lightning shone across their path. Under these circumstances I was not unwilling to yield to their request, and they accordingly set me down, under the arch of a bridge. Here we remained nearly two hours, till the rain ceased, and the storm had abated; but I had scarcely set out with the bearers of the third station, when a second, equally violent thunder storm overtook us, and I was obliged to take refuge in a village.

Notwithstanding this delay, I reached the bungalows of Cawnpoor, amid fine weather, at seven o'clock in the morning. The tempest had been equally severe here, and thunder storms prevailed during the whole day, although they are quite uncommon at this season of the year. In the evening, however, when the sky cleared up, we were all astonished to see a comet in the western horizon, with a tail thirty-five degrees in length. At first this remarkable phenomenon, which the natives consider a token of unusual events, was mistaken for a luminous cloud.

I spent the evening with General Gray, in a circle of experienced and intelligent officers: they were my last cheerful hours at Cawnpoor, for the following morning, the 6th of March, at 7 o'clock, I commenced my palanquin journey to Allahabad, which is 129 miles distant. The forty-eight hours' storm was succeeded by a glorious day, which renovated all nature. The dark blue vault was unclouded, the air pure and cool, and the foliage and the corn-fields rejoiced in unwonted freshness.

The road to Allahabad runs through the fruitful Doab, which is situated between the Jumna and the Ganges, only a few miles distant from the latter river; and its peculiar freshness in this dry season was very remarkable. It is a boundless garden, in which sugar-cane, indigo, cotton, poppy, wheat, barley, and many vegetables flourish. Beautiful groves of mangoes, tamarinds, and bananas, overshadow the villages, pagodas, mosques, and tanks, and give an ever-varying beauty to the landscape, which is animated by pilgrims, peasantry, travellers on foot and horseback, heavily-laden carts, and camels—altogether this district presents one of the most original and picturesque scenes of Indian life.

Before reaching Allahabad, we passed through a fine avenue of Neems (*Melia Azadirachta*), acacias, and mangoes, extending several miles in length, which led to the bungalows, and after journeying for the space of thirty-two hours, I found myself in the handsome villa of Mr. Woodcock, to whom I had a letter of introduction from one of his friends, and who had been expecting me for several days. Mr. Woodcock who holds a high civil office, possesses one of the finest bungalows, where every thing which can contribute to the comforts of life were again placed at my disposal.

Allahabad (situated 25° 27′ N. lat., and 81° 50′ E. lon. from Greenwich) consists, properly speaking, of three quarters: first, the fort, which is situated on a tongue of land on the large Bhat Prayag of the Doab, where the clear waters of the Jumna join the dull yellow waters of the Ganges; secondly, the town, situated to the north-west on the Jumna, which is here 1400 yards broad; and, thirdly, the bungalows and barracks which extend to a considerable distance to the north and east.

Allahabad is one of the most frequented places of pilgrimage, because the Hindoos consider it most meritorious to rush into the purifying waves of the sister streams, and to carry some of the waters to their most distant homes. As soon as the pilgrim arrives, he sits down on the bank of the river, and has his head shaved in such a manner, that every hair may fall into the water, because the holy books promise for every hair so sacrificed, a residence of a million of years in heaven! After he is shaven he bathes, and on the same day, or at latest, on the following day, he performs the funereal rites for his deceased ancestors. Many of these fanatics here put an end to their existence: they go in a boat to the spot where the two sacred streams meet, and, after having concluded certain prescribed ceremonies, and tied three large water jugs round their bodies, they sink into the stream. Others have thrown themselves with such impetuosity into the sacred depths, that they were not seen to rise again.

In the month of February, especially, thousands of these devotees, rich and poor, come here together: they regard the sacred stream with the same sensations, as the thirsty wanderer in the desert beholds the well of the oases. Their souls seem to be ravished, their exhausted frames are invigorated by a new strength, and, with redoubled steps, they praise the name of their god, with increasing fervour. A rajah, attended by a large train, was still here on our arrival, and had pitched his tents under mango trees.

The fort, which was built by the Emperor Akbar of blocks of red stone, is situated on the tongue of land at the junction of the river, which is rather elevated. It is now a bastioned quinquangle: the ancient walls, with semicircular bastions, face the two streams; the land side is quite regular, and consists of two bastions, and a half bastion, with three ravelins. In the middle of the fort stands the ancient granite-column, with inscriptions in Pali and Sanscrit, upon which, in conformity to ancient tradition, a lion passant has lately been placed. On the side next the water the spacious palace is fitted up for residences for superior officers, and the cool vaulted subterraneous apartments afford a welcome shelter against the hot winds. On the other hand, the barracks for the European troops, though built with great attention to the climate, do not at this season of the year afford sufficient protection to the soldiers, who here often suffer from fever.

An ancient Hindoo temple lies upon the beach below the level of the sacred river: its subterranean chambers are paved with flags, and rest upon columns; the Lingam Patalpuri is preserved here, and lighted by lamps. I must not omit to mention the arsenal in the fort, one of the very largest in India, which supplies all the northern provinces with arms and ammunition; it contains arms for 30,000 men and 30 pieces of cannon of different calibre. All is ranged in the most complete order.

The city, which has 30,000 inhabitants, consists of brick houses, of two and three stories high, and has in these latter times become more cleanly, but it is still called by the natives Fakirabad, that is, "the beggars' town," partly on account of its poverty, and partly on account of the great resort of fakirs and pilgrims. Trade and commerce have very much increased, since the establishment of a communication by steam boats between this and Calcutta. The numerous villas, and bungalows of the civil and military officers, surrounded by beautiful gardens, give a grand appearance to the place; for there are, probably, few other spots in India which have such handsome, and richly fitted up buildings of this kind. Roads, planted with avenues, wind between them and lead to the fort, the city, and several places of the principal circumjacent localities, as Allahabad is the seat of a high court of justice and a great military station of two regiments, some depôts, and two companies of artillery.

The whole district of Allahabad contains 2760 English square miles, of which, however, only 984,951 acres are cultivated, and is inhabited by a population of 949,446, of whom 651,877 are Hindoos, and 297,569 Mahometans.

Being at the seat of a great tribunal, I will take the opportunity of saying a few words on the administration of civil justice in India. All complaints that are brought before the court must be on stamped paper; engagements, documents, &c. to the amount of 32*s.*, must have a stamp of three halfpence; and up to 6*l.* 8*s.* 0*d.* the stamp of three pence; and this charge rises progressively, so that for 10,000*l.* sterling, a stamp of 5*l.* is required. In matters appertaining to a court of justice, and in appeals to a superior court, when the object in dispute is not worth more than 32*s.*, the stamp is 2*s.* and also rises progressively, so that for a value of 10,000*l.* the high stamp of 200*l.* sterling is required. Answers and replies must have a stamp from 1*s.* to 8*s.*; petitions and complaints to magistrates, relative to calumny, adultery, theft, &c. are likewise on stamped paper; namely, to a collector or magistrate one penny, to a provincial court 2*s.*, and to the board of revenue, or the Sudder Dewanny, 4*s.* Farmers, who have to pay rent to the government, are exempt from stamp duty, in matters relating to that subject.

In the north-western provinces (the government of Agra) the administration of civil justice is as follows:—first, that of the moonsiffs or native judges in the lowest court; whose decisions are limited to suits for personal property, not exceeding 30*l.* sterling, and in which no European is interested. The next court is that of the Sudder Ameen, the judge in which is generally a native, and where the matter in dispute does not exceed 100*l.* value. The third court, that of the superior Sudder Ameen, can receive any complaint of unlimited value. The next in order is the district, or Zilla court, the judges in which are Europeans, and the last instance, is the Sudder Dewanny Adawlut.

In these north-western provinces, which have a population of 32,000,000 inhabitants, there were in five years, from 1836 to 1840, on the whole, 261,154 complaints before all the tribunals, of which only 2314, were decided by European judges; all the rest were left to the native judges. Of 31,931 appeals, 17,090 were decided by European courts, the others by the native judges. In Bengal, the population, which is 40,000,000, there were, on an average of three years, 105,000 complaints, before all the courts, that is, one for every 381 souls.

The administration of civil justice in the Presidency of Madras is different. The village Moonsiff decides in matters to the value of ten rupees without any appeal. The district Moonsiff receives all complaints to the amount of 100*l.* sterling, but those above that sum, to 500*l.* sterling, come before the Zilla (European) tribunal. The Sudder Ameen, consisting of native judges, receives complaints to the value of 250*l.*: the registrars (European) to 300*l.* sterling. The superior Sudder Ameen, or the Zilla judge, up to 500*l.*; and the Provincial Tribunal decides in all matters of higher value. In this Presidency, with a population of more than 13,000,000, there were, in four years, 195,816 complaints before all the tribunals, of which only 5291 were decided by European judges.

In the Presidency of Bombay, civil justice is administered almost exclusively by native judges, in which it is not a little remarkable, that there is a tribunal resembling our arbitrators, the contending parties being obliged, prior to bringing their affair into court, to lay it before the Panchaeet, a jury of five confidential persons, to be decided, if possible, in an amicable manner. From the 1st of July, 1837, to the 1st of January, 1842, with a population of 6,270,461 inhabitants, 309,783 complaints were brought before the tribunal; of which only 8848 were not settled, and 713 appeals were made to the superior tribunal.

I made excursions in the neighbourhood every morning and evening, in company with Mr. Woodcock. Though the country about Allahabad is planted with mangoe groves, tamarinds, figs, and bananas, and the bushes are full of wild roses, yet the character of the country is quite peculiar, from the species of grasses which are introduced from the neighbouring mountains, and from the bamboo, sugar-cane, andropogon, and other plants, and a variety of corn, which luxuriate here. Indigo, cotton, wheat, barley, rape-seed, potatoes, turnips, poppy, rice, and jowary, flourish in the fields, and the gardens produce, not only bananas and mangoes, but likewise European vines, figs, apples, and plums. During our first ride, I had an opportunity of seeing the method of gathering opium, which is done in the following manner:—In the evening, incisions are made in the poppy heads, from which the opium exudes during the night, and is taken off before sun-rise, by old and young, with knives, and collected in poppy leaves. The price of a seer of fine opium is three rupees eleven annas, of which, however, the collector seldom gets more than one rupee. According to the statements of the country people here, an acre of land produces in good years only ten or twelve seers; as the opium is a monopoly, the quantity collected must be delivered to the appointed officers. There are two great opium stations: the opium agent of Benares is at Ghazipoor, and the agent of Bahar at Patna. The former has the superintendence of all the districts from Ghazipoor to Simla; the latter has under him the eastern and south-eastern district. These agents have their deputies in all parts of the country, who conclude the contracts with the opium planters, receive the opium collected, and send it to the principal stations, with a list of the names of the growers: there the opium is tasted, classed, and valued, it is made up into balls, and packed up in poppy flowers.

Among the ancient buildings in this city is the sepulchre of Shah Khasro, son of Akbar the Great. It lies to the north-west of the city, in a garden recently laid out by the English residents, who repair hither in cool days, to enjoy the shade of the fine tamarinds, figs, and orange trees, which abound in it. High arched gates lead first into a large court, which was originally intended for the caravans and travellers, but now serves for the residence of pilgrims; a second court is fitted up for bazars. The tomb is built of red sandstone, but it is far inferior both in splendour and in elegance to the tombs of Delhi and Agra.

In the vicinity of this tomb is the prison for the criminals of the district. And nearly 1000 of them are now here, under the guard of a detachment. When not employed out of doors on improvements in the city, they work at various trades in the airy apartments of their prison, by which means the cost of each individual is only 1¼ rupees per month. There is also a sick ward, where the greatest order prevails, which indeed is the case throughout the whole establishment.

The cool of the evening always invites the English into the open air; and the many carriages and parties of ladies and gentlemen on horseback strongly remind us of home, and we might almost fancy ourselves transported thither, did not the grooms running by the side with chowrees, and the coachman and servants in gay turbans and white garments, convince us that we are in Hindoostan, the second home of the English. The tone of society likewise affords many reminiscences of Europe. Since my arrival in India I have daily experienced the hospitality of the English, and am indebted for many agreeable hours to some of the first families. As the heat is very great during the day, the usual dinner hour is 8 o'clock, when each guest brings his own servant. The evening is generally passed with music and social conversation.

The distance from Allahabad to Calcutta, by way of Benares, is 488 miles by land, and by water 800 miles, on account of the many windings of the Ganges. By means of the steam boats which take a passage boat in tow, and proceed only by day, you seldom reach the capital of the country in less than ten days, though the expense is nearly the same. The passage down the river costs 350 rupees. I had to pay nearly 400 rupees for my dawk, because the bearers in the south of Bengal are accustomed to receive higher pay.

I took leave of Mr. Woodcock on the 12th of March, and was carried along a shady dam on the right side of the Ganges, which is here enclosed in banks of thirty to forty feet high, across the bridge of boats to the opposite village of Daraganga. The Ganges was, at this time, scarcely 600 paces wide, but in the rainy season, its waters fill the entire bed, which is a mile in width. As soon as we had crossed this sandy bed, we entered upon a road which, with very few exceptions, is in an excellent condition the whole way to Benares; but in the rainy season, it is often a good deal worn by the very heavily laden carts and waggons which traverse it.

The sun sunk behind heavy black clouds, with a temperature of 88° Fahr., and the lightning played in the south-eastern horizon during the whole night. Although the bearers proceeded very leisurely along this road, they performed the whole journey of seventy-five miles in less than twenty-four hours; for at 12 o'clock on the following day I reached the bungalows at Benares. Major Carpenter had sent his servant to meet me, with the request that I would take up my abode at his house: an invitation for which I was indebted to the kindness of Mr. Maddock, who had introduced me to this distinguished officer.

Benares is situated 25° 21′ north latitude, and 82° 40′ east longitude. It is called Varanasi in Sanscrit, from two small streams, the Varana and the Asi, which here empty themselves into the Ganges. This ancient, celebrated city, called the Casi, or "the Splendid," in the Ramayana, lies in a plain, and is built in a semicircle, on the left bank of the Ganges, at an elevation of sixty feet. Four miles beyond the concave of this extensive semicircle, which forms the city, lies the village of Secrole, in a northerly direction, and to the west, the numerous bungalows of the resident British. These are surrounded by gardens, and are connected with each other, and with the city, by good roads; pontine bridges are thrown across the deep beds of the Varana and Asi.

Towards the south are the villages and gardens

of Indians of rank, because, not only have many persons of great wealth, who await their death upon this consecrated spot, taken up their abode here, but many dethroned rajahs have fixed their habitation in this city. Among these, a branch of the royal family of the house of Delhi, the rajah of Benares, the ex-rajah of Coorg, the rajah Durjan Saul of Bhurtpoor, and the ex-rajah of Sattara, live here in retirement, under the special superintendence of Major Carpenter, on pensions which have been granted to them. Though we should be naturally led to suppose that their common misfortunes would induce them to sympathise with each other, it is painful to see the very opposite spirit manifested by them.

Whenever one of these noble Indians goes abroad to enjoy the fresh air, his attendants strut on before, and he reposes very comfortably in a takt-i-rawan, fanned with the cow's tail by his chowree burdar, who keeps close at his side, and is followed by several suwars.

The number of houses in Benares is estimated at about 30,000, of which 12,000 are strong and massively built, and 8000 belong to the priests alone. The latter residences are inhabited by the families of the Brahmins, who subsist chiefly on the daily offerings of the rich and pilgrims. There are no less than 1000 temples (Sivalas) and 333 mosques. It is very difficult accurately to determine the number of inhabitants, but according to the last census, which may be pretty well depended upon, they amount to 200,000*; among which there are 2000 students, and 7170 Hindoo fakirs and religious beggars. The population of the entire district of Benares, which comprises an extent of 1008 square miles, is 519,903, of which about 457,417 are Hindoos, and 62,486 Mahometans; and, in the city and its immediate environs, there are from 200 to 300 native Christians.

The Hindoo population is divided into four great classes; the Brahmins, the Kshatree or Rajahpoots, the Vaisyas, and the Sudras. There is also a fifth class, called Shankar Baran, to which the present Rajah of Benares belongs, who asserts that they are of the Bhumeehar Brahmins, *i. e.* of the Brahmins who cultivate the soil. They consider themselves the purest and most distinguished descendants of the highest Brahmins, but they, in fact, owe their origin to a Brahmin father and a Rajahpoot mother, and therefore cannot enter into a matrimonial alliance with the higher castes, of a wholly pure descent.

Among the lower classes are the Domes, Passees, and Bhars, who are indisputably the legal possessors of the soil. They are, however, at present employed in the meanest services, such as burning the dead, watching and cleaning the streets, &c. They are looked upon as unclean by the higher castes, who consider themselves defiled if they approach, or accidentally touch them. Besides two upper schools, there are several Hindoo schools,

* Mr. Princep states the population in 1822 and 1823 at 181,482.

two hospitals, and a blind institution; the latter of which was founded by the late rajah, and is supported by the British government.

On the evening of my arrival, Major Carpenter introduced me to many of his friends, whose intellectual conversation gave the true zest to the splendid entertainment, and kept up our cheerful circle till the hour of midnight. We arranged that I should visit the city, and its many places of interest, the next day, in company with General Simpson. The best and most undisturbed mode for a European to inspect so large and animated a place as Benares, is on the back of an elephant; and we accordingly proceeded to the entrance of the city, where we mounted the majestic animal that was awaiting our arrival.

The exterior of Benares, does not betray any of the splendour, the riches, and the curiosities which it contains; the streets are narrow and crooked; the houses, which, for coolness and shade, rise to the height of five and six stories, are built in the strangest and most singular style of architecture, being ornamented with verandas and projections of all kinds, and fretwork galleries, which run round each story. The lower stories are usually built of hewn stone, and, like the galleries and verandas, are very richly painted. In the suburbs, the houses are constructed of clay or bricks; they are seldom more than two stories in height, and are thatched with palm leaves or reeds. Glass windows are very rarely seen, even in the largest buildings, their place being supplied by wooden lattice-work, which is carved in every variety of pattern. The streets became narrower and more animated the farther we penetrated the city; indeed they were sometimes so confined that there was scarcely room for our elephant. Fearful ravages must be caused, if the cholera or small pox, or any other infectious disease, breaks out in these close, narrow places.

At the first market-place, numbers of Hindoos and Mussulmans were offering sacred collars, composed of horn, ivory, and flowers, for sale, and we saw a great many devotees, and lame and blind persons, and crowds of the most impudent beggars, mingled in the throng. Groups of people, from the Brahmin down to the lowest caste, were assembled round various houses, listening to the most wretched music, or gazing at the distorted countenances of different fakirs.

In another quarter of the city our attention was allured by wily bayaderes, who came to the lattices, or on the galleries, and endeavoured to attract our notice. Benares is famed for training the most beautiful bayaderes, who are also consecrated within the walls of this city: they are very proud of the place of their birth, but go into the most distant provinces of the empire. Their life is frittered away in dress, folly, and dancing; and, as long as their charms have the power of attracting, it is interwoven, as a privilege, with a succession of fleeting, transient amours; yet this established custom not only gains them the esteem of the people, but even the protection of the priesthood. When they parade through the streets, seated on a carriage, drawn by fine oxen, and dressed in rich and gaily-coloured costume, the populace are quite delighted to get a sight of these beauties, who group themselves with the most singular grace and attraction, and, in the most seductive manner, suffer their elegant and voluptuous forms to appear to advantage beneath their aerial dress, or their light shawl, flung carelessly over their shoulders. As they pass along the streets they sing a plaintive, monotonous song, accompanied by a tambourine, and a small trumpet, and, as they seem ever ready for sport, give vent to their mirth in humorous observations, while their fine large black eyes, which are encircled with antimony, gleam like sparks of fire.

Benares, however, is also the seat of learning and of the arts and sciences. It possesses schools and colleges for the priests, in which the laws and doctrines of Menu are commented on in Sanscrit. I was extremely interested in seeing the gravity and dignity of the learned Brahmins and their scholars, with their painted faces, and their fine expressive eyes, and all attired in pure white garments.

In the bazars, again, the attraction is an exhaustless store of the richest goods of all kinds; indeed the beautiful gold and silver work, the fine muslins and silks wrought with the same costly material, the elegant vessels of metal and copper, and the neat fancy work made of peacocks' feathers, might engage the attention of a stranger for days together.

After wandering about for more than an hour in

this singular little Hindoo world, which has hitherto maintained its purity and originality, we rode to the sacred fountain of Gyan-bapee. In the same manner as the Emperor Aurengzebe endeavoured to celebrate the triumph of the Koran over the law of Menu, by building a mosque on the site of a Hindoo temple which he had destroyed, in the middle of the city, on the banks of the sacred Ganges, so Akbar intended, by the erection of a mosque on this most sacred of all the Hindoo fountains, to proclaim the triumph of Islamism. "But the gods," say the Brahmins, "descended into the neighbouring well, and prevented his design." The Gyan-bapee is surrounded by pagodas and places of prayer, and it is so closely encompassed with buildings, that we were obliged to dismount from our elephant several streets before we reached it. It is impossible to conceive any thing more dirty, disgusting or repulsive, than the sight of this Hindoo sanctuary, which amply proves how much this religion has degenerated.

Several priests conducted us into the interior. The well is thirty feet deep, and is surrounded by a wall of hewn stone and fret-work, round which there are stone seats; the water was dirty and green. Close to the well there is a platform, composed of blocks of granite, on which the holy cow stood. On one of the stone benches, by the wall of the well, sat a very aged little man, crouched together: and though silvery locks hung over his temples, and his countenance was furrowed and wrinkled, his eyes sparkled with youthful fire, and he spoke with enthusiasm of the sanctity and wonders of this sacred spot. He was resolved, he said, to await his death here, as he was convinced that this would facilitate his way to heaven. At his side stood a naked fakir, whose hair hung like ropes from his head to the calves of his legs, and who had painted his body and face in such a strange and hideous manner, that I could not take my eyes off him. He appeared to answer our compassionate looks with scorn and contempt.

Adjoining the well are several small, dark temples, and places of prayer, which are lighted only by lamps: one of these temples is set apart for childless women. As we were considered unclean, we were not permitted to enter the sanctuary, in which their god, hewn in stone, was surrounded by numerous lamps; and we were obliged to content ourselves with looking at it through the narrow door. Sacred cows and calves were walking about in several apartments: two of these animals lay dead upon the floor, and the pestilential smell quickly drove us into the open air.

These pagodas, are covered with painted stone roofs, one of which was overlaid by Runjeet Singh, with plates of gold to the value of three lacs. Though the impression which the sight of this Hindoo temple made on us, was not calculated to tempt us to visit any other, yet, as I wished to see some of the most holy places, we proceeded to a pagoda, at a short distance, where they were in the act of performing worship, as we entered. A dirty Faquir, wearing the band of a brahmin across his shoulder, held his right hand elevated, and in his left a writing, from which he read, in a low voice, some prayers in Sanscrit: he stood the whole time on one leg, and occasionally struck his breast, with a violence approaching to fury. He was surrounded by a number of penitents, who listened to him with devotion and tokens of contrition.

The observatory founded by the celebrated Rajah Jeysingh of Jeypoor, is built of blocks of red sandstone, and is situated at the southern extremity of the city, close to the left bank of the Ganges. Like that of Delhi, it contains colossal gnomons and quadrants, but is not on so magnificent a scale. Being placed on an eminence, it commands an extensive prospect over the sacred streams, the city, and part of the environs. We here took a boat, to enjoy the fine view of the city from the water, and to observe the habits of the Hindoos, on the purifying stream of the Ganges. During this little excursion on the river, which is undoubtedly one of the most interesting in the world, most of the manners and customs of this remarkable people passed in living pictures before our eyes.

The splendid flight of stairs, called Ghauts, which runs far down into the river, were crowded with people, who stood on the steps by hundreds, in picturesque groups, bathing, or pouring water over themselves; at other points, along the banks, rose the flames of the funereal piles, of those who had died during the day, while the relatives, clothed in white garments, sat around in solemn silence. Here was a man, who, feeling his death approaching, had caused himself to be brought, on a couch, to the sacred stream, there to breathe out his spirit. I was informed that if a man, under these circumstances, should recover, he never returns to his family, but dedicates the remainder of his life to the service of the temple. Lamps were kindled in front of the pagodas, and brahmins and devotees surrounded the consecrated places. But a most revolting sight was presented by the many dead bodies, which are borne down the stream, a prey to the fish and vultures, and which taint the air to a considerable distance around. These corpses were those poor persons, whose families do not possess the means of defraying the expense of a funeral pile.

As all the Hindoo princes of India, and even the chief Hindoo families, here possess their own pagodas, sanctuaries, and palaces, which have very handsome wide marble stairs, leading down to the water's edge, the whole shore is covered with the finest buildings of this kind, which rise in terraces from the bank of the stream. They are inhabited by ambassadors, Brahmins, and Vakils, who daily perform their prescribed expiatory usages, and bring their sacrifices. Some of these palaces have been much rent by earthquakes, and the shattered fragments of several of the steps have fallen into the stream. The palace of the Rajah of Gwalior has suffered the most: a circumstance which the pious Hindoos regard as an evil omen for this princely family.

We left our boat, and landed opposite to a

mosque erected by the Emperor Aurungzebe, in order to take a survey of the building, and of the Mahadeo temple, as well as of the many sacred places in its vicinity. Several Hindoos conducted us through dark, narrow, dirty passages to the most holy of these places of pilgrimage, which are the daily resort of thousands of people, and took us to the entrance, where we saw the idol lighted up with lamps. It is impossible that any, but the credulous Hindoo, can feel himself elevated and edified by the sight of this monster. Indeed it appears incredible how any people can tolerate such a degrading idol service as this.

The mosque which is built of red hewn sandstone is situated on an eminence which rises 100 feet above the level of the water. The principal cupola is flanked by two lofty minarets, which are ascended by winding stairs. We mounted one of these, as we were told that the upper gallery commanded a fine distant prospect. The wide expanse of the most sacred stream in the world winds through a boundless valley, which is covered in the greatest luxuriance with all the varied productions of this Indian region. Mangoes, banyanes, acacias, bananas, pipala, and tamarinds, rear their splendid and umbrageous crowns above the rich undergrowth. Here the eye traces village after village, embosomed amid luxuriant foliage, and in the north-east it rests upon the immense throng of closely built houses of this vast city, which stretches out in a semicircle, and is surrounded by the most beautiful gardens, villas, and bungalows.

Standing on the pinnacle of a towering minaret, we seemed so far removed from the bustle and activity of Benares and the Ganges, that the strange, foreign appearance of the people and their occupations produced an unreal, dream-like impression upon my mind. We were not able to indulge ourselves by prolonging our stay upon this attractive spot; for the sun began to decline, and we were anxious still to visit the neighbouring village of Durgakund.

This village is about three miles distant from the city, and is the resort of old and young, on account of the sacred monkeys which are kept there. On our road thither we passed a very handsome school-house, which has been recently finished, and which owes its origin to the benevolence of a wealthy Hindoo. Close to the school we met two missionaries, who were preaching the Gospel in the open air, to an assembled multitude of Hindoos and Mussulmans. One of them seemed to produce a powerful effect upon his hearers, for the greater part listened to his words with the most riveted attention, nay, some with even evident devotion; but I was informed that their high and holy work takes but little root here, although there are fourteen mission schools, one of which is for girls.

We now rode for about a mile between high garden walls, which enclose the country seats of the rajahs, and the principal inhabitants of Benares. Durgakund is a little village reposing peacefully beneath the shadow of bananas, mangoes, and other fruit trees: it contains a small pagoda, which stands near a walled tank, with a remarkably fine flight of steps. Here many hundreds of monkeys play their pranks, they pluck the flowers and fruits, and break off the branches of the trees, nay, they even destroy the roofs of the houses, and have greater immunities than the people themselves, under whose protection they are placed. Devotees were standing on the steps, and feeding these impudent creatures; and even the cottagers, who were sitting at their doors, shared their meals with the monkeys and their own children. I can bear witness that this community is not altogether a peaceful one, for I saw a young fellow lose all patience, when a huge monkey, not content with his dinner, seized him so furiously by the hair, and scratched his face, that he was obliged to use violence and roar lustily for help, before he could get rid of his audacious guest.

Very early in the morning of my last day's sojourn here, I rode with General Simpson to the village of Sarnath. It is six miles north-east of Benares, and three, of the cantonments, and evidently lies on a classic soil, for, that a large and mighty city must have stood here, is amply testified by the numerous ruins, and beautifully-formed bricks, with which all the ground, and especially the banks of a lake, which extends from east to west, are covered. The only fragment which has been preserved, is a vaulted tower about sixty feet high; it is built of granite and blocks of red sandstone, which are let into one another, and fastened without any cement, and in the upper portion some bricks have been introduced. The diameter of its base is about 100 feet, and the whole of the exterior, forms a round domed cone, similar to the Manikeeala in the Punjab. This remarkable tower is a compact mass of stone, without any open space in the interior, and merely covers a deep well, into which the corpse of a king was probably let down. A copper tablet found upon its highest summit bears an inscription, which, as far as I know, has not yet been deciphered: it is now in the museum of the Asiatic society at Calcutta.

At an elevation of about twenty feet from the ground are several niches, surrounded by elegant arabesques, in which statues of men, women, and children, the size of life, formerly stood: some of these have been removed to Calcutta, to save them from the destructive spirit of the natives; seven statues of red sandstone, which were sadly mutilated, were, however, lying about. They are the figures of a people, with flat noses, thick lips, and unusually large eyes. The hair lies perfectly smooth to the head, and falls in innumerable curls over the neck and shoulders. Some of them were quite naked, others wrapped in light garments, which are very curiously wrought, and fit tight to the body, or fall in picturesque folds. One of these figures wore a cord round the waist, exactly similar to that which distinguishes the brahmins.

The question naturally arises, as to the epoch of this ruined city, and of the singular structure, which owes its origin to a people of whom no traces are to be found either in India or in Ceylon. It is not improbable that it may have been destroyed during the severe struggles between Bhooddism and Brahminism, or, perhaps, even anterior to that period. A small temple and a caravansary erected close to this tower, by a Hindoo, as an expiatory act, is now quite desolate and forsaken.

According to Mr. Princep's observation, Benares lies 231 feet higher than Chowringi, near Calcutta, and has a mean temperature of 76¼° F., for, two years' observation gave the highest mean temperature, 85½° F., and the lowest 63½° F. But the extremes of the temperature in May, when it rises to 111° 15′ F., and in January, when it falls to 45° F. (when ice is often found early in the morning), are favourable to the cultivation of European fruits and flowers. I here tasted the finest strawberries and potatoes, and saw the most beautiful pinks and carnations. During my stay from the 13th to the 15th of March, the thermometer was between 65° F. and 67° F. in the morning; at noon, between 89° F. and 90½° F., and in the evening, immediately after sunset, 79° F. or 79½° F.

LETTER XI.

TO CARL RITTER.

General observations respecting the criminals of India.— The Thugs.— The Thuggee or Phansigary system.— History of the Thugs.— Their religion and language.— The Jumaldehee Thugs.— The Mooltanea Thugs.— The Sooseeas Thugs.—The Phansigars and the river Thugs. —The usages of the Thugs. — Their enterprises and mode of strangling.— The tracking and prosecuting of the Thugs.— Statistics respecting the criminals of India.

Lucknow, March 2. 1844.

AMONG the Indians every branch of life has its peculiar caste: thus, as some men are educated for trade, and others for mechanics, there are also men who are trained to robbery and murder, as an hereditary occupation, and who form a particular caste; nay, even a peculiar nation. Most of the mountain districts on the borders of cultivated tracts of country, harbour such criminals, who, in subtlety and daring, exceed all the thieves on the face of the globe. They will dig through houses and walls; they will rob a traveller who is surrounded by his guards; slink into a tent and carry away the very bed on which a man is sleeping. These thieves are generally naked, their bodies are smeared with oil, and the dagger which they carry between their teeth is their only weapon: a safe retreat is of the first importance to them, and, therefore, when they force their way into an inner apartment, they always take care that they may have a loop-hole, through which they may effect their escape. So great is the power of these men, that the traveller is generally supplied with a guard of village watchmen, who belong to this class of thieves, by which means alone he is secure, as their presence is always sufficient to protect him against robbery.

Under the government of powerless princes, bands of robbers obtain the mastery, as the Pindaries did in former times, and the Decoits more recently. They form a secret society who assemble in the night, and attack villages: those who offer resistance are put to death; the wealthy are tortured, and the stolen property is rapidly carried off. On the following morning they mingle with the inhabitants, and, even if the injured party recognises them, he meets with no support. Their numbers, however, have been greatly diminished by the wise and persevering measures of the English.

Of all classes, that of the Thugs is the most formidable, and the most cruel; their life and proceedings fill the mind with horror and the most profound disgust, and prove how far man may depart from the right way. They surprise the unsuspecting traveller and strangle him, in order that no blood may flow and betray them, and then rob him of all his money and property. They accompany travellers on long journeys for many days, and even weeks; nay, they can eat and sleep with them, take part in their religious duties at their respective sacred places along the road, and live with them on the most friendly footing, till a favourable opportunity offers for the execution of their murderous deeds.

The Thuggee or Phansigar system is extremely ancient, and perhaps had its commencement in India, in the same manner as the Mussulman hordes that infested the environs of ancient Delhi, and who threatened the lives of travellers. In the caverns of Ellora, some say there are representations of most of the actions of the Thugs; at one place, a Thug is sitting in familiar conversation with the traveller on the same carpet; we next see how the noose is thrown round the neck of the victim, and how he is strangled; in another representation again the murdered man is being buried, &c. Feringya, the leader of the Thugs, attesting this, said, "Here may be found the secrets of the life and conduct of all men: for all these representations are the work of God, and not of man, for the Thugs would never have revealed their own secrets."

Herodotus mentions a troop, in the army of Xerxes, who, armed only with a dagger and a noose, strangled their enemies; and Thevenot, in his travels in India in the 17th century, speaking of the road from Delhi to Agra, says, "Good as the road is, there are many inconveniences; the traveller meets not only with tigers, panthers, and lions, but also with the most crafty thieves in the world, who, by means of a peculiar rope, to which a running noose is fastened, strangle a traveller in a moment."

Colonel Sleeman, who, with great sacrifices and exertions, undertook the pursuit of the Thugs, is of opinion, that the seven Mahometan Thug tribes are descended from the robbers here spoken of. He who can trace his descent from one of these seven tribes is considered by the Thugs as a man of high birth. Since the death of Akbar, we find that the Thugs were never actively pursued, their number increased, and that thousands of persons fell every year under their murderous hands. They range from the Himalaya to the Nerbudda, and from the Ganges to the Indus.

This far extended organisation of crime, could only be founded and propagated on a religious basis; hence the Thug feels no qualms of conscience, no pity for his victims, nor is he disturbed in his dreams, in solitude, or in the hour of death, by the thought of the hundreds who have fallen a sacrifice to his abominable iniquity. In a Thug prison in this city, I met with a man, sixty-five years of age, who boasted to me that he had killed several hundred persons.

The Thug believes that he is appointed to his work by his goddess Devee (called also Durga, Kalee, or Bhawani). As the priest of Jupiter sacrificed oxen, and the priest of Saturn children, the Thugs say that a demon named Rackat Beej (seeds of blood), who was so tall, that the deepest ocean did not reach to his breast, spread terror through the world by devouring all the new-born infants. He was destroyed by the goddess Devee, but when she cut down the demon, a second demon arose from the drops of his blood. Upon this the goddess created two men, and gave each of them a handkerchief, wherewith they might kill demons without bloodshed. When their business was completed, and they were going to return the handkerchiefs, called rumals (with which the Thug strangles his victims), the goddess gave them to the men and to their descendants, with the prerogative of employing them for their own use, in strangling their enemies. The temple dedicated to this goddess, near Calcutta, is still the chief place of pilgrimage of the Thugs, because the demon is said to be buried there, and Devee performs the greatest wonders at that place.

Devee is worshipped by all the Hindoos, and, as Europeans were often present at these unhallowed ceremonies, the Thugs spread a report that they, too, offered sacrifices to this goddess! At the festival of Devee, which the Thugs celebrate among themselves, only those of this sect are admitted who have proved their skill as stranglers, or whose families have been Thugs for two generations.

Both Hindoos and Mahometans belong to the Thugs, and even Brahmins have often been found among them, as their leaders, but only one woman is known to have taken part in their enterprises. She assisted her husband in strangling, and once even saved his life, when he was overpowered by one of his victims. Mothers have, however, often encouraged their sons, and wives their husbands, to practise Thuggee, and a woman in the Deccan even had a troop of fifteen Thugs in her service.

According to the deposition of an old Thug, nine tenths of their number in the kingdom of Oude are Mussulmans; in the Doab, between the Ganges and the Jumna, four fifths are Hindoos; to the south of the Nerbudda, three fourths Mussulmans; in Rajahpootana, one fourth Mussulmans; in Bundelkund, Sangoo, Bengal, Behar, and Orissa, half are Hindoos, and half Mahometans.

The Thugs have their own language (Ramaseeana), and their particular signs, which are understood by all of them, however remote they may live from each other. There are various branches or sects among them, some of which are of higher rank than others; and, though they act together in the practice of their diabolical crimes, they keep themselves distinct in their modes of life. The Jumaldhee Thugs, in the kingdom of Oude, and to the east of the Ganges, are known as being particularly crafty, skilful, and mysterious. They are reserved even to their wives, and do not instruct their children in their murderous trade till they have attained mature age.

The Mooltanea Thugs are a Mahometan sect in the north of India. Accompanied by their wives and children, they undertake journeys under the character of Brinyares, take with them a train of oxen and cows, laden with corn or merchandise, which they offer for sale in their camp, to attract victims. In strangling them, they use, instead of cloths, the cords of their oxen. It is said that the

Mooltaneas kill their daughters as soon as they are born, or, if they preserve them alive, they do not permit them to marry out of their own tribe. They live in no kind of community with the other Thugs, though they use their language, signs, and customs.

The Chingarees, or Naiks, are a branch of the Mooltaneas, and above a hundred families of them live in the neighbourhood of Hingolee. They follow the manners and customs of the Mooltaneas, by whom they are considered as inferior.

The Sooseeas are a younger class of Thugs, of the lowest Hindoo castes; they live in Jeypoor, Kishunghur, Bandu, Joudpoor, Tonk, and other places in Malwa and Rajahpootana; all the other Thugs despise them as an inferior tribe, and though they often employ them in their enterprises, they never eat with them. They are seen to travel through the country as merchants, money-carriers, or sepoys, who are in search of employment. When they travel in the former capacity, their leader, in the garb of an opulent merchant, is on horseback, in a waggon, or in a palanquin, surrounded by his companions, who serve him in the most respectful manner, and manifest the greatest deference towards him.

The Phansigar sect, so called from the manner in which they kill their victims, undertake long journeys, under the pretext of looking after thieves and murderers. Their leader is generally on horseback: they are accompanied by children under twelve years of age, to obviate suspicion, and oxen, to bring back their plunder in safety. A band generally consists of forty or fifty men, who set out on their journey in small divisions of ten or twelve, and meet at certain fixed places of rendezvous. They are assisted by the petty Poligars, or landholders, and by the chiefs of the villages, to whom they give up a portion of their plunder. Fathers frequently bring their children to them, to be instructed in the ways of murder.

The Phansigars were once very numerous, particularly in the district of Chittor, and are among the most cruel of the Thug sects; for the Phansigar does not hesitate to murder a man for a rupee, and kills even Coolies and Faquirs. Many hundred travellers are annually murdered by them: they make particular signs with their hands, and have a language unknown to the other Thugs.

The Phansigars (Phansi, *i. e.* Noose) live also in Mysore, the Carnatic, and Chittor, and first became known to the English in 1799, after the conquest of Seringapatam, when about 100 of them were taken, in the vicinity of Bangalore. They consist of Mussulmans and Rajahpoot Hindoos, and there also are Brahmins among them. They compare themselves with the tiger, which they never kill, affirming that a good Phansigaree is never attacked by the tiger. They never murder boys and girls: the former are brought up to their own profession, and the latter intermarry with their sons.

The Phansigars generally undertake two long journeys in the year, for three or four months at a time, when they appear as harmless wanderers; while some of them endeavour to find out in the different villages whether there are any travellers, and what is their destination. In former times, their leader rode on horseback, having a tent and merchandise with him. For strangling they use a cord with a noose. One throws the noose round the victim's neck, another lifts his feet from the ground, and a third stands by the side, to afford assistance, if required; some of them, however, boast of being able to strangle a traveller without any assistance.

The goddess Kalee or Murnee (the goddess of the small pox in the Carnatic) is the chief object of their adoration. Before the Phansigars set out on an enterprise, they make a feast, to ask counsel of the goddess. A silver or brass image of this idol, with her attributes, is set up in a solitary place, and sometimes that of the god Ganesa; an image of the serpent, of the lizard, a noose, a knife, and the sacred axe, are laid beside it, and strewed with flowers; fruits, confectionary, and spirituous liquors, are brought as offerings; fragrant essences are poured into the flames, and prayers are made. The head of a sheep is then cut off, and the dead animal laid before the image of the goddess, so that her right foot touches its mouth. Near it is a burning lamp and the image of Jayee.

The goddess is then asked by the leader, whether she approves of the enterprise: the answer is indicated by the convulsive movements of the sheep; if none take place, the enterprise is deferred, and the ceremony repeated, ten or twelve days afterwards.

A very peculiar sect is that of the River Thugs, who live in the district of Burdwan, on the banks of the Hooghly. There are said to be between 200 and 300 of them, who have possession of about twenty boats, with which, in the months of November, December, January and February, they go up and down the Ganges, even as far as Cawnpoor, under the pretext of making a pilgrimage to holy places, such as Benares, Allahabad, &c. Every boat is manned by about fourteen Thugs, each of whom has his own especial duty; some tow the boat, others land on the bank, to invite travellers to go with them, or to be carried across the river, while others who sit in the boat pretend to be pilgrims. The leader, who is generally the owner of the boat, sits at the helm, and gives the signal for the stranger to be strangled. In this act, no blood must be spilt, lest the murderers should be discovered by passing vessels, and as soon as the victim is strangled, his back is broken to prevent the possibility of his recovering, and the body is then thrown into the river, through a window, of which there is one on each side of the boat.

Several boats belong to the same society, and follow each other at the distance of five or six miles; in order, that if a traveller should not be inclined to take the first boat, he may be induced to yield to the solicitations of the men in the next boat, who have been instructed by signals. The leader in this boat speaks with contempt and distrust of those in the first boat, and thus endeavours to gain the confidence of his unsuspecting victim.

Although these River Thugs consist of Mussulmans and Hindoos, they never kill women. The Lodahas, Moteeas, and Jumaldehee Thugs, who live in Behar and the Bengalese, are in connection with the River Thugs, because the most frequented roads lead along the banks, and they hasten to the assistance of the River Thugs, if a good booty may be hoped for.

The Thugs do not obtain the privilege of strangling till they have proved by several undertakings that they possess the necessary courage and the requisite coolness. At first most of them are timid and fearful, but after strangling a few persons, the Thug, they say, loses all pity and compassion. They take their children for the first time, at the age of fourteen, without permitting them to be witnesses of the murders. They receive presents, and every thing is done to give them pleasure, and according to the degree of courage which they display, they receive some intimation of the circumstances to which they are indebted for their enjoyments on this occasion. On the second journey, the boy is permitted to see the bodies of the persons strangled, and it entirely depends on his behaviour then, whether he may be allowed to be present at the next murder.

On a journey of this kind, a leader of the Thugs lost his son by his appearing too soon. The boy was on a pony, which was held by one of the band, at a distance from the scene of slaughter, where more than twenty travellers were to be killed; but the pony escaped the man's hand, and galloped to the fatal spot. He arrived the very moment the travellers were strangled: this horrid sight so overcame the boy, that he fell in convulsions from his horse, and died in a few hours.

A leader of the Thugs being asked, whether his conscience never reproached him for having killed so many innocent persons, answered, "Does any one feel remorse for having carried on his business or trade? Are not all our actions justified by Providence? Is it not God's hand which kills, and are we not the instruments of his will?"

When a youth feels himself strong enough for his profession, he requests the oldest and most respected Thug (Gooroo) to take him for his disciple: if he is accepted as such by the leader, he must try his skill on the next traveller. As soon as the traveller is asleep, the Gooroo, with his disciple and three experienced Thugs, repair to a neighbouring field. When arrived there, he places himself with his face towards the spot whither they mean to go, and the Gooroo exclaims, "O Kalee! Kan-kalee! Bhud-kalee!" *i. e.* if it seems good to thee that the traveller shall die by the hand of this slave, grant us the omen, or sign. If the expected sign comes within a certain time, from the quarter to his right hand, the goddess is supposed to announce her consent; if not, other Thugs must kill the traveller, and the candidate must wait for the honour, till a more favourable opportunity.

If they receive a propitious answer, they return to their camp; the Gooroo takes a handkerchief and turning to the west, makes the fatal knot, a piece of silver coin being fixed at the other end of the cloth. The disciple, in a humble posture, receives the handkerchief with his right hand from the head priest, and leans over the victim. Under the pretext that a serpent is crawling about, the traveller is wakened, the noose is thrown round his neck, and he is strangled in an instant. As soon as the work is completed, the disciple bows before his Gooroo, touching, with both hands, his feet, and afterwards those of his relations and friends. A feast, and presents made by the disciple to the Gooroo and his family, conclude his initiation and reception into the society.

Before the Thugs set out on a journey, they consult the auspices. The most experienced among them, the Pundits, with the leader, and four of the principal Thugs, sit down upon a white cloth; the other members of the band being ranged in a circle beyond. A brass vessel containing rice, wheat, and two pieces of copper coin, is then placed before the Pundit, who is respectfully asked, by the leader, what day will be the most favourable for the enterprise. After performing some ceremonies, the Pundit declares the day, the hour, and the direction of the journey.

At the time appointed, the leader repairs to a field, or garden, beyond the village, raises his eyes towards heaven, and exclaims, "Great goddess, mother of all, if this our intended enterprise is justified in thy eyes, afford us assistance and the signs of thy approbation." All the Thugs present repeat this exclamation, and unite in praises and adoration of the goddess. If the sign is favourable, the leader remains for seven hours on the same spot; his companions bringing him food, and making all the necessary preparations for the journey. If the sign is not favourable, the ceremony must be repeated in a week.

The most sacred instrument of the Thugs is a pick-axe which is borne by the most cleanly, most temperate, and careful man of the band. According to the Thugs, it indicates, if buried, the direction in which the journey is to be undertaken, and, in former times, when, as they say, all the Thugs held together in conformity with the will of the Goddess, the pick-axe, if thrown into a well, rose again to the surface. The oath by the Kassee, is considered more sacred by the Thugs, than that by the Ganges or the Khoran.

This frightful mode of life is, on the whole, full of superstition. If the turban of one of the party catches fire, or falls from his head, the band must return and wait seven days; but if they are far from home, only the man returns who has met with the misfortune. The cry of a vulture, in the night, is likewise an evil omen: the Thug hastily leaves his camp and flies, even if he is sure of his victim. On the other hand, it is considered a very good omen to meet a woman with a child in her arms and a pitcher full of water, but if the pitcher is empty, it forbodes evil.

The howling of a wolf, the crossing of any game from the right side of the road to the left, the mere touching a lizard, &c. are all esteemed bad signs.

A new band of Thugs breaks the back of their first victim five times, as this is said to insure future sucess.

In the first seven days of the enterprise, the Thug abstains from Ghee, and flesh, and subsists entirely upon fish and rice. He does not shave his beard, nor permit a Dhobee to wash his clothes, nor does he bathe, or give alms. During a whole enterprise, even if it is protracted to the space of a year, they take no milk, nor do they clean their teeth; but if they succeed in finding a victim within the first seven days, they are freed from these restraints. On the seventh day, they all partake of a repast in common. In former times the first person killed was not to be a brahmin, a poor man, a bayadere, or a bard. A traveller who wore gold or had a four-footed animal with him was also spared. Persons who have lost a limb are never touched; and if a Thug meets such an one, on the first day of the journey, he returns home. Women, too, are never killed by them — but this rule is observed only by the Hindoo Thugs. The Thug will not strangle any female with whom he has been intimately acquainted — yet their love of murder is so great, that they have often resisted the seductions of great beauties, and sacrificed their victim.

In their enterprises, the Thugs are indefatigable, cunning, and prudent, so that, according to their motto, "Dead men tell no tales," no victim, and no witness has escaped them. A band of Thugs, consisting of more than an hundred men, travelled 160 miles, with 60 persons, among whom were some women, till they succeeded in strangling them all in a moment near Chitterkote. Another band accompanied a native officer and his family for 200 miles, till they found a favourable moment for executing their diabolical purpose. The wild, solitary jungles, are generally the places where most victims meet their fate; and the Thug remembers such places, as a sportsman does the most productive hunting ground, or an old man the happiest days and hours of his youth.

Two or three Thugs, as I have before observed, are employed in strangling a traveller. As soon as every one is at his post, the spies set, and the act of strangling is to take place, the leader exclaims, *Bajid*, *Bajid*, *Khan* or *Deo*. If the traveller is on horseback, one of the men throws the noose round his neck, the second lifts his feet out of the stirrups, and the third seizes the bridle. The corpses are either thrown into wells or buried; in the latter case, they cover the grave with thorns, or with the seeds of fleabane, to keep off the dogs and jackals.

If they do not succeed in strangling the traveller, when he is roused from sleep, or cannot get him into a convenient position, one of the Thugs falls into a swoon, some of his companions hasten to his assistance, others fetch water, or feel his pulse, and as nothing avails in bringing him to himself, one of the Thugs affirms that a charm or exorcism alone will relieve the sufferer from this evil. A pitcher full of water is placed on the ground, and every one present is requested to kneel in a circle, to take off his girdle, to bare his neck, and look up to the sky, and count a certain number of stars. In this position the noose is of course very easily thrown round the neck of the unsuspicious traveller.

It seems almost incredible that such a sect should have been able, for centuries, to murder, undiscovered, several hundred travellers every year. But the Thug finds constant facilities for the perpetration of his crimes, from the manner in which the Indians are in the habit of travelling: for they do not halt at the towns and villages, but stop under shady trees, where they cook and sleep, and the road often lies for many miles together through solitary jungles.

Almost every body in India is married; the younger sons of poor, but respectable families seek employment in the civil or military service, and while they are doing duty at a great distance from home, their wives and children remain under the protection of the father, or elder brother, so that the bands of love and affection are preserved unbroken. They submit, in their office, to all possible privations, in order to send, or to bring, as much as they can save, to those whom they love at home. Such families especially, have suffered by the Thugs; for if the officer who has obtained leave of absence does not return at the appointed time, another is put in his place, and the relations perhaps do not learn, till long afterwards, that one of their family has disappeared from the world, they know not how. Almost every native regiment lost annually several of its men, who were absent on furlough, and of whom no trace could be found; and in spite of all warnings, new victims continually fell under the murderous hands of this fearful sect.

In the west of India, the Bhats and Charans, a caste of Rajahpoots, possess the sacred privilege of taking the property of other people under their protection. Nobody ventures to touch them, or the large sums, in gold and silver, which they carry, especially in the province of Guzerat, through tracts which others cannot venture to traverse without a strong escort. In Rajahpootana, in the character of bards or heralds, they accompany the caravans which are then, not only secure against robbery, but even exempt from the usual taxes. Even this sacred caste has not been spared by the Thugs: in the year 1826, fourteen money carriers were murdered at one time, near Chupparah, and robbed of a sum of 25,000 rupees. In the following year, seven of them, with a sum of 22,000 rupees, fell into the hands of the Thugs near Malagaon, in Candeish. In 1823, three persons, who had 12,000 rupees with them were killed, near Dhor Kote, in Candeish, and nine persons with 40,000 rupees near Burwahagat, on the Nerbudda. In the following year, six gold bearers were murdered near Dhoolia, in Candeish, on whom the Thugs found the large sum of 82,000 rupees.

It is remarkable, that the Thugs have never attacked Europeans; for which they assign the following reasons:—first, because the European carries little or no money about him; secondly, because he always has loaded pistols, and is ever ready to make use of them; and, lastly, because a European is soon missed, and the rigorous and careful researches made in consequence might easily lead to a discovery.*

* Only one European, a sergeant in an English regiment, was strangled by the Thugs, in a state of intoxication, and his body was found in a well.[1]

---

[1] Shortly before this sheet went to press, the following lamentable news was received by the India mail:—

"The deputy quartermaster-general, Captain Alcock, left Cawnpore by palkee dawk for Agra on Thursday last, from whence he intended to march to Nusseerabad. He took an early dinner at Mrs. Clarkson's house at Mynpooree, on Saturday, and left in high health and spirits towards evening. At Bhooreah Tallao he was attacked by a Dacoitee gang: he got out of his palkee and defended himself with his sword, until they cut him across his wrists, when he ran towards the village, calling for assistance, and one of the Dacoits then shot him dead. He was, it is evident, mistaken for the magistrate, Mr. Unwin, who had been hunting after this gang; and he (Mr. Unwin) had also left Mynpooree by dawk alone, that evening, and arrived at the village two hours after, and was shocked to find Captain Alcock sacrificed to the vengeance of these wretches, for him. He returned with the body to Mynpooree, which was buried with all due honours on Sunday. The same leader of the Dacoits attempted Captain Tucker's life last year! Is this not a dreadful outrage in the midst of our own territory?" —*From the Calcutta Englishman, Nov.* 1844.

"The murder of Europeans by Dacoits," as the Friend of India observes, "is calculated to excite a great sensation in society: it is, indeed, a new and bold feature in their proceedings; the more surprising when we recall the decision of the

It is a strange fact, that the native princes, their chiefs and ministers, were the principal obstacles to the pursuit of the Thugs. Very few of the princes care for any of their subjects who do not belong to their own tribe, nor do they feel themselves bound to protect them against banditti and thieves. Added to this, many of the superior officers and landowners are often in league with such criminals, and afford them protection and shelter in return for a portion of their booty. Thus, in the dominions of Scindia, for instance, a secure asylum was afforded to the Thugs, for which they had to pay the sovereign an annual tax of twenty-four rupees and a half, for every house which was occupied by them. In the year 1797, this tax amounted to 7641 rupees for 318 houses; and the number of Thugs who went out in search of plunder, in that country alone, was estimated at

Thugs on this very point, by whom the question of the policy of attacking European travellers was regularly discussed and debated, and decided in the negative, on the ground that the practice would be too dangerous, on account of the great sensation which the murder of a Gora would excite. * * * In the murder of Captain Alcock, mistaken for Mr. Unwin, it may be observed, that the Dacoits have been evidently influenced by revenge against an active magistrate: they have suffered their vindictiveness to get the better of their usual prudence. But the proceeding is not the less new and daring; and if these men escape, especially Kansuhaee, the leader of the gang, the Dacoits may be emboldened to make attacks on Europeans a regular part of their system; the more so, as it cannot be unknown to them, that our countrymen travel about the country very commonly altogether unarmed." — *From the Delhi Gazette.* — [TRANSLATOR.]

954. The deliverance of India from these inhuman monsters was reserved for the indefatigable exertions, the wise and just measures, of the English. This important undertaking has, to a very great extent, been already accomplished; and, if the political agents continue to watch the Thugs with the same zeal as heretofore, there can be no doubt that they will eventually be entirely extirpated.

The discovery and capture of several bands of Thugs took place after the seizure of a band of an hundred and five men, by Mr. Molony, in the valley of the Nerbudda; of a second by Captain Wardlaw, and of a third by Major Borthwick. The latter, with 200 irregular cavalry, undertook a march of thirty miles by night, and in this manner surprised a whole troop of forty-six Thugs, who were returning from Hindoostan to the Deccan, with a booty of the value of 12,000 rupees.

Though the Thugs are bound to inviolable secrecy by a most solemn oath, the proofs of their guilt were so manifest, that they confessed every thing; and many, in order to save their own lives, became approvers and witnesses against other bands. When Feringhea, one of the most notorious leaders of the Thugs in Saugor, was brought before Major Sleeman, he offered, on condition that his life should be spared, to assist in the capture of several bands. On Major Sleeman expressing some doubts as to the sincerity of his depositions, Feringhea promised to give him a proof of his good will, and begged the Major to take him to the village of Selohola, two stages beyond Saugor. On their arrival at that place, Major Sleeman caused his tent to be set up in a mango grove; but how great was his horror, when, on the following morning, Feringhea caused five dead bodies to be dug up, under the small space covered by the tent, seven others immediately without-side, and five on the spot where his horses were fastened for the night! Major Sleeman relates, that, during the night, his wife, who of course was totally unconscious that she was sleeping over the graves of so many murdered victims, had been tormented by the most frightful dreams.

Above 2000 Thugs were called to account, in five years—at Indore, Hyderabad, Saugor, and Jubbulpoor; 1200 were examined in the two latter towns alone; and the murder of 947 travellers was fully proved. Of these criminals 382 were condemned to the gallows; 909 to transportation, and 77 to imprisonment for life.* The Thug

* Captain Meadows Taylor received from Captain Reynolds the following statement:—

From 1831 to 1837 inclusive, there were

Transported to Penang, &c. - - -	1059
Hanged - - - - - -	412
Imprisoned for life, with hard labour - -	87
Imprisoned in default of security - -	21
Imprisoned for various periods - -	69
Released after trial - - - - -	32
Escaped from gaol - - - -	11
Died in gaol - - - - - -	36
	1727
Made approvers - - - -	483
Convicted, but not sentenced - - -	120
In gaol, in various parts, not yet tried - -	936
	3266

dreads transportation — "to be sent over the Black water" as he calls it—much more than death. It is a law among the Thugs, that if one of them is discovered he ceases to be a Thug.

I visited a Thug prison at this place: several hundred of them were in chains, and had the word "Thug" branded on their cheeks; but as they were subjects of the King of Oude their punishment was subject to the will of the king, who did not seem disposed either to inflict the extreme penalty of the law, or even to keep them to hard labour. During my stay at this place, a new sect of thieves was discovered; but it was not fully ascertained whether they were Thugs. They stupified travellers by giving them narcotic potions, and robbed them, when in this condition, but never attempted to murder them. At present, however, the traveller in India, is more safe: it is seldom that persons are missed; and the regiments have the satisfaction of seeing their comrades return from furlough uninjured.

It would be very unjust to form an unfavourable conclusion of the moral state of the whole people from these criminal sects; on the contrary, it appears from the statistical notices respecting the criminals of India, compiled by Colonel Sykes, that those people have the advantage of civilised Europe.

Added to the above, Captain Reynolds stated, that, at the time he wrote, upwards of 1800 notorious Thugs were at large in various parts of India, whose names were known: how many besides existed it is impossible to conjecture.—*Confessions of a Thug. By Captain Meadows Taylor.* 1839.—TRANSLATOR.

It may, indeed, be questioned, whether the police can be so strictly exercised in India as in England and other European countries.

In the presidency of Bengal, the population of which is forty millions, the number of persons sentenced to death was 38 in the year 1838, 25 in 1839, and 27 in 1840, exclusively of the Thugs; whereas in England, during the same years, the numbers were 116, 56, and 57. In the same years, 81, 72, and 103 criminals were sentenced, in Bengal, to transportation or imprisonment for life; and in England, the numbers who suffered the same punishment were 266, 205, and 238. The number of persons condemned in 1837, including offences against the police, amounted to 38,902, which makes 1 to 1028 of the population; and in the year 1840, in which 42,785 were sentenced, 1 out of every 935 souls.

In the presidency of Madras, the population of which is 13,050,000, there was in the first half of the year 1839, 1 criminal to 609 souls; and in the latter half, 1 to 633, of whom 21 were sentenced to death; while, in England and Wales, 56 persons were condemned to death: in 1840, 20,622 were found guilty in this presidency, of whom 31 were condemned to death, and 69 to transportation; in England and Wales 27,187 were sentenced, of whom 77 were punished with death, and 238 to transportation.

In the presidency of Bombay, which contains 6,300,000 inhabitants, in two years and a half, from the 1st of January, 1838, to the 1st of July, 1840, 15 on an average were annually sentenced to death, 45 to transportation, and 7 to imprisonment for life. The total amount of all crimes and misdemeanours, including those under cognisance of the police, was 91,999 in the space of four years in this Presidency, making nearly 23,000 in a year, or one criminal to every 273 souls.

LETTER XII.

TO ALEXANDER VON HUMBOLDT.

Journey from Benares to Calcutta. — The Hooli festival of the Hindoos.—Description of the road. — The Puhari. —Burdwan.— Description of Calcutta. —Fort William. — The revenues and expenses of the administration of India. — The palace of the Governor-General. — A visit to Dwarkanauth Tagores.—Hindoo festivals.—Excursion to Dum-Dum.— Trip to Hooghly and Barrackpoor.— The Botanic Garden.— Social life at Calcutta.—Preparations for my departure to Bombay and the Indus.— Embarkation on board the Pluto steamer. — Departure for Bombay.— Stormy voyage and return to Calcutta.

Continuation of letter from Aden.—Embarkation on the steamer Hindoostan for Madras. —Madras.—Point de Galle.— The Maldive Islands and their inhabitants.— Aden.

Conclusion of letter on board the Oriental steamer.— The Red Sea. — Residence at Cairo. — Ascent of the Pyramids. —Journey to Alexandria.— Audience of Mehemet Ali.— Embarkation in the Oriental, and voyage to Malta, Gibraltar, and Falmouth.

Calcutta, 14th April, 1843.

I TOOK leave of Major Carpenter on the afternoon of the 15th March, and set out in a palanquin on my journey to Calcutta. On the road thither there are thirty-three dawk stations, and between twenty and thirty bungalows. In less than an hour, I was carried across the Ganges, which is 3000 feet wide at this part; but its waters scarcely flowed over the half of this breadth, though the mean depth was about thirty-five feet: the current of the Ganges at this place is, at the surface, at the rate of 2910 feet an hour, and the under current, below the surface, only 1410 feet an hour. I travelled through the fertile, richly cultivated valley of the Ganges for the first eighteen hours of my journey: the road, which is very good and broad, gradually ascended as I approached the offsets of the Vindhaya chain, and the country was as highly cultivated as on the previous part of my route. The Vindhaya mountains are here called the Bindi hills, and are, on this side, the last offsets of that remarkable physical conformation which traverses India, in its greatest breadth of 300 geographical miles, and here separates the Sone and the Ganges from each other.

At the earliest dawn of the morning of the 16th, while the moon still shone in the greatest splendour, my attention was attracted by bright lights dancing and flitting about in every direction as far as the eye could reach. I soon discovered that they were straw torches in the hands of the men and children of the villages, who were running about the fields, swinging and throwing their burning torches, and at the same time shouting and singing with all their might. It was the Hooli, one of the principal Hindoo festivals, which lasts three days, and appears to have much similarity with the bacchanalia of the ancients; for, at this time, the gentle Hindoos, who are much disposed to rejoicing and wantonness, are at full liberty to indulge their fancy, and to play foolish pranks and frolics even on women and strangers. The consequence to myself was not very agreeable, for at almost every stage I had several drunken bearers.

During the noontide heat of the same day, which was extremely oppressive in the mountains, being 98° Fahr., I rested for some hours in the bungalow beyond Sassaram. It is situated in the shade of beautiful mango trees, at the entrance of a mountainous tract, the elevation of which is scarcely more than 600 feet above the Ganges. The cheerful little village, which is adorned with the ruins of several Mahometan buildings, is most picturesquely ensconced under mangoes and bananas, among which the Fan palms lift their proud and elegant crowns. After luxuriating in a bath, and partaking of a good breakfast, I proceeded on my journey at three o'clock, and at sunset reached the village of Deury, where the river Sone flows in a bed 5000 paces in breadth, but the main stream was scarcely 360 paces broad, and not eight feet deep. The bed of the Sone is a deep stratum of sand, which is traversed by small streams and pools; but these were so shallow, that the bearers had no difficulty whatever in passing through them.

On the 17th I was quite among the mountains; the loftiest summits of which, according to my estimation, were not more than from 800 to 1000 feet in height, and were for the most part covered with brushwood. The inhabitants are a totally distinct tribe from any I had before seen: they are a short, stout, and dark-brown people, and live in houses covered with tiles or reeds. They are the Puharri, a race quite different in appearance, language, and religion from the Hindoos of the plain: there are no castes among them, nor do they worship idols, but they pray every morning and evening to a supreme being, whom they call Budo Gosai, and to whom they offer buffalos and other animals, as propitiatory sacrifices. They subsist principally on the produce of the chase, in which they employ bows and arrows. Their chiefs are under the protection of the English, and have entered into their service. All the Hindoos, my bearers not excepted, had on this day sprinkled their turbans and white dresses with a bright-red colour; and on the following days they all appeared in orange colour.

The bungalows at Dhunwah, where I rested and refreshed myself, lie on a small plateau, surrounded by steep rocks, with the most picturesque views towards the west. On the 18th the country appeared still more beautiful, and more diversified in the grouping of the mountain chains, the lofty summits of which were sometimes jagged and sometimes rounded, now forming perpendicular walls, and then declining in terraces to the plain: the situation of the bungalows at Dumry is particularly delightful.

As soon as we issued from these mountains, the appearance of the country and of the people was totally changed; the land was gradually more cultivated, and the people were handsomer, taller, more slender, more cleanly, and of rather a lighter complexion than those of the mountains. On the 19th I stopped for two hours in the bungalow at Hyrasone, and then proceeded in my palanquin with a temperature of 89° Fahr.

About half a day's journey from Burdwan, which is situated in a rich delta of the Ganges, and is surrounded by handsome seats and gardens, the country becomes like a boundless park: corn fields of every description alternate with plantations of sugar, indigo, cotton, and banana, interspersed with mangoes, banyans, tamarinds, bamboos, and pipala, sometimes standing singly, or forming pretty groups, and sometimes clustered in small groves, adorn this incomparable landscape. The roads are shaded with trees, and the villages consist of clean and neat brick houses, furnished with a veranda enwreathed with climbing plants, and surrounded by small gardens, in which bananas and flowers flourish in extraordinary beauty. The country is irrigated by means of tanks, wells, and ditches, from which the water is drawn in ox hides, and thrown over the land. The riches and luxuriance of nature quite astonish the European, and evidence the inexhaustible source which yields so large a revenue to the government.

The district of Burdwan is divided into sixty-four pergunnahs, and extends sixty-five miles from north to south, and about forty-five from east to west. It is one of the most populous and fertile districts in Bengal, and is perfectly level, with the exception of the western part, where the ground is undulating and less productive. In that direction there are jungles, consisting chiefly of willows, which serve for fuel, and for spars in building. The Damada and Adjy, which traverse the district from west to east, often inundate the land during the rainy season, and have several times done immense damage. A sixth part of the inhabitants of the country are Mussulmans; a great number of Brahmins, however, live here, and nearly one seventh of the Hindoo population belongs to that caste; next to them, the Koyst caste is the most active and intelligent portion of the people.

In this neighbourhood and at Hooghly, there is a very remarkable sect called Kurta Bhojah, to which many of the inhabitants in the north and east of this district belong. This sect consists of all castes, who have entirely renounced idol worship, and embraced a more pure religion. They assemble by hundreds at night in certain places, and unite in singing hymns and psalms: they lay aside every distinction of caste, and eat and drink in common. This religious feeling has, however, not taken deep root in all the members, and some, when they return home, being impelled by fear, or other motives, go back to the worship of idols. The sect, however, is daily increasing: a considerable number of them propagate Christianity in the district of Kishnagur: their leaders travel about the country, and are particularly successful, in the conversion of the Boishuors, the worshippers of Vishnu.*

* The following interesting account of this sect is given in the "Protestant Missions in Bengal," by the Rev. J. J.

The road from Burdwan to Hooghly and Calcutta is probably the most frequented of any in India.

Weitbrecht, and it was deemed important to subjoin it in this place. — TRANSLATOR.

"The first families who applied for baptism belonged to a sect who call themselves 'Kurta Bhojahs,' that is, worshippers of the only God. This sect appears to be extensively spread in Bengal, along the Ganges and its various branches. The founder of it is said to have lived in the beginning of the present century in a village near Culna, and to have become acquainted with the Scriptures by one of the first Protestant missionaries, either Carey, Foster, or Thomas. The doctrines and precepts of Jesus appear to have come home to his conscience; and possessing a considerable knowledge of the Hindoo shasters, he undertook the task of preparing a new religious system, retaining in it a considerable portion of Hindooism, but rejecting the worship of idols entirely, and substituting the worship of the only true God, as the foundation of his system. This new teacher succeeded in enlisting disciples from among his friends and neighbours, and the sect increased every year. Hindoos of all castes, Mahomedans, and even Indo-Britons, and descendants of the Portuguese, are now found among the Kurta Bhojahs.

"This brotherhood seems to manifest a very uncommon degree of energy and vigour: they have their missionaries, whom they send out in all directions to make proselytes. I met with one of them in the neighbourhood of Burdwan; and if they have many agents possessed of the same talents and lively energy as that individual, I am not surprised at the rapid increase of their disciples. He was a handsome young Brahmin, polished and dignified in manner, very agreeable in conversation, and eloquent. He assured me that the sect numbered above one hundred thousand members, and promised to introduce me to their private evening assemblies. They meet every Thursday in certain villages, after sunset, two or three hundred together; sitting cross-legged, in a circle, on the ground. They sing hymns in praise of their Creator. Every distinction of caste

The merchants generally send their goods by land, as a waggon is not more than six or seven weeks in performing the journey from Burdwan to Cawnpoor, and costs only 110 rupees; whereas a boat is four, and even six months in accomplishing this distance. But as this road is made chiefly of gutyn, a calcareous substance, which is soon pulverised by the heavily-laden carts, travelling is rendered exceedingly uncomfortable in dry weather by the clouds of dust, and in the rainy season, by the slough and mud.

The great abundance of coal in the vicinity of Shigar is very remarkable. It is so near the surface, that the strata stand out in many places.

From Burdwan the traveller is conveyed by the best and most rapid palanquin bearers, who trot four or five miles in an hour, singing and

ceases at these nightly meetings; the Brahmin is sitting in brotherly fellowship by the side of the Sudra and the Mahomedan. They break bread together, and a cup passes round the circle, from which all are drinking: doubtless this is an imitation of the sacrament of the Lord's Supper.

"Thus is an obscure sect, by the wise and gracious providence of God, destined to break through the chain of caste, and to become the pioneers to our mission work in Bengal. The people composing this sect are, as it were, already in a transition state. Some of these Kurta Bhojahs hearing Mr. Drew preach at Kishnagur, exclaimed, 'Surely this is our own religion;' and were shortly baptized. Moreover, I received from our brethren labouring in that place the interesting information, that their converts from that sect are the most consistent Christians, and give them the greatest satisfaction, evidently from this simple reason, that purer ideas of a Divine Being had previously been implanted in their minds."

shouting all the way. I arrived at the little town of Hooghly, at noon, on the 19th, just as the children were coming from school. Here is a temple, which, during the Rath festival, is visited by thousands of pilgrims, and where, in former times, as at Juggernauth, devotees suffered themselves to be crushed by the car of the idol, which has thirty-six wheels, and others were suspended till they died, by an iron hook, which was thrust through the hips of these unhappy fanatics. But I am thankful to say, that of late years the British government has prohibited this cruel custom.

The road from Hooghly runs between houses and gardens, near the river of the same name. At Pultah-Ghaut I was conveyed over the Hooghly in the evening twilight, while continued and bright flashes of lightning, in the south-east, illuminated the whole country. It was midnight before I reached Calcutta, and as I could not go to the residence of my friends at that late hour, I repaired to an hotel. Being almost tired to death, for I had had no sleep for five nights, and no refreshment for twenty-four hours, I lay down after a slight repast to take some rest; but the heat and the musquitos prevented me from getting any sleep, and in a feverish excitement, half awake and half dreaming, I impatiently longed for the day.

Before I enter upon an account of my proceedings here, I must give you a description of Calcutta. It is built on a perfectly level alluvial soil, on the left bank of the Hooghly, called by the natives Bhagirathi, or the "True Ganges," about 100 miles from the sea. Fort William, which commands the river and the surrounding country, lies at the most southern point, in 22° 34′ 49″ N. L., and 88° 28′ E. L., from Greenwich. Viewed from the Hooghly, Calcutta has the appearance of a city of palaces. A row of large superb buildings extend from the princely residence of the Governor-General, along the Esplanade, and produce a remarkably striking effect, by their handsome verandas, supported by lofty columns.

On the site of a wretched village, situated amidst jungles and impenetrable forests, Job Charnock founded, 120 years ago, the capital of the now mighty Indian empire; but though the jungles and woods have vanished, though the roads and pools are dry, yet a dangerous, infectious air often blows over the city from the Sunderbunds. At high water the Hooghly is a mile in breadth, but at the ebb, there is, on the opposite shore, a long road of dried sand banks, which are increasing greatly. To the south of Chandpaul Ghaut there was once a thick forest, between which and Kidderpoor lay two villages, the inhabitants of which were induced to settle in the city by the Seths, a wealthy mercantile community. Fort William and the Esplanade were erected on the site of the forest and of the abandoned villages in 1758; and where the splendid houses of Chowringhee now stand, a miserable village, surrounded by marshy pools, existed in 1717; and even in 1756, when Surae ud Dowlah took the place, only seventy houses were inhabited by Englishmen.

The present city of Calcutta extends nearly six

miles northwards from Fort William, along the left bank of the Hooghly; but its breadth varies very considerably. The Esplanade forms a large verdant square, with several handsome walled reservoirs, between the fort and the city, and on two sides is bounded by the Chowringhee, which consists of the grandest and most splendid buildings. At the most northern point the Maharatta Ditch surrounds the city from Chitpoor to the distance of a mile beyond the Fives Court, close to Chowringhee.

The city is divided into two distinct parts, formed by a line drawn from Bebee-Ross-Ghaut eastward, to the upper circular road, and from Hastings Bridge to the Tollys-Nallah in the north-eastern direction, to the lower circular road. This portion of the city is chiefly occupied by the Christians; whereas the natives have settled in the district from Bebee-Ross-Ghaut eastward, to Chitpoor Bridge and the Maharatta Ditch, including all the streets of the northern portion of the city.

Here, as in all Oriental cities, the streets are narrow and the houses lofty; the lower portion contains the bazars, and the upper the dwelling-house; the place of windows being supplied by curtains or shutters. The residences of the merchants are between Champaul Ghaut and the New Mint, along the river side, and those of the principal inhabitants are in Chowringhee, which is two miles in length, and forty paces in breadth, and occupies two sides of the esplanade. As the limits of the city are not marked by walls or ditches, an uninterrupted series of suburbs and villages are attached to it on every side. The dwellings consist for the most part of neat bamboo huts, covered with palm leaves; but they are excessively liable to take fire, and during my stay here, no less than 700 of them were burnt to the ground in three days.

If we were to take the number of houses and huts in Calcutta, amounting to 71,532, as a basis, from which we might infer the number of inhabitants, as has been done in former times, we should arrive at an exaggerated result. After eight months' researches, in the year 1837, Captain Birch, the superintendent of the police, succeeded in ascertaining the population of Calcutta to be 229,705 inhabitants. It appeared, at the same time, that a fluctuating population of 177,000 persons daily frequent the city. Of these inhabitants there are 3138 British, 137,651 Hindoos, and 58,744 Mussulmans; 3180 Portuguese; 536 Americans; 49 native Christians; 160 French; 203 Jews; 40 Parsees; 35 Arabs; 362 Chinese; 509 Moguls; 683 Mughs and Burmese; 4746 Eurasians, (children of a European father and a native mother,) and 19,804 of low castes. For the preservation of personal security, there is a police, with a magistrate at its head, and to which 8147 Thannadars, Naibs, Chokidars, Jemadars, and Burkandazes belong.

The climate of Calcutta may be inferred from its situation in a damp hollow, on the banks of one of the largest rivers in the world. Each season has its peculiar dangers; in the hot months, fevers and cholera prevail, and when the rainy season begins, dysentery and other painful diseases of the stomach are added to them. Even in the cooler season, the adult population suffers from dyspeptic fevers, and the children from catarrhs and coughs.

The most unhealthy part of Calcutta lies near Elysian Row, and is surrounded by the lower circular road, and Theatre Street; here dirty bazars, and the dwellings of Europeans, are built upon a marshy spot, filled with numerous half-drained ponds. When the other parts of the city are in the most healthy state, you may be certain that all kinds of diseases prevail here; nay, it not unfrequently happens, that in many houses not one of the inmates is exempt from fever. The ground is here so soft, that the houses often sink eight inches in a few hours. The most salubrious parts of the city are the Chowringhee, the Esplanade, and Tank Square.

The hot or dry season begins in the middle of March, and continues till the middle of June, when the wind blows very regularly from the south or south-west; the thermometer then rises in the shade, to 95° Fahr., and in the open air to 100°, or 110° F. The inhabitants suffer from a constant state of perspiration during this time; and the Europeans cannot sleep by night unless the punca, or fan, which is suspended over their beds, is kept in constant motion. During my three weeks' stay here, we had very regularly, in the morning before sunrise, 78° Fahr. in the shade, at noon 95½°, and in the evening, at sunset, 90°, Fahr. Various experiments of sinking the thermometer in the earth, at different times of the day, gave a temperature of 77° and 78°, at the depth of eighteen inches.

The finest season of the year, and the most favourable to the European constitution, is from the 1st of November to the 15th of February, when the sky is always clear, and cool refreshing winds prevail. The mercury then falls to 45° in the morning, and seldom rises above 75°. The sunbeams, however, are so powerful, that it is dangerous to be exposed to them at noon.

Though Calcutta has four large hotels, of which Spencer's hotel is the most distinguished, where a stranger is very well accommodated for 250 rupees per month, Mr. Maddock had very kindly invited me to take up my residence at his beautiful villa at Allipoor, where Warren Hastings matured his great plans. Mr. Maddock's charming seat was, however, not yet furnished; and I had, in consequence, the privilege of being received as an honorary member of the Bengal Club, where my friend had already prepared a lodging for me, and where foreign members have the privilege of a free residence.

The Bengal Club, which is in the very centre of the city of palaces, possesses the largest and handsomest buildings on the Esplanade, and overlooks the most splendid parts of the city, and the port of the Hooghly, with its numerous ships. It contains reading rooms, a library, and dining rooms, all of which are fitted up in the most convenient and elegant manner. From one of the windows of my apartment I see our Mussulman servants assemble for prayer every morning and evening: they all kneel on a retired grass plat; and Mr. Maddock's Hoockaburdar, a handsome man with a silver-grey beard, always takes the lead. Though the only business of this man is to bring the hookah to his master three or four times a day, he one morning, to our great astonishment, requested to have an assistant, and seemed rather surprised when his master paid no attention whatever to his request.

The Mahometans regulate the times of the day according to their religious duties. As soon as the sun sets, the night, whether it be long or short, is divided into twelve hours, and the time from sunrise to sunset likewise into twelve hours, whence it follows that, in the winter months, there is of course a great inequality. At the equinoxes alone their reckoning agrees with ours; yet the Mahometan's twelve o'clock is always one o'clock with us. Among the Hindoos, the day and night are divided equally into four parts. Their day begins at sunrise and ends at sunset: each of these times is divided into Ghurees of twenty-four minutes each, consequently the times of the day are longer in summer than in winter, and *vice versâ:* however, where the natives have become connected with the English, they have adopted their division of the day.

Immediately after my arrival, my friend introduced me to the principal families, which gave me an opportunity of seeing the splendid houses and costly furniture of the resident British. The forecourt, or garden, is surrounded by a wall: the dining room and drawing rooms are on the ground floor: the middle story surrounded by a veranda, supported by pillars, contains the sitting rooms of the family, and the upper stories the bed chambers. Bath rooms are universally introduced; and all the apartments are supplied with a punca to cool the air at will.

I had the pleasure of calling upon Dwarkanath Tagore, whom I had met in London at the Drawing Room, when this intelligent Hindoo, with remarkable gracefulness and dignity, for the first time paid his homage to his Queen. While I had been inspecting the Indian world, he, with acute penetration, had examined the manners of Europe, and he considered the time which he had spent there as the brightest period of his life. Though differences have arisen between him and his family on that account, he seriously thinks of returning to Europe, and of having his second son educated in England. Next to Ram Mohun Roy, Dwarkanath Tagore is one of the most distinguished men of his nation; he, too, contends against their errors and corruptions; but he wants the energy of mind and the moral courage of his illustrious and lamented countryman. Judging by his intelligence and sentiments, he appears to me to be more of a Christian than of a Hindoo, although he has not renounced his faith, and still observes some of its usages. His wife lives in strict seclusion, and his eldest son does not participate in the religious views of his father. It is exceedingly interesting to observe this remarkable man in the course of conversation, when he passes his small, delicate hand over his beard, and his fine large eyes look intelligently around, and reveal the quick succession of thoughts that arise in his mind. Dwarkanath Tagore, who, by his ability and enterprising spirit, has become one of the wealthiest merchants in India, is also one of the most hospitable men in that hospitable country: he had the goodness to invite me to a fête at his villa.

In the evening we took a ride along the Strand, where the fashionable world of Calcutta, both Europeans and Indians, go to enjoy the cool of the evening, as they do in London in Hyde Park. Here, however, the handsome equipages, and the ladies and gentlemen on horseback, are surrounded by a crowd of servants, which imparts a foreign air to this scene, which otherwise reminded us of our own country.

Those, however, who wish to enjoy the beauties of nature, repair to Garden Reach at Allipoor. Both sides of the road thither are enlivened by a succession of magnificent country houses, surrounded by lovely flower gardens and small parks; the verdant carpet of which is diversified by groups of mangoes, tamarinds, figs, neems, and teak; among which tower the lofty bamboos, whose delicate foliage flutters with the slightest breath of air. The notes of the Indian nightingale (the bulbul or Hazardasitana, *i. e.* the bird with a thousand songs) resound from amid the refreshing shade, and hundreds of luminous insects hover about like little lamps or ignes fatui; the air is filled with the most delicious perfumes, which are diffused all around by the evening breezes.

As I spent the forenoon in visiting the most remarkable buildings, I will, in the first place, give you some account of them. As a military man my attention was, of course, primarily engaged by Fort William. It is built in the form of an octagon, and is fortified according to Vauban's system; three of the fronts, however, which are turned towards the Hooghly to command the river, deviate from the regular form. The five regular sides are inland; the bastions have all very salient orillons, behind which retire circular flanks; the moat is dry, and has a lunette in the middle, but it can be laid under water by means of two sluices. In front of every courtine is a ravelin, the faces of which mount 26 pieces of heavy artillery at once. The demi-bastions which terminate the five regular fronts on each side are covered by a counter-guard, the faces of which are likewise defended by 26 guns.

This citadel was begun by Lord Clive after the battle of Plassey, and cost, on the whole, two millions sterling; but it is on so great a scale, that a garrison of 15,000 men is required for its defence. In the interior of the citadel are the bomb-proof barracks, the arsenal, and the magazines. The garrison consists of two European regiments, one of sepoys, and a few companies of artillery; because the principal station is at Barrackpoor, 13 miles distant, where there are 7000 men. The arsenal contains arms for 80,000 men. Close to it some works have been erected, by means of which the whole may be laid under water in a very short time. This has been done, because a few years ago a fire, which was supposed to have been caused at the instigation of the Rajah of Nepaul, burnt down one of the side buildings, and threatened the whole arsenal with destruction. An artesian well was begun; in boring which, the bones of dogs were discovered at the depth of 150 feet: this project, however, has been abandoned.

One of the most remarkable building in Calcutta is the Mint. It was commenced in the year 1824, on a plan proposed by Major Forbes, and was finished in six years. This Mint, which is undoubtedly the largest in the world, is erected on the Strand, 26½ feet below the surface of the ground, and 60 above it: it is built in the Doric style, and the centre portico is a copy of the temple of Minerva at Athens. The various machinery for coining and stamping the money are set in motion by six steam engines. Nearly 3000 workmen, chiefly natives, are employed in this establishment. Two lacs can be coined daily in seven hours; and since the year 1831, 200 millions of rupees have been issued from this Mint. As I have mentioned the source from which the current coin is spread over India, I will add an account of the revenue and expenditure of this vast empire.

The following are the results of a view by Colonel Sykes, of the Revenue and Expenditure of India at the four decennial periods: 1809–1810, 1819–1820, 1829–1830, 1839–1840:—

STATEMENT OF THE REVENUE derived from Land Sayer and Abkarry—Customs, Salt, Opium, Tobacco, Stamps, and Postage in the Upper and Lower Provinces of BENGAL, at MADRAS and BOMBAY, in the Years 1809–10, 1819–20, 1829–30, 1839–40, showing the Charges of collecting each Branch of the Revenue, and the per Centage on the separate Receipts; also distinguishing the Stipends and Allowances paid out of the Revenues, and the Amount of Net Revenue after these Stipends and Charges of Collection have been deducted from the Gross Revenue, showing likewise separately the several Heads of other Charges, and the final Results of Surplus or Deficit in each Year, converted into Sterling at 2s. the Sicca Rupee.

BENGAL AND AGRA.

	1809–10.				1819–20.			
	Revenues and Receipts.	Charges of Collection.	Net Receipts.	Rate ₩ Cent. of Collection.	Revenues and Receipts.	Charges of Collection.	Net Receipts.	Rate ₩ Cent. of Collection.
Revenue.	£	£	£	£	£	£	£	£
Land Sayer and Abkarry – Lower Provinces	2,872,484	207,883	2,664,601	7·237	3,310,408	304,030	3,006,378	9·184
Land Sayer and Abkarry – North-western do.	3,108,318	236,977	2,871,341	7·624	3,756,866	263,706	3,493,160	7·019
	5,980,802	444,860	5,535,942	7·438	7,067,274	567,736	6,499,538	8·033
Customs – Lower Provinces	211,565	22,663	188,902	10·712	347,455	50,137	297,318	14·429
Customs – North-western do.	230,228	33,860	196,368	14·673	288,971	39,623	249,358	13·714
	442,293	56,523	385,770	12·779	636,426	89,770	546,656	14·105
Salt (deducting cost)	1,284,334	131,792	1,152,342	10·261	1,348,359	227,228	1,121,131	16·852
Opium (ditto)	646,485	24,513	621,972	3·792	632,753	32,480	600,273	5·133
Stamps	52,990	8,237	44,753	15·547	125,972	56,173	69,799	44·592
Post Office	38,707	31,635	7,072	81·729	48,937	34,770	14,167	71·050
	8,445,601	697,560	7,748,041	Average 8·259	9,859,703	1,008,157	8,851,546	Average 10·225
Revenues of Prince of Wales' Island			69,940				48,860	
Ditto of ceded territory on the Nerbuddah							*177,183	
Tributes and subsidies								
			7,817,981				9,077,389	
Allowances and assignments payable out of the revenues – Lower Provinces		164,335				171,544		
Allowances and assignments payable out of the revenues – North-western do.		502,109				429,607		
			666,914				601,151	
Net revenue			7,151,067				8,476,238	
Charges.				₩ Cent. of other Charges to Net Revenue.				₩ Cent. of other Charges to Net Revenue.
Civil and political charges including contingencies			543,054	7·594			838,676	9·894
Judicial ditto – Lower Provinces		323,947				398,427		
Judicial ditto – North-western do.		160,452				178,324		
			584,399	8·172			576,751	6·804
Provincial police do. – Lower Provinces		63,534				69,735		
Provincial police do. – North-western do.		85,012				94,346		
			148,546	2·077			164,081	1·936
Mint ditto			22,249		Excess of receipts		2,669	
Marine ditto			64,783	0·906			90,790	1·071
Military ditto			2,972,738	41·571			3,822,309	45·099
Buildings and fortifications			94,680	1·324			146,566	1·729
Charges of Prince of Wales' Island, &c.			170,307				172,709	
Deccan prize (included in revenues of former years)								
Interest on debt			1,385,881	19·352			1,551,045	18·298
Total charges including interest on debt			5,984,817	83·692			7,360,658	83·834
Surplus			1,166,250				1,115,580	
			7,151,067				8,476,238	

	1829–30.				1839–40.			
	Revenues and Receipts.	Charges of Collection.	Net Receipts.	Rate ₩ Cent. of Collection.	Revenues and Receipts.	Charges of Collection.	Net Receipts.	Rate ₩ Cent. of Collection.
Revenue.	£	£	£	£	£	£	£	£
Land Sayer and Abkarry – Lower Provinces	3,274,384	319,733	2,954,651	9·765	3,528,289	384,212	3,144,077	10·589
Land Sayer and Abkarry – North-western do.	4,041,090	313,208	3,727,882	7·800	3,883,289	454,044	3,429,245	11·692
	7,315,474	634,941	6,680,533	8·679	7,411,578	838,256	6,573,322	11·310
Customs – Lower Provinces	311,707	56,611	255,096	17·831	374,206	41,545	332,661	11·102
Customs – North-western do.	340,424	36,760	303,664	10·798	187,024	61,081	125,943	32·659
	652,131	93,371	558,760	14·318	561,230	102,626	458,604	18·285
Salt (deducting cost)	1,387,037	216,033	1,171,004	15·575	1,841,334	196,655	1,644,679	10·680
Opium (ditto)	1,225,903	114,362	1,111,541	9·326	398,689	92,992	305,697	23·321
Stamps	276,618	54,092	222,526	19·554	309,324	27,532	281,792	8·901
Post Office	73,745	66,762	6,983	90·530	84,272	77,239	7,033	91·654
	10,930,910	1,179,581	9,751,329	Average 10·791	10,606,627	1,335,320	9,271,307	Average 12·589
Revenues of Prince of Wales' Island			28,559				13,808	
Ditto of ceded territory on the Nerbuddah								
Tributes and subsidies			173,168				232,869	
			9,957,856				9,517,984	
Allowances and assignments payable out of the revenues – Lower Provinces		120,790				165,466		
Allowances and assignments payable out of the revenues – North-western do.		312,488				399,670		
			433,278				565,136	
Net revenue			9,524,578				8,952,848	
Charges.				₩ Cent. of other Charges to Net Revenue.				₩ Cent. of other Charges to Net Revenue.
Civil and political charges including contingencies			791,036	8·327			855,130	9·541
Judicial ditto – Lower Provinces		375,312				482,078		
Judicial ditto – North-western do.		183,640				364,647		
			558,952	5·874			846,725	9·457
Provincial police do. – Lower Provinces		48,845				80,153		
Provincial police do. – North-western do.		94,346				128,473		
			143,191	1·503			208,626	2·328
Mint ditto			30,106		Excess of receipts		30,530	
Marine ditto			90,709	0·952			137,606	1·200
Military ditto			3,498,462	36·731			4,115,150	45·915
Buildings and fortifications			268,103	2·731			120,878	1·349
Charges of Prince of Wales' Island, &c.			133,066				33,963	
Deccan prize (included in revenues of former years)			341,689					
Interest on debt			1,334,851	16·113			1,252,873	13·978
Total charges including interest on debt			7,385,707	77·544			7,531,645	84·143
Surplus			2,138,871				1,421,203	
			9,524,578				8,952,848	

* Net receipts, the charges not exhibited in the Indian statement.

MADRAS.

1809-10.

Revenues and Receipts.	Revenues and Receipts.	Charges of Collection.	Net Receipts.	Rate ℔ Cent. of Collection.
	£	£	£	£
Land Sayer, Abkarry, and Moturpha revenues	3,694,755	169,215	3,455,540	4·608
Customs	251,279	48,499	202,780	19·301
Salt	228,572	41,516	187,056	18·163
Opium	-	-	-	-
Stamps	8,214	2,491	5,723	30·376
Tobacco	-	-	-	-
Postage	14,689	17,161	Excess Charge 2,472	116·829
	4,197,509	278,882	3,848,627	Average 6·756
Subsidies from Mysore, Travancore, and Cochin			393,756	-
			4,239,383	
Allowances and assignments payable out of the revenues			618,816	-
Net revenues, after deducting allowances and assignments and charges of collection			3,620,567	-
Charges.				℔ Cent. of other Charges to Net Revenue.
Charges of the civil and political establishments including contingencies			164,069	4·511
Judicial charges			216,668	5·984
Provincial police			71,987	1·988
Mint charges (deducting Mint duties)			-	-
Marine charges			-	-
Military charges			2,581,107	71·290
Buildings and Fortifications			57,063	1·576
Interest on Debt			372,416	10·286
Total charges, including interest on debt			3,463,306	95·636
Net surplus at Madras			157,261	-
			3,620,567	

1819-20.

Revenues and Receipts.	Revenues and Receipts.	Charges of Collection.	Net Receipts.	Rate ℔ Cent. of Collection.
	£	£	£	£
Land Sayer, Abkarry, and Moturpha revenues	3,400,844	323,321	3,077,523	9·507
Customs	441,868	90,033	351,835	20·375
Salt	298,299	60,766	237,533	20·361
Opium	-	-	-	-
Stamps	42,590	2,923	39,667	6·863
Tobacco	-	-	-	-
Postage	18,144	19,704	Excess Charge 1,560	108·597
	4,201,735	496,717	3,705,018	Average 11·821
Subsidies from Mysore, Travancore, and Cochin	-	-	320,728	-
			4,025,746	-
Allowances and assignments payable out of the revenues	-	-	595,928	-
Net revenues, after deducting allowances and assignments and charges of collection	-	-	3,429,818	-
		Net Deficit	327,537	-
			3,757,355	
Charges.				℔ Cent. of other Charges to Net Revenue.
Charges of the civil and political establishments including contingencies	-	-	206,416	6·018
Judicial charges	-	-	247,506	7·216
Provincial police	-	-	96,456	2·812
Mint charges (deducting Mint duties)	-	-	10,693	-
Marine charges	-	-	5,499	0·160
Military charges	-	-	3,033,654	88·449
Buildings and Fortifications	-	-	65,712	1·916
Interest on Debt	-	-	91,419	2·665
Total charges, including interest on debt	-	-	3,757,355	109·550

1829-30.

Revenues and Receipts.	Revenues and Receipts.	Charges of Collection.	Net Receipts.	Rate ℔ Cent. of Collection.
	£	£	£	£
Land Sayer, Abkarry, and Moturpha revenues	3,189,523	375,515	2,814,008	11·773
Customs	485,338	38,184	447,154	7·867
Salt	342,157	23,619	318,518	6·903
Opium	-	-	-	-
Stamps	43,438	8,875	34,563	20·431
Tobacco	50,624	3,344	47,280	6·605
Postage	26,838	24,009	2,829	89·460
	4,137,898	473,546	3,664,352	Average 11·444
Subsidies from Mysore, Travancore, and Cochin	-	-	322,357	-
	-	-	3,986,709	-
Allowances and assignments payable out of the revenues	-	-	585,014	-
Net revenues, after deducting allowances and assignments and charges of collection	-	-	3,401,695	-
	-	-	44,215	-
			3,445,910	
Charges.				℔ Cent. of other Charges to Net Revenue.
Charges of the civil and political establishments including contingencies	-	-	273,623	8·044
Judicial charges	-	-	231,769	6·815
Provincial police	-	-	63,052	1·853
Mint charges (deducting Mint duties)	-	-	16,833	-
Marine charges	-	-	11,078	0·326
Military charges	-	-	2,635,600	77·480
Buildings and Fortifications	-	-	46,772	1·375
Interest on Debt	-	-	169,183	4·973
Total charges, including interest on debt	-	-	3,445,910	101·299

1839-40.

Revenues and Receipts.	Revenues and Receipts.	Charges of Collection.	Net Receipts.	Rate ℔ Cent. of Collection.
	£	£	£	£
Land Sayer, Abkarry, and Moturpha revenues	3,337,840	410,884	2,926,956	12·309
Customs	384,645	48,466	336,179	12·600
Salt	349,259	32,157	317,102	9·207
Opium	-	-	-	-
Stamps	45,362	4,738	40,624	10·444
Tobacco	57,504	5,744	51,760	9·989
Postage	30,693	35,626	Excess Charge 4,933	116·072
	4,205,305	537,615	3,667,688	Average 12·785
Subsidies from Mysore, Travancore, and Cochin	-	-	325,609	
	-	-	3,993,297	
Allowances and assignments payable out of the revenues	-	-	560,077	
Net revenues, after deducting allowances and assignments and charges of collection	-	-	3,433,220	
	-	-	45,327	
			3,478,547	
Charges.				℔ Cent. of other Charges to Net Revenue.
Charges of the civil and political establishments including contingencies	-	-	302,763	8·818
Judicial charges	-	-	249,955	7·280
Provincial police	-	-	62,392	1·817
Mint charges (deducting Mint duties)	-	-	1,164	-
Marine charges	-	-	2,813	0·08[illegible]
Military charges	-	-	2,764,963	80·5[illegible]
Buildings and Fortifications	-	-	47,318	1·378
Interest on Debt	-	-	47,179	1·374
Total charges, including interest on debt	-	-	3,478,547	101·320

Revenues and Receipts.	BOMBAY. 1809–10. Revenues and Receipts.	Charges of Collection.	Net Receipts.	Rate ₽ Cent. of Collection.	1819–20. Revenues and Receipts.	Charges of Collection.	Net Receipts.	Rate ₽ Cent. of Collection.	1829–30. Revenues and Receipts.	Charges of Collection.	Net Receipts.	Rate ₽ Cent. of Collection.	1839–40. Revenues and Receipts.	Charges of Collection.	Net Receipts.	Rate ₽ Cent. of Collection.
	£	£	£	£	£	£	£	£	£	£	£	£	£	£	£	£
Land Seyer and Abkarry	444,585	52,173	392,412	11·735	1,048,075	132,485	915,590	12·641	1,515,337	218,933	1,294,404	14·468	1,731,436	273,537	1,457,899	15·798
Customs	101,853	19,391	82,462	19·038	225,633	35,410	190,223	15·694	403,193	27,831	375,362	6·902	220,876	43,709	177,167	19·788
Salt	1,711	-	1,711	-	-	-	-	-	22,829	-	22,829	-	130,963	11,693	119,270	8·929
Opium	-	-	-	-	-	-	-	-	-	-	-	-	18,451	7,481	10,970	40·545
Stamps	-	-	-	-	14,973	-	14,973	-	31,734	15,632	16,102	49·259	46,073	3,054	43,019	6·629
Post Office	5,189	4,283	906	82·540	5,295	3,875	1,420	73·182	10,893	14,741	Excess Charge 3,848	135·327	16,641	26,098	Excess Charge 9,457	156·829
	553,338	75,847	477,491	Average 13·707	1,293,976	171,770	1,122,206	Average 13·276	1,982,006	277,157	1,704,849	Average 13·985	2,164,440	365,572	1,798,868	Average 16·889
Subsidy from the Cutch government			-	-	-	-	-	-	-	-	24,507	-	-	-	18,588	
			477,491	-	-	-	1,122,206	-	-	-	1,729,356	-	-	-	1,817,436	
Allowances and assignments payable out of the revenues in accordance with treaties or other engagements			10,775	-	-	-	11,872	-	-	-	455,624	-	-	-	471,164	
Net revenues after deducting allowances and assignments and charges of collection			466,716	-	-	-	1,110,334	-	-	-	1,273,732	-	-	-	1,346,292	
Deficit			1,161,785	-	-	-	706,319	-	-	-	1,002,010	-	-	-	637,926	
			1,628,501	-	-	-	1,816,653	-	-	-	2,275,742	-	-	-	1,984,218	
Charges.				₽ Cent. of other Charges to Net Revenue.				₽ Cent. of other Charges to Net Revenue.				₽ Cent. of other Charges to Net Revenue.				₽ Cent. of other Charges to Net Revenue.
Charges of the civil and political establishments including contingencies			104,568	22·563	-	-	115,862	10·255	-	-	293,067	23·009	-	-	531,941	39·512
Judicial and police charges			47,850	10·252	-	-	83,421	7·513	-	-	229,659	18·030	-	-	230,238	17·102
Mint charges (deducting Mint duties)			Excess Receipts 97		-	-	Excess Receipts 1,610		-	-	774		-	-	Excess Receipts 20,[illegible]	
Marine charges (deducting receipts)			113,672	24·391	-	-	67,616	6·087	-	-	141,322	11·095	-	-	121,[illegible]	9·014
Military charges			1,063,837	227·724	-	-	1,512,003	136·175	-	-	1,501,080	117·849	-	-	1,052,145	78·151
Buildings and fortifications			32,431	6·948	-	-	16,635	1·498	-	-	92,200	7·238	-	-	28,022	2·082
Interest on debt			267,750	57·369	-	-	24,726	2·226	-	-	17,640	1·384	-	-	40,720	3·025
Total charges including interest on debt			1,628,501	348·928	-	-	1,816,653	163·615	-	-	2,275,742	178·667	-	-	1,984,218	147·384

A COMPARATIVE VIEW of the Rate per Cent. at which the Indian Revenue was collected in the Years 1809–10, 1819–20, 1829–30, and 1839–40, showing also the Rate per Cent. which the other Charges bore to the net Revenue in each of those Years.

		BENGAL.				MADRAS.				BOMBAY.				INDIA.			
		1809–10.	1819–20.	1829–30.	1839–40.	1809–10.	1819–20.	1829–30.	1839–40.	1809–10.	1819–20.	1829–30.	1839–40.	1809–10.	1819–20.	1829–30.	1839–40.
		£	£	£	£	£	£	£	£	£	£	£	£	£	£	£	£
Land Sayer and Abkarry	Lower Provinces	7·237	9·184	9·753	10·589												
	North-western do.	7·624	7·019	7·800	11·692												
	Mean of do.	7·438	8·033	8·679	11·310	4·668	9·207	11·775	12·509	11·735	12·641	14·468	15·798	6·629	8·858	10·230	12·[illegible]00
Customs	Lower Provinces	10·712	14·429	17·811	11·102												
	North-western do.	14·675	13·715	10·798	32·639												
	Mean of do.	12·779	14·105	14·318	18·985	19·301	20·375	7·867	12·600	19·038	13·694	6·902	19·788	15·641	16·303	10·345	16·696
Salt		10·261	16·832	15·575	10·680	18·163	20·361	6·903	9·207	-	-	-	8·929	11·442	17·488	13·679	10·359
Opium		5·792	5·133	9·326	23·324	-	-	-	-	-	-	-	40·545	3·792	5·135	9·328	24·086
Tobacco		-	-	-	-	-	-	6·605	9·989	-	-	-	-	-	-	6·605	9·989
Stamps		13·547	44·592	19·554	8·901	30·326	6·863	20·451	10·444	-	-	49·259	6·629	17·531	32·198	22·343	8·814
Post-office		81·729	71·060	90·530	91·654	116·929	108·397	89·460	116·072	82·540	73·182	135·327	156·329	90·601	80·619	94·645	105·990
Average charge of collection		8·259	10·225	10·791	12,589	6·756	11·821	11·444	12·785	15·707	15·276	13·985	16·889	8·016	10·919	11·920	13·186
Civil and political charges including contingencies		7·594	9·894	8·327	9·341	4·531	6·018	8·014	8·818	22·362	10·255	23·009	39·512	7·221	8·900	9·575	12·296
Judicial ditto		8·172	6·804	5·874	9·447	5·984	7·216	6·813	7·280	10·252	7·5[illegible]3	18·030	17·102	7·325	6·880	7·107	9·565
Provincial police ditto		2·077	1·936	3·503	2·328	1·988	2·812	1·858	1·817	-	-	-	-	1·991	2·093	1·555	2·062
Marine ditto		0·906	1·071	0·955	1·200	-	0·160	0·326	0·082	24·291	6·087	11·095	9·014	1·585	1·251	1·712	1·687
Military ditto		41·371	45·099	36·731	45·913	71·290	88·449	77·420	80·336	227·724	136·175	117·849	78·151	58·877	64·290	53·754	57·721
Buildings and fortifications		1·324	1·729	2·731	1·349	1·576	1·916	1·375	1·378	6·948	1·498	7·238	2·082	1·639	1·758	2·810	1·428
Total charges exclusive of interest		64·340	68·537	61·429	70·165	83·370	106·884	96·326	99·904	291·557	161·386	177·282	144·359	80·551	86·561	80·018	84·874
Interest on debt		19·352	18·298	16·115	13·978	10·286	2·666	4·973	1·374	57·371	2·226	1·384	3·025	18·010	12·805	12·124	9·756
Total charges including interest on debt		83·692	86·835	77·544	84·143	93·656	109·550	101·299	101·278	348·928	163·6[illegible]2	178·666	147·384	98·561	99·366	92·142	94·650

NOTES ON A FEW OF THE HEADS OF CHARGE.

BENGAL AND AGRA.

Land.—The increase in the per centage for collecting the land revenue in 1839–40, as compared with 1829–30, is partly accounted for by the augmentation of revenue surveys, the excavation of canals, and for additional native officers and establishments employed in investigating and conducting resumption cases.

Customs.—The large comparative augmentation in the per centage on customs in Agra in 1839–40 does not result so much from an increase in the charges, as from a reduction of receipts, occasioned by the abolition of the transit duties.

Opium.—Although the charge on opium was less in 1839–40, than in 1829–30, the per centage borne to the receipts is greater, in consequence of the reduction in the price of the drug, and diminished sale from our hostilities with the Chinese,—the net receipt from opium in 1829–30 having yielded upwards of 1,100,000*l.*, whilst in 1839–40 it produced little beyond 300,000*l.*

Stamps.—The apparent decrease in the per centage for collecting this duty is merely nominal, a portion of the charge being included in the judicial branch in 1839–40.

Judicial.—The large increase in the charges of this branch of expenditure is almost wholly attributable to the additional means employed for improving and extending the administration of justice amongst the people.

MADRAS.

Land.—The increase in the per centage of charge in 1839–40 is occasioned principally by additional surveys. The small per centage remarkable in 1809–10 is the result of an accidental credit in that year of large sums for refunded charges on audit, combined with some miscellaneous revenue receipts which are brought in reduction of the charges of that year.

Customs.—The increase in the per centage on the customs will be seen to accrue more from a diminution in the receipts, than from an increase of charge, occasioned, it is presumed, by the abolition of transit duties.

Salt and tobacco.—The variations in the per centage on these sources of revenue are evidently occasioned more by the different modes adopted for separating the cost of the articles from the charges upon them, than by a positive increase in the latter.

BOMBAY.

Land.—The per centage for collection is apparently 1½ higher in 1839–40 than in 1829–30, but if service pensions and some extraordinary payments were excluded in both years, the actual charge in 1839–40 would be rather less than in 1829–30.

Customs.—The increase in the per centage for collection is accounted for by the diminution of receipts, owing to the abolition of the transit duties.

Salt.—This is a new source of revenue at Bombay, and may be regarded as partaking of the nature of a custom duty. The receipts and charges on account of the tax should, therefore, be considered in connection with that duty, and hence would result an amelioration in the per centage on customs in 1839–40.

Civil charges.—The large increase under this head in 1839–40 is occasioned by the writing off in that year of the accumulated balance standing to the debit of "Wardens Official Fund," amounting to about 200,000*l.*

Marine.—The diminution in the per centage charge of the Marine in 1839–40, as compared with 1829–30, appears to be owing to a smaller outlay at Bombay for building and purchase of vessels and timber in that year than was incurred for the same purposes in 1829–30.

INDIA.

Military.—The high per centage of military charge upon the revenues of India in the year 1819–20, as compared with the rate in the preceding and succeeding decennial periods, is to be traced to the augmentation of the army a year or two previously, consequent upon the great Mahratta war about that time.

Interest.—The diminution of the per centage charge for interest is the result of redemption of debt by means of the Company's commercial assets, and reduction in the rate of interest, by substituting new loans for old ones, which bore higher interest.

The above explanations show that there is considerable difficulty in establishing exact comparisons in the heads of charge between the decennial periods, partly owing to novel or temporary charges, and partly owing to changes in the modes of keeping account, but the total charges nevertheless, both of collection and for carrying on the government of India, show an increase under the former heads from 8 per cent. on the gross revenue in 1809–10 to 13 per cent. in 1839–40, and under the latter heads from 80.551 per cent. in 1809–10 to 84.874 in 1839–40.

The palace of the Governor-General lies on the north side of the Esplanade, facing the city. It is three stories high, and has four wings, one at each corner of the building, surrounded by a colonnade of Ionic pillars, behind which are the narrow verandas. On the north side is a fine flight of steps, under which carriages drive to the entrance. Though the proportions are certainly not correct, this palace is a fine and magnificent building. Captain Wyatt the architect, who erected it at the expense of 130,000*l.* sterling, has combined perfect convenience, with great taste and elegance, in the interior arrangements. The lower story contains the council chamber and other public rooms. In the centre of the first floor is a large marble hall surrounded by pillars, and three splendid apartments, which are used for state dinners; and, above them, in the third story, is the ball room. All the apartments are furnished with divans, large mirrors, and handsome chandeliers. The four wings which are connected with the main building by covered galleries contain the private apartments of the Governor-General and his attendants.

The column which was erected in honour of General Ochterlony is near this palace: it rises to the height of 163 feet: the basis is in the Egyptian style, and the upper part is in imitation of a pillar in Syria. A winding staircase leads to the top, which commands an extensive view over the city and the banks of the Hooghly, as far as Barrackpoor and Fort Gloucester. The cathedral and the six churches of Calcutta (three of which are Roman Catholic) are by no means remarkable as specimens of architecture, and the theatre is even still less distinguished.

After I had been present at several entertainments, and at a grand dinner given by the Deputy-Governor in honour of my friend Mr. Maddock, at the palace of the Governor-General, I was invited by Dwarkanath Tajore to visit him in his fine villa, and I accordingly repaired on the 26th of March to this interesting Indian, who has adopted many of the manners and customs of Europe.

The villa is situated about five miles from Calcutta, in a small park laid out in the English style, combined with the beauties of tropical scenery. This quiet solitary abode is surrounded by a lawn, the bright verdure of which is adorned with a mosaic of flower beds, enlivened and refreshed by a beautiful sheet of water, along the margin of which are groups of mangoes, tamarinds, and bananas; the whole is bounded by plantations of cocoa and fan palms. This seat is a favourite resort of young married couples, who are often invited by the hospitable owner to spend the honeymoon here. The villa is two stories high, and is fitted up entirely in the European style, and it is ornamented with many works of sculpture and painting. Among the latter I greatly admired an extremely interesting portrait of a beautiful Indian lady reclining on a cushion. Dwarkanath pointed out the portrait of this accomplished beauty with a degree of pride, and he evidently appeared to have been very much attached to her. The brothers and a nephew of our host joined us at dinner, at which there was no lack of the richest wines, and even roasted joints of the sacred animal. After dinner six bayaderes appeared with their musicians. Their dance as usual was not so much to be admired as their pretty delicate feet and hands, and their fine contour. At length, however, their movements became so offensive, that we requested that the dance might be concluded. The notions of morality and decorum entertained by the Indians, even when they have acquired that degree of refinement which our host undoubtedly possessed, are still so different from ours, that they are quite insensible to that impropriety which so much shocked us. Two of the bayaderes, who were very pretty, sat down by us after the dance was over: one of them, a girl of thirteen, the orphan daughter of Mahometan parents, told me that she had been compelled by necessity to adopt this mode of life.

As I was riding to the Strand before sunrise, on my way to Dwarkanath, I witnessed a Hindoo festival, and saw numbers of men, women, and children, in neat white garments, hastening to the Ganges. It was one of those days when they consider it as a particular merit to wash away their sins in the waters of the sacred stream. Girls, selling flowers, offered elegant garlands, wreaths, and nosegays, for sale to the passers by; and numerous beggars and cripples had spread white handkerchiefs on the ground, and implored the pity of the charitable by begging and singing: almost every body, even the poorest, threw them some money, corn, or rice. The scene of the greatest animation was about the river itself, where numbers were assembled in picturesque groups, and men, women, and children, plunged into the stream. The women, several of whom came in handsome carriages, or in palanquins, were attended by their female servants; they went into the river in their delicate garments, closely veiled, strewed some flowers on the surface, and then dipped into its healing waters: mothers poured the purifying element over their daughters and little children.

As soon as the ladies of distinction had completed this work of penance, they were closely surrounded by their female attendants, and very dexterously and modestly changed their wet garments for dry ones, and then, to avoid observation, instantly stepped into their carriages and palanquins. Yet still an opportunity was afforded of casting a glance on the beautiful women of India; and our admiration is not only called forth by the higher classes whose noble and lovely forms, and lighter complexion, strike the eye, but also by the unveiled females, who, when in the flower of their age, in their fifteenth year, have very fine figures. In some places I saw several hundred men sporting in the water, to the sound of the drum, the cymbal, or the violin; while on the bank, near the bathing places, were various comical groups of barbers, who were busily engaged in exercising their profession on the heads and beards of their customers.

This festival reminded me of another very

poetical one, which is celebrated chiefly by the Hindoo women and girls. On a certain day in the year, when the sun is near setting, the women, with little boats, carved of wood, come from a great distance to the Ganges. Thousands of females, dressed in white, are then seen launching their little boats, each of which is supplied with a small lamp. Anxiously does every one watch her little boat, with its flickering light dancing upon the buoyant waves; for the completion of some cherished wish depends upon this light: if it remains visible as long as the eye can follow it, the secret wish confided to the stream will be fulfilled; but if it be extinguished before she loses sight of it, her fond hope will be disappointed; and though thousands of such little lamps are often tossed up and down the river, yet every woman maintains that she can distinguish her own. The many white figures moving about, backwards and forwards in the evening twilight, and the numerous lamps floating on the broad surface of the river, appear like the spirits and magic lights of fairy land.

A whole day was taken up in an excursion to Dum Dum, the Woolwich of India. Accompanied by Captain Mackintosh one of my acquaintances, I drove first to the cannon foundery, situated at the extreme north end close to the river, where I breakfasted with Captain Wilson, the director. This cannon foundery is, in every respect, better contrived than that of Woolwich: it contains a boring-room, in which twelve brass guns may be bored at the same time; for the government procures the iron guns from Europe. During the time I was there, six guns were cast; and the arrangements are such, that three times the number might have been manufactured.

We reached Dum Dum about noon; and here I was indebted to the kindness of Captain Buckle for several instructive and interesting hours. All the young officers arriving from Europe, as well as the recruits, are practically trained in this depôt of artillery, and then sent to their regiments; so much haste is, however, often made, that the officer must have completed his course of study in one year, and the private in seven months. The officers' rooms are handsomely fitted up; and besides the dining or mess-room, comprise a billiard-room, a select library, a model room, and a collection of remarkable arms.

The Elephant Battery, which I had an opportunity of seeing in operation, appeared to me to be very original and unique in its kind. Two elephants harnessed behind each other, or sometimes only one in shafts, draw a nine-pounder with the greatest ease. The movements are executed with great rapidity and precision, which is not without difficulty, because the Mahouts are not the most judicious people in the world. It has also cost much trouble to make the harness, &c., sufficiently solid; for the incredible bodily strength with which the elephant throws himself into the harness requires that the materials should be both strong and elastic. It seems very doubtful whether this elephant battery can be employed in battle, because the elephant is very timid, and is excessively afraid of fire; he is, however, a most serviceable draught animal, for bringing up heavy guns, especially in swampy soil.

My friend made arrangements for me to pass two days in the enjoyment of a country life in India, at the summer villa of the Governor-General at Barrackpoor; and, at the same time, to combine, with this little excursion, a view of the schools at Hooghly, which Mr. Bayley, under whose immediate direction they are, had kindly promised to show me. Accompanied by that philanthropic young man, I accordingly drove one cool morning to Hooghly, which is twenty-six miles distant. One of the finest roads I have seen, lined with avenues of beautiful mangoes, tamarinds, banyans, neem, and teak trees, varying in their foliage, colour, and form, led us through the paradisiacal valley, past many pretty country houses, some embosomed amid the umbrageous foliage, and others surrounded by little cocoa plantations. Beyond Barrackpoor we crossed the Hooghly, then passed Tranquebar, which belongs to the Danes, and soon afterwards Chandernagore, where the French nation was vividly brought before us; not only by the 100 sepoys in their French uniforms, but also by the countenances of many of the natives.

As I intend, in a subsequent letter, to give you a separate account of the schools, I shall now pass over what I saw and observed here. After stopping four hours at Hooghly I returned to Barrackpoor, where a room had already been prepared for me in the house of the Governor-General, and a few hours afterwards Mr. Maddock arrived. This little villa, which is built in very good style and taste, lies close to the Hooghly, at the end of a large park. The lower story, appropriated to the servants, is surrounded by a vaulted colonnade; in the upper story are large handsome saloons for social entertainments, and the private apartments. At the four extreme corners are four bed-chambers and as many baths: on the north and south there are airy verandas. All the rooms are fitted up with perfect convenience and princely magnificence.

Three neat bungalows, at a short distance, are designed for the residence of the immediate attendants of the Governor-General. This villa is surrounded by a small flower-garden, which joins the park, with its verdant lawns and fine groups of trees. At the extremity is a menagerie, which might be one of the finest in the world; but the keeper very justly observed, " One Governor-General takes an interest in it, and another none whatever."

The view towards the Hooghly is really enchanting: the broad river with many country seats, gardens, pagodas, flights of steps, and palm groves, present an uninterrupted busy scene of boats and bathers; and in the evening the banks are illuminated by innumerable lamps. On beholding this glorious scenery, I again felt the often-cherished wish that I could send to my friends at home, as if by magic, a picture of this diversified view of land and water, which quite overpowers the feelings: but, alas! the power of the fairies is long since broken; and it is granted to only a few favoured mortals, like Prince Pückler, to follow nature into her most secret recesses, and to give to language that charm which Claude Lorraine gave to colours.

I passed two days, which can never be forgotten, with my valued friend, in the silence and solitude of the country, amid this wondrously beautiful scenery. The evenings were spent in the family circle of Mr. Grant, who resides in a beautiful villa on the Hooghly, and, notwithstanding his advanced age, enjoys the best health, and the possession of his intellectual faculties in full vigour.

We returned to Calcutta in a handsome gondola, which a wealthy Parsee had sent for us. An excursion on the Hooghly, especially at sunrise, is most delightful: the landscape, when seen from the river, displays its greatest charms. Here we were greeted by the sight of beautiful country houses, peeping out beneath the shade of the most variously grouped trees or palm groves. Villages, with their pagodas, are erected on the banks, and fine flights of steps descend into the river; and the whole is most enchantingly reflected in the deep waters. On the flight of steps there are generally six small pagodas standing near each other, three of which belong to one village, and three to another, which is indicated by their being painted of different colours. Beyond these temples a colonnade runs towards the river, under the shade of which the bathers are protected from the burning rays of the sun; and here old and young are seen by hundreds sporting in the sacred stream. But our poetical reverie is painfully disturbed by the disgusting sight of the dead bodies floating down the river; a practice equally repulsive to the sight and to the smell.

As soon as we had passed the cannon foundery, the river became more animated by numerous men of war, merchantmen, and steamers; and suddenly the forest of masts, with their sails, rigging, streamers, and flags, gave a totally different character to the prospect. The commerce of Calcutta is so considerable that of late years 550 large merchantmen have annually arrived in the port.* We had to wind our way through this floating town in order to reach the esplanade, where our carriage was in waiting, and speedily conveyed us home.

One afternoon we made an excursion to the Botanic Garden, which is three miles distant. We drove along Garden Reach on the left bank of the Hooghly: both sides of the road are lined with the finest gardens and country houses, among which that of the chief judge, Sir Lawrence Peel, looks like a little fairy castle; opposite to it is the Botanic Garden, which extends to a great distance along the right bank of the river. It is undoubtedly one of the richest and most beautiful gardens

* The navy of the Presidency consists of 8 war steamers, of 722 horse power, two of which, each of 220 horse power, are equipped; there are besides 4 iron war steamers, each of 100 horse power: 4 iron steam tugs of 60 horse power, with as many iron passenger boats, and 18 pilot boats. In 1843, 571 merchantmen, whose total tonnage was 236,264 tons, entered the harbour of Calcutta.

in the world: besides a variety of European flowers and shrubs, all the trees and plants of India, nay, I may say, of all Asia, and southern Africa, are cultivated here. It was commenced about 50 or 60 years ago, by Lieutenant-Colonel Kyd, and after his departure, Dr. Roxburgh and Dr. Wallich continued to improve it with equal zeal and judgment. The object contemplated is not only to bring to the highest perfection all the fruits and vegetables of Europe and India, but also to raise tea and coffee, and medicinal plants, as well as the most useful kinds of trees, in order to supply the gardens of India and Europe. The number of species of culinary vegetables, fruits, and flowers, cultivated in the kitchen garden is 1200, or nearly a third of the whole number of species of plants raised in this garden: peculiar attention is paid to the cultivation of medicinal plants. Many hundred mahogany, teak, and sissar trees have been distributed among private individuals. Sixteen thousand plants were divided in one year, and 42,000 tea plants, raised from Chinese seed, were sent to Assam, Kamaon, and Simore. This incomparable garden, which concentrates the vegetation of half the globe, is not only a source of unceasing delight, but also of incalculable benefit to the inhabitants of Calcutta, who constantly resort thither as a retreat in hot weather: here they recruit after the fatigues of the day, and acquire fresh strength and vigour to resume their various occupations with renewed activity.

The mode of life in Calcutta is, like that of other cities of India, dependent on the climate, and only differs from it by its greater luxury and splendour. Calcutta vies in hospitality with all the other places I have visited; and I have been privileged to experience so many proofs of this, that the remembrance of it will be cherished throughout my whole life. With the first dawn of day both high and low are on the wing — the upper class to enjoy an excursion, and the lower to enter upon their day's work: in the hot season, the early hours of the morning and the close of evening are the only times of the day when the European can venture into the open air. At nine o'clock, after bathing, the family join at breakfast; after which they disperse for their several avocations till two o'clock. The ladies are engaged in domestic occupations, or in paying visits and making purchases, and the gentlemen are employed in their official residences. At this hour the whole party again assemble and partake of a hot tiffin, after which each returns to his business. Servants are every where employed to cool the air by means of the punca, or of a large fan; but in order that their masters may not be molested by their presence, the strings by which the punca is set in motion are passed over pullies, and conducted into the corridors, where the men keep the puncas in constant motion. As soon as the sun is near setting every body seeks recreation on horseback, or in carriages along the beach, or in excursions to Garden Reach and Allipoor. The natives also go out at this hour in their palanquins, and we frequently saw them reading the English newspapers. During our ride, we often met wretched persons who have been attacked by the cholera, and who would certainly have remained lying helpless on the road-side, had not some European taken pity upon them.

At eight o'clock the family meets at dinner, which does not give the hostess the smallest trouble, for the servants are so well trained, that it is only necessary to tell the butler and the kidmagar the number of guests that are expected, and a most capital dinner will be served. The ice is brought in large blocks from America, and is preserved in an ice-house. In the cooler season theatricals, concerts, and balls give a variety to the social entertainments. The rule that no dinner-party should fall short of the number of the Graces, nor exceed that of the Muses, is certainly not adhered to in Calcutta: only on one occasion I joined so small a party at dinner, which was that of the Junior Club, in the Town-Hall.

On the arrival of the news of the victory gained by Sir Charles Napier over the Ameers, at Hydrabad, I concluded that a lengthened war would ensue, and at once resolved to repair to the scene of action. I accordingly begged leave of the government to proceed thither in the Nemesis or Pluto, which were destined for the Indus; and was indebted to the kind intervention of Mr. Maddock for a favourable reply to my request. These two vessels had come into port a few weeks before from the Chinese expedition, and were to put to sea on the 6th of April.

I shall ever look back upon my sojourn in India with feelings of sincere pleasure and gratitude; for not only will the valuable and ample stores of acquired knowledge, furnish materials for agreeable and useful contemplation, to the latest term of my life, but the numerous proofs of kindness and friendship which I have enjoyed, will cast a bright halo over every reminiscence; those hours especially which I passed in the society of Mr. Maddock will never be effaced from my memory. This eminent statesman presented to me, at parting, a beautiful and valuable sabre, kindly expressing the wish that I would wear it in remembrance of my Indian friends; and this I shall ever do with feelings of the highest esteem and cordial attachment.

I took leave of him at midnight, on the 5th of April, and embarked on board the Pluto. This steamer is of 100 horse power, flat built, and draws scarcely four feet of water; it was therefore resolved that we should go through Manar Straits, over Adam's Bridge. The captain was an experienced seaman; and we had on board General Walker and his family, on his way to his new garrison at Madras, three other officers, and a surgeon. Our sailors were mostly Lascars, who had been collected from all parts of the world: — there were Mussulmans, Portuguese, Arabs, and Chinese, for the most part, lazy, careless people. The Pluto also had charge of a million of rupees, which were to be delivered at Bombay.

We weighed anchor at seven o'clock in the morning, on the sixth of April, in foggy weather, and proceeded down the Hooghly, amid the cheers of the crews. Towards nine o'clock we had a beautiful deep-blue sky, and the rays of the sun darted with increased power. We were carried forward so rapidly by the ebbing tide, the steam, and the sails, that we cast anchor at Kedgeree, at six o'clock: here we had to wait for the Nemesis, as we were to put to sea together, and the captain had appointed this as the place of rendezvous. That vessel, however, did not come in sight till nine o'clock the following morning, when we immediately set our engine to work, and, accompanied by the Nemesis, passed the first light. As we approached the sea, the wind became more violent, and the water more agitated, so that the Nemesis, whose engine had suffered some damage in China, could not keep up with us. On reaching the Pilot boat, at midnight, where we parted with our pilot, we could still see the lantern of our consort, but in the course of an hour we wholly lost sight of her.

On the eighth of April, the barometer fell considerably, and there was every indication of an approaching storm. The violence of the wind increased to such a degree, that our little vessel was continually covered with the waves, and tossed about in all directions. The motion was so irregular, that, for the first time in my life, I became sea-sick — an evil which most of the sailors shared with me.

On Sunday the ninth, the weather became quite stormy—not a speck of blue was to be seen in the sky: we were enveloped in a grey veil, through which the sun, shorn of its beams, shed a melancholy gleam, and, from time to time, was completely obscured by dense black clouds. Though our engine was worked to the utmost of its power, we advanced scarcely two knots an hour: the waves had already torn off the planks of the paddle wheels; and our stock of coals was so reduced, that even, under the most favourable auspices, we could not reach the nearest harbour, that of Coringa, which was 300 miles distant.

The captain having determined the position of his ship at noon, and having duly weighed the circumstances, found that it was impossible to gain that port, and he therefore considered it his duty to return to Calcutta — a resolution which he took very reluctantly, but which necessity compelled him to adopt. The wind was now in our favour, and we were able to spread our sails, and were carried along with such rapidity by the constantly increasing storm, that we accomplished in the space of fourteen hours the distance which we had been three days in making; for we descried the light of the Pilot boat at midnight, and came up with it at three o'clock in the morning ; but we had to cruize about the boat nearly three hours before we could take a pilot on board. We entered the Hooghly at one o'clock in the afternoon, and at six anchored off Sultanpoor. The telegraph had already transmitted information of our return to Calcutta.

On the eleventh of April, at ten in the morning, we reached the Esplanade, and I hastened to look for my friend. Some anxiety had been felt about us, because there was a stormy wind at Calcutta, and still greater fears were entertained for the Nemesis, which, according to the statement of the pilot, had steered towards the coast, because it was no longer able to keep out at sea.

Mr. Maddock immediately informed me that news had just been received of a second brilliant victory, obtained by Sir Charles Napier in Sinde, in consequence of which, that brave General considered the affairs in that country as finally settled. This induced me to resolve to return to Europe, in the Hindostan steamer, which was to put to sea in a few days. If, however, on my arrival in Egypt, I find permission to make a longer stay in India, I shall return to Bombay, and from thence undertake my cherished plan of a journey to Cashmere and the Himalaya mountains.

Aden, 8th May.

I arrived safely at this desolate harbour two days since, and am now at a bungalow, at the extreme north-west end of the Peninsula, built on a high rocky point. The little, closely built town, lies at my feet, in a hollow, enclosed by bare, jagged masses of rock, surrounded by the barracks and bungalows of the troops stationed here. In the far distant

Arabia a few trees, which look like little specks, indicate that there is still some vegetation, and to the west and south I enjoy the sublime prospect of the boundless ocean.

I passed three happy days at Calcutta, in my friend's villa at Alipoor, revelling in the enjoyment of the luxuriant scenery. The Hindoos celebrated three of their greatest holydays, the last of which, on the 13th of April, concluded with a fête, something resembling our Christmas fair in Germany. As we rode along the Esplanade in the evening, throngs of men, women, and children, were crowding round the sellers of sweatmeats, fans, paper lanterns, and children's toys of every description. All the people were dressed in clean white garments, and many of the women and girls, who walked about unveiled, or had carelessly flung their veils back, were distinguished by fine figures and handsome countenances, lighted up by the most brilliant eyes.

The last evening was spent, till midnight, in the company of friends, when I again took leave of Mr. Maddock, who is so justly endeared to my best affections, and proceeded, by bright moonlight, to the place of embarkation, at the end of Garden Reach.

In spite of all forebodings, the Hindostan was to weigh anchor on Good Friday, the 14th of April; but in consequence of the necessary repair of the machinery, the departure was deferred to the following day, and even then, the Hooghly, which has proved fatal to so many vessels, nearly defeated our plan; for our large steamer was torn from its anchor by the force of the current, on the very point of being dashed against one of the banks, and then carried a mile down the river.

With the first voyage of the Hindostan, a new communication was opened between India and Europe, direct from Calcutta to Suez. What had been deemed by most persons, only twenty years before, as a mere visionary scheme, was now realised. The Oriental Steam Navigation Company, supported by the East India Company, undertook this great enterprise, with two steam-boats, the Hindostan and Bentinck of 550 horse power. The Hindostan is commanded by Captain Moresby, who has gained an imperishable name in the navy by his admirable surveys of the Red Sea, and of the Maldive Islands. It is 250 feet long and 42 broad, and draws nearly three fathoms of water, and cost 110,000*l.* in building. Though it is not exactly adapted to the hot climate, the cabins being rather too small, it is however extremely convenient, and furnished in a very handsome manner. In the large saloon, which alone cost 5000*l.* sterling, there is every accommodation, and a well-chosen library. There are even baths in the vessel.

The upper deck in its whole length affords ample space for the passengers to take exercise. The engine consists of two separate works, with two chimnies, and contains four boilers, and besides the usual life-boats, the roofs over the paddles form two large boats, in each of which thirty persons may be easily accommodated.

Our company, consisting of above 100 passengers, was extremely miscellaneous, civil and military officers with their wives and children, captains of ships, merchants, and Indian adventurers. Most of my English comrades, among whom I will mention only Colonels Shelton and Wyld, and Captains Trower and Houghton, were going to recruit their strength in their native country, after the exertions of the war. The latter, one of the bravest officers in the army, had lost an arm, and was the only survivor of a regiment that had perished in the disaster at Cabool.

Among the passengers was a relation of the Begum Somroo, who is known all over India, and of whom I will say a few words. When the Maharattas threatened the empire of the Great Mogul, a Silesian, named Sommer, whom the most romantic adventures had brought to India, found means to rise to the dignity of one of the first chiefs, and was placed by Najaff Khan, the principal counsellor of Cassim Ali Khan, King of Delhi, as tributary governor in the province of Sirhind, in the centre of the Doab, eighty miles north-east of Delhi. Sommer had his own troops and twenty pieces of cannon, at the head of which were some Europeans, among whom were Levasso, an Italian, and Levois, a Belgian. Whenever this fortunate adventurer was not engaged in war, he sought recreation and amusement in the pleasures of the people, in dancing and music.

Soon after the death of his wife, some bayaderes requested the favour to be allowed to dance before him: among them was a Mussulman girl thirteen years of age, of singular grace and beauty, who made such an impression upon Sommer, that he made her a proposal to remain with him. This bayadere, afterwards the Begum Somroo, declared herself ready to remain with him if he would take her for his wife, and promised that her attachment to him would induce her to embrace the Roman Catholic religion. The itinerant bayadere was artful enough to perceive that Sommer was desperately in love with her; and as she saw there was some hesitation on his part, she pretended that she was going away, upon which Sommer was induced to marry her. The Begum was in the bloom of youth, and succeeded so completely in centering the affections of her husband, that in his hours of solitude he was often overwhelmed with the idea that he might survive her. But the ambitious Begum soon grew tired of her fond husband, though she endeavoured to confirm him in his belief that her heart was animated with a similar affection. In one of these happy moments, the Begum conceived the idea of having two rings made, each filled with poison, and gave one of them to her husband, with the mutual promise, that, if they should ever be separated, and one should hear of the death of the other, the survivor should take the poison which was concealed in the ring.

Sommer was soon after seized with a severe illness, which confined him to his bed. While in this state he received intelligence of a rebellion in the province; and as delay would be dangerous, the Begum, mounted on an elephant, put herself at the head of the troops, and at parting reminded her husband of their reciprocal promise.

A few days after her departure a battle ensued, during which the Begum sent a confidential person to Sirhind with the news that she was killed. Sommer had scarcely received the melancholy intelligence, when he opened his ring, took the poison, and died, in 1770.* The rebellion was soon suppressed; the troops did homage to the Begum, who obtained the Pergunnah from Najaff Khan, on condition of keeping three battalions under arms, for the security of the district.

Soon after the death of Sommer, the Begum married Levasso, the General of her troops. Having no children by her husband, this infatuated woman was seized with jealousy bordering on frenzy, which she carried to such a degree, that Levasso, having on one occasion manifested an interest for a young person among her attendants, she caused her to be walled up in a place under her own apartment, and inhumanly rejoiced in listening to her moans, lamentations, and mortal anguish.

Levasso possessed neither the prudence, talent, or knowledge of mankind, so eminent in his predecessor: vain and revengeful, he attempted to make use of his position to ruin General George Thomas, who was in the service of the Maharattas, and who had on several former occasions made him feel his superiority. The General enjoyed a great reputation as a commander: his enterprises had always been successful, and brought his men large

* Other accounts, however, say that Sommer died a natural death.

booties. Levasso unexpectedly advanced against him, and he instantly collected a body of men, inferior, indeed, in number, but far superior in military skill.

Levois counselled Levasso to come to terms with the General; but Levasso, who had been long jealous of the devotion and attachment of the soldiers to Levois, considered this advice as treachery, and degraded his brave officer. The enraged troops hastily summoned Zaffer Yab Khan, a son of Sommer, by his first wife, from Delhi, and placed him on the throne of Sirhind.

Forsaken by her troops and dependents, and destitute of every means of succour, the Begum saw, when it was too late, the imprudence of her husband in marching against the General, and she at once resolved to get rid of a man who had no power to protect her, and of whom she had long since become weary. She therefore told him that she considered their case desperate, and that she expected from him that he would die with honour, rather than ignominiously fall into the hands of his enemies.

They accordingly fled from Sirhind, accompanied by their most faithful attendants: the Begum was in a palanquin, followed by her husband, who was mounted on horseback; but they had proceeded only a few miles when they were overtaken by the soldiery of Zaffer Yab, and carried prisoners towards Sirhind. On the road thither, the Begum desired one of the attendants to give her a dagger: she bared her breast, and punctured it, so that the blood flowed, and then fainted away. Her husband, roused by the cry of distress which arose among her attendants, anxiously inquired the cause, and being told that the Begum had killed herself, he drew a pistol from his girdle and shot himself.

The Begum remained a prisoner at Sirhind, but she eventually succeeded in persuading General Thomas to take up her cause: he approached Sirhind, effected her restoration, and carried Zaffer Yab prisoner to Delhi.

From this period, the Begum governed with unlimited power, and with singular prudence and wisdom, till she attained her seventy-fourth year. She resided in a very large palace at Sirhind, which was fitted up partly in the Oriental, and partly in the European style. She was perfect mistress of the Persian and Hindostanee languages; and, during certain hours of every day, she seated herself behind a curtain, and transacted the affairs of the government with her officers. She never appeared unveiled, even at the public durbars. To Europeans, however, her conduct was the very reverse: she was extremely fond of giving them splendid entertainments, where none but female domestics were in attendance, and she then always appeared without a veil, and was dressed in the richest Oriental style, covered with gold and jewels. She was a very small figure, and rather stout, but light and active: the expression of her countenance was harsh and severe; but even in old age her beautiful black eye sparkled with all the brilliancy of youth. She appears to have had some compunctions of conscience in the latter part of her life, and endeavoured to find consolation from her father confessor: at her death, she left a part of her wealth to the Romish church.

The Begum frequently complained of her keen sense of loneliness and isolation, which she sought to alleviate by adopting the two children of a Gorawalla (groom). The boy was sent to England as a wealthy heir, under the name of Deysommer, where he afterwards married the daughter of a nobleman; and the girl was married to Major Regalini, who was in the service of the Begum. A son, who was the offspring of this marriage, and had been invited by his childless uncle Deysommer to visit him in England, was our fellow-passenger on board the Hindostan.*

Although the Hooghly is navigable at all times of the year, even for the largest vessels, it is however considered to be one of the most dangerous rivers in the world, on account of its varying descent, its shifting bed, and its rapid currents. The vast mass of water soon spreads from one, to a couple of miles in breadth, and, half way between Calcutta and the sea, attains such a width, that

* He was a handsome, animated, and gentle youth of sixteen, and was exceedingly fond of exhibiting himself in the most splendid dress of the Orientals. When he arrived in London, at the residence of his uncle, he found that his unhappy relative had at that very moment been declared a lunatic, and was confined in some asylum. The poor, lonely youth was immediately sent back to Liverpool, where a ship was on the point of sailing for Calcutta: the unhappy lad was put on board of her, and at once taken back to India.

the palm-clad shores look like dark lines and the numerous ships and vessels which traverse it appear only like black spots. The banks and islands are covered with towns and villages, surrounded by palms, plantations of rice, sugar, mulberry, pine-apple, fine orchards and fields of vegetables.

We commenced our voyage on the 15th, at ten in the morning, but we were able to use only half our power, and came to anchor when we had made forty knots. On the 16th, we set out with the tide; but notwithstanding the utmost care, and every precaution on the part of the pilot, we were within an ace of being dashed against the bank, by the incredible force of the bore; and, had not the pilot, with the rapidity of lightning, seized the helm, we should certainly not have escaped this catastrophe. We cast anchor in the afternoon in Diamond harbour.

It would certainly have been better, if the Hindostan had taken her departure from this point, and the passengers' baggage and coals had been sent thither from Calcutta, in small steamers. On the 17th, we again weighed anchor, and proceeded on our voyage, with a small quantity of steam; but, after sailing only six hours, the pilot was obliged to cast anchor near Kedgeree. At last, on the 18th, when we had made scarcely an hundred knots in three days, we neared the bay of Bengal. Favoured by the finest weather, and a tolerably calm sea, we put our pilot on board the

Pilot boat, and full of hope, steered to our next goal—the harbour of Madras.

The passengers were all in the highest spirits—for we were hastening to our native land, where we each hoped to meet beloved friends and relations, and were already enjoying a foretaste of the happy hours which we should spend in converse on the past. We were a very sociable party; music and singing kept us together on deck till a late hour of the night; and in the daytime, the hours were whiled away in endeavouring to descry distant vessels, or in watching the movements of the hapless flying fish.

The fine weather still befriended us on the 19th; but the wind and the current were so much against us, that we could not make more than eight knots an hour. On the following day, the current was so very contrary, and at the same time turned towards the west, that instead of advancing 228 knots, we had made only 192 in the last twenty-four hours.

On Friday the 21st, the captain expected to be able to see the light-house of Madras at about eleven o'clock at night. There was a complete calm: the sea was perfectly quiet; and it was one of those glorious tropical nights when the firmament is studded with countless myriads of shining orbs. Charmed by this great splendour, and enjoying the cool evening air, most of the passengers, including some of the ladies, were assembled on deck, and every eye was directed to the point where the light was expected to appear. The captain had stationed a sailor at the mast-head, and scarcely had he called out that he clearly perceived a gleam from the light-house, when this welcome intelligence was re-echoed by us all. We accordingly steered towards it: when a fearful shrill voice suddenly exclaimed, "Captain, there are breakers!" and at the same moment, the vessel turned in a contrary direction, and the engine was stopped. Captain Moresby himself had providentially discovered the dangerous mistake, turned the ship with his own hand, and ordered the engineers to stop the engine. The lead was immediately let down, and it appeared that we had only five fathoms water. We found, contrary to our expectation, that the current had carried us twenty-seven miles to the west in the midst of the dangerous Pulicat reef, where two vessels returning from China had perished only a few weeks before.

Some naval officers among the passengers advised the captain to cast anchor and wait till break of day; but Captain Moresby, in a calm, decisive manner, declared that he perfectly knew his position, and would bring his ship safely to Madras. With the lowest power of our engine, and continually sounding on both sides, we began to move slowly onward. The coast was scarcely a mile distant on the right hand: we continued our voyage not without anxiety, having sometimes 6, then again 12, or 7 fathoms, till at length we had 18, and eventually 40 fathoms water, a sure sign that we had happily wound our way out of this fatal labyrinth.

Towards four o'clock we got sight of the lighthouse: at the first dawn of day we entered the roadstead of Madras; and before six o'clock we cast anchor, at a distance of about 400 paces from the shore.

Madras, which is situated 13° 4′ 11″ N. lat., and 80° 22′ E. long. from Greenwich, was built in the first half of the seventeenth century, on a flat, alluvial spot on the sea-coast, in the vicinity of the ancient Mandaraja. Although the town contains above 250,000 inhabitants, (the town and district, 30 square miles in extent, contain 462,051 souls,) it possesses nothing of the grandeur and royal splendour of Calcutta. It looks more like a row of handsome country houses than a great city: only the façade towards the bay, where the citadel lies, the palace-like edifices of the supreme courts of justice, the custom-house, and the warehouses, have any thing approaching to this character.

The citadel, or Fort St. George, was built in the year 1689: the sea was above a mile distant from it only six years ago, but now the bulwarks are almost washed by the waves. It is admirably situated for the defence of the harbour, and may be easily defended by 5000 men. It contains a church, the barracks, and an arsenal, with arms for 50,000 men: a marble statue of Lord Cornwallis is erected in the court-yard.

Workmen were at this time employed in constructing a raised causeway along the strand to check the inroads of the sea; a new lighthouse, also, has been built opposite to the middle of the roadstead. The streets of the town, in which the Europeans and principal natives reside, are broad, and planted with avenues of trees; but the houses are not more than two stories high, and consequently they have not a free current of air during the prevalence of the hot burning winds, against which the inhabitants can only protect themselves by screens kept constantly wet.

The mean temperature, notwithstanding the vicinity of the sea, is said to exceed even that under the equator, and to be 81° 69′ Fahr.

The greater part of Madras is occupied by what is called the Black Town, which is separated from the Fort, towards the north, by the Esplanade. It is very closely and irregularly built, and consists of brick houses and bamboo huts. From this town a navigable canal runs northwards along the coast, by way of Enore to Pulicat, for the purpose of conveying coals and provisions to the capital.

Though Madras has only a roadstead, and no safe harbour, the commerce in Asiatic and European goods is very considerable, and it is the principal seat of the trade in pearls and jewels in the East.

The natives of Madras are far inferior in their external appearance to the Bengalese; they are, indeed, more muscular, but they are shorter, darker, and of a less noble countenance, and are very subject to elephantiasis. There is about an equal number of Mahometans and Hindoos; many native Christians, and a community of Armenians. The female servants, with very few exceptions, are descendants of the Portuguese. It is very remarkable that the hookah, which is so generally used in India, is rarely seen here.

The rope-dancers, serpent-tamers, and sword-swallowers of Madras are celebrated throughout India; they will leap over elephants and even five camels standing side by side; their bodies are so pliant, that they twine themselves like snakes up and down between the steps of a ladder; they walk over sharp swords; raise heavy burdens with their eyelids, and, like Ramo Samy of old, are said to be able to float in the air without any visible support. Even the children exercise themselves in swallowing small sticks of bamboo, in order that they may eventually do the like with swords and daggers.

We had scarcely cast anchor when we were surrounded by Massula and Catamaran boats: the former are large, light, deep boats, the planks of which are fastened with elastic coir (the fibres of the cocoa-nut husk) instead of nails; and it is only by the help of these boats that it is possible to pass through the heavy breakers. But from October to the end of December the breakers are at times so violent, that the Massula boats cannot approach, and a landing can only be effected with the Catamaran.

To remedy the great danger which at present attends landing, an Englishman has proposed to the government to build a pier, consisting of jointed pieces, and extending into the sea like a mole; but his proposition has not yet been acceded to. The Catamarans are small rafts of elastic wood, on which the men are bound, or sit cross-legged; they convey letters and papers in their conical, waterproof caps. Bold and skilful as these sailors are, and excellent swimmers into the bargain, they must be constantly on their guard against the numerous sharks, that they may be able quickly to reach their float, when the waves have swept them off from it.

Our time in Madras was exceedingly limited, for we were to stop only so long as was necessary to take in coals, and were to put to sea again in the night; some of my companions and I, therefore, took the first Massula boat that came up, and were rowed to land amid the shouts and songs of the boatmen. The nearer we approached the shore, the heavier the breakers became, and the towering waves frequently threatened to engulf us; but, with extraordinary skill, and the exertion of all their strength, the naked boatmen watched the moment when the foaming wave neared us, and we happily reached land without a dipping.

I immediately hired a palanquin, and desired the bearers to carry me to the house of Mr. M'Clean, to whom I had been introduced by letters from Calcutta, and who holds one of the highest civil offices here. His villa is in the Mount Road, the handsomest and longest street in Madras, for it is eight miles in length, studded with country-houses and gardens, and runs from the Fort to St. Thomas and the cantonments of the artillery.

I saw the equestrian statue of Sir Thomas Monro, formerly Governor of Madras, which was erected on the Esplanade in honour of this eminent man, by the voluntary contributions of the presidency, which amounted to 120,000 rupees. It was executed by Sir Francis Chantry, the sculptor, who has represented him bareheaded, wearing his uniform, and a cloak. The horse is in a perfectly quiet position, neither is there any appearance of motion about it. The memory of Sir Thomas Monro is held in such veneration by the natives (who are much displeased that he is represented bareheaded), that, even now, they salute the statue as they pass it.

The country round Madras has the appearance of a fine park; for although the soil is strongly impregnated with saline efflorescences, flowers of every kind grow in it, and the roads are bordered with very fine avenues of trees, interspersed with the bungalows and the residences of the English.

Mr. M'Clean and his lady received me with British hospitality, and did their utmost to make my day pass as agreeably as possible. I was not a little delighted at here meeting Captain Cunningham, who, after a tedious voyage of sixteen days on board the Nemesis, and a providential escape from many dangers, had arrived here, only the day before. We passed the forenoon together, in viewing the citadel and the most remarkable parts of the city. Mr. M'Clean kindly promised to show me his stud, which enjoys great reputation, and we accordingly set out in the afternoon and drove across the arched Marmalong bridge, which is 500 paces in length, and is thrown over the Adigar, which flows in a broad and stony bed, and then on to Guindy, passing the summer residence of the Governor. A small stone house, built upon a rising ground, was pointed out to me as having been erected to indicate the spot where St. Thomas the Apostle is said to have been stoned by the people. At the end of the Mount Road, small rocky eminences rise in the background, on the highest of which stands a Roman Catholic church, with a monastery for priests and monks: the cantonments of the artillery are in the valley.

The stabling for Mr. M'Clean's beautiful and valuable Arabs is in a park two miles to the south of the cantonments. There were only eight horses, which, however, are said to have cost him 27,000 rupees. We did not return to his residence till dark, and our cheerful dinner almost made us forget that nine o'clock was drawing near, at which time Mr. M'Clean accompanied me to the place of embarkation. When I reached the roadstead, I saw that the blue light was already burning as a signal that the anchor was weighed. Our boatmen exerted themselves to the utmost against the breakers, which had become more violent since the morning; indeed, our boat was twice completely covered by the waves, and it was full twenty minutes before we reached the steamer, wet through and through. A few minutes afterwards, between nine and ten, we put to sea. The weather was extremely fine, and the stars shone brilliantly.

The following day was equally propitious, and the sea was calm and almost motionless; but on the 24th the sky was clouded, and we had a south-east wind, in the forenoon, though it cleared up towards evening. In the following night we approached the coast of Ceylon; and when we were in the latitude of the two reefs, the Great and Little Basses, the captain took the precaution of sounding, for several hours.

Early on the morning of the 25th, the coast of Ceylon lay shrouded in a mist, at our right hand, and at ten o'clock we had a full view of this paradise of an island, with its picturesque mountain chain, wildly-grotesque projecting rocky walls, boundless cocoa forests, and verdant vallies. We passed so near to the coast, that we could form a very clear picture of the fruitfulness which nature has so lavishly bestowed here. Whichever way the eye turned it rested upon the finest palm forests, the most charming vallies, the most luxuriant corn-fields; and the very highest summits of the mountains were adorned with verdant slopes, enamelled with bright flowers, herbs, and creeping plants, whose delicious perfume spread far and wide.

At eleven o'clock we came in sight of the lovely bay, which forms the harbour of Point de Galle, and consequently had made 1189 knots in 150 hours. Towards the south a low promontory with a small wooden lighthouse runs into the sea; and numerous beauteous islets, covered with palms, rising scarcely above the level of the water, are sprinkled over the deep, and a thick forest of cocoanut trees, extending far inland, surrounds the bay which forms the harbour. Numerous rocky islands, overgrown with palms, lie scattered in picturesque groups, and the waves of the sea dash incessantly against their indented shores. The harbour is defended by a small rampart with bastions, and is connected with the little town, which extends towards the south. The entrance to the harbour is so narrow, being scarcely 100 feet in breadth, that we gladly availed ourselves of the assistance of a pilot, surrounded by small boats, which kept close to our side, taking soundings. Before casting anchor, our vessel was encompassed by numerous Urna boats, laden with cocoa nuts, pine apples, bananas, and vegetables. These small boats are built of the wood of the jack fruit tree (*artocarpus integrifolia*) and ropes of cocoa-nut fibres: they are from twelve to sixteen feet long, and four feet deep, but so narrow, that only one man can sit on each of the four seats. On one side of the boat there is an outrigger made of two pieces of elastic wood eight feet long, bent in the form of a bow, and attached at the opposite end to a beam of light wood, of the same length as the boat, floating in the water, by which the boat is secure from upsetting even during the most violent storm. The larger craft, which are built in the same manner, sail along the coast as far as Madras.

As we were to stay here three days, to take in coals and provisions, I immediately went on shore, to visit the town and its environs. The Cingalese are a small, mean-looking race, of a dark-brown complexion, low forehead, and inexpressive physiognomy. Both the men and women wear a garment which fits very close round the hips, and falls to the ankles. Their hair is plaited and fastened at the back of the head with a large tortoise-shell comb, and very few of the men suffer their beard to grow. Every body, even the very poorest person, carries an umbrella, made of Chinese paper or the leaf of a tallipot palm, as a protection against the scorching rays of the sun. The wives of the principal inhabitants were dressed in richly embroidered white muslins, or a coloured silk skirt and a slight bodice, and never appear unveiled. The costume of the women and girls of the lower classes is the same, only that their garments are made of white calico: they are distinguished from the men by their bodice, or by a scarf thrown over the shoulders.

The Cingalese of Point de Galle are greedy of gain, and very servile. The people every where bowed to us, with the utmost reverence, humbly calling us "Hamdrueneh" (Sir). They importuned us to purchase gold and silver chains, precious stones, ivory, and elephants' teeth, for which they asked three times their value.

The little town immediately joins this citadel: the streets are paved with flags; and though the houses are only one story high, they are very cleanly, and have a piazza in front, as a protection against the sun. The population amounts to about 3000 souls, most of whom are Portuguese and Dutch: a battalion of English troops, and several companies of native soldiers, form the garrison. The trade is chiefly in the hands of the Mussulmans, who are here called Murimen.

We commenced our excursions into the environs

early on the morning after our arrival. There are two roads from Point de Galle, one to Colombo, which runs along the coast, and the other to the interior and the neighbouring villages. I chose the latter, as I was desirous of visiting one of the largest Bhoodist temples (Panzela). Immediately behind the town are thickly-wooded eminences, covered with cocoa palms, teak, jack, banana, and bo, or bobaha trees, with an under-growth of wild cinnamon, pine-apples, climbing plants, and a profusion of flowers. Wherever little streams run down from the mountains, the vallies are planted with rice, or sugar-cane, and, at the most picturesque points, on the declivities, or in the plains, are neat wooden houses, thatched with palm leaves, under the shade of cocoa-nuts and bananas. The character of the vegetation of the island is every where very apparent: in some parts are forests and plantations of the finest tropical trees, rice fields here and there, along the irrigated vallies, and in the more level parts, are cinnamon trees, while all the rest of the island is wild and uncultivated. Villages are rarely met with, and the isolated dwellings in the midst of forests, are surrounded by fruit trees, both wild and cultivated.

After proceeding about six miles, I left my carriage, and went by a footpath through an intricate forest to the temple, which is situated on a hill. The priests (*unanzeh*), who reside in a small dwelling near the temple, came to receive me. They were dressed in yellow garments: one of them understood Hindostanee, and appeared to be an intelligent young man, desirous of information, and expressed himself much pleased at this unexpected visit. The temple is surrounded by a wall with two entrances, and is furnished with niches on the inner side, in which lamps were placed: a small stone basin with holy water stood at the chief entrance. The temple itself is small, and possesses nothing peculiar in the style of architecture: several stone steps lead to a vestibule, from which we entered the proper place of prayer.

Opposite the door of this apartment was a seated colossal statue of Bhooda, with very long ears, and a lotos flower on his head. The statue was either of wood or stone, painted yellow, and had a curtain suspended before it. Bhooda was surrounded by his relatives, who were painted in grotesque forms on the walls. A small image of Bhooda, made of gold, stood on a table under a glass shade, in front of the large statue, and flowers, especially the yellow blossoms of the bobaha tree, with rice, fruit, and spices, had been brought by the people as offerings to the god, but of course they were afterwards taken possession of by the priests. In conclusion, the priests took us to their dwelling, a small house of one story: it was furnished with several articles in the European style, and the greatest cleanliness and order prevailed throughout. In a large cupboard were the prayer books (Banapotha), which are written on tallipot leaves: the leaves of some very valuable prayers were covered with black lacker, and the writing was in very elegantly formed gold letters. On taking leave of the priests, they requested permission to see "the Hindostan," and I was glad to be enabled to gratify their wish.

I next proceeded along the fine road to Colombo, which runs parallel with the sea through a cocoa-nut tree forest, twenty-seven miles in length, and several miles broad. The road soon turned from the dense forest to the coast, close to masses of rock, against which the breakers dashed with a thundering noise. But again I found myself in the profound shade of a primeval forest, broken only by smiling mountain streams, which ran to the sea, and flowed between narrow green vallies, or rugged banks. After following this most delightful road for several miles, I left the carriage to examine a cinnamon plantation. The trees were on a sandy soil, under isolated cocoa palms, bananas, and jack fruit trees. The shoots are planted at the commencement of the rainy season, and in the space of six months they send out such vigorous branches, that the bark maybe used; but in order to strengthen the stem, the young shoots are cut off, and it is not till it has attained due girth, that the shoots are cut off, scraped, and the bark stripped off and dried. An acre may be managed by one man, and produces an annual revenue of 10*l.* sterling: after the lapse of three years the shrubs are no longer productive, and are rooted up.

Not far from this cinnamon plantation, under the shade of lofty cocoa trees, is a celebrated Bhoodist temple, which I would not leave unvisited. Here is a wooden statue of Bhooda, twenty feet long, which represents him as lying down asleep. The priests presented me with flowers and cocoa nuts, the outer shell of which was soft, of a bright red colour, inclining to yellow. The milk was sweeter, and had a more aromatic taste than that of the common cocoa nut. The tree differs from the other species only by a smoother bark, and by more delicate leaves. The Cingalese have a certain reverence for the cocoa-nut tree, because, as they say, "it serves for ninety-nine things, but man is not able to discover the hundredth." On the last morning of my stay here, I visited the bazar of Point de Galle, where there is abundance of the fruit of the island offered for sale — pine apples, bananas, cocoa nuts, bread fruit, vegetables, and flowers of the most diverse and rare species.

At noon, on the 27th of April, we weighed anchor, and within an hour lost sight of Ceylon. In the evening the horizon was illumed with flashes of lightning from all quarters: on the following day, and on the 29th, when we descried the Maldive Islands, the sky was clear, the sea calm, and the air balmy. At eleven in the morning we passed through the Gulandre channel, which is six miles broad: the northern group of islands, the Heawandu Pholo (between 7° and 8° N. L.), with its 23 islands, lay on our right hand, and the Tella Don Matte Atoll, and the Milla Don Madre Atoll, consisting of 155 islands, on our left. The latter are joined on the south by the seven islands of Malcolm Reef, next to which lie the Mahlos Mahden Atoll, 166 islands, which are divided by the Moresby channel into the southern and northern.

The four islands of Horsburgh Atoll, and the two Cardewae islands, lie to the south, joined by the northern Male Atoll, with fifty-two islands, of which the most southern is the fortified King's Island, and the southern Male Atoll, with twenty-seven islands. In this direction, there are no less than eleven groups, consisting of 523 islands, extending as far as 2° N. L.

These remarkable groups of islands are of coral formation, and are adorned with the most luxuriant cocoa palms. They are inhabited by a civilised race of above 20,000 Mussulmans, who are governed by a sultan: his ancestors were expelled by the Portuguese, 200 years ago; but he has maintained his authority here to the present day, and his title and rank are hereditary. He is an ill-informed man, and lives in total ignorance of what is passing in the rest of the world; but, like his subjects, he is hospitable, and is always ready to assist the crews of stranded vessels. Under him are five vizirs, or ministers of state, a high priest, and a judge in civil and religious matters. Next to them, the Hendeggery, or director of the customs, is the most considerable public officer, and the Emir-el-bahr, the harbour-master, is the lowest of the principal officers.

Every Atoll, or group of islands, has two chiefs, called Atoll-warys, and a Catib, who acts both as priest and judge, whose business it is to deliver to the government at Malay, the tribute in silver and copper coin, and the productions of the country due from each Atoll. Permission to trade with foreigners can only be obtained from the seat of government. The inhabitants, who are a very harmless, good tempered, and friendly race, resemble the Cingalese in their persons and dress. Their women live secluded, but they are ugly and dirty. The men are noted as experienced and enterprising seamen, and carry on a considerable trade in dried fish, turtles, shells (*cowries*), cocoa nuts, and mats, with Ceylon, Bengal, the coast of Malabar, and Java. In their frail boats, which are built with great skill and care, of cocoa wood, they steer across the wide ocean with compasses, quadrants, sextants, and other instruments of their own making, the glasses for which have been taken from old instruments.

In several of the islands are schools for instruction in the art of navigation, in which the English navigation tables are used, the signals and regulations of which have been translated into their own language. Crimes are very seldom heard of: murders never occur, and drunkenness is unknown. The islands are extremely unhealthy: out of a dozen inhabitants, eight suffer from fevers, dropsy, or elephantiasis scroti. Capt. Moresby, who surveyed these islands in 1835, and to whom I am indebted for this information, told me that in the first two months he had lost sixteen men, and that, in consequence, he never ventured to spend a night on shore. When the sickness of his crew obliged him to go back for a time to Bombay, he allowed two officers to await his return on King's Island; but they were taken so ill with fever, that the sultan, in order to save their lives, immediately sent them to Ceylon.

We met several fishing boats, and were in hopes that we might obtain a supply of fish for our table; but no sooner did our monster, spitting forth fire and smoke, approach them, than the terrified fishermen fled to the shore with great precipitation, and in evident alarm. As we doubled the island of Kila, we saw the wreck of a brig, which had been stranded a few days before, on the white coral reef: it had very probably perished here in the darkness of the night.

We had a continuation of fine weather for several days. Our monotonous way of life was somewhat diversified by the numerous flying fish, and by the appearance of the sea, which, for many miles, was tinged with a red colour by animalculæ. On the second of May we had the novelty of a sale on board; for the effects of eight seamen, who had fallen victims to the cholera, immediately on their arrival at Calcutta, were disposed of by auction. On the 4th we saw an Arabian vessel coming from Bombay, with a cargo of cotton, and which had on board many Mussulmans, who were going on a pilgrimage to Mecca.

In the afternoon we clearly perceived the rocky island of Socotora, and on Friday the 5th, we passed within three miles of the extreme north-east coast of Africa, off which the Elephant rocks projecting into the sea resemble an elephant kneeling down, ready to be mounted. We kept in sight (till three o'clock in the afternoon) of the bare, variously formed calcareous rock, which rises from 300 to 3000 feet, and in some places declines almost quite perpendicularly to the sea. In the evening the head cook died, and was committed with much solemnity to his watery grave on the following morning. The engine was stopped while the captain read the burial service: the sudden silence which prevailed upon the sea, which was as smooth as a mirror, rendered the ceremony peculiarly impressive.

At five o'clock on the 6th of May we anchored in the harbour of Aden, and consequently had run 2158 knots in 220 hours. We cast anchor near the Tenasserim steamer, which had come from Suez, and having burst a boiler in the Red Sea, was obliged to stop here and have it repaired. The evening and the night were incomparably beautiful: the moon, and constant flashes of lightning over the mountains of Arabia, showed us the strangely formed masses of rock, sometimes in a magic, and then again in a dazzling light, while cool sea breezes refreshed the air. The glorious night was an indemnity for the deprivation of sleep, for we were unable to obtain any rest: we were taking in coals, and the negroes and the Sumaly, who were employed in the work, kept up an unabated wild singing and dancing, which continued throughout the whole night. Though on these occasions they are always so excited, and at the same time so completely wearied, that some of them generally fall down perfectly exhausted, and half dead, they cannot renounce this practice.

The harbour of Aden has much resemblance in point of form to that of Gibraltar, with the exception that it is enclosed by rude, naked rocks (of which the Shamsan rocks are the highest), which rise to the height of 1718 feet, in the most rugged and bold outline: the entrance is above a mile broad, and the harbour is so large, that a whole fleet can conveniently anchor in it. No vegetàtion, however, is any where visible: there is neither soil nor disintegrated rock to afford nourishment to plants or trees; of late, however, some indefatigable English officers have caused mould to be brought from Arabia, in order to make a trial whether bananas and flowers cannot be cultivated. These masses of rock, which are composed of granite, porphyry, syenite, crystals, and lava, have evidently been raised by the agency of volcanic power, which is every where visible. The coasts are, besides, remarkably rich in rare shells, and the most beautiful white coral, which is used for lime. Close to the harbour, an enterprising Parsee has built an inn of stone, bamboo, and reeds, in which there are airy apartments for forty guests.

Here I hired an ass, and proceeded to the bungalow of Dr. Scott, a distance of about three miles from the town. I traversed a road which has just been completed, and which first runs along the bay, near which lie several small rocky islands, where some officers had pitched their tents, to pass the hot months; then, gradually rising, the road leads through an artificial door in the rock, about 400 feet high (the entrance to which is defended by small turrets and a battery), into the valley, which is surrounded on three sides by steep, inaccessible rocks, and contains the little town of Aden, the barracks, and the bungalows of the officers and troops, which amount to 2000 men (partly Europeans and partly sepoys), who compose the garrison.

The town, which has now from 18,000 to 20,000 inhabitants, consists of three parts, the Arab, the Sumaly, and the Jews' quarter. The first two are built of bamboo, thatched with reeds; the latter, consisting of buildings two stories high, of masses of rock, has an uncivilised appearance, and is very dirty. A mean mosque stands at the extreme end of the Arab quarter. The Jews, of whom there are 2000 in this place, affirm that they came here on the first dispersion of the tribes. They are servilely civil, and in their appearance and manners have much affinity with the Afghans. Though they are chiefly engaged in trade, and are skilful builders and mechanics, they very rarely cross the sea.

The Sumalys have settled here as a wandering tribe from the African coast, and hire themselves to all kinds of services, as mechanics and grooms; but their nomadic life, which has accustomed them to independence, renders them unsteady, and little reliance can be placed upon them. The upper part of their body is well made, but they have very thin thighs and calfs. Their features are noble and delicate, their dark lively eyes are expressive and mild, and they usually dye their curly black hair light red, which does not look at all amiss with their dark complexion. The greater part of the inhabitants are Arabs.

There is only one well in the whole of this peninsula, the water of which has a brackish taste; and we may here, every morning and evening, see groups of handsome, graceful women who come to draw the clear element. The cisterns are of use only during a very short period of the year, because rain may be reckoned among the greatest rarities; yet the climate is healthy, and the heat is moderated by the sea-breezes. Might not an Artesian well be bored at a trifling expense, and be of indescribable benefit to the inhabitants?

As nothing thrives in Aden, there is a constant intercourse with the neighbouring Arab tribes, with which the British government has lately concluded an amicable convention. Camels arrive daily, laden with corn, fruit, and vegetables for sale; rice, potatoes, wine, and other necessaries of life indispensable to Europeans, are brought from Bombay. Though the English have been only five years in possession of this remarkable and important place, the commerce has greatly increased, especially in Mocha coffee; and it may be expected that in time many productions of Arabia and Persia will be brought hither. The importation of dates from the Persian Gulf, along the coast, has already become so considerable, that above 100,000 barrels are annually sold in this district.

In the erection of the new barracks, many remains of ancient buildings were discovered, whence it is inferred that this place must have been more important in former times: at present there are only the ruins of a Turkish tower, some walls, and a few turrets on the highest points of the rock. Where the peninsula is connected with Arabia, by a narrow isthmus, there are two advanced batteries of four and eight guns, which command both the land and the sea. The building of the barracks, which were lately begun, and of the powder magazine, has been stopped, because the site chosen is now considered unsuitable to the purpose. The occupation of this place costs the East India Company 90,000*l.* sterling per annum.

It is remarkable that here, as in Ceylon, there are neither crows nor sparrows. The sea produces abundance of fish, some of which are rare, and others monstrous; thus I was shown a fish with a bull's head, which was caught here. Sharks and electrical fish render bathing very dangerous: an officer received so violent a shock from one of the latter, that he was in a state of insensibility for some hours, and unable to move his limbs for several days.

On board the Oriental, in the harbour of Falmouth,
June 8. 1843.

We left the harbour of Aden on the 8th of May, at three o'clock in the afternoon, amid the salute of artillery, and proceeded along the Arabian coast towards the Red Sea. In twelve hours we had passed from the calm southern ocean, through the Straits of Babel Mandeb to the agitated Red Sea; and at seven in the morning we sailed by Mocha.

The Red Sea is 920 (1400) miles long, and 140 (180) miles broad in its greatest breadth. In the summer time northern winds prevail throughout the whole extent of the sea; but in the winter, from October to May, those winds blow only over the upper part of the sea, while the south winds prevail in the lower part, and the currents then flow in an opposite direction with great rapidity. The water is of a deeper blue than that of any other sea in the world, which is attributed to the quantity of saline particles; for, while in other seas a gallon of water contains two parts, that of the Red Sea has five parts. The numerous bare and rocky islands are of volcanic origin, and are uninhabited. The shores on both sides are bounded by sterile, calcareous rocks, or desert sandy flats. Some of the Arabian fishermen are celebrated as divers and pilots, and Captain Moresby affirmed that he had seen the father of our pilot, dive to the depth of thirty or forty fathoms to pick up money, when he remained nearly two minutes under water. He likewise succeeded in stripping the copper off a stranded ship, which had sunk in eighteen fathoms water.

The neighbouring tribes point out a spot, about twenty miles from Suez, as that where Moses led the children of Israel through the sea, and where Pharaoh and his host were drowned; but, as the sea is between twenty and thirty fathoms deep at that spot, the place must probably be looked for more to the north, perhaps in the vicinity of the present town of Suez.

Having the advantage of the finest weather, a calm sea, and bright moonlight nights, we cast anchor on the fourteenth of May, at three o'clock in the afternoon, four miles from Suez, and were conveyed on shore in small boats; but we had scarcely embarked when a violent south-wester suddenly arose, which blew with great violence against the Bay of Suez, tore the sails of our little boats, and drove us to the opposite coast. We were thoroughly wet through by the dashing of the waves, and drifted about till midnight, when our boatmen at length succeeded in landing us safely at Suez. At six o'clock on the following morning I set out with three of my companions to cross the desert to Cairo. On this route Mehemet Ali has erected a line of telegraphs: the horses were excellent, and the arrangements so contrived, that we arrived safe at the English hotel in Cairo, on the 16th of May, at five in the morning. Here I received the first account from home, after an interval of five months, which compelled me to relinquish my projected return to India.

Travellers who come from Calcutta by the steamer are obliged to wait at Cairo till the steamer from Bombay has arrived with the mail: in consequence of this arrangement we had nearly a week to view the curiosities of Cairo and its environs. My first excursion was to the pyramids of Ghizeh. Accompanied by my fellow-travellers, I set out on the 17th, in the afternoon, with a dragoman: we mounted small asses, and rode through the southern part of the city towards the Nile.

On the way we met Ibrahim Pacha, driving himself in an English cabriolet. He is very corpulent, and filled the whole seat: he has remarkably fine eyes, and looked around with an air of command, otherwise his physiognomy was expressive of cruelty and indolence.

On reaching the country houses on the left bank of the Nile, I felt so exhausted by the heat, that I requested our dragoman to procure me some water to drink: to our surprise, he conducted us to a pretty villa, alleging that we should meet with the best accommodation there. We had scarcely dismounted, when an officer, in the Turkish costume, with a diamond star on his breast, came to meet us, and cordially bid us welcome in French, inviting us to rest ourselves upon an ottoman. It was Soliman Pacha, a robust man, of middle size, with a short beard, blue eyes, and a most good-natured countenance. The conversation soon became very animated, and was carried on by the hospitable renegado, with the pleasing courtesy of a Frenchman. Pipes and coffee were set before us, and when we took leave, Soliman Pacha offered to supply our kitchen, which we declined, heartily thanking him for his kind reception, and hastened to reach the Nile. We had scarcely set off when the servants of our hospitable entertainer came running after us, and begged a bakshish, which, after so good a reception, was justly due to them. In the hurry of the moment, however, I distributed my gifts rather unequally, which caused a dispute among the recipients, but I did not stop to see the end of it.

As soon as we had been conveyed across the Nile, the immense pyramids rose before us, and it was three o'clock before we reached them. Surrounded by about twenty Bedouins and Arabs, and some girls with pitchers of water, who claimed the right of assisting travellers to ascend the pyramids, we were to commence the difficult ascent to the summit of the highest of these wonderful monuments. You are aware that the outside of the pyramids consists of large blocks of calcareous stone, often six feet in height and breadth, which, in different places, have been loosened, partly by violence, and partly by the lapse of time: they form a kind of steps, by means of which it is possible to ascend; but these steps are so high and narrow that it is difficult and wearying to reach the summit without the assistance of the Bedouins, who are accustomed to it.

One of the pyramids, where these steps are wanting in some places, has hitherto been ascended only by a very few persons. One of my companions, however, performed the feat without any assistance whatever! In sixteen minutes we reached the little platform of the highest pyramid, the pyramid of Cheops, where we enjoyed at sunset the incomparable view over the desert, the ruins of Memphis, the other pyramids, the fertile valley of the Nile, and the city of Cairo, with its numerous mosques and minarets. The sight of this sublime but melancholy picture excites the imagination of the beholder in the highest degree: surrounded by the colossal monuments and ruins of a strange, mysterious people, by a gloomy wilderness, and the most luxuriant fertility, his soul is more moved by contemplation of the past, and the mutability of all human deeds and works, than by any circumstance connected with the present moment.

Almost every traveller has endeavoured to immortalise himself on these monuments, and my companions followed their example; in which I was the less inclined to join, because, to my great surprise, I found my name already carved there! We descended these stupendous creations in the evening twilight; but the descent is still more difficult than the ascent, and he who makes a false step runs the risk of being precipitated from that fearful height. After we had rambled among the pyramids and tombs till it was quite dark, we sought for rest in a chamber at the foot of the pyramid. On the following morning we viewed the interior of the great pyramid and some of the tombs, and at ten o'clock set out on our return to Cairo.

To the great satisfaction of all friends of humanity, Mehemet Ali has founded a new hospital for lunatics, where those unhappy persons are, in every respect, well taken care of. The quarantine establishment for the plague, which commits dreadful ravages in Cairo, is in the front part of the Lunatic Asylum. During my rides through the city, I often saw deserted houses, half in ruins, the inmates of which had fallen victims to this frightful disease. One morning I rode through the city, along the cemeteries and sepulchral monuments, to the petrified forest lying in the desert to the south. I here found five different kinds of wood, and saw two trees in pretty good preservation lying in the sand, one of which was twenty-one feet in length.

On the road to Suez, in a garden belonging to Boghos Bey, is a large handsome obelisk, which is forty feet above the surface of the ground, and twenty below it. This was the last place of interest I was able to visit, for an indisposition, which had been occasioned by our stormy landing at Suez, obliged me to keep my room.

On the 21st, a steamer conveyed us in twelve hours to Atfeh, whence we put ourselves into a gondola, and were towed along the canal to Alexandria, which we reached the next morning at six o'clock. During our stay of two days in that city, our Consul-General procured me an audience of Mehemet Ali. We drove to his palace, which is situated close to the harbour, at nine o'clock in the morning. His Highness was seated cross-legged upon an ottoman, in one corner of a large apartment, and welcomed us with a motion of his right hand; and his interpreter, a little Armenian, stood before him. Mehemet Ali is in the evening of his life. His silvery beard completely covered the lower part of his face, and fell below his breast. When he smiled, an expression of coldness and cunning lurked about the corners of his mouth, but his eyes looked around with youthful fire. He invited me to a seat on his right hand, and when we had taken our place, pipes and coffee were brought to make up any deficiency in conversation.

Mehemet Ali inquired, with the most lively interest, about the Afghans, the king of Delhi, the ameers of Sinde, and other Mahometan princes. But when I told him that their power was now at an end, his brow immediately became clouded; he seemed lost in thought, and uttered something to himself, which was scarcely audible, but the words "decline" and "ruin" could be distinguished. He appeared to feel the most bitter vexation that he had failed in his object of raising Islamism to greatness and power. He then asked, with an air of surprise, how it was possible that the British government could have allowed me to serve in their army, and to become acquainted with its operations. I replied that the English had no reason whatever to make a mystery of their proceedings, and the less so, because we, more than any other continental power, were their natural allies, and had been on terms of friendship with them from the earliest times. "Yes, as long as it is their interest," replied Mehemet Ali, with a sarcastic smile. On my observing that I had seen with admiration the works in the citadel, and had found many advantageous changes in Cairo, he replied very abruptly, "That will all fall to the ground after my death." His countenance, however, brightened up, when I spoke of his fleet, the good order of which had greatly surprised me. This is his only delight, and the hours which he generally spends every morning in surveying it are among the happiest of the day; but, at the same time, one ship after another is decaying, and the whole fleet, without being of any advantage, is fast falling into ruin. We took leave of his Highness after passing more than half an hour with him.

Meantime the steamer had arrived from Bombay, by which our company, including children, was increased to 148 persons. The "Oriental," on board of which we were to proceed to England, had not accommodation for so large a number, on which account several travellers, myself included, were obliged to submit to the greatest inconveniences. We left the harbour of Alexandria on the 24th, at two o'clock in the afternoon, reached the quarantine harbour of Malta on the 28th, Gibraltar on the 3d of June, and steered the same evening towards the Atlantic Ocean.

When we were off the Bay of Cadiz, a hurricane suddenly arose, and raged with extraordinary fury for nearly eight hours. The towering waves rose majestically above the watery surface, sometimes ascending in lofty columns, then rolling over each other in long ridges, crested with silver foam, and then approaching us with gigantic strides, broke over the vessel, and saturated us with their white spray. The wind at the same time whistled and roared among the masts, chimnies, chains, and tackling, and rent our topsail in an instant. Such a furiously raging sea is one of the sublimest phenomena in nature, and the more so, contrasted with the perfect calm which succeeded as suddenly as the tempest had set in. The sky cleared up, and the ocean became more tranquil; but on the seventh of June we again encountered an agitated sea. A favourable wind, however, drove us so rapidly towards our destination that we reached the coast of England at three o'clock in the afternoon of the following day. We here again encountered a tempest, which was no less violent than that in the Bay of Cadiz, and the more dangerous, because we had steered fifteen miles too much to the west, and, instead of being opposite to the harbour of Falmouth, were on the coast of Cornwall, off Blackhead. Against such a raging sea, whose waves continually dashed over our vessel, our engine, though of 450 horse power, could not carry us more than four knots in an hour, and every thing depended on our reaching the harbour of Falmouth before dark.

It was just dinner-time, and most of the passengers had assembled in the great saloon, when the storm and waves suddenly rose very high. At some moments the sea raged with such fury, that the vessel laboured in vain to make way against it: the fury of the elements was the greatest at the spot where the Conqueror is said to have contended with them five months before. On that melancholy occasion, one of our company had lost his only son, a hopeful boy, only eight years old, and he mournfully gazed upon the miserable, cold, watery grave, with an expression that seemed to say, "Shall the father here join his child?" But Providence decreed otherwise: the disk of the sun just descended into the sea as we entered the harbour; and a shout of joy and exultation was raised by the passengers when, at eight o'clock, the rattling of the chains announced that the anchor was safely dropped on their native shore.

LETTER XIII.

TO ALEXANDER VON HUMBOLDT.

Religion of the Hindoos.— Their deities.— Castes.— Establishments for education.—General committee, and sphere of operation.—State of the schools in 1835, *and statistical reports relative to them up to the year* 1842.—*Influence of European education on the youth, with respect to morals and religion.*

On board the Hindostan steamer,
May, 1843.

In no country in the world does the religion of the inhabitants appear so prominent as in India, where every town has its different temples, from the meanest building which encloses the rudest idol, to the most gorgeous deities enshrined in pagodas with lofty towers, spacious court-yards, splendid colonnades, and walled tanks. While priests and devotees crown the idols, and bring offerings of fruit and flowers, the people perform their devotions at sunrise, standing in the water, bathing, or throwing water over their heads. During the daytime the men are attracted by singing to the sacred place, as well as graceful groups of veiled women, who bring their offerings to the divinity.

A strict Brahmin is occupied four hours every day in the performance of all his superstitious ceremonies; but if he is engaged in worldly pursuits, he may fulfil his religious duties in half an hour; and a man of a lower caste is content with frequently repeating the name of his god while he is bathing. On holydays, the people go in procession with palm branches, flowers, pictures of idols, cars, flags, and lanterns, made of silk, or of coloured and gilt paper, on long poles. The gaily dressed multitude in their picturesque costume, and the tastefully decorated symbols of their worship, impart an extremely animated, cheerful, and splendid appearance to such processions. Pilgrims, fakirs, and religious mendicants, on the way to their sacred places, meet the traveller at every turn, some in the dress of their order, and some carrying the symbols of the god whom they are going to worship, and with whose name they salute every body they meet.

But with all this external religious pomp and splendour, with the strict observance of usages and ceremonies, since the time of Menu, Hindooism has deviated and fallen away from its original purity. Several of the deities have been neglected, others have been substituted, the dead are worshipped, sects have been formed, monotheism is fallen, and the belief in a god who pardons sin, without the necessity of repentance, as well as the neglect of the Vedas, has become general.

The Vedas assign four great periods (Yags) to the development of the world; and to the Almighty the three great qualities; first of creation (Brahma); secondly, of preservation (Vishnoo); and, thirdly, of destruction (Shiva). They say that the angels assembled before the throne of the Almighty, and humbly asked him what he himself was. He replied, "Were there another besides me, I would describe myself through him. I have existed from eternity, and shall remain to eternity. I am the first great cause of every thing that exists in the east and the west, in the north and the south, above and below: I am every thing, older than every thing, King of kings: I am the truth: I am the spirit of the Creation, the Creator himself. I am knowledge, and holiness, and light. I am *all mighty.*"

Though this fundamental principle no longer prevails, though the objects of devotion are no longer the same, yet this religion still exercises as powerful an influence over the people as in the most remote ages; and, though the deism of the Vedas as the true faith, including in itself all other forms, has been displaced by a system of polytheism and idolatry, has been nearly forgotten, and is recollected only by a few priests and philosophers, yet the belief in a Being far exalted above all, has not been obliterated. The visible and symbolical part of religion gained the superiority over the pure and sublime, by the obstinate and blind adherence of the priests to antiquated forms, and by their encouraging the adoration of new deities and symbols. In the Shasters of this new creed, the eighteen Pooranas, which are not by Veisia, the compiler of the Vedas, but by different authors about the ninth century after Christ, and partly compiled from more ancient traditions, we find accounts of the creation, philosophical speculations, instruction in religious ceremonies, genealogies, historical fragments, and innumerable legends, of the deeds of the gods, heroes, and sages.

Besides many millions of gods, there are seventeen deities who are chiefly worshipped by the Hindoos. Brahma, the god of creation, the only one mentioned by Menu, has but one temple in India, and though invoked in the daily prayers, is altogetner passed over in special devotion. His wife Saraswati, on the contrary, the goddess of learning and eloquence, is held in high esteem. Vishnoo and Shiva, and their incarnations, have become the chief objects of worship. Shiva, say the Pooranas, wanders about upon earth, sometimes laughing, and sometimes screaming, surrounded by spirits and goblins, intoxicated, naked, with his hair clotted and dishevelled, and strewn with the ashes of a funeral pile, and his neck and arms hung about with human bones and skulls. His wife, who appears under three distinct names, Doorga, Parbattee, and Kallee or Devee, is held in equal veneration, and is represented in a still more revolting form. In the south of India, she appears as a handsome woman riding on a tiger, in a haughty and threatening attitude, as though she would destroy the demon; but in Bengal, and other parts of India, she is represented as a black woman, with a hideous physiognomy, smeared with blood, her head entwined with serpents, and, like her husband, ornamented with human bones and skulls. A thousand goats and other animals are sacrificed every month in her temple at Calcutta; and in Bindhya-básini, the blood shed in front of her image is never permitted to dry. Equally bloody sacrifices are offered to Shiva; for on certain days in the year martyrs are seen going in solemn procession to the temple, with their lips and tongues slit, and knives sticking in them, and their bodies entwined with living serpents; while others hang suspended by a hook fastened in their flesh, from a lofty tree, in momentary peril of falling from the dizzy height and being dashed to pieces.

Vishnoo appears as a pleasing young man, of a dark complexion, dressed in sky-blue, like a king of ancient times, or in the form of his ten principal incarnations or avatars. First of all, he was a fish, which snatched the Vedas from a demon, who had got possession of them during an inundation; then he was a boar, which raised the earth with its tusks, from the bottom of the ocean into which it had sunk; then again he was a tortoise, which supported a mountain. In the fourth, Vishnoo becomes at length more closely connected with mankind by saving the life of a believer whom his father was going to kill, because he asserted that Vishnoo was in the pillar which supported the hall in which they were. Vishnoo, in human form, with the head and paws of a lion, sprung out of the pillar, and destroyed the unbelieving tyrant.

In the fifth incarnation, it is said, that a king, by means of sacrifice and penance had obtained such power over the gods, that they were obliged to give up to him the earth and the sea, and looked forward with anxious foreboding to the moment when his last sacrifice would put him in possession of heaven. On this occasion, Vishnoo appeared as a dwarf Brahmin, and begged for as much ground as he could measure in three steps. The rajah made no difficulty in granting the modest request of the little being, and poured into his hand some water from the Ganges, in confirmation of the oath; but while he was doing this, Vishnoo suddenly became a giant, and with his first step traversed the whole earth, with the second the ocean, and with the third took possession of heaven; and thus, craftily depriving the rajah of his dominions, he permitted him to descend into hell, as king of the lower regions. His sixth incarnation is a Brahmin hero, Parasu-Ram, who extirpated the Kshetryas. Rama, a king of Oude, was his seventh avatar, of whom it is related that he was expelled from his paternal dominion, and lived for many years in a forest, secluded from the world, devoted to religious duties, while his wife Sita was carried off by a giant, Rawana, king of Ceylon. In order to deliver her, Vishnoo passed through the Deccan, penetrated to Ceylon, and supported by an army of monkeys under the deified leader Hunnooman, he triumphed over his adversary. Having, however, unjustly put to death his brother Lachmana, who had shared all his dangers, he was overpowered by the stings of conscience, and threw himself into a river, and, as the Hindoos assert, was received among the gods. Vishnoo's principal incarnation was that of Krishna, the son of a king of Mathura; but he was brought up by a shepherd, in order to conceal him from a tyrant who sought his life. His youthful sports and deeds, in stealing milk, and killing serpents, are held in undying remembrance by the Hindoos. He was exceedingly beautiful, and he was adored by women and girls of all ranks, whose hearts went forth to meet him whenever he appeared. He is held in such high veneration by the people, that when the Governor-General was on his march from Delhi to Agra, they requested him to pass through Mathura. Vishnoo's ninth avatar was Boodha, and his tenth is yet to come.

Among their principal deities are also the following:—Lakshmee, the wife of Vishnoo, and Goddess of Plenty and Good Fortune: Indra, the God of the Air and of Heaven: Varuna, the God of Water: Pavana, the God of the Wind: Agni, the God of Fire: Yama, the God of the Nether World, and Judge of the Dead: Cuvera, the God of Prosperity: Kartika, the God of War: Cama, the God of Love: Surya, the God of the Sun: Soma, the God of the Moon; and Ganesa, the God of Wisdom. Rama and Krishna are, however, held in far higher veneration than all the others, especially in Hindoostan.

Very few of the above-named gods have temples; but, on great religious festivals, their symbols or images are carried about on poles, and afterwards thrown into the water. The images of the gods in the temples, as well as on the highways, have a brutal, savage, and disgusting appearance — nothing whatever of dignity or greatness. Some are represented with four hands, and several heads, and are painted red, blue, or yellow. Equal, and often greater veneration is shown to the planets, and sacred rivers, especially the Ganges, which represents a goddess.

All, in the midst of this confusion of idol worship, are animated by hope — eternal reward is reserved for the good, and punishment for the wicked: the former are to go to Yama, to wander amid delightful paths, under the shade of fragrant trees, between streams covered with the lotos, and unceasingly have flowers showered down upon them. The air will resound with the hymns of the blessed, and the melodious songs of angels. The way of the wicked, however, is on a narrow, dark path, now over burning sand, now on sharp stones, which cut their feet at every step: they are naked, tormented with thirst, covered with dirt and blood, and have hot ashes and burning coals poured upon them; and, troubled by the most frightful visions, they fill the air with their cries and lamentations.

The religious life of the Hindoos is not more alien from the spirit of the European than their social separation into classes or castes. According to Menu, Brahma created four kinds of men: — first, the Brahmins, who issued from his mouth, to lead and teach mankind; secondly, the Kshatria, or the caste of warriors, from his arms, to defend and protect them; thirdly, the Vaisya, or caste of merchants, from his breast, to feed and to preserve them; and, fourthly, the Shoodras, from his feet, to serve and obey the others.

The Brahmin is the first of all created beings. The world, and all that is in it, belongs to him; by him all other mortals enjoy their life, because his curse can destroy kings; therefore, a Brahmin is to be treated with more respect than a king. His life and property are secured by the strictest laws in this world, and threats of the most dreadful punishments in the next. His youth must be passed in self-denial and chastisements, and devoted exclusively to the study of the Vedas: obedient, and serving his teacher, he is to beg his subsistence from door to door. In the second period of his life, we find him surrounded by his family and his children, performing the usual duties of a Brahmin, in reading and teaching the Vedas, sacrificing and praying, giving and receiving alms. He is not, however, permitted to accept any services; he is to renounce all the pleasures of life, such as music, singing, dancing, play, &c., and to shun worldly honours and enjoyments like poison. Even his external appearance and his dress are strictly prescribed. He is commanded to appear frank and modest, pure and chaste, without passion; his hair and beard cut, and his person cleanly, with a staff and the Vedas in his hand, and bright gold rings in his ears. If he has read the sacred books, brought up his son, and performed the holy sacrifices, he is allowed to confide every thing to his son, and to live in his house, as arbitrator. His third period of life is the most laborious. Clothed with the skin of a black antelope, or with leaves, with his hair hanging down, and his nails suffered to grow very long, he is to sleep out of doors, on the bare ground, without fire, to live only on fruits and roots, but to perform all religious duties with the greatest scrupulosity. Lastly, he concludes his life in self-contemplation, and, in meditations on his God, he is to breathe out his spirit, as the bird flies into the open air from the branch upon the tree.

The Kshatria or caste of warriors, though below that of the Brahmins, is held in high honour, because the latter live and act under their protection, and, as Menu says, the weal of the world depends upon their union. Many princes, and most of the ministers, belong to this caste, whose business it is to defend the people, to give alms, to offer sacrifices, and to refrain from sensual enjoyments.

The Vaisyas, notwithstanding their inferior position, enjoy the privilege of being hospitably entertained by the Brahmins: their business is to keep the flocks, to carry on trade, to lend money on interest, and to till the ground. The duty of the Shoodras is to serve, first, the Brahmins, and then the other two classes; but a Brahmin must never touch food that has been prepared by a Shoodra. If a Shoodra insults a Hindoo of the higher caste, his tongue is to be slit; if he sits down on the same seat with a Brahmin, the latter is to chastise him; and if he attempts to instruct him in religious duties, boiling oil is to be poured into his mouth and ears. But this slavish relation of the Shoodras to the Brahmins and higher castes, is no longer so severe: he offers his services to whomsoever he will, is protected by law against their tyranny, and is often in possession of property. Upon the whole, the castes are no longer so strictly separated, and more especially so in camp, where a Brahmin, serving in the army, has intercourse with the Shoodra, in a manner which he would avoid in ordinary life.

Among a people entertaining such religious and social principles, it must be difficult for the English to introduce Christianity and European learning: the former makes but comparatively slow progress, through the labours of the missionaries, while the latter daily gains ground, and promotes the Christian spirit and manners. Though it is only within the last twenty years that the British government has begun to provide for the establishment of schools and popular instruction, yet much has been effected within this short period. Deeply impressed with the vast importance of the subject, the government has prosecuted the undertaking on a truly noble scale, and with an energy and zeal commensurate with its end. The Directors of the East India Company as far back as 1824, in a dispatch to India, said, "We wish that you may be entirely penetrated with our zeal, with which we desire the education and training of the natives of India to be promoted, and rest assured that we are ready to make considerable sacrifices for this object."

There were two systems of instruction in India. In the presidency of Bengal the English language was chiefly used in teaching, and in that of Bombay the language of the natives. The first system was much censured; but when we consider that there are various dialects in India, that the languages of the country are by no means sufficient to teach the subjects of instruction in a lucid manner, and conformably with the present state of learning, and that the English literature is so rich in all that is good and useful, we might feel disposed to give the preference to the system adopted in Bengal; but it has been modified, and the vernaculars are now attended to.

In the presidency of Bombay, the Elphinstone institution, founded in the year 1837, and so called in honour of the Governor, Mountstuart Elphinstone, is the principal establishment for the instruction of the natives. It consists of two divisions, one for the English, and the other for the native language. The former is subdivided into the upper and lower school; in the first of these mathematics, natural philosophy, mechanics, chemistry, political economy, geography and history, are taught, and, according to the report of 1842, there were 30 scholars in this division: the lower school was attended by 587 boys. There are besides, several schools belonging to this institution, in which instruction is given in the native language, and in which there are 719 boys.

The government has likewise established English

schools in the following places: at Poonah, where there were 81 boys, and where 61 young people had already been prepared for various offices in the country; in Tannah 58 boys, and in Surat 35 were under instruction. The English school at Panwell was dissolved on the report of the Board in 1842. Lastly, there is at Poonah a Sanscrit gymnasium, in which 85 students are educated gratis, and 68 pay the fees.

In connection with these superior institutions are the schools of the natives in the district, under the superintendence of the Board. They are such as aim chiefly at influencing the civilisation of the people, and therefore confine themselves to the simplest elements of instruction. To the first division belong those in the collectorates of Poonah, Ahmednuggur, Sholapoor, and Candeish.

In the collectorate of Poonah are 19 schools, which are attended by 1257 boys; in that of Ahmednuggur there are 16 schools, with 1243 scholars; in Sholapoor, 4 Marattee and 6 Canarese schools, with 250 boys; and in Candeish there are two Mahrattee schools, with 80 boys. The state of the schools in these last two collectorates is reported as being much neglected.

The second division is formed of the collectorates of Surat, Ahmedabad, Kaira, and Tannah. The collectorate of Surat contains 13 schools, with 1142 scholars; Ahmedabad 6 schools, with 414 scholars; Kaira 7 schools, with 456 boys; and, in the northern Concan and the collectorate of Tannah, there are only Mahratta schools, 10 in number, which are attended by 661 children, between the ages of five and 15. The third division consists of the southern Concan and the southern Mahratta country. In the collectorate of Ratnagherry, there are 9 schools, with 782 boys, the establishment of four new schools, has been granted.

The variety of dialects in the southern Mahratta country renders instruction very difficult there. Mysore is the seat of the Canarese language in its original purity; but in the district adjoining that territory the language becomes corrupt and almost unintelligible, by the mixture with Telinghee in the east, Mahrattee in the north, Malabar in the west, and Dravid in the south. Now, as in the collectorates of Darwar and Belgaum, Canarese is the language of the natives, and at present employed for the communication between the government and the people, (though Mahratta was formerly made use of for this purpose, and is still used in some of the Jaghires,) the council of education at Bombay has decided that the Mahrattee language shall be entirely excluded in the Canarese schools: in the same manner as in the schools of the Deccan, instruction is imparted only in the Mahrattee, and in Guzerat in the Guzerat dialect. In the collectorate of Darwar there are two Mahrattee and five Canarese schools, which are attended by 531 boys. In Belgaum there are 18 Canarese schools, and one Mahrattee school in the little town of Khanpoor, in which there are 669 scholars.

According to this account the presidency of Bombay numbers 120 schools for natives, in which 7750 boys are instructed. The Council of Education has caused a census to be taken, as far as possible, of the number of boys fit to attend school, from which it appears, that of 100 boys above five years of age, about 18 on an average enjoy public instruction.

In the presidency of Madras, the only institution for superior branches of education is the university, founded in 1841. It consists of a higher or academic, and a preparatory school: the academic department is intended to comprehend a medical and an engineer school. Children of natives of all castes are admitted into this institution, and receive instruction seven hours every day. The fee for the high school is four rupees, and for the preparatory school two rupees per month. According to the last report, the first was attended by 100 young people, and the latter by 38. The Board does not deem it advisable to give any admission gratis, because in that case poor children would, for the most part, make use of it, who, after attaining some knowledge, and before they had completely finished their education, would be compelled to leave the institution. The Board also complains that the results and practical importance of education are not better understood and appreciated by the natives, even among the superior classes.

Since the year 1823 a general committee, consisting of 17 members, has been at the head of all establishments for education in the presidency of Bengal. The secretary of the government is, *ex officio*, a member of this committee. Two natives are annually chosen from the Council of Administration of the Hindoo college, and the other members are elected from the higher classes of European functionaries at Calcutta. The secretary, alone, has a salary of 500 rupees a month. The general committee is a superintending and controlling board: every member has a right to make proposals, on which the majority decide. Sub-committees, consisting of three members, are formed from it, and have the care of the finances, the choice of books and instruments, and the appointment of teachers, subject to the approval of the general committee.

The general committee, in its report to Lord Auckland in the year 1835, states, that it is endeavouring to extend, to confirm, and to improve, the basis of the system, and that it contemplates, as soon as there are sufficient means, "to establish in every village of the country a school, where instruction shall be given in the native language." When a school has been found to answer in the principal stations, the committee will form a college, and take care that the professors and teachers shall reside in the vicinity of their respective spheres of action; for which purpose it is intended to build houses for their accommodation rent free. In every college there shall be a professor of mathematics, of natural philosophy, and of law: "but this branch of knowledge," remarks the committee, "has to encounter great difficulties from the number of conflicting systems of law, and their composition in so many different languages; we hope, however, that the law commission will shortly furnish us with a succinct and sufficiently comprehensive work on Anglo-Indian law, in the English and native languages." This being accomplished, every thing would be done to form practical officers for the administration of justice and finance, so that every Zillah, and every civil tribunal, shall have the assistance of one or two.

With a view of promoting English writing and literature, an edition of a selection of the best English authors, both in poetry and prose, was set on foot. Besides this, every institution contains a library, for which the Rajah Bejai Govind Singh alone gave 20,000 rupees, and private persons made considerable presents in books. In order, however, that the native languages might not be neglected, while the study of the English was being pursued, the council caused translations of the best English works to be made. The Governor-General also declared that the diffusion of European literature and learning among the natives was to be kept in view as the principal object, without, however, interfering with the instruction in the languages of India. It was, therefore, the special object of the committee to educate schoolmasters and translators, and to give such a direction to the seminaries, that the young men might be employed in the departments of justice and finance. This desirable object was to be promoted by scholarships and prizes of books, medals, and money, which were to be bestowed upon the best scholars in every branch of learning.

In the year 1835, we find the following seminaries already established: In Calcutta, an Anglo-Hindoo college, a Mahometan, and a Sanscrit college; in Benares, an English seminary, and a Sanscrit college; in Delhi, an English and an Oriental college, and schools at Maulmain, Hooghly, Moorshedabad, Bhaugulpoor, Saugor, Allahabad, and Agra. In the same year the following were established: A medical college at Calcutta, and seminaries at Pooree, Gawahatee, Dacca, Patna, Ghazipoor, Meerut, Rajshahee, Jubbulpoor, Hooshungabad, Furruckabad, Bareilly, and Ajmeer. Each of these twenty-seven institutions were under the special superintendence of a committee of Europeans and natives, chosen from among the inhabitants of the district in which the school was situated.

In these schools were 3398 pupils, among whom were 1881 Hindoos, and 595 Mahometans, educated, maintained at an expense of 25,427*l.* 6*s.* 6*d.* Of these 1818 learned English, 218 Arabic, 473 Sanscrit, 376 Persian, and 40 Mahrattee. If I observe that this small number of scholars, from a population of 73,000,000, is only one pupil out of 18,250 inhabitants, it must not be forgotten that three times the number of children are instructed in other establishments. Experience, however, had already shown at that time that the scholarships, and the grants of school-books free of expense, did not promote the intended object. The committee, therefore, proposed, that every boy should provide himself with books; and the plan had so far a good effect, that, in the same year, we find at Maulmain 106 scholars, among whom there were 48 Burmese, and 16 Chinese. At Meerut the seminary increased in eight months from 19 to 112 scholars; and at Dacca, where, at the opening of the school, so many children came, that it was necessary to hire another house for them, a native made a present of 1000 rupees*; and a collection made among the natives and Europeans amounted to 5000 rupees. In the Oriental college at Delhi there were in that year 197 scholars, of whom 61 boys, divided into nine classes, belonged to the Arabic division: 80 boys, in eleven classes, were instructed in Persian; and 56, in nine classes, in Sanscrit. The directors of this institution, in their report, mention a scholar who did great honour to the establishment, and who had thoroughly studied the chief works on the principles of Mahometan Jurisprudence; on Mahometan law; on natural philosophy; on ethics, logic, and on rhetoric.

* The following fact, communicated by the Rev. J. Weitbrecht, gives a pleasing view of the interest manifested by another native in the education of youth:—

"I requested the Rajah of Burdwan for some assistance in building an English school in that town. To my surprise he presented me with two bank notes, amounting to 1500 rupees (150*l.* sterling). The same wealthy individual once attended an examination of our orphan and infant schools, and was agreeably surprised in hearing the little boys and girls sing and repeat portions of Bible history from the prints suspended round the school-room; for he, with many of his deluded countrymen, had the idea that females are unfit for, and incapable of, intellectual and moral improvement."—*Translator's note.*

The result of education on the mind and sentiments in Bengal will be most clearly shown by some extracts from the best essays of scholars produced on their examination in the presence of their teachers. In the Hindoo College at Calcutta, "The Art of Printing" was given as a subject, and the prize was adjudged to Kylas Chander Datt, a scholar of the first class, seventeen years of age. He expresses himself in the following terms:—

"To preserve from oblivion the religious ceremonies, laws, and renowned actions of sages and heroes, mankind, in the primitive ages of the world, had recourse to metre. The simple and crude laws of the early inhabitants of ancient Greece were set to music, and chanted in fairs and other public places, in times of festivity and merriment. But experience taught our barbarian ancestors that oral tradition could hardly be credited after the lapse of a few centuries. So many and so extravagant were the errors, that crept into unrecorded but genuine history, that a more lasting monument of their exploits was deemed requisite. Amongst the variety of objects with which men are surrounded, it is natural that those should be selected, which are, comparatively speaking, of an imperishable nature. The decrees of Solon, the laws of the twelve tables, contracts, wills, epitaphs, treaties, and conventions, were all engraved on stone, metal, or wood. Before the invention of the Divine Art of Printing, as it has been emphatically called, men were absorbed in the grossest superstition. Alfred and Charlemagne, by erecting schools and endowing monasteries, had shed only a temporary lustre over the intellectual horizon of Europe. The monks being the only instructors of youth, the communication of knowledge was very slow and imperfect. Incredible legends, unedifying homilies, and trite expositions of the Scripture, were the only learning at that dark period. The contracted ideas of the monks, their outward austerity, their religious opinions, and their depraved morals, rendered the communication of knowledge in their hands utterly unfit. Science degenerated into barbarous sophistry, and genius remained mute and inglorious in the fervour of theological controversy.

"Printing was invented in the middle of the fifteenth century, and in the course of a hundred years attained its noonday splendour. This wonderful invention was at first of a rude and simple nature, consisting of whole pages carved on blocks of wood or marble. The formation of movable type was a grand step towards its present improved state. The clergy, finding it inimical to their interests, became its inveterate foes. They attributed its origin to the prince of darkness; the thunders of the Vatican were directed against it; it was called the great dragon, the antichrist foretold in sacred history. But still it flourished. It soared with unwearied wings far above the artillery of malignant monks. Ere a century expired, Europe saw the embers of learning in a blaze, saw the expiring lamp relumed, witnessed the decay of popery, of abject despotism, and a material change in the habits and opinions of mankind. In short, the invention of printing made a complete revolution in the human mind. Happy is it for mankind that it has withstood all the artifices and hostility of its selfish opponents. Had it been strangled at the very moment of its existence, had some dreadful fatality, some unaccountable intrigue checked its growth, in what a state would the world have been now!

"The world has been filled with such an infinite number of idle books, tending to increase the love of pleasure, of dissipation, and of vice, such trashy articles have gone abroad, amongst which can be numbered the present essay, that instead of instructing, they distract the attention of mankind; such heresies have been propagated, such private scandal has been published, that we cannot but lament that with so glorious an invention there should have been wedded such injurious consequences. But the advantages far outweigh the disadvantages. What though there has been an infinite number of worthless publications? What though there has been a partial perversion of morals and primitive piety, what though there have been wanton innovations to gratify the avarice, the vanity, or the misanthropy, of hungry, foolish, and wicked men! The extensive general beneficial effects on morality and religion will endear it to the latest posterity! The evils will pass away in the triumph of time, of civilisation over barbarism, of truth over falsehood. Three centuries only have elapsed since the invention, and behold the mighty consequences. Is it possible that from a commencement so feeble, there has gone forth a progress so steady, an expansion so gigantic, a benefit so glorious? During the middle ages, the universities, the monasteries, and the libraries only of the great, contained books. But now behold the splendid saloons of the lords of hundreds of manors in England, and the hut of the poor cultivator of one acre of ground, and tell me whether or not you will find in both the works of Scott and Lardner. The invention of printing, then, may be deemed the most glorious in the annals of mankind. May angels continue to hover over its safety, and may that God in whose hands are the issues of all things, perpetuate to us the inestimable boon, which, through the agency of some obscure men of Germany, he has bestowed, and continue to render it the happy instrument of exposing the enormities of kings, of the heinousness of private individuals, of the diffusion of knowledge, and the increase of civilisation!"

In the College at Delhi, "The Advantages of Education" was given as a subject, and the prize adjudged to Umed Singh, a youth who had been only three years and four months in the school. He says,—

"Education is the art of cultivating the mind, and of rectifying the affections and dispositions of the heart. It stores the mind with the knowledge of a great many arts and sciences, and fills the heart with a due sense of what we owe to God and man.

"When we look at our own country, how can we avoid being touched with a sensation of regret and pity. While other nations provide foreign countries with innumerable useful things, the inhabitants of India are unable to supply their own wants. It is universally acknowledged, that necessity is the mother of invention, but the poor Indians are proper examples for the reverse. They do not exert their minds to produce something that is useful, nor stir their hands to make something which they stand in need of. They rather squander their time in play than devote it to study, and starve in want rather than be useful. Here we see a great many native gentlemen of noble families reduced to the brink of starvation, and yet they never exert their bodily or mental powers. But let me ask you, can these miseries be imputed to their idleness? no, their idleness proceeds from the want of a good education. Had they been taught to know the advantages of industry, had education excluded from their minds the blind and superstitious belief of predestination, and taught them to consider the value of that time which might have produced a very noble equivalent, had it not been thrown away, I am certain they would not be so despicable a body of men. I cannot conclude this essay without observing, that a man without education is but a mere animated being, or (if I may say) a living stone cut into a human figure: he appears as a man, but in reality is only a few steps above the brute creation in the scale of existence. He can do good neither to himself nor to the society he lives in. He can neither be religious nor virtuous. He may, perhaps, be possessed of some brilliant endowments of nature, but they are like pearls lying hid at the bottom of the sea, which it is not in his power to fetch out and make them shine with proper lustre."

In the year 1836 we find already 30 institutions for the education of youth, attended by 3298 Hindoos, 670 Mahometans, and 198 Christians, of whom 3511 received instruction in English, 381 in Sanscrit, 256 in Arabic, and 358 in Persian, at the total expense of 35,519*l.* 11*s.* The committee insisted, that every boy, who at all possessed the power, should procure his own school books, because by this means many useful books came into the hands of the people, and the regular attendance at school was promoted. A great obstacle to instruction was found in the many holydays of the natives; so that a schoolmaster at Ajmeer complained that there had been twenty-one holydays in two months. The deficiency in able teachers was sought to be remedied by enlarging the classes in which teachers were trained; but one great drawback was occasioned by the circumstance that many children left school before their education was completed, because the parents wanted their assistance.

The committee were also much to be commended for the care evinced in the improvement of the physical powers of the pupils, by giving instruction in gymnastic exercises, and by providing that the younger children should not sit in the school so long as the elder.

In the year 1837, we find 38 institutions, in which there were 170 teachers and 5196 scholars. At that time the expense of one scholar in the Arabic school at Calcutta, per month, was 15 rupees, 9 annas, and 7 pice; in the Sanscrit college, 11 rupees, 2 annas, and 1 pice; in the colleges at Delhi and Agra, between 8 and 9 rupees; but in the schools at Allahabad, only 1 rupee, 8 annas, per month.

In the following year, there were in the presidency of Bengal seven colleges and 33 schools, in which 100 professors and teachers, and 115 Pundits (teachers of Hindoo law) and Moulavies (teachers of Mahometan law) were engaged. They were attended by 5727 scholars, and cost 38,179*l.* 11*s.* The subjects taught in the colleges were, mathematics, book-keeping, engineering, architecture, drawing, surveying, mechanics, ethics, natural philosophy, chemistry, jurisprudence, technology, history, geography, and poetry; in the preparatory schools, reading, writing, grammar, geography, and the first rules of arithmetic, were taught in the English and native languages. The desire of being instructed in English became so predominant in consequence of the situation which the best scholars obtained in the service of the state, and of private persons (thus in only one year forty scholars of the College of Delhi obtained situations), that Persian and Arabic were quite neglected. In the province of Assam, as ardent a thirst for knowledge was manifested as there was in Europe in those ages when learning revived. Yet out of 100 children of an age to go to school in Moorshedabad, only 8 came; in Burdwan 16; in Behar five; in Tirhoot only 2; and in Arracan many of the inhabitants considered education as a mark of slavery.

In the year 1838, there were forty-four schools and colleges in the following places: in Bengal, at Calcutta, the Hindoo-Sanscrit Medical College *, and the Madressa; at Hooghly, the College of Mahomet Mohsin, a branch school, and a school for young children; likewise schools in Seedapoor, Tribanny, Umerpoor, Jessore, Dacca, Comillah, Chittagong, Dinajpoor, Bancurah, and Bauleah; in Orissa, at Cuttack and Midnapoor; in Assam, at Gowahatty; in Arracan, at Akyab and Ramree; in Behar, at Patna; two schools at Bhaugulpoor, Arrah, Chaprah, and Maulmain; in the district of Allahabad, at Benares a college and a seminary; schools at Ghazipoor, Allahabad, Saugor, Jubbulpoor, Hossingabad, Azimghur, and Gorruckpoor; in the north-western provinces, a college at Agra, a college and institution at Delhi, also schools at Bareilly, Meerut, Furruckabad, and Ajmeer. In these establishments there were 6550 scholars, viz. 4952 Hindoos, 1400 Mussulmans, and 198 Christians. The expense was 38,179*l.* of which only a little more than 24,000*l.* sterling fell to the provinces of Bengal and Agra, which alone have a nett revenue of nine and a half millions sterling.

* Dr. Goodeve and Mr. Frederick Mount have especially exerted themselves to promote and improve this institution, which is already placed on an equality with the better class of medical colleges in Europe.

It appears from the report of the committee to the Governor-General, that the boys were beginning to attend school at an earlier age, yet, notwithstanding every effort, the higher and middle classes manifested less interest in education; and it appeared extremely important to form a respectable class among the natives, acquainted with the English and native languages, who might have a favourable influence over their less educated fellow-countrymen. In drawing up a uniform plan of instruction, it was intended to take care that the master should teach well, and not too much, and that he should influence the minds of his scholars, as well as promote their intellectual advancement; and corporal punishments were prohibited, but rewards were to be given, as well for moral rectitude as for improvement in learning. During the last year of their stay in the colleges, the scholars were to be chiefly instructed in practical subjects which are of the most frequent occurrence in India. It was found difficult to retain many pupils of the higher classes, because they left the colleges as soon as they thought themselves capable of filling some small situation under the government or in the service of private persons. To remedy this inconvenience, a trifling gratuity was given to the best scholars of the lower classes; and those scholars in the colleges who most distinguished themselves by their diligence received every year, after the examination, a gold medal, and those in the schools, a silver medal. The general committee was likewise careful for the erection of convenient schoolhouses, with airy apartments and shady playgrounds; and to every superior institution a museum of natural history and a model room were to be attached.

In the years 1840 to 1842, there were seven colleges and 33 schools under the superintendence of the general committee, which cost 56,843*l.* In the Medical College at Calcutta, the monthly expense for each scholar, in the years 1840 and 1843, was respectively* 58¾ and 51 rupees; in the Hindoo College, 9 rupees, 2 annas, and 6 pice; in the Sanscrit college, 11 rupees, 15 annas, and 7 pice; but in several of the lower schools, not quite 2 rupees. The total number of boys in all the schools was 7391; viz. 5435 Hindoos, 1507 Mussulmans, 240 Christians, and 209 of different sects, who were instructed by 87 head masters, among whom were two professors of the university of Cambridge, and 233 under masters.

In the year 1843, there were 10 colleges and 41 schools, which were attended by 8609 scholars. If we add to this number the 900 scholars of the General Assembly's institution at Calcutta, we have only one scholar for about 10,000 inhabitants; on which, however, it must be observed, that the female sex receive no education in India. If we adopt the estimate of Mr. Adams for some districts, as applicable to the whole presidency, we shall have for every 100 boys, above five years of age, 15½ who receive instruction in the schools.

* In the Report it was 73 rs. 10 an. 4 pice per head, but this was to the exclusion of the lower school; the students of which should have been brought in to diminish the average cost.

To this statistical view, I will add a few observations which occurred to me on my visit to several of these institutions. It has unfortunately hitherto been very apparent that most of the boys attend the colleges and schools only in the prospect of obtaining a situation, and that the majority belong to the lower classes; for, with the exception of Calcutta, people of rank and fortune do not send their children to school.* Scholars who have raised themselves above the general mass by their intelligence and virtue stand alone, and abandoned in their own families and in society; and they feel themselves unhappy and discontented if their hopes are not realised.

On the foundation of the Medical College at Calcutta, Dwarkanath instituted an annual prize of 2000 rupees, for three years, for the best scholar, and expressed himself, in a letter, as follows:—" My own experience has taught me that no motive is

* In the Protestant Missions in Bengal, before alluded to, Mr. Weitbrecht says,—

" We have just heard the gratifying news that a wealthy Brahmin, in the city of Benares, has lately given up his son into the hands of one of our missionaries, with these remarkable words: " I feel convinced, sir, after reading your holy Shasters, that they contain the true religion. I have not the power to come up to the purity of its precepts, but here is my son; take him as your child, feed him at your table, and bring him up a Christian." At the same time he made over the sum of 10,000 rupees (1000*l.*) into the hands of the missionary, to defray the expense of his son's education. This event is a new era in the history of our North Indian missions; the effect of it will be incalculable upon the minds of the Hindoos at Benares; a greater blow has never been inflicted upon the stronghold of idolatry."— *Translator's note.*

more powerful with the natives than pecuniary rewards, and I am convinced that the difficulties will vanish in proportion as young men are encouraged in this manner." This frank and sincere acknowledgment clearly intimates the motive which induces many parents to send their children to school; but, on the other hand, it is not to be denied, that occasionally a thirst for knowledge and a desire of improvement lead the youth to school. Thus, in the Hindoo College at Calcutta, I met with the only son of distinguished and wealthy parents, of Assam, who by his ardour for improvement, and his good moral conduct, was honourably distinguished among his collegiates. Two scholars, in the Hindoo College at Hooghly, had likewise devoted all their energies to the study of astronomy, and, from their own scanty means, had themselves made the requisite instruments for observing the stars; with small magnifying powers, indeed, but answering the purpose.

Boys of all ages, above seven, and of every religion and caste, from the highest Brahmin to the lowest Shoodra, are found in these schools. The scholars themselves make no distinction whatever on this account, though, in order to avoid giving offence, there is a regulation that if the parents or children of the higher caste should insist upon it, a child belonging to the lowest caste must be removed from the institution; but such a case has never occurred. Only in children of the highest caste of the Brahmins a partial separation is made when they take their meals, which are brought to them by servants of their own caste. These boys then retire to a place appropriated to them, where they sit down apart from their fellow-scholars. In other respects, they live together in a familiar and friendly manner, both in and out of school. Almost all the scholars of the higher classes are married, but it is seldom that one of them lives with his wife, who as yet is betrothed to him. Most of them are too young, in fact, they are sometimes mere children, and they seldom form a household establishment till they have obtained a situation.

A very striking fact among the boys, especially the children of Hindoos, is their quick comprehension, their intellectual activity, and their love of European learning, especially metaphysics and the belles lettres. Of ten children of the higher classes, you will find nine who are fond of poetry, and have made themselves familiar with the best poets of England. With this passion for poetry, however, they find it difficult to make verses, though they are inexhaustible in ideas for poetical subjects. In the other branches of learning, particularly mathematics, history, and geography, I find as much knowledge among the scholars of the first class as among our first class at the Gymnasia.

It rejoiced my heart, and surprised me not a little, when to my question, "In what country is the education of the people the most advanced?" I was answered, "In Prussia;" with a tolerably correct statement of the method pursued. These youths comprehend, with far greater facility than our young men, propositions and metaphysical theories: they are persevering and indefatigable, and grieve much when their attendance at school is interrupted or forbidden them. When I visited Mohamed Mohsin's College, at Hooghly, the scholars of the higher class had presented a petition against the numerous holydays, but at the same time requested the removal of a teacher, whom they declared to be incompetent. This little conspiracy was of course strictly inquired into, and the instigators were to be removed from the College. In all the schools which I visited, the boys of all classes unhesitatingly expressed their satisfaction at remaining in the school till six o'clock in the afternoon.

Though it cannot be doubted that there are boys of remarkable talent among the scholars, it is equally true, that no men of distinguished eminence have arisen among them. They appear like tropical plants, which rapidly arrive at maturity: they attain their physical and intellectual perfection too prematurely to be vigorous and durable: they are tall and slender, but their nerves and muscles are weak, and they have no stamina. It is evident, that among them brilliant schoolboys seldom enter into life as eminent men; and it is to be feared, that the mind of the Bengalese will never acquire any very great depth, or be endowed with much activity. The few exceptions, among whom Rammohun Roy cannot be wholly excluded, are distinguished only as Hindoos, and would never have been considered great men in our own country.

This indolence and apathy which comes over them with manhood, and which must be mainly attributed to the climate, is the melancholy cause why so many of the young men, when they enter upon active life, become indolent, vain Baboos, whose whole efforts are directed to the acquisition of money; for a very small number only pursue their studies after leaving school. Some of them obtain situations under government, as deputy collectors with a salary of from 150 to 400 rupees per month; others become teachers, merchants, clerks in great commercial houses, or secretaries to private wealthy individuals, with monthly salaries from 200 to 600 rupees. In general, he who has obtained an office and dignity has not only to provide for his parents, but is also expected to maintain the whole family. This circumstance was very characteristically indicated by an exceedingly hopeful boy, in the Hindoo College at Calcutta, who, on my asking him who his parents were, and how they maintained themselves, replied, "My father sits at home, and does nothing; but I have a brother in office."

A very important question is, What influence has education produced on the religious sentiments of the Indians? It has hitherto appeared that the young people grow up as Deists, and, in some cases, have even converted their parents and relations to deism; yet, with very few exceptions, neither they nor their families have neglected the religious usages of their ancestors. Their adherence to them, and their great respect for them, seem to be an innate custom, from which they cannot wean themselves, though they profess their disbelief in them, and prefer the Christian religion. The case is otherwise with the scholars of the General Assembly Institution, which is founded on the principals of the Scotch church, and has for its object not only the propagation of learning, but also of Christianity.* Nine hundred boys are now

* Captain Von Orlich appears not to have seen, or to have received any authentic information respecting the numerous missionary schools in India, or he would certainly have noticed them, as well as the admirable Scotch school under the care of Dr. Duff. He would then, perhaps, have been inclined to entertain more favourable opinions of the progress of Christianity in India. However, to complete in some measure the interesting detail on education which he has given, we add a summary of the schools under the Church Missionary Society up to April, 1844.

CALCUTTA AND NORTH INDIA MISSION.

Commenced 1816.

Mission Establishment.

24 European missionaries.
1 Indo-British missionary.
1 European catechist and schoolmaster.
10 Indo-British catechists and schoolmasters.
117 Native catechists and teachers of all classes.
2 Indo-British schoolmistresses.
4 Native schoolmistresses.

Summary of the Calcutta North Indian Mission.

Stations - - - - - -	10
Communicants - - - - - -	644
Attendants on public worship - - - -	2180
Seminaries - - - - - -	8
Seminarists - - - - - -	204
Schools - - - - - -	45

instructed in this institution, which was founded only in 1830, and is maintained by the benevolence

Scholars:

Boys - - - - -	2155
Girls - - - - -	265
Youths and adults - - -	373
Sexes not distinguished - - -	40
	2833

MADRAS AND SOUTH INDIA MISSION.

Commenced in 1814.

Mission Establishment.

1 Clerical secretary.
19 European missionaries.
1 Indo-British missionary.
3 Native missionaries.
7 European catechists and schoolmasters.
1 Indo-British catechist.
382 Native catechists and teachers of all classes.

Summary of the Madras and South India Mission.

Stations - - - - - -		13
Communicants - - - - - -		2103
Attendants on public worship - - - -		13995
Seminaries - - - - - -		3
Seminarists - - - - - -		99
Schools - - - - - -		194
Scholars:		
Boys - - - - -	4376	
Girls - - - - -	1081	
	5457	

BOMBAY AND WESTERN INDIA MISSION.

Commenced 1820.

Mission Establishment.

6 European missionaries.

of the Scotch church, and of private persons. It consists of a school department, and of a college;

1 European catechist and schoolmaster.
20 Country-born and native schoolmasters.

Summary of the Bombay and Western India Mission.

Stations		2
Communicants at Bombay		3
Schools		20
Scholars:		
Boys	882	
Girls	2	
	884	

HIMALAYA MISSION.

Commenced 1844.

Missionary Establishment.

1 European missionary.
1 European catechist.

Summary of the Himalaya Mission.

Stations	1
Schools	1
Scholars—boys	18

CEYLON MISSION.

Commenced 1818.

Mission Establishment.

9 European missionaries.
2 Native missionaries.
1 European lay-agent.
104 Native catechists and teachers of all classes.
18 Native schoolmistresses.

Summary of the Ceylon Mission.

Stations	4
Communicants	182

the first has seventeen classes: in the latter, the course of education occupies four years. I here heard from the lips of the scholars, how they estimated the Christian religion above all others in the world, and considered Hindooism as idolatry. At an examination, the following subject was proposed, "The Comparison of Christianity and Hindooism," which was answered by one of the pupils in the following manner:—

"The theology of the Hindoos recognises in

Attendants on public worship		3870
Seminaries		3
Seminarists		65
Schools		82
Scholars:		
Boys	2110	
Girls	601	
	2711	

—*Report of the Church Missionary Society*, 1844.

With respect to the probable effect of the preaching of the Gospel in India, the following remarks by the Rev. J. Weitbrecht will be found interesting and encouraging:—

"I do not calculate the result of the labours in Bengal so much by the number of those we have baptized, as by the moral impression which Christian truth has produced among the people. It is true, that of three or four thousand who have heard the preaching of the Gospel, only a few comparatively have been converted to Christianity; but most of those young men have carried home with them a clear knowledge of the mos important doctrines of Christianity, and have thereby obtained a decided conviction in their own minds that our religion contains sound and saving truth, and that the very groundwork of Hindooism is made up of lies and falsehood; that the one darkens and deteriorates, while the other improves and sanctifies the heart."—*Translator's note.*

theory, as its supreme God, a being without attributes or moral feeling, who is neither our Creator, Preserver, nor Governor. In fact, this theology is supernatural absurdity. According to this, man must leave the world, go into the jungles, and become an inactive being, no better than a stone. If every one were to act in this manner, no children would be born, and the world would be destroyed. How can we compare it with Christianity? Christianity raises man to his proper dignity—to glory: purifies his moral nature, and, instead of obliterating the properties of man, sanctifies and purifies them; in a word, converts an immoral, weak, sinful world into a paradise, animated by enlightened, purified, and sanctified human beings, who live together in endless and undying love in joy and happiness. Popular Hindooism is the mother of ignorance, of superstition, of vice, impiety, and misery: it is the grossest idolatry. Neither this nor the former can be compared with Christianity."

Dr. Duff, who conducts this institution with indefatigable zeal, and with rare devotedness and self-sacrifice, had the gratification, some years ago, of seeing two of his scholars of their own accord, and against the will of their parents and relations, publicly embrace the Christian religion. But as soon as the news was spread among the people, most of the parents kept their children from school. So great, however, was the desire for knowledge and instruction, that Dr. Duff had the pleasure of soon seeing the number of his scholars complete again; and not only the sons of inferior castes and poor parents, but even those of Brahmins and rich persons, desire to hear the word of the Lord. A Hindoo scholar of the first class concluded his essay on the Influence of sound general Knowledge upon Hindooism with the following words:—

"The resplendent Sun of Revelation hath darted forth to the eyes of benighted India. But, alas! alas! our countrymen are still asleep—still sleeping the sleep of death. Rise up, ye sons of India, arise, see the glory of the Sun of Righteousness; Beauty is around you; life blooms before you! why, why will ye sleep the sleep of death? And shall we who have drunk in that beauty—we who have seen that life—shall we not awake our poor countrymen? Come what may, ours will be the part, the happy part, of arousing from slumber, slumbering India."

INDEX.

A.

B.

C.

D.

E.

F.

G.

H.

I.

J.

K.

L.

M.

N.

O.

P.

Q.

R.

S.

T.

U.

V.

W.

Y.

Z.

THE END.